THE GUN DIGEST BOOK OF KNIVES
5TH EDITION

W9-BXN-573

By Jack Lewis
and Roger Combs

DBI BOOKS
a division of Krause Publications, Inc.

Staff

SENIOR STAFF EDITORS
Harold A. Murtz
Ray Ordorica

PRODUCTION MANAGER
John L. Duoba

EDITORIAL/PRODUCTION ASSISTANT
Karen M. Rasmussen

ELECTRONIC PUBLISHING DIRECTOR
Sheldon L. Factor

ELECTRONIC PUBLISHING MANAGER
Nancy J. Mellem

ELECTRONIC PUBLISHING ASSOCIATE
Laura M. Mielzynski

GRAPHIC DESIGN
John L. Duoba

COVER PHOTOGRAPHY
John Hanusin

MANAGING EDITOR
Pamela J. Johnson

PUBLISHER
Charles T. Hartigan

ABOUT OUR COVERS

Beginning at upper right, there's a near-ultimate high-tech expression, a Spyderco-Walker-Klötzli liner lock, made in Switzerland in ATS-34, titanium and carbon fiber; below that, in purpled titanium and mother-of-pearl, is another liner lock, handmade by Ralph D. Harris; and then a Bill Defreest GORDON drop-point hunter in hollow-ground ATS-34 and warm cocobolo, nicely shaped. The charming engraved folder at the bottom is by A.A. Darakis, made in the '80s, all work by him; and above the Darakis is an S.E. Serafen utility boot knife in rag Micarta and chisel grind. At upper left, the unmistakable Howard Viele has collaborated with Spyderco on a dangerous-looking liner lock; and at the top is the SOG Microclip tool, very nearly the very smallest of the useful devices of this nature. Underlaying all of those, we see an Applegate-Fairbairn dagger as made by Blackjack in Illinois of A2 steel and a just-one-of-its-kind R.W. Loveless working straight edge, naked lady trademark and all.

Knives: From the study collection of Ken Warner, Editor of DBI's *KNIVES* Annual and of *GUN DIGEST*.

Photo by John Hanusin.

Copyright © 1997 by Krause Publications, Inc., 700 E. State St., Iola, WI 54990. All rights reserved. Printed in the United States of America.

No part of this publication may be reproduced, stored in a retrieval system, or transmitted in any form or by any means, electronic, mechanical, photocopying, recording or otherwise, without the prior written permission of the publisher.

The views and opinions contained herein are those of the authors. The editors and publisher disclaim all responsibility for the accuracy or correctness of the authors' views.

ISBN 0-87349-188-2   Library of Congress Catalog #73-83465

Contents

Chapter 1: Knives: The Third Oldest Tool
Sticks and stones were first, then a rock was split 6
    Caught Knapping 10

Chapter 2: New Designs, New Materials
Blade materials and knife designs are constantly evolving 14

Chapter 3: Military Knives
*Knives, swords, sabers, bayonets—armies have used edged
weapons for thousands of years* 19

Chapter 4: The Navy SEAL Knife Controversy
Will the real SEAL Knife please stand up? 26

Chapter 5: A Matter of Survival
What is a survival/fighting knife, and how might it be used? 31

Chapter 6: Keeping It Sharp
No doubt about it, a sharp blade is a good blade .36

Chapter 7: A Study in Steel
*Ever in search of a sharper edge, veteran cutler David Boye has come
up with new information and techniques* 45

Chapter 8: Custom Knifemakers
*In a series of profiles, some of the latest and greatest
makers of today are given their just due* 52
    Jim Hrisoulas 53
    Tim Hancock 60
    Mike Franklin 65
    Phill Hartsfield 70
    Chris Reeve 77
    Mike Tamboli 82
    Bob DeFeo 87
    Tim Alverson 91
    Charles Weiss 95
    Bud Nealy 99
    Allen Elishewitz 103
    Alex Collins 105
    J.W. McFarlin 109
    Ken Hoy 113
    Dr. Lawrence Wilson 117

Chapter 9: A Matter of Collection
*Reasons for cutlery collecting seem to number on a par
with the collector population* 120

Chapter 10: Fathers and Sons
Knifemaking skills are handed down to the next generation 131

Chapter 11: Lady Knifemakers—Only a Few
Paula Anzel is a novice who's as good as her teacher 138

Contents

Chapter 12: American Bladesmith Society
*In twenty years, this group has grown from the four
founding members to more than 550* 141
Teaching the Basics of Forging 149
Emil Morgan's Railroad Spikes 155

Chapter 13: Knifemakers Guild
*More than a quarter of a century ago, these custom
craftsmen had a meeting of the minds* 160

Chapter 14: Decorating Knives
A beautiful knife can be made more attractive with the right artwork 165
A Horn-Handled Damascus Knife 171

Chapter 15: Sheaths and Pouches
*The right container protects and carries—and has
the knife always ready for use* 174

Chapter 16: New Developments in Folding Tools
Folding knives, blades and locking systems are changing 181
Year of the Multi-Tool 187
The Gentleman's Pocketknife 197

Chapter 17: Bird Hunter Blades
There are subtle design variations that make the difference 201

Chapter 18: Knives for Sale
Cutlery is made and sold by large and small businesses everywhere 204
Buck Knives 211
Imperial Schrade Cutlery 217
GT Knives' Two-Man Team 224

Chapter 19: Art Knife International
A sophisticated and profitable way to market high-value knives 227

Chapter 20: Knife Restoration
Some old knives just need help to live longer lives 230

Chapter 21: A Matter of Design
*It took nearly four decades for Rex Applegate's and
William Fairbairn's thoughts to crystallize into reality* 235

Chapter 22: Long Knives, Swords and Sabers
For some cutlery forms, big is considered best 241

Chapter 23: Machines for Handmade Knives
Modern knifemakers use power tools to save both time and effort 249

Chapter 24: Dixie Gun Works' Knives
For the do-it-yourselfer, these partially finished blades offer many possibilities .252

Introduction

THIS IS THE Fifth Edition of THE GUN DIGEST BOOK OF KNIVES. As has been the case when we finished each of the first four editions, we have turned off the word processors, leaned back in our chairs and wondered whether we have exhausted the supply of new and pertinent information. A few years hence, when the publishers want a Sixth Edition, will we find enough material to fill another 256 pages?

But after reviewing the contents of this Fifth Edition and comparing it to the earlier editions, it becomes obvious that progress is a universal thing that includes knifemakers—both custom and factory—and the techniques and materials they use.

There still are countless knives being made from carbon steel, and both the maker and the buyer realize that special pains must be taken to see that this material does not rust, thus ruining the value of an expensive custom blade.

Going a step beyond, Damascus steel for custom knives has found an increasing number of collectors who want this type of blade in the knife they order. Here, there no doubt is the desire to have a knife that is one of a kind and will not be duplicated in exact detail for someone else. That desire comes under the heading of "pride of ownership" and is a powerful force when it comes to marketing custom knives.

More and more companies turning out mass-produced factory knives are seeking to develop an additional market by dressing up a standard with cosmetics to become a "commemorative" or "special issue" that will appeal to a particular level of collector interest.

There are some dangers in this approach, of course. Said danger inevitably is the result of corporate greed. Several major firearms companies, chiefly Winchester and Colt, followed the same approach, starting some three decades ago.

In 1961, Colt made twenty-five Sheriff's Model nickel-finished and appropriately marked single-action revolvers for Centennial Arms Corporation. In those days, these guns retailed for $139.95. Today, if you can find one in pristine, unfired condition, it will cost you somewhere in the neighborhood of $5000. Reasons for all this come under the heading of the laws of supply and demand.

Colt, however, looked at this instant sellout and launched into a commemorative program that same year, issuing five more commemoratives. In 1963, they issued ten different commemoratives.

By comparison, in 1984, Winchester issued 15,000 copies of a 22 rimfire rifle, suitably decorated and marked, which they dubbed the Boy Scout Commemorative. Seemingly, there were not many Scouts willing to pay $595 per copy, and even today, you can buy these dressed-up Model 9422s at considerably less than $500 each.

Several knife manufacturers have made similar mistakes in judging buyer interest in so-called commemorative knives. By now, most have learned that it is best to produce small numbers at a proper price than to grind out thousands upon thousands and expect buyers to stand in line for them. By the time we get around to doing the next edition of this tome, we suspect that there still will be factory-produced commemorative knives, but they will be produced in limited numbers.

We also have touched on some new materials that are being used to make knife blades, and we all are aware that some custom makers and factory personnel are attempting to develop improved steels and tempering techniques. Surely, many of these new approaches will be in use by the time we want to write about them.

Then there is the computer. It is a recognized fact that knives now are being designed by computer, so is there any reason to deny the possibility that, by the time the next edition is ready, you will be able to sharpen your pet blade with a new program for your PC? Think about it!

Jack Lewis
San Clemente, California

Roger Combs
Fallbrook, California

KNIVES: THE THIRD OLDEST TOOL

Sticks and stones were first, then a rock was split

MOST LIKELY, THE first knife was a broken rock, split with a sharp edge. Some caveman discovered it cut fingers if not handled correctly and it could help butcher a mastodon, trim tree limbs and would do a job on enemies better than what he had before.

The evolution from cracked rocks to the finest stainless steel art or hunting knives of today took probably hundreds of thousands, if not millions of years to accomplish—and that evolution is not finished. New blade materials, cutting techniques, handle materials, heat treatments, chemical processes, machines and computers are being developed and tried by craftsmen all over the world. Old, forgotten methods of construction and forging are being revived, just as Damascus steel was rediscovered a generation ago.

All manner of materials have been used as knife blades. One might guess—and some research shows—that flint rocks have been the basis of the most common and successful knives, even today. No doubt, some primitive person came upon some recently cooled volcanic rock or lava. Maybe it reached a body of cold water that caused it to crack, leaving a sharp edge that caused a cut. Maybe, in another part of the world, a being came upon a meteorite, still hot and glowing red. What could he do with it?

Knapping or chipping flint rocks became an art that lasted for thousands of years. It is still practiced today. In many parts of the world, the ground is littered with flint arrow and spear heads in various stages of work, offering modern scientists an insight into how our ancestors did their work.

Although used only by hobbyists today, a correctly knapped arrowhead is still the sharpest and deadliest available, even in modern times. The problem is that it takes a lot of skill and

practice to make good arrowheads and they are subject to breakage when shot. Most of us do not have the skills and patience to create flint heads. Most of us use replaceable-blade, stainless steel broadheads. They can be resharpened, but most archers simply replace the old, dull ones with new, sharp blades.

We do not know if the knife or the spear point came first; somebody probably realized that a large flint point fastened to a long, stout stick was safer to use against a wooly mammoth than trying to hold the flint in a bare hand. That must have been about the time it was learned that your enemy could not reach you as easily if you kept your flint on the end of a six-foot pole.

Another variation was holding the flint blade with a piece of leather, woven plant material or even hardened clay. When the spear shaft broke off just behind the flint, somebody had a hafted skinning knife.

All sorts of substances have been used for knife blades. Before the Iron Age, bronze, fired clay, green wood, fire-hardened wood, as well as rocks and stones were used. According to some extensive research by knifemaker Phill Hartsfield, one of the earliest references to quenching sword blades to harden the metal was about 900 B.C., in Homer's *Odyssey*. Mention is made of tempering the shining, red-hot sword and pole-axe in water. "The red-hot metal hisses in the lake..." Aristotle wrote about the production of Wootz steels of India from about 350 B.C.

Evidence indicates that the Chinese began production of steel by melting and solidification long before Indian Wootz. The Wootz steel was made directly from iron ore in Catalan forges. The forge produced crucible steel, according to some of what Hartsfield has learned.

The Iron Age began somewhere in what is now eastern or middle Europe, perhaps in Asia, too. It spread through much of

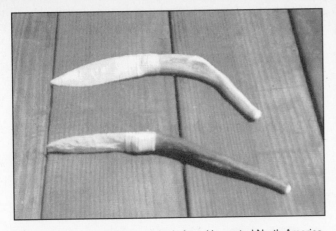

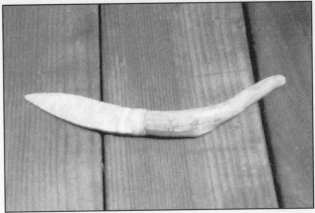

This pair of knives replicate originals found in central North America, the product of early American craftsmen. The originals are in museums, but these replicas are as accurate as possible.

Another view of an early American knife. The handles were antler, bone or wood; the blades knapped from flint of other materials. The tribal group that controlled the flint supply usually exerted power over its neighbors.

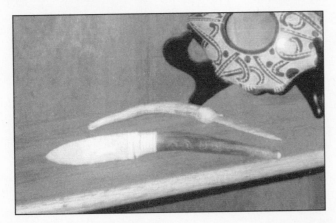

A slightly different version of an authentic American knife, crafted before the arrival of Europeans to the New World. It has a decorated handle that "personalized" the knife.

what was the known "civilized" world carried by traders, smugglers and explorers.

In most of North and South America, the arrival of iron and steel technology awaited the arrival of European explorers in the late 15th century. Despite that, most of the edged weapons and tools of our hemisphere continued to be made of knapped flint, rather than metal, for the next several hundred years. Many hobbyists and traditionalists continue to practice the art, insisting that even today, the sharpest blades and arrowheads are still made of flint, rather than steel. Big game is killed using flint-tipped arrows and then field dressed using flint knives, even into the 21st century.

The Romans brought the world of iron to the Britons, and the Normans brought their smiths and metalworkers. The first centers of European cutlery production were situated along strong-flowing rivers so that waterwheels could provide the power required to make knives before the advent of electricity. Great Britain, Germany and France had their cutlery centers, and soon did America along the streams of New England. Switzerland, Scandinavia and Italy have their traditions of knife production.

The first crucible-cast steel works was opened in Sheffield, England in 1740. Steel was produced by dissolving carbon in molten iron. The English cutlers declared the steel was too hard to be used for knife blades and would not work with it. However, they soon learned their competition in central Europe was

producing better products and taking away the market. They learned to work with carbon steel.

The so-called stainless steel was developed in 1912. Carbon steel is relatively easy to forge when red hot. It is soft and pliable and may be worked by hand hammers or mechanical devices. Stainless steel must be heated to much higher temperatures and must be held within a tighter range of temperatures before it can be forged. When the stainless steel begins to cool below the required range, forging has to stop. High-speed mechanical forging hammers were developed so that the work could be finished during the relatively short period of time when the steel was at the right temperatures. As steels and machines were improved, the mass production of millions of knives per year from a single factory has become a reality.

With all the advances in technology and materials, the past few years have seen a resurgence of interest in old materials and old methods of construction. Several modern custom knifemakers have developed markets for knives that are hand-forged in coal fires, hammered Damascus steel blades, knives that are made with flint blades, meteor metal, combination metals, hand-polished sword blades and many other reversions to the past. Perhaps their popularity is a reaction to technology moving too fast. Perhaps it is an appreciation of the makers' skills and artistic abilities. Whatever the reason, there are plenty of collectors and knife users who are willing to pay top dollar for new knives that look old.

Many custom knifemakers and even some cutlery factories pride themselves in their artistic creations. They have found many buyers for their output. Some of these buyers seem to be investors as well as collectors; others are interested in art knives in appreciation of the work and skill that went into the production. A large audience is becoming aware of the increase in value of, say, a Bob Loveless or a Bill Moran knife made twenty or forty years ago, for instance. Watching some of the frenzied buying at knife shows leads one to conclude that many knives are purchased with an eye toward the potential profit, rather than an appreciation of art.

The situation is not necessarily bad. It certainly is a boon to the knifemakers whose work sells that way. And plenty of other art forms have been sold with the same excitement. Paintings and sculpture of the Masters have sold in the multi-millions in recent years, although that run-up of prices seems to have paused recently. Nevertheless, art is art, no matter the form. A small piece of steel can be hammered and ground into a pleasing shape and be called art, just like oil paint on a small square of canvas.

But the bread and butter—pardon the pun—of knives is that they are tools, useful tools. Knives are portable tools that cut

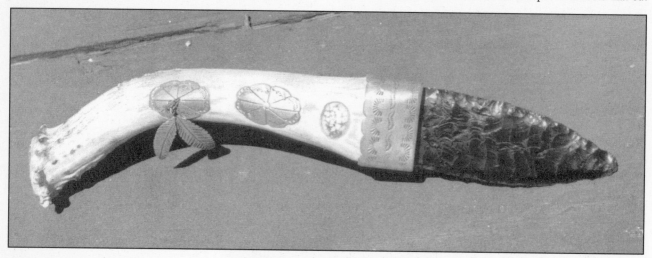

(Above) A modern replica of another early American design. The blade is chipped or knapped obsidian. Although somewhat brittle, the chipped blades are unmatched for sharpness.

(Right) The details of this antler handle with silver decorations show good work here, although the hanging feathers would be less than ideal on a working knife.

A skilfull craftsman could knap a blade to nearly any shape, length and thickness, depending on the intended use.

With light behind it, the obsidian blade is somewhat translucent in the thinner edge portion. Obsidian was made into knife blades, arrow heads, spear points and other useful tools before the development of bronze or iron.

Elsewhere in the world, in what is now Iraq, craftsmen were developing Damascus steel. These are modern Damascus blades, hand-made for Damascus USA Co. The blades are forged to shape, rather than cut from blank stock.

things. They may be large or small, designed to slice bread or cut enemies in half, poorly made or precision produced, expensive or cheap. In their simplest form, they are primarily cutting tools. We could not get along without them.

Perhaps another of the reasons knives are so universally favored by all civilizations and all nationalities is, aside from their usefulness, is the relative ease of manufacture. Knives may be made of almost any material, from broken glass, tin cans, aluminum, steel, screwdrivers, plastic and anything else that will hold an edge, for as little as one slice or stab. While local and national governments all over the world continue to attempt to restrict the access and ownership of firearms by citizens, controlling the distribution of knives would seem impossible.

Not that governing law enforcement bodies do not try. There are many local, state, provincial and national laws and rules regarding the use and possession of certain types of knives. The importation and manufacture of so-called switchblades, butterfly knives, daggers, dirks, and long-bladed locking knives is illegal or subject to many restrictions in several areas. Too often, local law enforcement officials interpret the rules as they wish, arresting people and confiscating their knives, because they might be dangerous or they fit some sort of threat criteria. At one time or another, even the ubiquitous Buck knife with a locking blade of more than 3 inches was considered a concealed weapon and its possession prohibited in some jurisdictions.

Knives are everywhere. All kinds, sizes and types of knives.

They are in our kitchens, tackle boxes, glove compartments, pockets, handbags, on belts, in boots and attached to the front of some rifles. They are used to cut string, fingernails, cardboard, wire, rope; to open letters, slice ham and turkey, butter bread, split kindling, repair leather reins, clean fish, cut hoses, open boxes, perform emergency operations, rescue accident victims, slash through undergrowth, open rations, graft fruit trees, and protect life and limb, every day throughout the world.

There are cheap knives and expensive knives; knives to collect and look at and knives to use in jungles and underwater. There are tiny knives and huge, long knives that we call swords, heavy knives and lightweight knives. They have blades made of traditional tool steel and of the latest Space Age lightweight alloys.

Knives are turned out in backyard shops by artistic craftsmen one per month, made to order, and at the rate of thousands per day from modern computer-controlled cutlery factories. Blades are hammered out by squatting Third World workers, much as they have done for hundreds of years, making them for sale in the most modernized countries. They are shipped thousands of miles to market or put to use in the same workshop in which they were produced.

The shape, size and uses of knives is limited only by the mind of those producing and using them. In the chapters ahead, the authors will discuss the variety of makers and users of knives, as well as provide you, the reader, with some idea of how and from what many knives are made.

KNIVES: THE THIRD OLDEST TOOL

Caught Knapping

Before the Bronze Age—before any kind of "Metal Age"—the Stone Age saw the development of knives, arrowheads and spear points chipped or knapped out of rocks. This progression probably occurred over tens of thousands of years, in several parts of the world.

Nobody knows where and how the first of these artifacts were made, but there is a similarity among the ancient tools found in all parts of the world where early man is known to have existed. Was there trade or did the skills evolve in several societies or groups at about the same time?

We will never know the answer to these questions, but the tools of those early times are duplicated today by a few dedicated students. With practice, they say, almost anybody with rudimentary manual skills and some rocks can produce the tools of our forebears.

John L. Sloan is a Tennessee writer and bowhunter who believes in getting back to basics in all his activities. During one of his hunting seminars in Indiana, Sloan encountered a man who still prefers the old ways.

Norm Blaker makes all his own bows, arrows and arrowheads. He knaps the arrowheads out of flint and other traditional stones, and has successfully taken deer and other game with these tools each year he hunts. Sloan interviewed Blaker and the following report is the result:

SEVERAL HUNDRED YEARS ago, a Native American, maybe a Huron or a Muskegon, passed through what is now Michigan on his way north to better hunting and fishing. He camped for a while as he traveled and made a few arrow points to use on the hunt. A day later, needing food, he loosed an arrow at a whitetail deer, but the arrow missed. He would have to wait awhile longer for a venison dinner on this trip.

Hundreds of years later, a seven-year-old boy, prowling the same trail after a heavy rain, found a strange-looking piece of rock. Thin and chipped along the edges, it was shaped like an arrowhead. For young Norm Blaker more than forty years ago, a love affair with tradition began and led to the development of a modern flint knapper.

There definitely is nothing new about making arrow points and knives out of flint or other rocks such as obsidian. My research into the history of man has taught me that those who could work rock were revered in every culture from the time man first learned to make things from the natural materials around him.

My North American Indian anthropology professor at the University of Wyoming was an excellent flint knapper. He also was exceedingly boring, until he started making skinning

Norm Blaker, flint knapper, displays some of his bows, arrows and flint tips. The black bear trophy was mounted by his son, Dave.

knives in class. There is something about the fashioning of things from raw materials that draws interest and crowds wherever it is done. That was true then, and it is true now.

It was that interest that drew me to study a slender, quiet man making things at a traditional archery tournament held in Indiana a couple of years ago. That same fascination drew me to him again at the Anderson Archery International Bowhunting Clinic in Grand Ledge, Michigan, a couple of summers ago.

Norm Blaker is from Hillsdale, Michigan. He loves to tinker with things. Certainly, he has no fear of experimenting and learning different ways to do things or, for that matter, to live a different lifestyle. He learned flint knapping—the art of making usable tools from flint—pretty much by trial and error and through continuing experimentation. By his own admission, from the moment he picked up that crude arrow point at the age of seven, he was hooked.

Norm (left) and Dave Blaker look over some of the finished work during the Anderson Archery Bowhunter Clinic in Grand Ledge, Michigan.

"I was intrigued with finding out how it was made," he remembers. "I had heard that perhaps Indians dropped the cool rocks in boiling water, then again cooled them rapidly, causing them to split. I quickly found out that was not the way to do it.

"So I started banging away on flint with hammers and things. I tried just applying pressure to the edges. Then, pretty much by accident, I stumbled upon the technique of using deer antler as a working tool. I started using different sizes and shapes of antlers, until I was able to get tools to fit my hand that did the job I wanted."

To look around Norm Blaker's exhibitor's booth at an out-door show is a little like being a kid in a candy store. You have the urge to handle everything you see, but at the same time, you are apprehensive that such beautiful items might be fragile.

In addition to arrow points—they are not called arrowheads by those who make them—the tables are adorned with knife blades, spear points, hatchets, pipes, bows and arrows, earrings and, oh, just all kinds of super stuff. Blaker, you see, is a master craftsman.

"It took a while to produce points that, in my opinion, were as good as the Indians made," he said. "Indians were not as concerned with their points as they were with their arrow shafts.

Two of Blaker's finished flint arrow and spear tips. No doubt, they could be also used as knives should the need exist.

Flint products are not simply pounded to shape. The work is more skilled, relying on firm pressure rather than sharp strikes. It takes a long time to develop the proper technique to be a good knapper.

A customer examines some of the flint-knapped products. Blaker displays his wares at a number of archery and blackpowder events around the Midwest.

For the most part, they took only close shots at game. Their points did a tremendous job. But to reach perfection in knapping, a point or a blade might require several years of experience. In fact, I have not reached that stage yet. As I started to use the antler for a tool, just pressing it along the flint edge, things began to get better.

"There was not much reading material on the subject available in those days. I've been doing this for more than forty years, and when I started, there just was not a great deal written on how to do it. Fortunately, there are more references available today."

Picking up tips here and there, and learning by doing, Blaker began to produce marketable items. His hobby began to grow and, in time, became a paying proposition. Norm Blaker is a retired carpenter. He and his wife, Jeanne, often accompanied by son, Dave, a master taxidermist, and Dave's wife, Penney, travel a great deal, attending traditional archery tournaments and buckskinner rendezvous.

"We are not getting rich," he says. "It is still just a hobby, but being retired, living on a fixed income, the shows allow my wife and me to travel and meet old and new friends. The sales we make usually just about pay for our trip."

Blaker is purely a traditionalist. He makes his own bows and arrows, points, knives and clothes. And he uses them.

"I hunt with the flint points in states where it is legal," he revealed, as another chip of flint fell at his feet. "Most of the laws regarding arrow points are rather archaic. States that have laws dictating the use of steel points do so only as a result of some broadhead companies offering the results of experiments with aluminum and plastic heads. For the most part, those heads

were designed to be practice heads only, but most lawmakers do not understand that.

"Believe me," he said with emphasis, "a flint point is every bit as lethal as any commercial steel broadhead on the market. But I also make steel arrow points, much like the early Indian trade points, to use in states that specify steel heads."

Blaker's bows usually are made to draw between 50 and 60 pounds draw weight at $27\frac{1}{2}$ inches draw length. He uses cedar or cane arrows and has deer, bear, boar and sheep to his credit.

"I am not a trophy hunter," he said quietly, as he flipped a strand of long hair from his face. "I kill animals for the freezer. I do it to eat. There is pleasure in hunting, yes. There is pleasure in using tools I made myself, too. But I don't just go out and

Norm and Dave Blaker look over some of the basic flint knapper's tools. They have not changed in thousands of years!

Flint blade knives are much in evidence on Blaker's table. Archers and bowhunters are natural customers for the products.

(Below) Blaker covers the ground under him to catch the flint chips while working in public showgrounds. The tiny chips are extremely sharp!

hunt all the time. I hunt with bow and arrows, and occasionally a flintlock rifle. I used to be the president of the Sauk Trail Long Rifles Club years ago. That was a good club. I still enjoy going to some of the blackpowder rendezvous. I make my own clothing and do quite a bit of leather work. Everything I make is done by hand."

Blaker says there is a tremendous explosion in a return to traditional values today.

"The young are getting interested in flint knapping," Blaker. "In fact, they are getting interested in all phases of traditional living. My main concern is to ensure that the young ones and the interested older, learning the trade, do it right. If they don't, it hurts everyone."

Norm Blaker buys most of his flint from a supplier. "I used to travel to Indiana and other places to find flint, but it takes too much time. Today, I get good flint in shorter time by just buying it."

In the days long gone, flint was a valuable trade commodity. Tribes—Indian and otherwise—who had access to flint carried it on their travels. It was a much sought-after trade item by the tribes who lived in areas where flint was scarce or non-existent.

Blaker looks like the typical mountain man of the 1800s. His hair is long and he wears a full beard and an earring. He is concerned about image:

"We have to pay attention to ethics and to our image. We, as hunters—not just traditional hunters, but all hunters—must present the right image," he said as he lightly fingered a beautiful arrow point that a few minutes ago was a rock.

I sure am glad I had the time to catch Norm Blaker knapping!

NEW DESIGNS, NEW MATERIALS

Blade materials and knife designs are constantly evolving

Most knifemakers, whether they work in the largest factory or in a little shop behind the garage, seem to be tinkerers, experimenters and investigators. They always are trying to improve their knife designs and find new ways to do old things. They always are trying out new materials for blades and handles. Each time you talk to one, he seems to have a new idea on how to decorate a knife or how to lock open a folding blade. Everything to do with knives, it seems, including the sheaths and pouches we carry them in, has changed over the years and continues to change.

One major continuing trend is the development and use of Damascus steel, especially by custom knifemakers. We will take a close look at the process in another chapter, but basically Damascus steel is produced when a piece of steel is heated until soft, hammered, folded, heated again, hammered and folded again perhaps hundreds of times. The patterns the process produces are always different from one blade to the next. Some makers have been able to manipulate the layers of steel to produce extraordinary designs and patterns. The process is slow, tedious and often requires great skill and strength on the part of the forger. To compensate for all that work, most good Damascus knives are quite expensive.

According to legend, the technique of producing Damascus steel was lost to European makers for hundreds of years. As the name implies, the process may have gotten its start in what is now known as Damascus, Iraq. As with most such technologies, others probably had developed it in other areas, too. The steel became famous for its cutting ability in swords and knives. Some of that reputation may have been the result of the ferocious Arab fighters who were wielding those weapons, as well as the cutting ability of the blades.

Bill Moran is generally accepted as the man who revived and repopularized Damascus steel for knife blades. His knives are highly prized by collectors.

Modern Damascus can take a number of fascinating patterns when produced by a skilled hand such as Jim Ferguson.

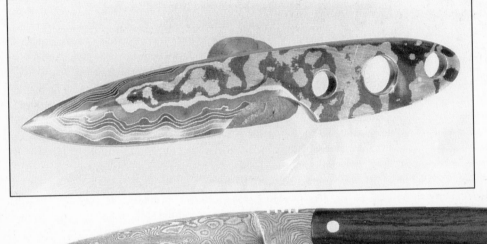

Jim Ferguson is the maker who produced this unusual Damascus blade. He calls it Twisted Nickel.

Damascus USA contracts out the task of hand-forging modern Damascus steel blade blanks, forged to shape. The knives are finished by other craftsmen. They are relatively inexpensive and, therefore, quite popular.

At any rate, the Damascus reputation spread over much of the Middle East, Europe and Asia—but not the formula for making it. The steel no doubt was produced in many small shops by dedicated, skilled workmen, who probably handed down the technique only to their close relatives—the old father-to-son routine. Somewhere along the way, as more modern and efficient steel-making techniques became common in much of Europe and America, the makers of Damascus were less in demand, and most ceased production. There was no longer a market for the product.

Over the years, collectors and craftsmen everywhere continued to be aware of Damascus steel. Plenty of examples of the ancient craft still are to be found. Some craftsmen attempted to duplicate the steel, but there were no instruction booklets to show them how. The increased interest in all things of a knife-like nature that followed World War II seems to have added further curiosity about Damascus. The reputation of the sharpness and quality of the steel grew to mythical proportions. It was probably never as good as the legends remembered, but reproducing Damascus steel was a challenge worthy of some of the best knifemakers of the middle of the century.

The man who is generally credited with rediscovering and

producing modern Damascus steel is William Moran. Others were involved in the rediscovery process, but it's generally agreed it was Bill Moran's work and the interest in it that brought the old/new process back to popularity. Moran also has been instrumental in renewing wider interest in hand-forging steel as a method of making custom knives.

There were others experimenting with Damascus. But today, there are many, some of whom hand-forge their blades, while others rely on power hammers and presses to fold the heated metals.

All manner of metal combinations have been tried, producing some fascinating Damascus patterns for blades and other art works. Every blade is different, just as every handmade knife blade produced by grinding and sanding is different from its predecessor. The types and properties of the various steels heated and hammered are what determine the outcome of the blade. Almost any two metals that have approximately the same melting point may produce a Damascus blade. The number of layers varies from two up to ten or twelve. Somewhere, some maker has experimented with many more layers than that. Tim Hancock, the Arizona blacksmith, makes knives with more than 300 layers.

The more dissimilar the various steels to be forged, the more distinctive the resulting pattern. Some makers use tool steel combined with stainless steel for a bright, contrasting look. Others use their skills to produce what is known as ladder Damascus, with the folded pattern running across the blade, rather than along its length. Designs, patterns, even complicated pictures may result from the blade maker's forging skills. These blades tend to be collectors' items rather than hunting knives. Most are highly desired by collectors and investors.

As the popularity and cost of Damascus has grown, a market for less-expensive blades of the material has developed. A number of suppliers are able to produce Damascus blade blanks and finished blades on a production-line basis, selling for far less, but presenting some beautiful patterns for knives. These can be produced with powerful machines in modern factories, but most are contracted out to craftsmen who are not necessarily custom knifemakers, but who forge the metal by hand. Essentially, these craftsmen make blades, while somebody else produces the finished knives.

Another old/new development in recent years is the interest in replicas of knapped flint knife blades, and several artists are practicing the skill (or art) of producing blades and arrowheads from stone. Examples of originals are common in many parts of North America, and thousands are found in private and public collections in museums and elsewhere.

Writer C. R. Learn has encountered a knifemaker who combines two of the ancient knife blade concepts, Damascus and flint, certainly an unusual concept. This is what he found:

LEROY REMER OF Triple R Knives lives about a hoot down the road from me. Once in a while, Remer and I get together and play "what if." This is a game where you take an idea, work it up into a project and sometimes you end up with a great end product. Other times, we come up with a great idea that just doesn't work out as we expect, even though the experience and techniques are fully utilized.

Over the years, I have become fanatic about Damascus or layered steel. The main problem is that it is perhaps one of the more expensive steels with which to work. And no two blades will ever be the same. There are craftsmen in the layered steel business who can come closer to uniformity than the eye can detect, but that quality of steel blade material is even more than expensive.

Damascus has some good points and only one bad one, as far as I am concerned. It cuts like no other steel, holds a good edge and is fantastic in appearance. The bad news is that unless it is layered of stainless steel, it can and does rust, so it behooves the knife user to keep the blade oiled. With proper care and handling, Damascus blades will last as long as any other.

Remer makes knives of the flint steel style by grinding the simulated flint chip configuration into the blade using a small arbor on his belt sander. He does it smoothly and fast.

I asked, "What if you made a Damascus flint steel blade with a horn butt handle? Would the Damascus pattern show with the flint-chip pattern?"

Not too long after that, I dropped by and he asked me what I thought of his flint-chipped blade.

"Looks great," I said, "but what was the steel?"

The reply was, Damascus. The appearance was not exactly what we had expected. The blade had been flinted or knapped, the Damascus etched and antiqued just Remer would treat any Damascus knife blade. It came out a dark color, but there was no visible pattern or figure of the layered steel.

Once you make a blade, you might as well use it, so we came to an agreement and I asked him to put a horn handle on it. I have lots of deer and other types of antler material on hand. He suggested a small additional section of the handle to be made of oosic. This takes a simple horn handle out of the normal routine, because oosic is not cheap, but does make a unique and good-looking handle material. The oosic, along with a brass finger guard offset with some black paper spacers, made a unique knife that most likely will not be duplicated again.

There is nothing wrong with the steel and the workmanship, but it just doesn't *look* like Damascus. But I know it is, because I saw the blanked blade as the knife was under construction. It is often difficult to sell a product when it doesn't look like what it is called—in this case, Damascus without figure.

The next question was how to make a Damascus flint-chip blade that looks like Damascus. It is relatively simple if you have Remer's years of experience. He suggested two variations. The first appealed to me because it would have a radiused base section on the hollow-ground blade. That would be finished in the normal Damascus manner for the pattern to show. The upper section and the base of the blade near the handle would be flinted to give it a different appearance. It would be half and half, with the flint on top and the smooth hollow grind on the cutting section.

A second variation would be to make a bigger blade and reverse the appearance—flint-chip the hollow-ground section and smooth-finish the upper section and base near the handle to bring out the pattern of the Damascus. This meant the attempt to flint the entire blade had not been a loss of time and effort, and probably could be remedied. If Remer used a finer-grit sanding belt, he would get a smoother knapped pattern on the flint. He had used a 60-grit belt on this knife. Maybe by taking it down to 320 or finer, the pattern of the Damascus would show in the surfaces of the flint blade.

Other variations continued to surface, but there was neither time nor inclination to follow through. Ideas like this are fun; they increase knowledge. And as long as the idea man picks up the mistake, there is nothing lost.

If you find a knifemaker at a show who will talk with you, it might be interesting to run ideas by him to see the response. Some will not make anything but the shapes they like; others will tackle anything you want to have made. The more popular the maker, the higher the price, of course, but think of the fun you will have had.

Many other materials have been tried for knife blades. There are several substances, such as ceramic sheets, that will produce an extremely sharp edge. But the ceramic blades are brittle and easily broken if pressure is exerted from the side, rather than directly onto the edge. The ceramic material tends to shatter much like a thin piece of glass. Broken glass has seen common use as blade material, but usually only as an emergency procedure.

Knifemaker Leroy Remer calls this blade material Flint Steel Damascus. The unsual look is created with power tools and requires a close examination to detect the Damascus pattern.

Damascus blades are known to hold their edge well even under heavy use. Remer's Flint Steel Damascus design combines the old with the new for a different yet pleasing working knife.

An antler handle complements the early knife look on this Leroy Remer creation.

In recent times, all sorts of manmade materials including plastics have been tried as knife blades and handles. One of the most common handle materials continues to be micarta, a product originally developed as an electrical insulator. It is unaffected by most liquids; does not crack, chip or peel; and is easily shaped. However, rumor has it that the original manufacturer is no longer making micarta, so knifemakers must look elsewhere for good, tough handles.

Fiberglass-reinforced plastics, resins and carbon substances are sometimes used as blade material. Aside from their durability and utility, the use of these kinds of knife blades is questionable. They may be undetectable by normal airport or public building metal-detecting equipment. The penalties for possessing weapons of this type might be severe.

That said, knives of some of these materials have their uses. A.G. Russell, the catalog knife retailer, has offered a small self-handle knife for years, intended as a letter-opener. The knives are lighter in weight than a similar knife of metal. They are impervious to moisture, sweat, oil and most other corrosive chemicals.

Precious metals have been used as knife blades for centuries. Gold and silver are the most common. They are too soft to be of much use for tough cutting chores, and if you lose one, you have lost a lot of money. As artistic expressions of the maker, gold and silver knives are unmatched.

A few years ago, custom knifemaker Buster Warenski made a replica of a ceremonial knife found buried with King Tut in ancient Egypt. The knife is gold, inset with many precious stones and carefully follows the design of the original. It will come as no surprise that the knife was made for collectors only and is valued at tens of thousands of dollars.

It seems likely that the Space Age, Electronic Age and Computer Age will see the development of other materials that might be used as knife blades. Certainly, new products will be found for the handles. But for this century, nothing has replaced good steel—and nothing is likely to do so in the near future.

One of the contenders on the popularity chart is titanium, a lightweight and tough metal. Titanium has seen plenty of use in aircraft and space vehicles, because it is so light, yet it is as strong as steel. It resists staining and corrosion as well as stainless steel, but weighs about the same as aluminum. Space vehicles and rockets use a lot of titanium. One of the drawbacks is that it is difficult to work; it tends to resist machining and wears out cutting tools fast. It also is expensive to obtain and expensive to work. But titanium-blade

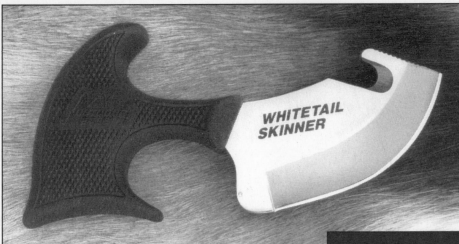

Outdoor Edge produces the unusual T-handle skinners with sharp gut hook blade. This is a very useful design for hunters and often imitated.

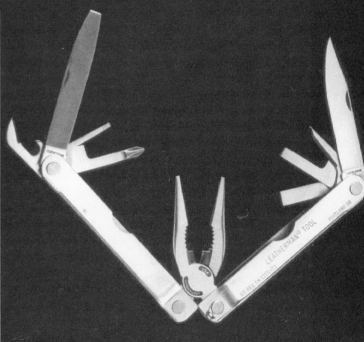

The original Leatherman tool contains a dozen or more tools folded into the handles. Many other makers now have variations on this theme, and they're all good sellers.

knives have found their way into military knives, diving knives, expensive folders and for other tools that may be exposed to corrosive situations.

Knife design trends currently seem to be moving in several directions at once. There are those who favor the traditional designs, such as the Bowie, the jackknife, daggers and fighting swords of a previous era. Others like fantasy knives that resemble next-century rocket ships, and multi-bladed hatchets, and multi-tool folders, both practical and impractical.

Perhaps one of the strongest trends is the so-called multi-tool. These are folding handles that contain handy tools such as pliers, screwdrivers, can openers, bottle openers, files, clippers, scissors as well as one or more knife blades. It seems every major North American knife brand is offering one or more of these multi-tools.

The liner-lock blade-locking system for folders is another new/old design that has gained considerable favor in recent years. Some of the earliest folding knives of more than a century ago used this design, but it has seen some major improvements lately. Most factories and many custom knifemakers offer at least one liner-lock folding knife.

Another trend noted is the rising popularity of swords and large knives. Perhaps it is due to the increasing interest in martial arts over much of the country. Schools teaching Filipino, Chinese and Japanese martial arts that utilize knives and swords are enjoying plenty of business. As you will note in another chapter, some custom sword makers are hard pressed to turn out blades fast enough to satisfy the demand. That has resulted in thousands of low-cost, lesser-value swords flooding the market from Europe and Asia. Some of these are satisfactory as display or decoration items, but their utilitarian value is questionable.

The best custom knifemakers, those who carefully build proven designs from the best steel and who use the greatest care when heat-treating the blades, produce the real thing. Their products are sought after by martial artists and collectors from around the world. High-quality swords and fighting knives never have lost their appeal nor their usefulness. Perhaps today's martial artist may never defend home and castle with a swinging sword, but they do want to have the best while practicing their art. Makers who can fulfill that require-

ment have no need to seek out more customers. Their customers seek them out.

The line between large fighting knives and swords is blurred, and there is little agreement about where one leaves off and the other begins. The difference may be one of employment. A sword generally is agreed to be a slashing, cutting weapon, held by one or two hands. A fighting knife usually is held by one hand and may be employed in a slashing or in a stabbing manner.

There are as many designs of fighters as there are practitioners of the art, with just as many ideas about what makes a good fighting knife. There are straight blades, curved blades, long blades, short blades, daggers worn up the sleeve or on the leg, folders and pocketknives. The technique of using the fighting knife is what dictates the design.

Later chapters will explore in detail some of those who are advancing the state of the art of knifemaking and knife using. Knifemakers and designers are constantly experimenting and modifying their products. What is new today will be old stuff in the next century—maybe even the next decade!

MILITARY KNIVES

Knives, swords, sabers, bayonets—
armies have used edged weapons for thousands of years

THE HISTORY OF military blades is shrouded in the same ancient mists as those that obscure the origins of knives themselves. The question of whether a chipped flint blade was used first to kill game or other humans never will be answered. Throughout history, blades of one kind or another always have been used to put down the enemy, whether it was the guy barricaded in the next cave or the soldier carrying an AK-47 who was trying to sneak through the barbed wire.

For many of us, the thought of military knives brings about a memory of bayonets. The bayonet, for its simplest definition, is a knife or short spear that is affixed to the end of a rifle. It is to be used as a last resort, when the soldier is out of ammunition, out of hand grenades, the radio is down and he must act to save his life or that of his buddies. In the days of muzzle-loading single shot rifles, a bayonet saw a lot more action than in more recent years. In the 20th century, the last great bayonet charges were conducted in World War I from the trenches of France.

Still, there were times during World War II and in the Korean War when the command, "Fix bayonets!" was given. No doubt, bayonets were used to kill enemies on both sides in those wars.

Most of the time, though, soldiers use their bayonets to open military-issue C-ration boxes and cans. They have dozens of other tasks, such as cutting rope and vines, digging holes and handling other duties. For the most part, militarily speaking, bayonets are defensive in nature, rather than offensive, but keep in mind those bayonet charges out of the trenches.

Through the late 19th century and into the 20th, the bayonet saw a great deal of evolution in its design. In the days of the American Civil War, the bayonet was strictly a dagger. It was intended to stab the enemy soldiers. There was no cutting and slashing involved. The cross-section of the bayonet blade was more or less triangular. The sharpened portion was the tip only, although there is little doubt that some infantrymen

Perhaps the best known military knife, from WWII to the present, is the Ka-Bar fighting knife, originally made for the U.S. Marine Corps.

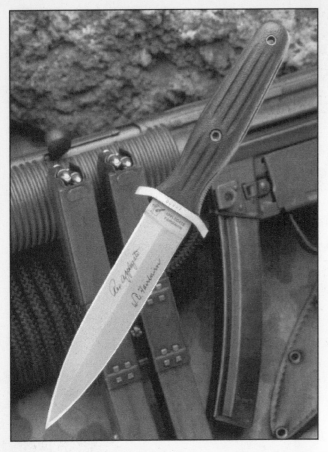

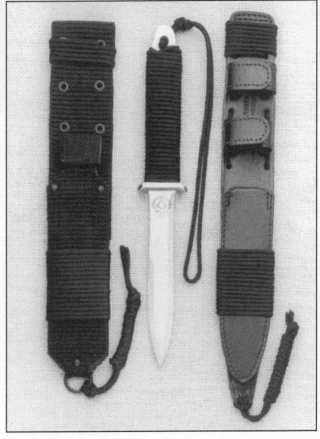

The Applegate-Fairbairn fighting dagger is another knife with a famous reputation. This replica is by Blackjack Knives.

The John Ek military knife design achieved fame in WWII. Ek knives are now produced by Blackjack Knives.

probably tried to put a knife edge on some bayonets. The triangular cross-section design remains with us today and may be seen on most of the bayonets affixed to the typical AK-47 and all its variants.

In modern times, the bayonets found on many of the short, lightweight, automatic and semi-automatic AK-47-type rifles and carbines are attached permanently to the rifle. When not in use, they fold back along the forearm or barrel, but they swivel out from the folded position, ready for use in an instant.

Because of the current ban on certain semi-automatic rifles

from civilian hands—the so-called assault weapons—buyers and collectors of these firearms often will find the bayonet attachments have been filed or ground off the rifles to satisfy legal requirements. Whether such acts will have any effect on the availability of bayonets remains to be seen.

Another philosophy of military knives was that of a small shovel or trowel that curved to a point and had the edges sharpened. The authors have seen several versions of this design in museums. These pre-dated the ever-handy entrenching tool by at least a century. Make no mistake, these entrenching tools,

The updated version of the Vietnam War SOG military knife was originally designed for Special Forces use. SOG Specialty Knives produces this replica with blued blade. It's highly popular with veterans and collectors.

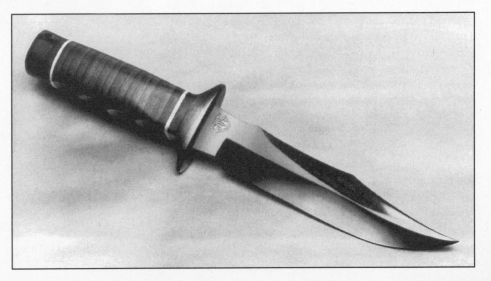

This photo dates back to Tunisia in WWII. A Gurkha soldier in the British army brandishes his issue Kukri military knife. The Gurkhas are fierce and respected fighters.

(Below) In more modern times, Marine Corporal Scott Wyble carries a 15-inch Ang Khola-style Kurkri for various uses in the field. It's still an efficient knife.

small shovels and spades, can be and have been used as weapons when necessary.

Early models of these spade-like knives/bayonets carried wide blades measuring about 8 or 9 inches in length and 4 to 5 inches in width. Some have concave-convex cross-sections. All appear to be quite sharp on the edges, but it must have been a task to keep them sharp for inspection and use. Most were made of carbon steel, and rust prevention was a problem for the soldiers who had them.

Bayonets have gone through several evolutions of design and employment. They have gone from long to short to long and back to short a number of times. The WWI and WWII versions were relatively long-bladed affairs. Later, as the M-14 replaced the M-1, then to be replaced by the M-16 rifle, the bayonet became shorter, with a more knife-like appearance, and was sharpened on both edges. In combat and bayonet practice, employment means more slashing than straight stabbing.

Reality began to manifest itself in the minds of the designers.

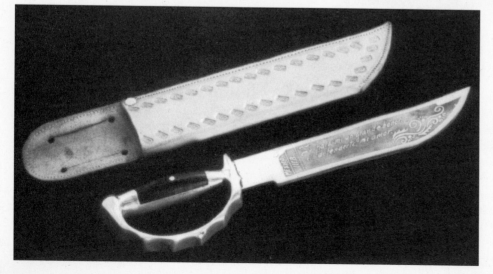

Buckle 'N Blade made this replica of the Mexican Iron Fist knife, complete with knuckle guard. It would be illegal in some communities.

Major Bruce "Doc" Norton, USMC (Retired), is director of the Command Museum, Marine Corps Recruit Depot, San Diego, California.

Apparently, the routine use of bayonets to open rations and ammunition boxes, dig out stubborn roots and rocks from fighting holes, opening gas and oil cans, and dozens of other non-combat functions dawned on the military designers. The latest official U.S. military bayonet, as manufactured by Buck Knives, is primarily a rugged military knife that fits onto the barrel of the M-16 rifle. It has specific functional design elements to serve as a barbed wire cutter, can opener, saw, large knife and several other tools. A hole in the blade fits over a lug pin on the sheath to form a strong leveraged wire cutter. Cutting wire and steel bands is not at all uncommon in today's military. With minor modifications, the Buck-made U.S. bayonet makes a terrific large camp or survival knife, as well.

Discounting swords, the military has long been called upon to use machetes and bolo knives, especially in the jungles of Central America, the Pacific islands, the Philippines and the countries of Southeast Asia.

The Philippines and Central America, in particular, have shown us the effects of a carefully wielded long machete. Their use and employment still is taught to U.S. servicemen in Central America.

As with most martial art weapons, these long blades have a practical agricultural as well as a military use. Machetes are great for chopping down sugar cane, cutting through thick jungle growth and slicing heavy bamboo trees.

Many modern armies have learned what seemingly primitive long knives can do in the hands of desperate and motivated peasants. The U.S. military forces have adopted and adapted a number of machete and bolo styles for official use since the days of the Spanish-American War, during WWII and through operations in Vietnam and Panama. No doubt, the future holds more situations calling for the military use of machetes.

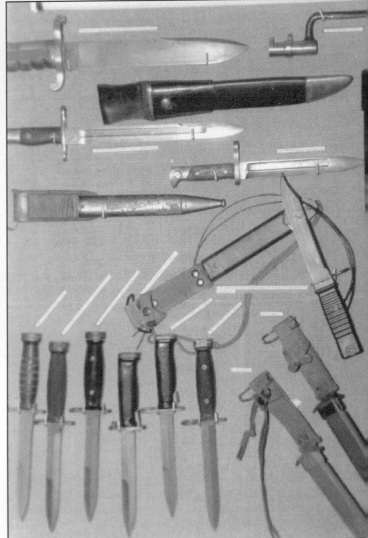

Cold Steel is the title of this display of bayonets dating back to the Civil War days. It shows an interesting evolution of the tool.

The trench knife of WWI fame, with a "brass-knuckle" hand guard, was listed officially as the Model 1917-1918, according to research by Bernard Levine. The "knuckle-duster" version with individual finger holes in the guard is still valued by collectors, although production stopped in 1918. Some were still in the supply system and issued during the early part of WWII. Today, in California and some other states, any brass-knuckle device, with or without a knife blade, is illegal to own or sell. Examples may be found in some military museums, however.

There are several well-known knife designs that gained fame in WWII. Some were handmade by Hoyt Buck, Bo Randall, John Ek, David Murphy and by several production factories such as Ka-Bar, Case, Camillus, Imperial and others. The U.S. Marine Corps version of the famous Fairbairn-Sykes Commando knife was made by Camillus and issued to the Marine Raiders fighting in the Pacific. In recent times, several manufacturers have produced updated replicas and commemoratives that still are favored by collectors.

More recent wars and "peace-keeping" operations have sparked the interest of some casual as well as dedicated collectors

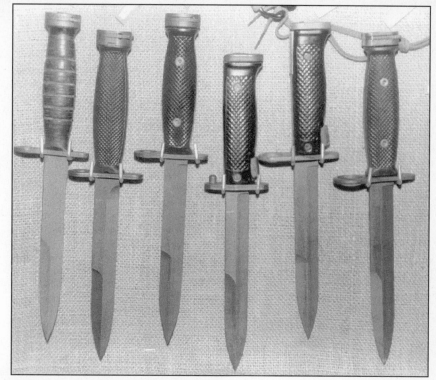

The MCRD Command Museum has comprehensive displays of modern military bayonets like these U.S. models.

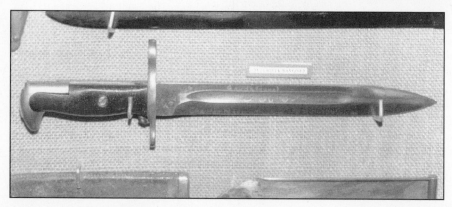

Bayonets and entrenching tools of a much older era are chronicled in the MCRD museum. This bayonet was used on the South Pacific island of Guadalcanal in WWII.

and history buffs. But that interest does not seem as intense as that shown in the knives of WWI and WWII. Most of those who had knives in Korea during the early 1950s had Ka-Bars and used them for everything from opening C-ration boxes, cutting wire, digging slit trenches and slicing food, as well as providing some entertainment to bored troops in knife-throwing contests.

As for Vietnam, the typical edged weapon in the hands of troops included the Ka-Bar, machetes and several models of the Swiss Army Knife. One of the most sought-after is the much-copied Studies and Observation Group knife, later known as Special Operations Group (SOG) type. Some were marked with the Army's Special Forces badge and appropriately inscribed. Many were intended to be used for covert-action operations. They were large, practical fixed-blade knives, but not many were made and issued during the Vietnam War. All, at the time, were sought after by GIs and civilian workers. Everyone wanted one as a souvenir of the war, especially those who had not been issued one. Some of these SOGs were made in Okinawa, but have no maker's identification on them.

Others, marked as made by Japan Sword, were longer and

slimmer than those of the original design. Legend has it that these were intended to be used by the CIA. The originals have a collector value of $1000 and up.

Since the Vietnam War ended, there continues to be a demand for the original issue knives, as well as replicas. Documented and verified originals continue to be highly sought. However, because of this, there are many unscrupulous makers and dealers who peddle fakes and replicas as the genuine article. Any buyer must beware of these and study the knife for clues of authenticity or of later manufacturing techniques.

SOG Specialty Knives is a manufacturer that has featured the SOG knife for several years. The design is a frank replica of the original, but probably of somewhat higher quality. As of this writing, they are still cataloged and include several interesting variations on the original SOG design.

Of even newer design, strictly to military specs but available to the public, is the Buck-made M9 military bayonet. The original design was by a small company called Phrobis III, although Buck Knives got the contract to manufacture them in the many thousands that were required. At last check, the M9 was still in

This is a numbered commemorative version of the modern, current U.S. M9 bayonet, as manufactured by Buck Knives.

production by Buck and is being sold to several foreign governments for their military.

One of the unique features is the oval cut-out near the tip of the blade that accepts a special lug designed into the sheath. Slipped together, the blade swivels on the lug to act as a barbed-wire cutter.

For civilian use, the M9 is a fine camp or survival knife. In fact, most modern military knives have plenty of practical civilian uses. Perhaps, that is one reason they remain so popular with all knife users.

Probably the best known foreign-made military knife is the famous Kukri. "Kukri" seems to be the American spelling for the curved knife. In Nepal, the spelling is "Khukuri." No matter the spelling, it is the official issue arm of the Nepalese Gurkha troops who serve in the British Army, although that may be history by the time you read this. The basic design dates back to ancient times and still is being produced in India and Pakistan as well as Nepal.

Quality of the available Kukris in the U.S. varies from poor, made-for-tourists to fine working and collectible examples.

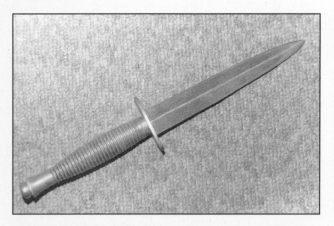

The Fairbairn-Sykes knife is one of the most famous designs to come out at WWII and has been updated today. Originals like this one are prized by collectors.

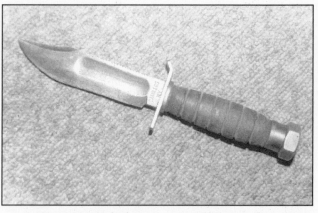

During WWII, Camillus Cutlery of New York turned out thousands of military fighting knives like this, and the design is still a viable one.

This old machete is marked USMC and may have seen service in Central America in the 1920s.

The long military machete is still in use in many parts of the world. The basic design is a good one and hasn't changed in many years.

There are several importers in the U.S. who sell through dealers and through catalogs. Most of the time, several models, sizes and qualities may be seen at gun shows throughout the country.

The best are made in Nepal. They are hand-forged and fired in yak dung. The handle has been painstakingly formed from the horn of Nepal's beautiful spotted deer. The scabbard is made of water buffalo leather, hand-worked and hand-sewn. Some wood sheaths are covered with leather or velvet and are built to hold one or two additional smaller knives.

Most Nepalese Kukris are made by workers who have access to only the most basic tools. They have no electricity or phones. They will use a charcoal pit, leather bellows, tongs and an anvil probably made from a section of railroad track. Steel is hard to come by, too, sometimes calling for a week's walk by the knifemaker to his source.

There is no such thing as 440C stainless steel blades used in the production of genuine Kukris. Because they are handmade, no two are alike. Each is a custom knife, made by hand. Fans of the Kukri claim a good one will last through 50 to 100 years of hard use in jungles, deserts, northern forests—and on the urban streets most of us inhabit.

One of the best places to see a lot of old and modern military knives and bayonets of all types is in a museum, especially a military museum. One of the best is the Command Museum at the Marine Corps Recruit Depot, San Diego, California. The museum is open to the public, usually seven days a week. The public is always welcome, and visitors have no problem being admitted to the historic recruit training facility. The recruit depot is just north of downtown San Diego, a block or two west of I-5, with plenty of directional signs to get the visitor to the museum, which is only a few feet from the main gate.

The director of the museum is one of our old Marine Corps buddies, Major Bruce "Doc" Norton, USMC (Retired). He still carries the nickname Doc, because during the Vietnam War, before he went to college and got a commission in the Marine Corps, he was a Navy medical corpsman, serving with a force reconnaissance company with some of the toughest Marines to be found anywhere. Doc Norton was the only Navy corpsman to be entrusted with a leadership role during many patrols in enemy territory. He has written books about his experiences, and they have become bestsellers within the non-fiction military book genre.

As one might expect, the MCRD Command Museum contains plenty of firearms and bayonets on display, in addition to a great deal of other artifacts of wars past. There are uniforms, dioramas, paintings, photographs, flags, films and equipment used by Marines over the past 225 years. It is the place to go for those interested in history or especially those interested in military knives and bayonets. The display items are all carefully identified and cataloged. Even those unfamiliar with the historic nature of the blades on display will be able to identify most of them and determine where they belong in the history of the Marine Corps.

For instance, several of the display cases chronicle the development of bayonets from Civil War days to the present. Others show machetes and bolo knives from various places such as the Philippines and Central America. There also are several examples of early entrenching tools that resemble modern gardening trowels rather than the small shovels that they actually are.

The museum's military knife displays take us right up to the present with examples of the current-issue M9 bayonet. Those with plans or a chance to visit Southern California will be rewarded if they add the MCRD Command Museum to their list of tourist stops.

Another extensive collection of old and new military bayonets, knives and other weapons is to be found at the Museum of Historical Arms in Miami, Florida. The museum features antique swords, daggers, firearms and accoutrements from all over the world, and is recommended by knife consultant and author Bernard Levine. His *Levine's Guide to Knives and Their Values,* now in its third edition from DBI Books, is the bible of knife collectors and buyers. We are indebted to Levine for much of the research material found in this chapter.

THE NAVY SEAL KNIFE CONTROVERSY

Will the real SEAL Knife please stand up?

ANYTIME A KNIFE manufacturer can add the term, "Official Knife of ..." to his sales literature and advertising message, it can mean extra sales in the civilian market as well as acceptance by other military organizations.

The Navy's SEALs, (SEa, Air, Land) personnel are probably the most specialized elite military group in the world today. SEALs must undergo a rigorous training program that has been devised to produce the consummate warrior for special duties and tasks. Only a select few endure and are accorded the right to wear the SEAL trident on their uniform. The weapons they use are the best available and often are non-traditional to the rest of the military establishment.

At least two U.S. knife manufacturers are claiming to produce the "official" knife for the SEALs. There is a bit of a problem with this designation, because it is the authors' understanding that the SEALs may use almost any weapon, any knife, they choose, within certain specifications. Each of these volunteers is free to select whatever knife he firmly believes will be the most efficient and serviceable in accomplishing his mission as part of the team.

The two contenders to the title are SOG Specialty Knives and Mission Knives. Both no doubt are selling hundreds of knives to SEALs and others, including civilians, who appreciate a large, tough, practical knife worthy of the name. Each claims to be making the official knife for SEALs. Perhaps it really does not matter to civilian buyers which knife is or is not the official design. Both are excellent and worthy of our attention and consideration. Let's take a look at the SOG offering first.

Spencer Frazer, the head man at SOG Knives, says the development of the new official Navy SEAL knife was one of the most extensive testing and evaluation programs ever undertaken by the U.S. government.

"The program," he relates, "included every cutlery manufacturer in the U.S. We are proud to announce that the SOG SEAL Knife 2000 has been appointed the one and only official Navy SEAL knife.

"This knife evaluation program included the following tests: tip-breaking strengths, blade-breaking toughness, sharpness and edge retention, handle twist-off limits, two-week saltwater immersion tests, gasoline and acetylene torch resistance, chopping, hammering, prying, penetration, cutting six different types of rope and nylon line, low noise and reflectivity evaluation, plus an intense hands-on competition in the field."

The accepted knife is made with a blade of 440A stainless steel, 7 inches long and 1/4-inch thick. The blade is powder-coated with black, scratch-resistant surface. It is hardened to Rockwell 55-56C status, and the blade has a 1 1/2-inch serrated edge near the handle. Overall length is 12 1/4 inches and the knife weighs 12.7 ounces without the sheath. The handle is made of deeply checkered, non-slip Kraton with a thong hole in the butt. The sheath is black nylon with hard plastic inserts, eyelets, two retaining straps and a quick-release belt loop.

"The SEAL-2000 has a nice heft in the hand and good balance. It may be employed in any of several holds or positions," says Frazer. "The checkered handle offers a firm grip with any hold, in either hand. We believe that any serviceman or woman, Navy SEAL, Army Ranger or Marine Recon member, will find the SOG knife giving many years of satisfaction. It is available on the civilian market without any changes to the military specifications."

A slightly different approach is taken by Mission Knives, a

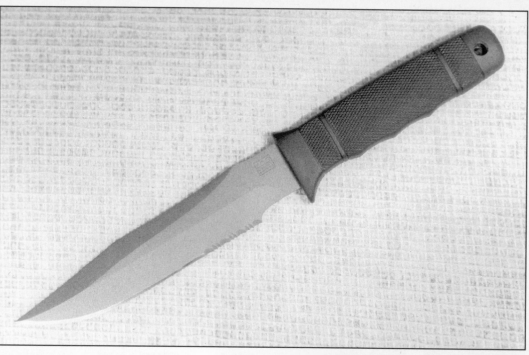

The SOG SEAL-2000 is a rugged, good looking knife. The handle is of deeply checkered, non-slip Kraton and has a thong hole in the butt.

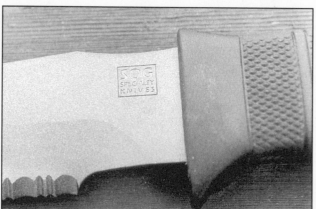

The SOG knife has a dull, non-glare finish on the blade that is scratch-resistant and long wearing.

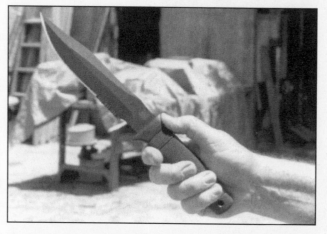

The SOG has nice balance when held in the straight grip. This is a tough, no-nonsense fighting knife, for sure.

company that specializes in titanium alloy blades. As a result, the knives from Mission are surprisingly lightweight and tough. The first time one picks up this SEAL knife, the lightness is obvious. The large Multi-Purpose Combat (MPC) model, for instance, weighs only 9 1/2 ounces. The knife is well balanced in the hand and cuts through things like jungle vines and medium-size branches with ease.

Richard Schultz is the vice president of Mission Knives. He says that some of the features of the MPC design are targeted to the Army Rangers and Marine Corps reconnaissance market. It also will be available on the civilian market with no changes after production has caught up with the hundreds of orders Schultz says were on the books by the end of 1996. Army Rangers and Marine recon troops are perhaps no less well trained for their hazardous missions, specializing in operations behind enemy lines, observing and reporting enemy troops, or taking out enemy commanders or other targets. None of it is easy, and they demand and receive the best equipment available. No commander would want to do less.

With the blade held along the forearm, the SOG knife is a deadly weapon. The serrated portion of the blade is clearly visible.

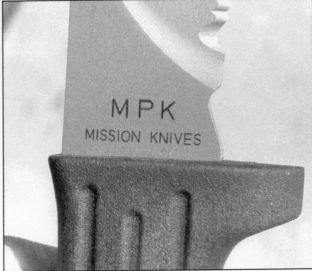

On the civilian version, Mission Knives clearly marks the non-glare blade. The titanium is impervious to corrosion, sea water and most other damaging environments.

Ready for action, the Mission Knives Multi-Purpose Combat knife will cut cleanly through most smaller vines and undergrowth.

The titanium blade makes for a lightweight knife. Note the clean lines, partially serrated edge and clear grind line.

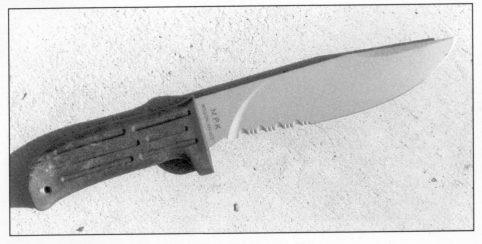

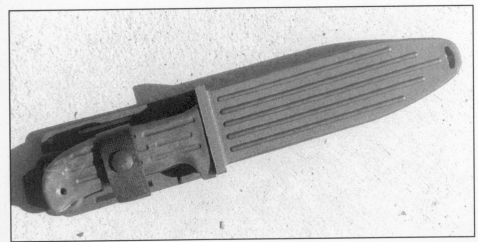

The Mission sheath is made of the same material as the non-slip handle using the same injection moulding methods.

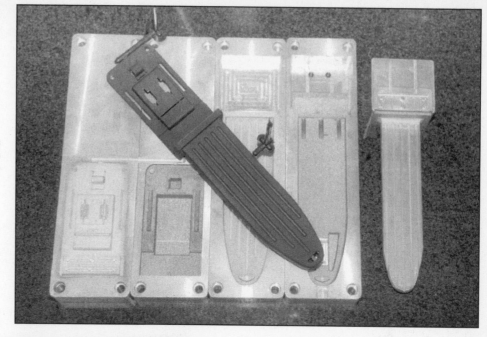

The hot Kevlar-Hytrel sheath material is injected into the moulds while in liquid form. It's flexible yet extremely durable.

This finished titanium blade blank is ready to receive a Kevlar-Hytrel handle. The blade is unmarked for military sale.

The most obvious feature of the knife is the 7¼-inch non-reflective titanium alloy blade that is sharpened with a V-grind for strength and has 2 inches of blade serrations.

"The blade is immune to corrosion, sea water and all natural environments," declares Schultz. "It is non-magnetic per the military MIL-M-19595 specs. It passed that test in 1993. Tests show a tensile strength of 250,000 psi at minimum. The blade is heat-treated to a Rockwell C rating of 44-46."

The blade is ¼-inch thick, and the knife is 11⅞ inches long. It has no markings when sold to the military market.

Titanium is much more difficult to work, as compared to steel. It certainly is more expensive. At this writing, Schultz and his people had not made a decision as to whether or not the MPC will have a blood groove in the top part of the blade. If so,

it will be for marketing purposes, rather than practical value. Mission Knives wants the new knife to be reminiscent of the Ka-Bar design that most Rangers and Marine recon people used in Vietnam.

One change they have made from the Navy SEAL knife design is to move the sharpened part of the blade forward ½-inch to accommodate a finger groove near the handle.

The handle is a one-piece textured and grooved Kevlar fiber in a black Hytrel base. It is formed over the full tang by a pressurized, injection-moulding machine. The knife tang is placed in one side of the heavy steel mould, and after the other side has been locked in place, the liquid Kevlar is injected into the cavity. The Kevlar substance cools and the mould halves are broken apart. Only touch-up cleaning is required to finish the handle.

The blade tang is placed in one side of the injection mould before the handle material is injected.

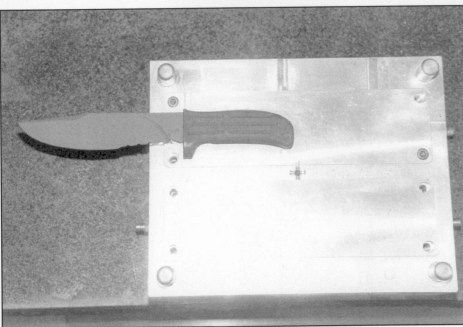

The completed handle cools and the mould is opened to reveal a finished knife.

The sheath is formed in the same manner, using the same Kevlar and Hytrel material as the handle. It is suitable for field, SCUBA (underwater) and jump operations. The knife is held firmly and safely in the flexible sheath. The sheath and handle are fire-resistant and electrically non-conductive. They are equally immune to saltwater or any other corrosive action caused by the environment.

Mission Knives already has shipped hundreds of its SEAL and MPC knives to military buyers. They have been through numerous field tests as well as actual employment on active duty. Rick Schultz anticipates many more orders from military and civilian buyers. It is easy to use, feels good in the hand and is noticeably light in weight.

Whichever knife gains official acceptance by SEALs, Rangers, recon Marines or the larger, entire military establishment, it will mean a great deal to that manufacturer. For the general public, it is a win-win situation. All this design and testing creates better knives for anyone who uses them. No doubt, we will hear more about the competition and the results as time progresses.

A MATTER OF SURVIVAL

What is a survival/fighting knife, and how might it be used?

The authors do not advocate fighting with a knife, and we hope you never have to protect yourself or a loved one with a knife. But should it come to a matter of life and death for you or a loved one, you might want to know what to choose and how to use it in self-defense or in a survival situation.

Knowing the rules and some techniques might just save a life someday—perhaps your own. With that in mind, we present these thoughts on what, when and how to use a knife in a confrontation, if there is no other alternative.

THERE IS A particular saying among knife fighters and martial artists who teach it. The saying is that the first rule of knife fighting is: "Run!"

That's pretty good advice, actually. You must assume that the bad guy—your potential opponent—has far more experience and strength; is in possession of a larger, sharper knife; has several armed buddies to take you down if something happens to him; and is a street-trained fighter. The obvious best and primary advice is to not let yourself get into a situation that would require you to defend yourself with a knife—or any other weapon.

However, it does happen to innocent, unsuspecting citizens in large cities and small towns. It happens all the time. You can read about it in the newspaper almost every day.

The Rule of Run is only slightly facetious. All things considered, most legitimate martial arts instructors and trainers tend to recommend taking the easiest and fastest way out, if there is one. It is not the way of a coward. Forget about honor; forget about saving face or appearing brave. Get out. But if you must save a life by using a knife to stop an assailant or defend against a knife attack, there are some things you should know.

Paul Vunak is a well-known martial arts coach and teacher, trained in Filipino stick fighting techniques as well as in the Jeet Kune Do concepts of the late Bruce Lee. Knife fighting should be taught by qualified teachers only.

Martial arts students wear protective gear and substitute sticks for knives during a workout under the eye of an instructor. Note the strong-hand lead.

There is no way we can teach the basics of knife fighting in this one chapter, or in a whole book on the subject, for that matter. Several excellent books and no small number of popular magazines and videos are devoted to the subject. It is a legitimate martial art and may be studied with any of several teachers around the world.

Make no mistake, however, about the fact that most courts and legal jurisdictions look upon almost any knife as a lethal weapon, much as is the case with a firearm, when it comes to the law. To claim self-defense in any confrontation, you must prove three things: First, the assailant had the means, the opportunity and the ability to kill or seriously injure you or some other party. Second, there was a threat to a human being. (Remember, if the assailant dropped his weapon, turned away or was much smaller, weaker, older or younger than you, he is not considered to be a threat to your life or health.) And finally, you must be sure the use of lethal defensive force was the only alternative.

You may not use lethal force to save or protect your property. If your car is about to be broken into or stolen, or you catch a burglar in the act of stealing the VCR from the house, he is not armed and makes no threats to you, you cannot use a knife to save your property. You can protect yourself with a knife only if there is a threat to yours or someone else's life. You may not like that and you may wish to debate the laws, but that is the way it is in today's courts.

There may be several definitions of a fighting knife, but they are similar to the definitions of a survival knife. The knife that will save your life is also the one you have with you when you need it. It could be a tiny folding pocket knife or a really large blade such as the huge Bowie type carried by Paul Hogan in the movie *Crocodile Dundee*. In most jurisdictions, however, local officials might want to ask you what you were doing with such a large knife.

Sometimes, the only thing you will have is a pocket folder. Remember, though, the knife you don't have with you will do you no good in a knife fight or in a survival situation.

To be realistic, the knife most of us carry is a folder. On a hunting or fishing trip, we probably will be carrying a larger sheath knife. But a folder with a 3- to 4-inch blade is possibly what most of us will have available when the need arises.

To be sure, in some areas around many hunting camps, particularly if in remote or rural neighborhoods, you might not draw a second glance when carrying a large sheath knife on your belt. Those with assignments in certain foreign countries or remote locations would not think of venturing forth without at least one or more so-called survival knives. Everyone else will have one or two, often carried in plain view. Many cultures have no hangups about that.

A large, strong, sharp knife has multiple uses beyond self-defense and combat. Such tasks might include opening a can of pork and beans, cutting kindling to get a campfire started, chopping a few pine bows for a softer bed, cutting through seaweed or kelp that has tangled the outboard motor propeller, cutting a fouled anchor line, severing a seatbelt to free a person in a wrecked car, hollowing out a small shelter from the wind in a sudden storm, field-dressing a deer—and a thousand other things we might be able to think of. Some of those uses might not be a matter of life and death or self-defense, but they certainly can be comfort and health considerations.

In a survival situation, the smallest pocketknife, if that is all you are carrying, can be a weapon or survival tool. If the knife is a folder, the blade-locking mechanism should be strong and foolproof. There can be no chance that it might close inadvertently, causing a cut or injury at best, or a loss of your life at worst.

There are several mechanical blade locking systems for folders that have been around for years. Most are safe and convenient, but the buyer should examine the mechanism carefully. Ask questions. Find out how it works. Make a decision to get the most rugged folder available.

In recent years, the so-called liner-locking mechanism has become popular with factory-production and handmade knives. Most are rugged enough that the other parts will fail before the blade will close accidentally. However, if the spring liner lock is too thin and weak, and if the design is flimsy, the locking mechanism can override and permit the blade to close when it should not. Test it by hammering the back of the blade smartly against the workbench, making sure your fingers are out of the way. In a poor design, the blade may snap shut. Incidentally, it would be a good idea to ask the knife's owner for permission before doing this research!

The folder, large or small, has one advantage in that it is likely to be carried most of the time. Therefore, it is most likely to be available in an emergency situation. For purposes of this discussion, let it be known that the folder has some inherent weaknesses. Usually, it will be on the small side and will not be the best tool for life-protection or survival use. Anything mechanical is subject to failure. The pivot pin may foul, rust or break. The locking mechanism may be clogged with dirt or may break. The folding blade must be opened before it can be used.

Those fractions of a second might mean the difference between success and failure. The current popular design of

This long blade tanto by Cold Steel is definitely a survival/fighting knife design.

While a long fixed-blade knife may be more effective, the one most likely to be carried is a folder such as these Spyderco pocket clip models designed by Bob Terzuola.

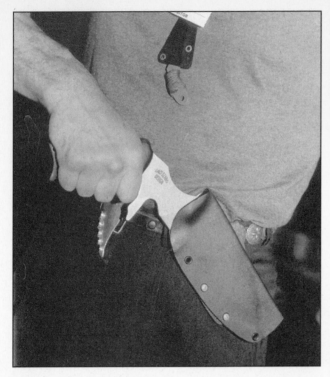

A different fighting knife design is the sheath model that is worn and drawn much like a pistol.

Laci Szabo is a respected martial arts instructor who designed the knife he holds. Note the extended finger guard.

In an emergency, any knife, no matter how small and light, may serve as a defensive weapon when the need arises.

using a button or hole in the blade to open it quickly and easily is a solution to the time-delay problem. Almost every knifemaker has one or more one-hand-opening folding knives.

A sheath knife is ready to be used as soon as it is in the hand. It usually will be larger and stronger than a folder, and more suited to the task at hand. Because there are no moving parts, the sheath knife usually will be lighter in weight than the same size folder. In these situations, bigger truly is better.

There are as many theories and schools of self-defense with knives as there are martial artists, it seems. Many of these schools are hundreds if not thousands of years old. The philosophies and the techniques have been passed down through hundreds of teachers and students, generation after generation.

The authors do not intend to summarize, categorize or judge any of these schools and their artists. All of them have far more knowledge and experience beyond anything we might discuss here.

As for knife fighting, there always seems to be the question of what grip to use in holding the knife. Some will say the best technique is having the tip pointed outward, toward the opponent. That will keep the opponent as far away from your body as possible. Others propose holding the knife with a reverse grip—the blade edge upward along and beneath the forearm. The movement is like an uppercut blow by a boxer. It is said to project plenty of power to the knife.

Instructor Paul Vunak (right) demonstrates the close-in technique of "defanging the snake" with a stick rather than a knife.

Becoming a skilled knife fighter takes years of training and practice. The basic moves may be learned, but not mastered, in a few days.

Most martial arts teachers will say that, if possible, the best defensive move is a slashing motion, rather than a stab. You are more likely to hit the target and do more damage with the slash. There are plenty of situations, though, that would dictate simply doing anything, making any move, that will ward off or damage an assailant, ending the attack against you.

For instance, if you are grabbed from the rear around the neck or head, the only thing you might be able to do is stab directly to the rear. There would be no chance of setting yourself up in a fighting stance, ready to fend off the attack.

If there is the time and opportunity, a defensive knife handler will attempt to present the smallest target possible to his or her attacker. You don't want to stand squarely facing the opponent. Some teachers advocate holding the knife in the strong or dominant hand, while turning the body to present only one side of the body to risk. The knife arm would be at about a 45-degree angle, ready to withdraw or spring forward as the situation developed.

The hand without the knife, the weak hand, should be held against the lower chest and upper abdomen area to at least partially protect the heart and lungs. You must move and turn, keeping the angle on your attacker, much as a boxer might. Footwork is as important here as it is for a boxer.

One school of martial arts teaches the knife fighter to "defang the snake." A cutting slash across the back of the assailant's knife hand will cut tendon and muscle, causing the opponent to drop the knife, stick, broken bottle or whatever is being used. This will happen no matter how big and strong the guy is, even if he is a raging drunk or stoned on drugs. Once the tendons are cut, the hand no longer can grip. The opponent still may be able to hammer you over the head with his other hand, but the knife action may buy you enough time to get away.

That is the extent of the advice we will give on protection or street survival using a knife. But remember, the first rule of knife fighting is worth repeating: "Run!"

Most of us prefer to think of a knife as a useful tool, rather than some sort of weapon. Knives perform hundreds of legitimate tasks every day for us, from cutting through a tender steak, buttering the bread, cutting string, opening packages, stripping wire, pruning and trimming our plants, sharpening pencils and many things other than saving lives. But saving lives is one of the tasks knives have been called on to perform for perhaps hundreds of thousands of years.

There will be more of the same in the 21st century. With preparation, we all should have a better chance of survival.

Take a careful look at some of the knife designs that are available in the survival and fighting categories. Talk to martial artists about the problem. If you are interested, there are hundreds of instructional videos, magazines, books and schools where you may increase your knowledge and your chances of survival in the future.

KEEPING IT SHARP

No doubt about it, a sharp blade is a good blade

"LOOK SHARP, BE Sharp" was an advertising slogan for a shaving product a few decades ago. It was a good idea then and a good idea now, at least when it comes to razor blades and other edged tools.

From the time of our Boy Scout days, we have known dull knives cause more accidental cuts than sharp blades. We know we don't keep those kitchen knives sharp enough, often enough to satisfy the spouse. Think about that little folder in your pocket. When was the last time you sharpened the blade? Carving the holiday turkey or Easter ham is a cinch if the knife is sharp, but a real chore with a dull blade.

In its simplest definition, sharpening a blade means removing the chipped, bent, worn or dulled metal from the blade and replacing it with a correctly tapered, properly angled and gritted sharp cutting edge. It is easy to say and define, but for most of us it is not so easy to do.

For some, getting a good edge on a blade seems easy. It comes naturally. For others, it is more difficult, almost impossi-

The hands of professional custom knifemaker Charles Weiss have decades of experience at sharpening knives. Weiss uses the traditional method of working on an oil stone to sharpen knives. The angle between the stone and the blade must be constant.

Final honing of a sharpened blade may be done on a leather strap. The blade edge is drawn away from the leather, to the left in this photo. The process removes any tiny wire edge left on the blade from the stone.

ble. The hucksters on late-night TV or at the county fair have knives that can cut paper-thin slices from any fruit or vegetable. "And that's not all..." How do they do that? Perhaps they use some of the techniques and equipment we discuss in this chapter. Perhaps it is a trick only they know.

The matter is complicated further when considering the type of material used for the blade, its thickness, width of the blade, the blade's designed use and its condition. Some edges need the finest-grit finish, while others should be sharpened only with coarse or medium sharpening materials. Some edges should be relatively rough, while others—a razor blade or a scalpel— should have the finest possible cutting surface.

Different blades, different blade sizes, steels, uses, thicknesses and materials require different angles and techniques to get it right. A hatchet blade requires altogether different cutting angles than does an arrow broadhead or a skinning knife, for instance. We must be aware of the intended use for the blade if we are to know the best edge angle. Then we have to obtain the most appropriate device for achieving and maintaining that edge angle, and learn how and when to use this particular device.

One of the most familiar sharpening devices is the bench or shop stone. These may range in size from 10 inches in length down to only a couple of inches. About 1/4-inch thick, the smaller size is intended to be carried in the tackle box or shirt pocket. Bigger is better, and those little stones are of dubious value.

A good bench stone is at least 6 inches long, thick and heavy enough to accommodate larger blades. It should be on a sharpener stand or bench holder so it will not slide around while the blade is being honed. Some will be sold with a metal or wood holder into which the stone fits snugly. Then the stand may be clamped or otherwise fastened to a sturdy workbench, countertop or heavy kitchen table, if necessary.

Another variation of the bench stone is an elaborate three- or four-sided device that holds stones of various grits. Each rotates on an axis to bring up the desired grit stone for sharpening use. On some, the side that is down rests in a reservoir of honing oil. The oil is intended to carry away the minute particles of steel from the knife blade as it is honed. The tiny pieces are held in suspension, off the stone surface, until wiped away. A three-sided apparatus will have coarse, medium and fine stones on the rotating axle rod. The idea is to start with the coarsest stone surface, honing away at the damaged or dulled edge, then move on to the finer stones. On some knives that are not too dull, the coarse stone surface may be bypassed.

Some of us will remember the Carborundum sharpening stones that used to be evident in many kitchens and workshops. Most of these are considered rather coarse, and thousands of craftsmen sharpened wood plane blades, screwdrivers and knife blades on Carborundum stones for many years. They still may be found in some hardware stores and cutlery supply outlets, but the more common stones might be made from natural noviculite, most of which comes from Arkansas. These stones are mined, cut to handy sizes and shapes, and sold all over the world. They are available in several grits or hardness ratings, from soft to extremely hard. All require thin honing oil to carry away the metal grit.

Another medium is a ceramic block or rod. The ceramic usually is considered hard or fine grit and is used for final-edge honing. It requires no liquid to carry away the filings. The ceramic is cleaned with kitchen cleanser when it becomes too dark and embedded with metal residue. A cleaning is supposed to return it to new condition, but some users have had difficulty in removing all the residue from the ceramic.

Ceramic material is typically used on sharpening rods, a more common application. The rods are set into drilled holes on a metal, plastic or wooden stand or bench, at an angle to sharpen the blade. The knife blade is held vertically as it is drawn down and across the ceramic rods in a slicing motion. As long as the blade is held rigidly, the sharpening angle remains the same and the edge is sharpened. Ceramic is ideal for final touch-ups on blades sharpened with coarser stone, but the material in block form is not as common as it was a decade or so ago.

A word of caution when using sharpening rods of any material: The rod angle is fixed by the holes drilled into the base of the sharpener and may not be the best angle for a particular blade. Furthermore, blades with deep or wide hollow grinds may be ruined if the grind line touches the honing rod as the edge is being sharpened.

Man-made stones or rods of various grits are available for sharpening. Their attractiveness is that the grit size is controlled and constant across the stone. Every stroke of the blade removes the same amount of metal, as long as the pressure remains constant. With practice, the person doing the honing can get a feel for just how long the operation will take on a particular blade.

Ceramic rods mounted in a base at a specific angle are popular with many knife sharpeners. A product of the Space Age, these sharpeners are available from several manufacturers.

Another popular manmade material is diamond dust on a metal or plastic surface used as a hone. The advantages of diamond stones are that the lubricating liquid is only water. That eliminates the need to carry honing oil into the field with the sharpener. Also, the diamond dust will hone the hardest blades consistently and repeatedly. They are relatively clean to use and, with care, will last for many years. These diamond stones are available in large shop sizes, small fold-up models to carry in a pocket or backpack, or tiny touch-up stones handy for arrowheads or fish hooks.

Metal filings are rinsed away with any water source, and the stones are not likely to break under hard usage. Their disadvantage may be the initial cost. Diamond dust, no matter how fine, is an expensive commodity. While the diamond sharpeners are tough, they can be broken if dropped on a cement floor or otherwise abused.

Most, although certainly not all, kitchen knives need a cutting edge angle of about 22 degrees. A skinning knife might require a more shallow angle of about 19 degrees; a razor or broadhead blade, shallower yet. Other edged tools may have an edge angle of 25 degrees.

If the angle of the knife edge is unknown, the simple answer is to follow that which is already on the blade. Unless the knife is quite old and badly dulled to the point that it is rounded or obscure, the angle will be visible. The challenge is to hone or grind the new edge with the blade held at the optimum angle long and carefully enough to make it right. That is the difficulty for most sharpeners.

How do you keep it at the same angle throughout the stroke, each stroke? When that can be maintained, the edge will be sharp and quick to cut. But if you let it roll or take a different angle for a few strokes, the edge will be rounded and the cutting surface will vary from end to end.

With steady, strong and experienced hands, the correct angle can be maintained on a sharpening stone or block. As mentioned, some of us can get the edge just right each time. While interviewing Charlie Weiss of Phoenix, Arizona, for a part of this book, he offered to restore the edge on a little Buck folder I carry. Weiss uses a medium-grit shop stone saturated with plenty of honing oil. He does not use a jig or other mechanical apparatus to hold the blade at the selected angle. He used considerable force when stroking down on the stone. His experience keeps the blade angle correct. Weiss maintains the correct angle throughout the stroke, particularly when nearing the blade tip. The blade is drawn upward from the stone as the round tip is sharpened.

Maintaining the requisite amount of pressure and angle is easy for experienced sharpeners, but some of us cannot seem to manage it. The knife blade tends to rock slightly as it is drawn across the stone. To compensate for this, we must rely on some sort of guide or holder to lock the blade and the sharpening medium correctly in relation to each other.

There are several products on the market to hold the blade and sharpening stone at a constant angle with each other. A couple of devices we've seen clamp onto the knife blade to hold it at the specified angle. A large ball- or roller-bearing rides the surface of the sharpening stone as the knife edge is drawn across the stone. As long as the blade and the bearing are held on the stone's surface, the angle can be maintained.

More popular these days are the ceramic rods and base holder, where the rods are held in drilled holes at predetermined angles. With this, the trick is to keep the blade exactly vertical during the honing stroke. The knife blade is drawn down and across the rods to sharpen it. The action should resemble an attempt to take a slice off the rod as the blade moves down it.

The rods will do a good sharpening job on most knives, and in particular those with serrated cutting edges. If the knife is an

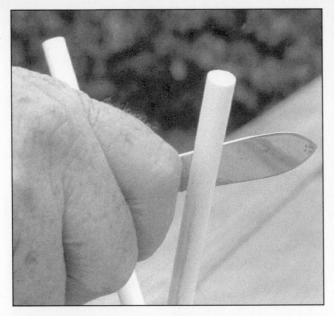

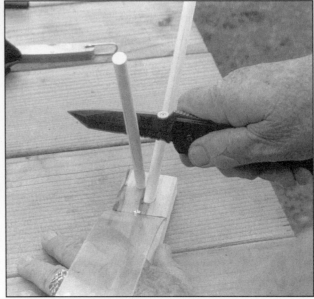

The technique with the rod sharpeners is to hold the knife blade exactly vertical while stroking it down along the ceramic rod. As the rod becomes embedded with metal residue, it is rotated within the base to reveal a clean area.

This wood base also mounts a plexiglass hand protector. The rods are ideal for sharpening serrated blade edges.

expensive custom-made model and/or has a deep hollow grind, one must use great care to not let the grind line come into contact with the rod. The finished grind line can be dulled or damaged as the blade is drawn down the sharpening rod. For most standard kitchen knives, there will be no problem.

Most of these rod sharpeners have built-in hand protectors. One hand holds the base firmly to the table or bench while the other draws the blade down along the sharpening rod. The user must prevent the blade from striking the work surface as the stroke is completed—especially if it is the dining room table!

The base may be made from wood, metal or plastic. Some models store the rods within the base. Others have a leather or nylon carrying pouch. Lightweight and portable, they are at home in any hunting camp or workplace where knives must be sharpened from time to time.

Most of the angled sharpeners utilize ceramics, but others have diamond-impregnated rods. Most are round, but some have triangular cross-sections. The flat surface is used for standard blade sharpening, while the edges of the triangles are fine for honing serrated-edged blades. Rod lengths vary from about 4 to 14 or more inches. They are not indestructible and can break if dropped on a hard floor.

Blades with serrated edges have come into favor in the past decade or so. Some of the newer knives from Buck have fully or partially serrated edges, so we asked Chuck Buck about sharpening them. He recommends using small-diameter ceram-

This Lohman sharpener combines a diamond sharpener with a ceramic rod, mounted in a plastic base. The kit includes two 4-inch diamond rods and two 4-inch ceramic rods that all fit into the storage case.

Another popular sharpening device is the bench-clamped, rod-mounted tool. The holder jaws adjust for most knives, except for the smallest ones. This model is from Gatco, but several brands are sold around the world.

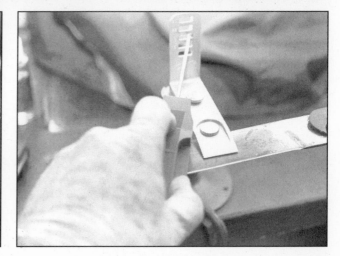

The flat sharpening stones range from very fine to extra coarse, and usually four or five gradients are included in a kit. Honing oil is applied to the surface of the stone.

The stone is stroked across the blade edge as the sharpening angle is maintained with the rod inserted in a numbered angle slot. The system works quite well.

ic or steel rods to work on the concave surfaces. They can be difficult to sharpen, and Buck uses considerable pressure and care with those edges.

Most of the serrated blades are flat on the back, and Buck says to just lay the blade flat on the sharpening stone or rod to knock off what is known as a wire edge. The wire is the slight turn-over of blade metal, extremely thin, left on the opposite side as the blade is honed. For best cutting, most of the wire edge should be removed.

For portability to the shop, office or in the field, a simple ceramic or steel sharpening rod mounted in a wood, plastic or metal handle is hard to beat. One never knows where or when a knife will have to be sharpened, and the little 4- to 6-inch rod may be carried like a pen or pencil. It can be stuffed in the bottom of the traveling case or even in a slot in your day planner. The little rods may not do the perfect job on your best carving

knife, but they are excellent for touching up a pocketknife or skinner, or even last-minute honing on broadheads for bowhunters. The ceramic rods usually will not give travelers problems at airport security points, if carried aboard a plane.

Another popular sharpening system consists of a holder and a clamp to hold the blade. The base is bolted or C-clamped to a workbench or table. The sharpening stones are about 6 or 7 inches long, about 1/2-inch wide, mounted on a plastic or wood base with a 6-inch rod at one end. The rod fits into one of four or five slots above the blade clamp that determine the sharpening angle. The slots may have marked angles of 25, 22, 19, 15 and 11 degrees on some brands. Other makers may offer slightly different angles.

To use this device, the knife is clamped solidly, and the sharpening stones are stroked along the edge of the blade. The clamp adjusts to fit the thickness of the knife blade. Most of these sharpening systems have three, four or more different grit stones permitting the sharpener to move from coarse to fine, depending upon the ultimate use of the knife. Some systems have a sharpening rod or angled stone for use on serrated blades.

Instructions call for the liberal use of light honing oil on the stones. The key to success in using these kinds of sharpeners is their ability to maintain the angle of the stone and blade throughout the honing strokes. The blade clamp must be tight, and care should be exercised that the guide rod doesn't slip out of the slot while stroking the blade. With a bit of practice, these systems produce excellent edges. One drawback of this type of system is that the operator cannot exert much pressure on the blade during the stroke. The stand may tilt slightly and the clamp cannot be tightened enough to prevent some blade movement when great pressure is applied.

Most knives are sharpened easily with this clamping system, but not all. Small pocketknives with blades of less than $1^{1}/_{2}$ inches may be difficult to clamp tight enough that they do not move while being honed.

Furthermore, small blades do not have enough of the blade metal protruding beyond the clamp, causing the stone to contact the clamp ahead of the blade. Blades longer than 7 or 8 inches will prove difficult, too. The stone will stroke along most blades of about that length, but if much longer, the stone will not reach. The longest kitchen, fighting or military knives will have to be sharpened on a solid bench-mounted stone.

Bowhunters using two-, three- or four-blade broadheads realize that, even when using replaceable blades, the edges must be touched up from time to time. This can be done with standard sharpening rods or stones, but one outfit, Eze-Lap of California, makes a little portable sharpener that will do it all. Everything is mounted in a flat plastic holder about 4 inches square. Small diamond-dust stones are mounted at the correct angles for two, three or four blades. The broadheads can be sharpened without even removing the heads from the arrow shaft. On top of this patented device is a small, grooved diamond-coated rod to touch up knife blades and fish hooks.

In time, some stones will become saturated with oil, so the user must remember to wipe them clean before and after each sharpening session. A build-up of oil and metal flakes will tend to mar the cutting surface of the blade.

Except for ceramic or diamond-dust surfaces, the best cleaning method is to simply wipe a honing-oil-soaked rag or paper towel across the surface. Clean off all the tiny metal and stone pieces and apply fresh oil for the next sharpening session on a cleaner surface.

It is important to wipe the stones before and after use, especially a bench stone left uncovered. The combination-type stones on an axle usually include some sort of cover to keep off dust and dirt, but some can get through. Dirt and dust are the enemies of good knife sharpening.

Those with the equipment and skill may prefer to sharpen knives using power tools. A sanding belt or power wheel will do a quick job of resharpening a knife, but it also can ruin a blade quickly.

The primary problem with any power equipment always is safety. A momentary lapse in concentration or a relaxed muscle can cause the belt or wheel to suddenly grab the knife out of the operator's hand and put it into another soft part of the body. The results can be deadly at the extreme! Many have injured them-

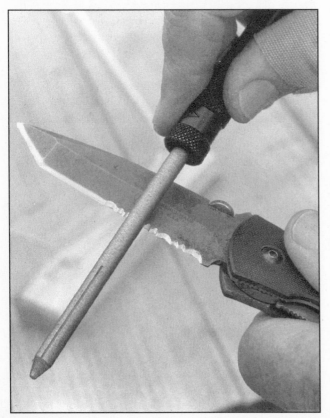

(Left) Serrated blade edges are often the most difficult to sharpen. A small-diameter coarse steel rod will get the job done, but the honing angle must be carefully maintained. This sharpening rod unscrews to fit inside the handle.

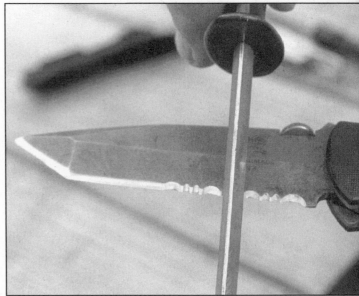

This tool used to resharpen the serrated edge blade has a flat oval-shaped rod. Maintain steady pressure and angle for best results.

A device called the Eze Lap Arrow Sharp is compact enough to be carried into the field. It also will hone a knife edge on the single bar on top of the holder.

The Eze Lap is angled to take care of most arrow broadheads and does a good job with a bit of practice.

selves while trying to sharpen knives on a power wheel. However, using a grinding or polishing wheel is a quick, easy way to resharpen axe blades and splitting mauls.

Aside from the safety considerations, a blade can be ruined with excessive heat. When sharpening a knife on power equipment, be sure to have a can of cooling water close at hand to dip the blade frequently during the work. Any blade can be "burned" by holding it in one place too long or too hard against a fast-moving wheel or sanding belt.

The blade should be kept moving along the surface with minimum pressure exerted. In skilled hands, sharpening a knife with power equipment takes but a few seconds, but it isn't a job for a beginner. Leave that operation for the professionals.

If sharpening serrated blades is so difficult, why buy a knife with half or all the edge having those grooves? There are some things that are cut more easily with a serrated edge. If you test the new serrated-edge blade with your thumb, it feels sharp, but not as ready to cut as a plain blade...until a slice is made. That is the big advantage to the serrated blades. Cutting or slicing through a heavy rope, a cardboard box or, as some emergency personnel must do, a seat belt is usually easier and faster with a serrated-edge blade. The key word is slice. Field dressing a deer, sharpening a pencil, and cutting a steak or a stalk of celery is easier and cleaner with the plain, sharp blade.

The half-serrated blades are a compromise, leaving the forward half of the blade with a plain edge. Much of the sales appeal of some serrated-edge knives is cosmetic. They look good, but the serrations must be kept extra-sharp to be most effective.

Some makers believe serrated edges tend to weaken the blade, each dip in the edge creating a potential breaking point. Also, there are more places that are difficult to clean, thus inviting corrosion, even on so-called stainless steels. For a fighting knife, dagger, bayonet or fish fillet blade, nobody would advocate anything but a plain, sharp knife edge.

Despite all the skill, practice and equipment at hand, some

(Above and below) The small All Rite sharpener is lightweight and small for easy carrying. The sharpening steel is a simple tungsten carbide piece fitted into the plastic handle.

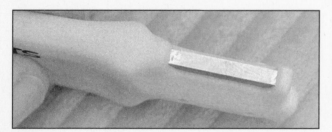

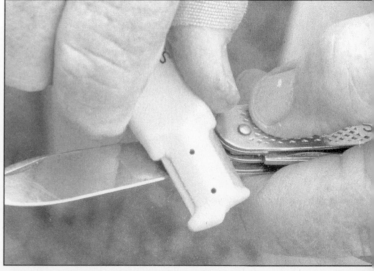

The tungsten carbide will take down a rough knife edge in a hurry.

This Lansky Sharpener solves the angle problem with a triangle-shaped holder that locks into two different angles. The device folds compactly for transport.

Still popular and used all over the world are the natural Smith's Arkansas Noviculite stones, found only near Hot Springs, Arkansas. Stones are available in various grits from fine to coarse. These oil stones are found in shops everywhere.

knives are easier to resharpen than others. Some of the difficulty is a function of the shape and size of the blade, but most of the time it is due to the type of steel and its hardness. It is an over simplification to say the harder the steel, the more difficult the sharpening, but it also holds a high degree of truth. On the other hand, hard blades will hold a sharp edge longer than will blades of softer steel.

Some makers produce knives following the philosophy that the blades should be as hard as practical so the buyers/users seldom will need to sharpen the edge. With normal usage, the knife may not need reworking for years. It dulls so slowly and gradually that the average user may not notice the change for a long time.

Some knife manufacturers offer free factory resharpening services. That keeps their knives sharp and working well, and ensures the customer continues to be satisfied with the knife. He or she will tend to say good things about the knife. Most custom knifemakers will resharpen any knives they have made.

There also are a number of machine shops, sporting goods dealers and knife retailers who offer knife sharpening at a nominal cost. We know of at least a couple of custom knifemakers who attend motorcycle gatherings. Motorcyclists tend to carry one or more knives much of the time. The knifemakers, with a small belt sander or wheel, can restore an edge in a couple of minutes. Charging only a few dollars per knife, the craftsmen may realize a fair profit for the weekend, not to mention good will.

Some skilled and frequent knife users, such as professional hunting guides and butchers, prefer a softer blade steel. They carry a sharpening stone or steel with them and are seen frequently touching up the blades after a few cuts. They are experienced enough to know what kind of edge works best for their work and are able to achieve it with a few strokes of the steel. In time, a butcher will completely wear away a knife blade, but he gets plenty of use from his knives in the meantime.

Most, although not all, stainless steel blades will be heat-treated and hardened more than one made from tool steel. The non-stainless blade needs more sharpening and more general care to keep it from corroding. It seems a natural part of the care to resharpen the edge more frequently. When wiping it down or cleaning off substances such as lemon or tomato juice, it takes little effort to clean it off.

Your grandfather probably had a razor strap, or strop, to put a finishing touch to his straight-edge razor blade. A generation or so ago, most barber chairs had the leather strop hanging from the back. Usually, they have a rough side and a final, smooth side. The barber would give the razor a few strokes across the first side, then a couple on the smooth surface before applying it to the customer's beard. For some blades, that finishing is necessary. Archery broadheads, for instance, need perfect edges without the tiny wire edge that prevents the best cutting. A skinning knife ought to have a razor's edge, too.

Some skilled sharpeners recommend the use of a leather strop to take off that final bit of unwanted metal. Charlie Weiss uses a tiny leather scrap on the bench for a few final strokes with the sharpened blade. As the leather turns black where the

The diamond sharpening stones from DMT use plain water as a lubricant when sharpening blades. They are available in several shapes and sizes.

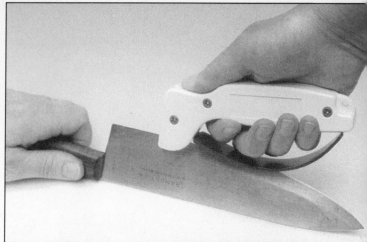

The Accusharp tool features a hand and finger protector. The sharpener uses twin tungsten carbide blades held in the plastic handle. It is drawn along the length of the blade to sharpen.

blade is drawn, it is proof that microscopic bits of metal are coming off. Others use an extra-fine muslin power wheel or a fine-grit belt sander.

Phill Hartsfield uses the simple technique of making a couple of slices through a piece of cardboard after he has sharpened his knives and swords. He says the tiny wire edge is knocked off by the heavy cardboard, leaving the knife edge razor sharp. Most

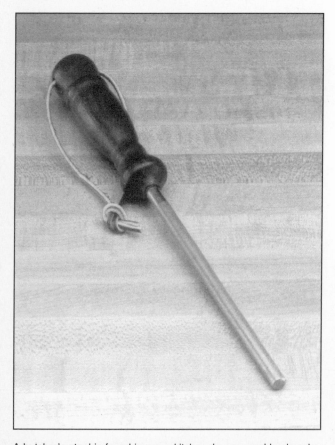

A butcher's steel is found in many kitchen drawers and backpacks. This Lohman model is 10½ inches long with a diamond-dust surface and wooden handle. Steels are used for final touch-up after sharpening or during a long butchering session.

knife people simply ignore that final step and are happy with the honing achieved by their careful work on a stone or rod.

How do you know when a blade is sharp enough? The obvious answer is to slice a hard-boiled egg, fresh tomato or hard salami. If the blade will easily cut thin, even slices, it is sharp. To detect irregularities in the blade, draw the edge slowly and lightly across your thumbnail. It will snag on an unsharpened portion and may need more work. Test the edge lightly with your finger tips, but don't slice or pluck the fingers along portions of the edge.

Other tests include slicing sheets of paper or shaving the hair off of one's forearm. Shaving can be dangerous to your arm and cutting through paper actually will dull the blade after it has been sharpened. Satisfactory performance is the best proof of a good sharpening session.

Sharpening a hatchet or axe blade is a different proposition. Here, the best splitting or cutting is done when the edge is more rounded, although some splitting mauls are straight-edged. The solution is to follow the original angle or type of edge. Axe heads are far too heavy to be clamped into a sharpening jig. Nicks or chips in the edge are first taken down with a file, then a round Carborundum stone, well oiled, will bring back the factory cutting edge. Rather than slicing or shaving wood, an axe splits with a wedge action. The edge cannot be thin. The angle may need to be 30 or 40 degrees to stand up to the hard pounding that cutting and splitting wood requires.

There is something satisfying about a newly sharpened knife, particularly in the kitchen. Thin slices of hard-boiled eggs and tomatoes are difficult to obtain without the sharpest blades. Cutting vegetables into small pieces for a salad is a whole lot easier with a sharp blade. A sharp knife will look better, work better, be safer to use and last longer than one that has become dull.

All the sharpening devices mentioned here will accomplish the task if properly used. Some of us can get a shaving edge on a blade in seconds; others can never get it right. The system that works for you may mean sending it back to the maker from time to time.

A STUDY IN STEEL

Ever in search of a sharper edge, veteran cutler David Boye has come up with new information and techniques

WHAT DO PSYCHOLOGY and steel have in common? Admittedly, not a great deal, unless your name is David Boye and you have relegated yourself to living in an out-of-the-way area of Arizona.

The same David Boye also is doing a great deal to restructure thinking among both custom and commercial knifemakers as to what is the best steel for building a blade. He envisions a blade that will stay sharp longer and require less sharpening to return it to top-grade cutting shape.

By now, you're wondering what this is all about, aren't you? Not surprising, really, but it concerns what David Boye has come to refer to as dendritic steel. What this amounts to is that the knifemaker has started investment casting knives, instead of forging them or using the stock-removal method with which most of us are familiar.

Through his studies which have extended over the past fourteen years, Boye has come to believe that any amount of forging or other type of stress is less than conducive to producing good steel. That includes what the rolling mills do to the metal.

Following this theory, David Boye now investment casts his knives, using a casting grade of 440C stainless. This, coupled with his own heat-treating, results in an edge that registers at 58C on the Rockwell scale. That hardness is more or less standard for the custom cutlery trade, but the Boye knives seem to boast an unusual degree of sharpness and are quite strong.

David Boye has been a recognized force in custom knifemaking for well over twenty years. He dropped out of graduate school where he was seeking a doctorate in psychology. As he recalls now, "I wanted to make tools, but I also recognized the fact that I was seeking some sort of art form, as well."

Tools he knew something about, having worked in his

This pile of hemp particles is the result of fifteen hours used to make 3000 cuts in 1-inch rope, using an 8-inch Boye dendritic steel knife. This was done without resharpening the blade.

These dropped-edge sheath knives are called the Boye Basics and are made totally of cast metal. They're sold with a brass-lined Cordura sheath. The wide, curved blade is ground to a .012-inch bevel for durability, cutting efficiency and sharpening ease.

(Below) The Boye Basics can be dressed up on special order with the addition of a cocobolo handle, sacrificing some of the lightness of the standard designs.

Boye taught himself the art of etching. This 2-inch dropped edge features a stick-like figure of a bowhunter etched on the blade.

father's heavy-equipment repair operation during college sessions. He also had taken a college course in jewelry making, because it offered him a "chance to work with the hands as well as the head."

Gone from college and puzzled about how to make a living, Boye came across an old two-man saw blade of the type used by lumberjacks. He decided to make a knife from this material. He sold it the same day he completed it and knew he had ended his search for a livelihood.

A native Californian, Boye studied the knives and swords displayed at a San Francisco museum, thinking in terms of the jewelry-making course he had taken earlier. The craftsman taught himself to etch metal, and this type of decoration soon was finding its way onto each of his knives.

During this period, he continued to make and sell knives, while he searched for better stock and improved techniques. At one point, he even tried a Swedish razor steel, AEB-L.

More than twenty years ago, Boye produced a book, *Step-by-Step Knifemaking.* His original plan, he recalls, was to turn out a pamphlet of perhaps fifty to sixty pages, selling it around Santa Cruz, where he then lived.

As the book grew, he was encouraged to submit it to pub-

lishers. Rodale Press snapped up the heavily illustrated manuscript and published it in 1977. Today, the book has sold more than 150,000 copies and, by the knifemaker's own admission, has kept groceries on the table during some lean periods. This volume, we have found, is in the technical library of most working knifemakers and has been the initial inspiration of any number of these craftsmen.

By his own admission, Boye had "achieved the burnout point on grinding knives" when Don Longuevan, a machinist friend, suggested casting them, thus reducing the grinding time of the stock-removal technique being used.

"I knew that gun parts and some cutting tools such as router bits were being investment cast," Boye recalls. He approached people in the casting industry, and most agreed his idea was feasible. The next step came in 1982, when he began working with Larry Venkeer of International Precision Casting. Venkeer has continued to the present to do Boye's casting in his plant in Linden, Utah.

The cast blades of 440C stainless invariably showed a strange grain pattern that Venkeer and Boye considered to be a sign of an inferior steel. What the two men were seeing was dendritic crystal formation, and Boye even built a drop hammer

Boye's little 3-inch blade skinner features some etching, but the craftsmanship in this piece is reflected in the cocobolo handle with its spacers of bone and sterling silver.

The names of both David Boye and Bob Loveless are etched on the blade of this model. It was cast from a pattern that Loveless developed in the mid-1970s.

that was intended to reduce the pattern in the knife casting.

There also were thoughts of forging followed by some experiments. However, the tests for cutting qualities and blade toughness that followed showed that forging reduced the aggressive cutting qualities of those blades.

"Neither of us realized at that time that the carbide crystal structure of cast steel contributed to better edge-holding qualities," Boye recalls today.

To determine just what they had discovered, Boye started out cutting heavy cardboard with his cast knives. That was like cutting butter with a hot knife, so he advanced through several other materials until he settled on using 1-inch manila rope as a test medium.

According to Boye, "When the knife edges were prepared identically, those of dendritic steel consistently outperformed the forged steels selected for the testing.

"Using an 8-inch chef's knife, I cut 3000 pieces of 1-inch hemp rope in 15 hours without resharpening, then I resharpened the knife in only 1 minute, using a small porcelain hand stone."

With the same chef's blade, Boye then went on to chop in half a 6-inch oak log, then cut 9 inches around a heavy steel barrel.

As a result of studies made with the aid of a microscope, Boye learned that the act of forging will break up the microscopic carbides in the steel, at the same time reducing them in size. Thus, according to Boye's theory, the smaller the grain size, as in forged steel, the sharper the blade should become when sharpened. However, it will not have what he describes as much "bite." With the forged blade, the carbide particles are removed from the edge of the blade in the sharpening process, thus reducing the ability of the edge to cut.

Boye contends that, with properly cast dendritic steel, what he calls "pop out" of the carbides does not happen. Thus, with the carbide crystals deep into the composition of the steel, the edge remains aggressively sharp. Photos of 440C knife edges that have been enlarged as much as 200 times lend credence to Boye's statements, for the iron-chrome carbides visible on the blade are much larger and form a rugged pattern in comparison to the deposits in the forged blade of the same material.

According to Boye, what he calls the "dendritic cutting effect" has great similarity to the so-called Damascus cutting effect. In the latter, the meeting of hard and soft layers of steel create a serration effect along the blade's edge. The hard formations of iron-chrome carbides that network throughout the dendritic steel is a good deal harder than the basic Rockwell hardness measurement of 56 to 58C, according to Boye's findings.

Old pro Bob Loveless heard of Boye's steel, and the two of them came up with a straight-edge design made of dendritic steel. Boye made some wax patterns based upon a Loveless design, which the latter said dated back to 1973. From these patterns, the casting proceeded and Loveless called the finished knife "one of the most useful for all-around work that I've ever come up with."

It was in the casting process that Boye's earlier education in jewelry making came into play. The so-called lost-wax process has been used for thousands of years in producing intricate jewelry of gold and silver. Only in recent times has it been introduced for such large items as handgun frames. William B.

David Boye specializes in chefs' cutlery tools and enjoys turning out such sets as this, complete with etched blades. All are of dendritic steel and have cocobolo handles. The price of each knife, however, is in the hundreds of dollars.

Ruger, the noted firearms designer, was one of the first to recognize the value of the process. His Sturm, Ruger & Company, Inc., now has a casting plant in New Hampshire and another in Arizona.

Today, hot wax is flowed into aluminum moulds and, when cooled, is removed. This wax creation is an exact replica of the knife sans the handle, in most cases. The wax models then are dipped in several applications of what is called slurry, a liquid porcelain. Between each coating, sand is added to the surface to give what will become the mould added strength.

Once this progressive operation is completed, the moulds are allowed to dry for up three weeks before going into a high-temperature oven where the wax is burned out, leaving the actual mould in the interior of the hardened porcelain. In the Utah casting plant, molten 440C steel is poured into the porcelain mould while it still is white hot.

According to Boye and Larry Veenker, as the steel cools in the mould, the network of carbide crystals is formed throughout the blade material. When cooled to handling temperatures,

the porcelain cast is broken away and each of the blades is trimmed, annealed and straightened in Veenker's Utah foundry.

According to Boye, "Pound for pound, this method of producing blades is more expensive than any other, but I've found that in the long run it is well worth the effort."

If nothing else, there is little in the way of waste. As might be expected, some of the cast blades are rejected, but these go directly back to the casting room to be melted down and reused.

The cast blades are shipped from Utah to Boye's operation in Dolan Springs, Arizona, where he goes about additional blade straightening followed by stock removal, the necessary heat-treating, final grinding and polishing. The blades then are etched with Boye's own designs and fitted with handles of what the craftsman considers a proper material for the knife's design and intended use.

His background in tools and art are combined in Boye's design work, for he makes an obvious effort to combine the

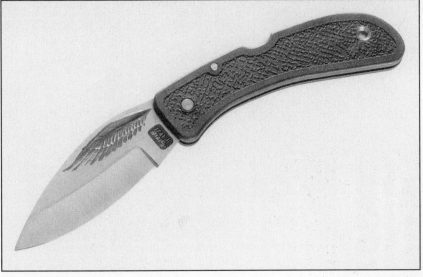

This is David Boye's lightweight lockback folder with unique 3-D art on the blade. Patterns cast into the blade from Boye's original art range from an eagle's wing to a range of mountains, a blue whale to a bowhunter. Other scenes are of a Celtic horse, a sunburst and basketweaving.

(Below) Shown are a typical hunting knife (from left) from Boye, an 8-inch chef's knife of the type he used in cutting 3000 lengths of 1-inch rope, and a version of his Boye Basic design with a fold-over sheath that becomes a handle.

best qualities of a cutting tool with aesthetics. He wants the buyer to like the way the knife fits the hand and does its assigned job.

Boye isn't hooked on "big," either. While some of his kitchen knives have lengthy blades, for daily tasks he prefers small blades and feels his customers do, too.

"The dropped-edge blade is the knife I want to use myself," he is quick to explain. "It affords maximum efficiency in cutting, it protects the user's fingers and it can be used as a skinner and a scraper."

David Boye has an opportunity to test his knives in the field. While he denies that he is an ardent hunter, he does hunt for food and does his own cleaning and butchering. "Whatever I shoot, I eat," he declares, offering his personal philosophy.

Following that philosophy, the craftsman produces a dropped-point hunter and a skinner that features an upswept blade in what he calls his Outdoor Line. He also produces two versions of his dropped-edge blade. All of these knives, incidentally, get handles of American hardwood.

The Arizona craftsman has still another philosophy that has to do with his work: "The most frequently used knife, day to day, is in the kitchen. I believe that using a beautiful, well-made knife goes a long way toward inspiring the cook and, in turn, adds something to food preparation."

Perhaps it doesn't need to be stated that the first knife Boye ever made was a kitchen knife. He considers his real specialty to be the creation and design of fine knives—paring, carving and utility styles—for chefs.

Boye's best sellers at the moment, however, are what he calls the Boye Basics. Sold in sets of three, he describes these as "bare-bones utility knives." These are all-metal sheath knives with blade lengths of $2^{1}/_{4}$, $2^{3}/_{4}$ and 4 inches respectively, all three packaged in a heavy-duty Cordura sheath. Cast as they are, the handles are thin and help to hold down the weight, but around the edge of each knife's handle is integral I-beam-shaped reinforcement for added strength.

Thinking back over his quarter-century as a custom cutler, Boye has come up with some pertinent thoughts on the various facets of his career, what he has learned, and information he is happy to pass on to others.

"My accidental discovery in 1981 of the so-called dendritic cutting effect opened the door for new theoretical considerations regarding edge performance," he states. "Cast dendritic 440C stainless was substantially outperforming forged and roll-forged steels in cutting aggression and endurance tests."

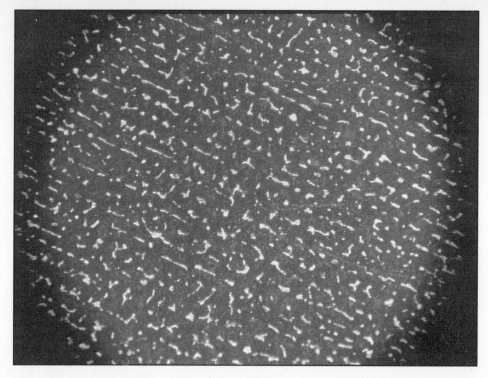

This is a 20x view of the etched flat surface of one of David Boye's cast 440C stainless blades. The light-colored spots actually are the network of carbides. Note that they are distributed quite evenly.

The following is an analysis of the phenomenon from his perspective of making blades from dendritic steel for over sixteen years and ten years of working with other steels before that.

As for cutting theory, "cutting occurs because the point-of-contact pressure breaks the bonds of cohesion and parts the heretofore unitary element of the workpiece.

"What knives do is concentrate pressure. A sharper knife takes the same amount of overall pressure and concentrates it into smaller points of contact, thus yielding higher pressure at the point of contact.

"In blade theory, we need to delineate clearly the factors that actually take part in this concentration of pressure," Boye explains.

Here are listed some of these factors, along with his commentary.

Pressure: "Here we have amount, direction, duration, concentration and speed of application."

Edge Geometry: "The angle of the juncture of the bevels. The narrower this angle, the more pressure is focused on the tip."

Sharpness: "This refers to the precision of the grind of the bevels of an actual knife and the condition of the edge."

Wear Resistance of Blade Material: "Resistance to the removal of blade material by the workpiece."

Cutting Action: "There are two kinds of cutting action: the blade can be pushed into the workpiece directly (vertically) like a razor blade, or it can be rubbed back and forth (horizontally) in the direction of the blade along with vertical pressure, thus producing a sawing effect. Sawing is lateral movement of tooth across the workpiece. This action dynamically increases the application of pressure at the workpoint."

Tooth: "High points along the cutting edge. This can be anything from a wavy edge, to serrations, to any variation of the blade due to sharpening implement, or to damask (patterns) within the steel. The general rule is that more tooth equals more lateral cutting performance."

According to Boye, "Hand-forged Damascus steels and Wootz metals have shown patterns in the steel to translate into more aggressive lateral cutting performance. This Damascus cutting effect derives from the relatively hard and soft steel alloys. Along the edge, tooth is created as the harder structures are exposed and produces a serrated cutting edge.

"Another source of tooth in forged steel," he says, "is the carbide microparticles (grain) which remain after being broken down during the forging process. These appear at the cutting edge and may vary in size from one forging treatment to another."

Boye contends that "with forged material, the limit of how mathematically sharp a blade can get is the size of the carbide particles. The smaller the particles, the sharper the edge can be made without dislodging the carbides along the tip of the edge during sharpening or use." (Such dislodging is known as "carbide pop-out.")

According to the craftsman, "The dilemma here is that the finer the carbide particles, the less tooth the steel has. With lateral cutting action, the fine-grained steel is too smooth to have bite and tends to slide, not cut.

"When the grain is large, it is not as sharp, but can cut more aggressively laterally, because the relatively fewer but larger carbides concentrate more pressure at fewer points than do many more smaller carbides. This is exactly like a saw with fewer, larger teeth that cuts more aggressively than one with many small teeth."

According to Boye, "Experienced bladesmiths and master forgers can reduce grain size or enlarge it. In general, hammering reduces grain size and heating enlarges it. Multiple heat-treatments can, as well. With precise reheating, the beginnings of re-dendriticization may occur. One of the facets of the bladesmith's art is to produce the appropriate microstructure for the given application."

As suggested earlier, with dendritic steel, the original skeleton of hard carbides formed from the molten state and 100 percent bonded throughout the steel is retained. The tips of these hard chrome carbides form tooth along the edge.

"With dendtritic steel, the toothy virgin carbide microstructures are at maximum abrasiveness, fully bonded and rooted, and do not pop out," Boye explains. "Therefore, a different kind of cutting edge and a new kind of cutting action are produced.

"In dendritic metallurgy, hard structures throughout the steel reinforce the matrix and produce more rigid mass; there is less willingness to deform, therefore less flattening at the blade apex.

"With forged steel, hardness decreases distortion and wear and retains carbides at the edge better. Thus, higher hardness produces better edge retention and cutting stamina," Boye declares.

"With dendritic steel, the bite derives from hard structures within the steel, and we have theorized that a softer matrix might result in greater differential in hardness between matrix and tooth," the Arizona cutler says. "I believe dendritic steel, to some degree, can in a way pseudo-sharpen itself, as the softest matrix wears away and exposes more tooth."

David Boye supports his concept with the 3000 pieces of 1-inch hemp rope he cut without resharpening the blade of that particular knife.

"To measure cutting performance, I mentally counted the number of lateral strokes it required to complete each cut. The edge was a Moran grind; that is, the sides of the knife came together right at the cutting edge, which was stropped with a buffing wheel and acid-etched to maximize exposed carbides.

"At first, the blade would cut the rope in one slice, without problem, but performance went downhill noticeably. After about 500 cuts, the blade was cutting in about four strokes. At around 1500 cuts, we were at around seven strokes. At 2000, we were at around nine strokes. At 3000, I was lucky to cut the rope in less than fifteen strokes.

"During the actual cutting," Boye recalls, "I had the feeling that the knife was not much duller during five hours of continuous cutting from around 500 almost to 1500 or so. My theory is that the matrix was wearing down a little faster than the tooth. Thus, the edge still may have been getting 'toothier' and duller at about the same rate, and thus performance was maintained."

Boye reports that at around 2500 cuts, he began to notice a more rapid loss of effect and attributed this to general wear on the edge, making it wide (translate, "dull"). After 3000 cuts, he says, "it was not fun to cut the rope." The total test, incidentally, required three five-hour cutting sessions.

Boye theorizes that had the blade been harder—perhaps 61 instead of RC 58—the wear of the steel might have been less and the tooth might have been exposed at a slower rate, resulting in lower performance."

But what about RC 52? Would this be even more aggressive? Boye says that, "until it is thoroughly tested, there is only opinion as to the ultimate effect hardness has on performance with dendritic material.

Today, Boye is aided by his daughter, Rachel, and an apprentice. His knives are available by mail order or they can be obtained from the Boye Knives Gallery in Davenport, California, a community about ten miles north of Santa Cruz. Copies of Boye's knifemaking book also are available at the latter site.

Expanding his efforts, Boye now is selling his dendritic steel to other knifemakers, either as billets or unfinished blades. It's been a long, sometimes rough road from that first kitchen knife fashioned from a used-up saw blade.

Through this entire essay, some readers have been asking, "What the hell is dendritic steel?"

Well, the molten steel is cast to the desired shape in a mould, and a network of chrome-carbide crystals are formed throughout the material. As Boye explains it, these crystals appear in branchlike patterns that resemble trees or ferns.

The name, dendritic, is derived from *dendron*, the Greek word for tree.

CUSTOM KNIFEMAKERS

In a series of profiles, some of the latest and greatest makers of today are given their just due

JACK LEWIS AND B.R. Hughes wrote the first edition of the GUN DIGEST BOOK OF KNIVES in 1973, almost a quarter of a century ago. The Knifemakers Guild was in its infancy and so were many of today's custom knifemaking stars. At the time, there were an estimated ninety custom knifemakers, who could be indentified as such, in the United States.

A poll of the 1972 Guild members, conducted at the time, listed their choices of the top fifteen makers of the era, in descending order: Bob Loveless, Bill Moran, D.E. Henry, Corbet Sigman, Ted Dowell, Lloyd Hale, Ron Lake, Clyde Fischer, Blackie Sewell, Bernard Sparks, Bob Dozier, George Herron, G.W. Stone, Chubby Hueske and Bo Randall. There were some ties on the list, but they are generally in order. That first edition of the book featured many of those (today) well-known makers, plus dozens of others who later have reached stardom in this art.

A modern-day poll would show some of the same names, along with many additions of those too young to have been part of the movement a quarter of a century ago. Some of those named have gone on to their rewards, and others have dropped out of sight.

Custom knifemaking and knifemakers were virtually unknown to most readers of the time. Many of the names, processes and the terms we now take for granted had to be shown and explained. Today, most readers know what a hand-made or custom knife is. Many are familiar with the products and the makers themselves. It is a matter of continuous education. New cutlers—artists in steel—are constantly brought to our attention. Their knowledge and skills are awesome.

The goal of the authors then, as now, was to locate and bring to your attention the skills and abilities of some of the best custom knifemakers to be found. In the following pages, some of the names will be familiar. Some have been making knives for twenty-five years or more, but somehow have missed out on the publicity. Some are quite young, and some are a bit older, although those terms must be viewed from the reader's perspective. Many will become the stars of the future, while some of those you will read about already have reached a well-deserved level of recognition for their skills. If we writers have done our job, we shall convey to you our excitement and admiration for these artisans. All deserve consideration by and the interest of the reader.

It is possible, although unlikely, that some of those original fifteen "best" knifemakers will still be around when the next quarter-century has passed. Newer makers will be on the scene to take their places. Take a look and offer them your support for their efforts. The authors believe that quite a few of the knifemakers featured in the pages that follow will be on your list of favorites twenty-five years from now.

Knife shows come in all sizes and shapes throughout the world. They are great places to "discover" today's and tomorrow's better custom knifemakers. A knife show also is the place to meet the makers, look at their creations, handle them, talk about them, and to sell and trade knives of all types.

CUSTOM KNIFEMAKERS
Jim Hrisoulas

MOST OF US are satisfied to concentrate on one career and hope it is a successful endeavor. Jim Hrisoulas has been successful in at least three careers and continues to fulfill his ambitions in all three. He is a respected custom cutler, he is the author of several books on bladesmithing in the modern age and he is a part-time trainer for Nevada police agencies.

The bladesmithing career came about in 1984, when the 300-pound, 6-foot, 1-inch Hrisoulas was involved in law enforcement. In a surprise situation, a suspect he had been investigating suddenly trapped him and had the muzzle of a handgun in the big man's ear. The felon pulled the trigger, but the round apparently was faulty. The gun did not fire.

After taking advantage of the felon's surprise and putting him not only on the ground but in handcuffs, Jim Hrisoulas leaned back to take a hard look at his life to that date. While serving in the U.S. Army and in law enforcement, most of those days had involved violence of one kind or another, he realized. It was time for a change of careers.

A native of Pennsylvania, Hrisoulas was born in 1956, later moving the California, where he made his first knife at the age of fourteen. He did his forging in the family barbecue. Later, in high school shop classes, he learned to handle a gas forge.

Having decided bladesmithing would be considerably less demanding on the nervous system than having people stick guns in your ears, Jim Hrisoulas put all of his savings into equipment and set up shop as a full-time knife- and swordmaker.

Working in his shop in Henderson, Nevada, a Las Vegas suburb, Hrisoulas' specialty has become pattern-welded, Damascus-type blades made from various types of steel and other metals. Included in his raw materials are wire cable, motorcycle chains, stainless steel strips interspersed with iron—virtually any material that can be welded and hold an edge! In inspecting this craftsman's work, we found his efforts impressive, and regardless of the raw materials used, there are exacting but exciting patterns in his blades once they are completed.

According to some sources, there are those who resent Hrisoulas' openness and they feel his books, *The Master Bladesmith* and *The Pattern Welded Blade*—not to mention the several videos he has made—give away what should be carefully guarded secrets of forging.

But Hrisoulas is and always has been free with his knowledge. Several other knifemakers scattered across Nevada and Southern California have benefitted from his instruction on either a formal or informal basis. The Nevada craftsman feels information should be shared and that such sharing will be to the ultimate benefit of all bladesmiths.

"If a knifemaker can make a better blade, based upon new information he can use, that is going to be a plus in his rela-

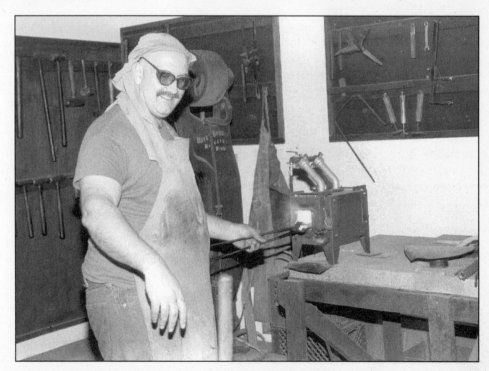

Jim Hrisoulas keeps himself well insulated against stray sparks and other hazards when he forges metal.

Hrisoulas' favorite tool is this extra heavy anvil, imported from Germany many years ago. The bucket and leather strap on the nose is a heavy weight used to reduce the amount of ring from the anvil when it is struck.

(Below) The basic ingredients of Damascus steel knife blades include strips of different metals, soon to be forged.

tionship with his customer, and that customer will be back," he contends.

The proof that not all others share his feelings is reflected in the fact that he has received anonymous letters and phone calls from persons claiming to be custom knifemakers. They say he shouldn't be giving out this valued information on Damascus creation and forging in general. There have even been threats—some not particularly veiled—regarding his future if he does not stop. Hrisoulas has not stopped.

Another Las Vegas cutler, Don Mounts, is one of those who is quick to praise Hrisoulas for his teaching. "Jim does not seem to mind interruptions and questions from other knifemakers, answering them with any and all the knowledge he has," Mounts says.

Over the years, Hrisoulas has built a complete forging and knifemaking shop behind his Henderson home. The structure is large enough to house all his forging, grinding and cutting tools with plenty of additional space for workbenches and storage.

Looking out the main door of the shop, one can see much of the city of Las Vegas 20 miles away, with its backdrop of brown mountains. Henderson is one of the fastest growing areas in the state, but Hrisoulas is situated so that urban sprawl is not likely to affect his operations.

His shop has a couple of forges, anvils, belt sanders, a bandsaw, a power hammer and a wide assortment of hand tools. All are neatly arranged to be accessible to the maker. To even the casual visitor, it is instantly obvious that this craftsman has a great deal of respect for his tools and other equipment, not to mention ultimate pride in his shop.

Hrisoulas is the first to admit he is not one to overspend on the raw materials for his knives. Following this philosophy, he tends to haunt auction houses, scrap yards and recycling centers, as well as production facilities. Such missions bring him worn-out blades from sawmill operations, wire cable, scraps of

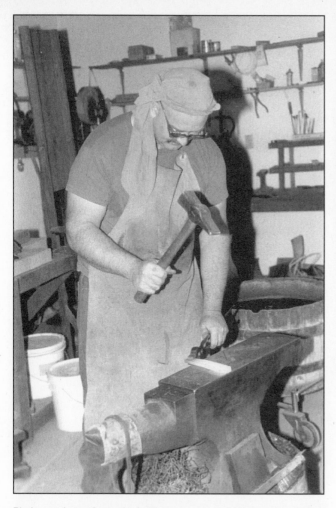

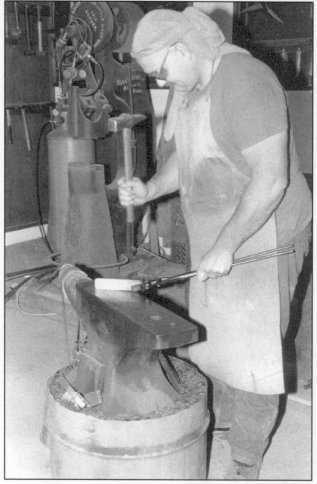

Blade metal must be worked at the correct termperature as it is formed and shaped. Hrisoulas says the skill must be learned and practiced. He keeps a wooden bucket of quenching water near his anvil as he works.

A casual look reveals that Hrisoulas has the arms and shoulders to be a strong forger. He says forging involves more technique than strength.

Most of the Damascus blades are shaped by forging, but some work is required on the belt sander.

sheet metal "and anything else that will soften when heated to a high enough temperature."

He forges on a huge, 300-pound German anvil that he has used from the time he first started serious forging. Born of respect for his own hearing and the neighborhood, he uses a heavy leather strap to hang a heavy weight on the nose of the anvil. This reduces the degree of ringing from the anvil when it is struck. This, of course, is a trick of the trade that every aspiring blacksmith and knife forger might use to advantage.

For most of his forging, Hrisoulas favors a small, gas-powered forge with which he is able to heat most metals quickly. This unit is surprisingly small, but is large enough for use in making most using and collector knives. It is not, however, of sufficient size to handle large knife blades and the swords that have become a Hrisoulas specialty.

The Nevada craftsman's technique is to pre-heat a piece of metal before attempting to bring it up to forging temperatures. He believes the pre-heating measure is important in that it sets the scene for bringing the length and thickness of the metal to its proper forging temperature on a uniform basis. This, in turn, reduces stresses in the metal that might be created by uneven heating.

Wire-wrapped handles are among Hrisoulas' and his customers' favorites. If you ever have tried it, you will recognize that wire-wrapping is a skill in itself, and while Hrisoulas makes the process look easy, it is not. It takes a great deal of

(Above) All sorts of metal may be used to produce knife blades. Hrisoulas haunts salvage and surplus sales yards to find things like wire rope for knives. Wire rope is thoroughly cleaned, then twisted before forging into blade shapes.

(Right) After the wire rope and stainless steel strips are heated, Hrisoulas forge-welds the ends to keep them from unraveling. He uses pieces of baling wire to temporarily hold the twisted wire rope together as forging begins.

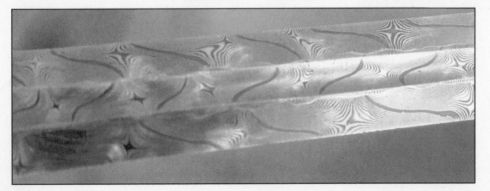

Various metal combinations and different forging techniques produce fascinating Damascus patterns for knife blades.

skill and practice to get an even, uniform and attractive handle on a knife.

Hrisoulas realizes there are those who find his size and looks somewhat intimidating. This may serve well when you're in a full-time law enforcement role, as he once was, but it doesn't do anything to bring in customers. Nonetheless, the bladesmith is a truly polite and kindly individual, big and strong enough to fill the role of the village blacksmith of poetry and legend.

Hrisoulas has great strength in his big arms and shoulders, so when he is hammering a knife into shape from a cherry-red piece of hot steel, he does not seem to be exerting himself. Perhaps he is not, for he appears to allow the anvil, hammers, tongs and other hand tools to do the job rather than forcing the work by means of muscle power.

Because of his years of experience, this bladesmith is highly safety conscious. During on-the-job interviews, when pictured in his books or seen in his video tapes, Hrisoulas always is careful to wear the appropriate eye protection, whether forging, grinding or welding metal. The floor of his shop is swept with a good deal more frequency than the average housewife's kitchen, and all work surfaces are kept free of scrap, tools and any other materials that could possibly cause injury through even a freak accident. For forging, he wears specially coated lenses that allow him to look into the flaming furnace without damage to his eyes.

The mark that Hrisoulas uses on his creations is a circle surrounding a salamander and a small sword. This is stamped into each of the blades that leave his forge.

While this maker puts every effort into producing a knife or sword that will equal or better the performance of the ancient Damascus blades used against the knights of old during the Crusades, we suspect that surprisingly few of them ever are put to a demanding outdoor test. The beauty of Hrisoulas' blades is such that a suspected majority are purchased by those who appreciate their looks and want them for display on the wall of a den or over a mantle piece rather than for use afield.

There is no doubt, of course, that the patterned blades, each one different, are as tough as they are beautiful and could be used in a hunting camp or even on a factory floor, if bought for such a purpose.

Hrisoulas has not rested upon his laurels, however. In his continuing search for knowledge and the bladesmithing secrets of past and present, he researches constantly, experimenting in his shop and carrying on correspondence with museums, collectors, other knifemakers and metallurgists around the world.

His interest in history and his research into methods of the past have led to him prefer making what have come to be called "period" blades, following the design styles of knives and swords that were made in a designated time period in a specific geographic location.

As a result, numerous examples of his work have been placed in museums to illustrate what this particular type of blade probably would have looked like. The Nevada-based maker has made a particular study of the ancient Vikings and the blades they carried. His reproductions of such knives and swords have brought praise from numerous museum curators.

Oddly, the majority of Hrisoulas' blades are left unsharpened, unless an edge is specifically requested. This is not without reason, of course.

"Back when I sharpened all of my knives and swords, there were several accidents in which individuals suffered bad cuts," the bladesmith explains. "Apparently, there are a lot of people out there who do not know how to handle a blade that has the characteristics of a straight razor." As a result of this policy, more than 70 percent of the period-type blades for which he currently receives orders specify that they be unsharpened.

When we met Hrisoulas at the Soldier of Fortune conven-

Hrisoulas is noted for his use of twisted wire carefully woven on some of his knife handles. It is a special technique that he freely shares with other makers.

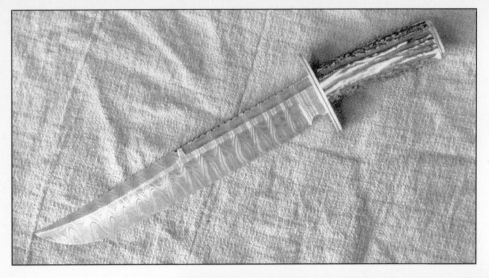

This Hrisoulas blade pattern is finer and tighter than some other Damascus forgings. The handle is stag.

This Hrisoulas dagger offers an almost symetrical Damascus patten.

The twisted handles are popular with Hrisoulas' customers. He has no trouble selling all the knives he can turn out.

Hrisoulas likes to use natural materials for his handles. This is an exceedingly nice using knife.

Jim Hrisoulas marks his blades with a salamander and sword logo. Note the details of the Damadcus steel after it has been etched to bring out the lines.

tion in Las Vegas in 1995, we made mention of his being a knifemaker. His correction was: "I'm a swordmaker." Considering the fact that more than 60 percent of his current output is swords of one kind or another, perhaps the designation is more accurate.

That does not mean he will not accept orders for knives to be made to a customer's specifications. He will. He also carries knives of his own design that he describes as "stock" items, but each boasts a forged blade and an unusual handle.

In the handle department, Hrisoulas prefers to use one of the various types of ivory, but he also uses buffalo horn, dyed beef bone, stag and impala horn. He also uses wire-wrapping as decoration on knife handles and some scabbards. The wire usually is of copper or brass, but on special order and for enough money, he can furnish it in gold or silver, too.

Hrisoulas' price schedule has been a source of amazement to hordes of knife fanciers, including your author. If you want nothing more than a carbon steel using knife, the price is less than $100. Or you can have a full-length carbon steel sword for as little as $375. Some makers won't even light up the forge for that kind of money.

Damascus, of course, is considerably more expensive, and rightfully so. There are hours upon hours of heating, folding and beating involved in getting an unusual Damascus pattern. Such artistic touches don't just happen. Because of this and other creative factors, the Hrisoulas-made Damascus knives and swords run from $1,500 to $5,000, he tells us.

Of course, all of this doesn't mean you can't try to make your own. After all, Jim Hrisoulas shares his own secrets in his books and his videos. The rest of it is just a whole lot of hard work!

CUSTOM KNIFEMAKERS
Tim Hancock

ARIZONAN TIM HANCOCK probably can be described best as part cowboy, part blacksmith and a whole lot knifemaker! Descended from a long line of blacksmiths and horseshoers, he revels in his Western upbringing and the custom-designed spurs and bits he makes for ardent horsemen. But his chief interest obviously is in his line of custom knives.

A certified master bladesmith of the American Bladesmith Society, he turns out handmade folders, sheath knives, miniatures and even swords in his well set-up shop in Scottsdale. He works with a variety of steels and produces his own Damascus. He does his own heat-treating in his shop, using a technique he developed on his own.

"My cutlery must meet the demands of superior performance, durability, and be of an elegant and functional design," he told us during a visit to his expansive shop. "As a bladesmith, I can be diverse in style and steel selection.

"Embellishments such as filework, inlays, sculpted fittings, precious metals, bluing, browning and exotic handle materials may be incorporated to create a more exquisite or personalized piece. I also enjoy complementing the knife with a custom sheath. Only raw materials of the highest quality are sought out for use in my creations."

Hancock was born in 1954 near Fort Collins, a college and cattle town in northern Colorado. His grandfather had been a farrier and wheelwright in Canada early in the century, and his father spent his early life as a farrier before attending college and becoming a highly respected large-animal veterinarian.

Young Hancock began learning farrier work (horseshoeing) at the unlikely age of ten. At the age of twelve, he was working summer school vacations as a horse wrangler, pushing a string of horses over 180 miles of mountains and open range. Horses are still part of his life, and when you see him leaning against the doorway of his shop, a silver belt buckle at his waist and a $100 Stetson on the back of his head, you know he's still part cowboy and mighty proud of his heritage.

Some years later, he turned to welding and ultimately became so proficient at the craft that he was hired to teach others the techniques.

Still later, Hancock learned the pipe-fitting trade. Obviously, he learned it well, for he eventually was hired by a large construction company to train others in the job. However, through all of this, he never lost his interest in working with hot steel and iron.

According to his own records, Hancock made his first knife in 1986. His father, a collector of Native American artifacts, had an old Sioux sheath knife he had picked up years earlier. The younger Hancock mentioned that he wished he had a knife like it.

"Simple," his father suggested. "Why don't you make one?"

That was a challenge that could not go unanswered, and Hancock began forging, using the knowledge and talents handed down by his father and grandfather.

"It wasn't an easy project," the craftsman recalls today. "I had to forge a number of pieces of steel before I had one I figured was worth finishing. I didn't realize it at the time, but in completing the knife, I was accomplishing every step in the most difficult manner possible."

Tim Hancock is a third-generation blacksmith and welder who has found that the artistry of knifemaking pays a lot better than shoeing horses. That does not mean he cannot shoe a horse. He can!

Hancock has the tools and has developed the know-how of inlaying silver wire in the handles of his knives. He admits he ruined a lot of silver before he developed his current expertise.

According to Hancock, he sent the knife to his father as a companion piece for the original Sioux-made blade. "My Dad was happy with the results, but I wasn't. I knew there had to be an easier, less time-consuming way to make a knife.

"So I decided to make another one on which I could try shortcuts and, hopefully, end up with a better knife. After that, things just happened, and I found myself in the custom knife business!"

By this time, however, Hancock had come to realize he was dreadfully short on production know-how when it came to knives, so he went looking for help.

First, he sought out custom cutler Jerrald Lambert, who offered advice and counseling, suggesting to Hancock he enroll in one or more of the courses conducted periodically at the Texarkana College School of Bladesmithing. For those unfamiliar with this course, it is overseen by the American Bladesmith Society. Instead of being taught on the school's Texas campus, the course is conducted in Washington, Arkansas, where James Black, creator of knives for Jim Bowie, had his forge well over a century ago.

In 1988, Hancock completed the performance phase of the journeyman bladesmith's test at the school. His progress and performance were overseen by Wayne Goddard, one of the truly respected custom forgers in the knife business.

It wasn't until 1993 that Hancock was able to attend the first major knife show of his experience. This was the noted Blade Show that was held that year in Atlanta. It was here that the young knifemaker had five of his completed knives submitted to the review panel of the American Bladesmith Society.

According to Hancock, his heart was somewhere in the

Hancock has assembled an array of equipment that is meant to make each step in his knifemaking easier, but there still is plenty of handwork to keep it interesting.

This twisted Damascus knife is recreated in the style of early California and is what Hancock calls his Baby Bowie. It measures 6³/₈ inches overall and has a blade of 3³/₄ inches. The handle is of mother-of-pearl with silver and blued steel fittings. The Damascus is a combination of 1095 and 203E, made by Hancock. He inlaid fifty-eight pieces of silver in the handle design. (Photo by Rodman Bittner.)

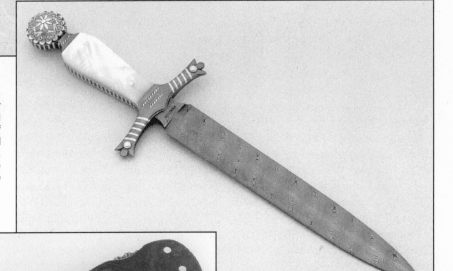

This Quillion dagger was built as the test piece for Tim Hancock's acceptance as a Master Bladesmith. It measures 12¹/₂ inches overall with a blade of 8³/₈ inches. The handle is of presentation-grade mother-of-pearl; the steel is Damascus with 336 layers of 1095/nickel. Fittiings include a blued steel handle frame inlaid with silver. Conchos on the pommel are handmade and handtooled.

The artist calls this his Life Long model, which incorporates 212 layers of steel in a twisted Damascus pattern. It measures 6¹/₂ inches overall with a 2³/₄-inch blade. The handle is of Arizona ironwood, and the fittings are of grooved iron and nickle. The lock nub is handfiled. (Photo by Rodman Bittner.)

This spear-point Bowie by Tim Hancock is 14 inches overall with a 9-inch blade. The Damascus blade is handled with curly maple and has nickel silver fittings. The handle and sheath are inlaid with silver wire. The sheath was formed from curly maple, too. (Photo by Rodman Bittner.)

vicinity of his Adam's apple during the time he was awaiting a decision as to whether he would be granted membership in the prestigious organization. Perhaps he should have had his answer earlier, though. Before the knives were sent to the review board for inspection, they were on display, and the Arizona craftsman had numerous offers to purchase them. He admits it was difficult to tell folks he could not sell the five until they had been evaluated by the ABS committee.

"Every time someone offered to buy one of the five, I had the inclination to take the money and run. I was really concerned about how the review board would view my work and whether I could qualify for membership," Hancock admits today, grinning at recollections of his feelings of inadequacy among the acknowledged masters.

Realizing he could make a full-time living with his forge, hammer and personal creativity, Hancock built a new shop in 1993, a model of what most knifemakers wish they had. The first thing one notices is that the structure is set behind his desert ranch-style home far enough that hammering is not going to bother his family or the distant neighbors.

The hallmark of the shop's interior is the cleanliness Hancock is able to maintain in the various departments, which include forging, grinding, heat-treating, et al.

Like other bladesmiths, Hancock does use some stock removal in touching up and sharpening his blades with a grinder, but he considers himself anything but a stock-removal maker. He is almost poetic in his description of his work, as he sees it.

"There are a lot of talented knifemakers who prefer the stock-removal method," he says, adding, "but the nostalgic origins of the cutting blade came from the fire of a forge and the tenacity of the bladesmith. That's why I prefer forging, I guess. My family has been a part of that origin."

Hancock favors forging 52100 steel for blades that are not his own Damascus creations, working his own patterns in the steel. As mentioned, he also provides filework, sculpted fittings and inlays, as well as exotic handle materials if the customer will pay the price. Actually, his charges are far from pricey. They simply reflect the toil, the hours and the talent that went into the production of each knife. The last we heard, one could buy a small Tim Hancock custom knife for less than $100. At the other extreme, some of his large Bowie styles with all sorts of adornments are priced at $3,000 or more. If you're in a hurry and want a knife for next week's moose hunt, this may not by your man. His delivery time, as we understand it, is somewhere in the vicinity of eight months.

For those who ask Tim Hancock what he expects of a knife he has made, he has a stock answer that makes sense: "Each knife should be better than the last one I made. Also, I seek to make each of my knives a functional piece of art, possessing both grace and character."

As for his hobbies, he still spends a lot of time on a horse.

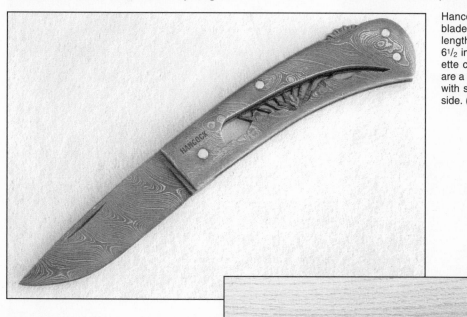

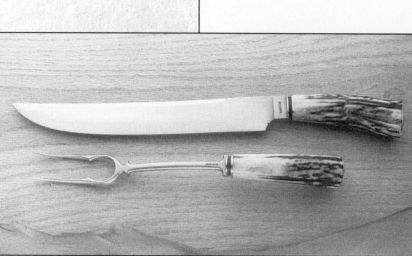

Hancock's Desert Sunrise folder has both blade and handle of Damascus. Blade length is 2³/₄ inches, and overall length is 6¹/₂ inches. This award winner uses silhouette cut-out frames. Engraved on the face are a saguaro cactus and a mountain range, with sunrise and mountains on the reverse side. (Photo by Rodman Bittner.)

Hancock also does custom carving sets such as this. The knife blade is of W2 steel; the fork of 51W. Overall length is 15 inches with a blade of 10¹/₂ inches. Handle material is stag; fittings are of brass.

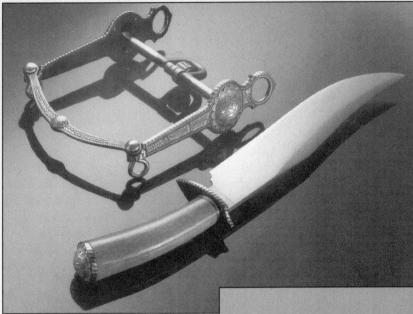

Hancock's Cowboy Bowie measures 17 inches overall with a 12-inch blade of 1095 steel and a handle of oosic. The guard is of iron inlaid with silver. The pommel is mounted with a hand-tooled silver concho. Hancock also made the accompanying Spanish-type bit.

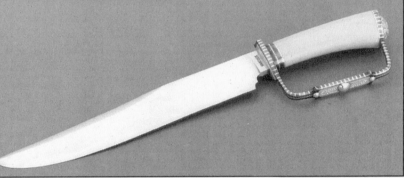

This Hancock D-guard Bowie is 16 inches overall with an 11-inch blade. The blade is of high carbon steel; the handle of mastadon ivory. The fittings are blued steel inlaid with silver. The concho on the butt cap is hand tooled from sterling sliver. (Photo by Rodman Bittner.)

This has led to a sideline that often threatens to take over the knifemaking facet of his career. He makes highly decorated but nonetheless functional bits and spurs for Western-style riders.

"These bits and spurs are expensive," Hancock admits, "and

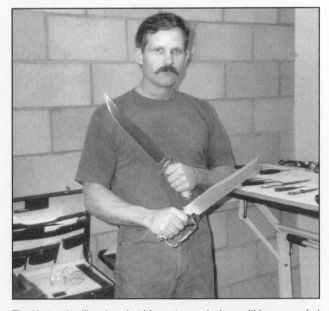

Tim Hancock will make what his customer desires, within reason, but his own favorites are one-of-a-kind Bowie knives for which he has found a continuing ready market.

not the kind you'll find in use on the average cattle ranch. A few—very few—of the spurs may end up on the heels of rodeo cowboys, but most of them are bought by collectors of Western art, with some being purchased by those showing expensive horses, and those people who like to ride in parades and can foot the expense of silver saddles, bridles and my bits and spurs."

When away from his forge, Hancock also enjoys hunting, mountain climbing and scuba diving, not to mention rock climbing and ice climbing. It would appear he is a well rounded daredevil as well as an artist.

Hancock enjoys working with a customer to turn that individual's ideas into a competent, beautiful knife, but he also is selective in taking on such assignments. If there is any indication there will be a clash between practicality, beauty and symmetry, he tends to pass on the project, suggesting the potential customer find another maker. It doesn't happen often, but it does happen.

B.R. Hughes, one of the founders of the American Bladesmith Society and a highly respected judge of custom cutlery, said several years ago, "Were I to list the ten best unheralded bladesmiths in American today, Tim Hancock's name would be near the top of the list. He's extremely good—and he's going to get better."

According to our own on-the-spot observations, Hancock no longer is unheralded. He has become known, he has gotten better, and he can be expected to get better still!

CUSTOM KNIFEMAKERS
Mike Franklin

"I WAS HAVING a discussion with a potential customer who had seen some of my knives on a dealer table at a recent show," Mike Franklin said recently. "He was obviously impressed with my work. 'Everyone in the knife business will know your name in the near future,' he said. I smiled and said that after only twenty-four years as a knifemaker I guess I might become an overnight sensation."

We have been aware of Mike Franklin's craftsmanship and skills for some twenty of those twenty-four years. He is a man with a sense of humor and a love of hunting, especially in his home state of Ohio, where there are plenty of deer to hunt. He is a long-time member of the Knifemakers' Guild and makes fine, expensive knives for collectors, as well as tough, using knives for hunters and others. He has been a full-time professional knifemaker since 1974.

"Although I offer a complete line of custom knives, including hunting knives, camp knives, fighters, folders and an occasional Bowie knife," Franklin declares, "most of my time is spent on folders.

"Some years ago, I invented my own version of the button lock. I call it my Double-Action Locker. It locks open and closed, and is a one-hand opener with either hand. I also offer the standard liner lock, and that accounts for a large percentage of my production."

Franklin says that, at one time or another, he has used 1095, O1, A2, M2, M4, D2, 440C, ATS-34, Stellite and CPM T 440V steels in his knives. His favorite, he says, is the little-known CPM T 440V. It has, according to the maker, no equal for cutting tools where stainless qualities are required. It is tough, holds and takes an edge much as a good tool steel, but is more stain resistant. On the downside, it is difficult to get a mirror finish on blades of 440V, and it is expensive to buy.

"Right now," says Franklin, "my standard steels are 440C stainless for most of my knives, and 1095 for my new HAWG! line of using knives.

"I offer virtually all of the various micartas for handles, including ivory, black linen, red linen, green canvas, plus pres-

Knifemaker Mike Franklin lives in southern Ohio and has plenty of hunting opportunities, including huge trophy hogs with bow and arrows.

Franklin also enjoys whitetail deer hunting with handguns. He tests all his knife designs on the game he kills.

Franklin uses his belt sander to flat-grind a blade blank. Heavy gloves are a must for this work.

The sparks fly as Franklin cuts out a titanium liner for one of his folding knife designs.

sure-treated wood on some. When I am asked, I will use elephant ivory, walrus ivory, fossilized walrus and mastodon ivory. My all-time favorite handle material is stag. Nothing looks as good on a small hunting knife as good, rough stag!"

Mike Franklin heat-treats all his own blades and has done so for several years. In this way, he says, he can control most of the process of making knives so as not to slow down production.

"I simply refuse to let my blades out of my shop until they are finished knives," he states. "With the relatively inexpensive equipment available to makers, just about any knifemaker should be able to afford to heat-treat all his or her own blades. On most knives, I quench on the high side in oil, aiming for a Rockwell C hardness reading of 58-60."

Franklin has been and is an avid bowhunter. Perhaps the abundance of deer, liberal tag limits and the long season in Ohio has much to do with that fact. His decades of bowhunting experiences are what led him to become a knifemaker.

"I had been a bowhunter for a few years and was not satisfied with any of the available knives more than two decades ago," he recalls. "I always loved to build things instead of buying them, even as a child. So I elected to build a knife. One thing led to another, and here I am."

His favorite blade shape always has been the drop-point for sheath knives and folders, although he also likes the semi-skinner and the clip blade. Today, however, the so-called tanto-type blade is most popular, and that is to what Franklin responds. Tantos have almost taken over his business, he says.

"I graduated from high school and college with honors," he

admits. "My field was vocal music through school. After college, I taught for five years before going into knives full time. I have no formal training in knifemaking, but have learned through trial and error.

"I was lucky enough to live near knifemaker Bill Pease during the early 1970s. He was a maintenance man for a local mill and drove by my shop on the way to and from work. He already had a lot of experience with machinery, and he was not afraid to share his knowledge with me. During the past few years, I have become friends with Mel Pardue, and we have spent a lot of time talking and exchanging ideas.

"The first custom knifemaker I ever met was Jimmy Lile. In 1973, I lived in Columbus, Indiana, the site of a blackpowder rendezvous. Lile came to the event and we talked. He gave me advice and help. We became friends and remained so until his death."

Franklin says his shop is small at present, built using concrete forms from a concrete wall behind his home. The shop is equipped with two Bader belt sanders, a floor model and a bench model. He uses two Baldor buffers, one running at 3450 rpm and the other at 1750 rpm. He also has the standard 2x72-inch belt sander, given to him by Bill Pease several years ago. Franklin also uses a Sears drill press, an Enco mill, Micro lathe, a 6x48-inch sander and a band saw. Says Franklin, "Recently I built a sandblast cabinet and bought a five-horsepower air compressor. I built a 4-inch dust-control system and installed inlets at all my machines that might make dust.

"My logo marks are put on my blades with a Marking Methods etcher. Any additional information is put on with a small

Vigor jewelry engraver. I mark the backs of all my blades with the month, year and type of steel used. My blades are heat-treated in a small ceramic kiln."

At this time, most of his leather sheath work and marking is done in his home. Franklin has plans to move his operations to an old farm house near his present shop. The old house should provide more space and allow him to set up a clean room for precision work, leaving another room for the rough, dirtier work.

Franklin recalls the first edition of the Gun Digest Book of Knives, reading about custom maker Jimmy Lile. He saw the pictures and began making knives, not having seen one before. He took some of his early efforts to a local gun shop to show to a friend. His friend knew of a man who collected knives and might be interested in Franklin's wares.

"The guy lived on my way home," says Franklin, "so I stopped and introduced myself. He picked out my favorite knife, a hidden tang, upswept blade with whitetail antler handle and large brass guard. He asked if I would sell it. It was my favorite and I didn't want to sell it, so I mentioned what seemed the outrageous price of $75. He pulled out some money and paid me. Later, he told me that he would gladly have paid twice that amount!

"After we finished our transaction, the man showed me some of his collection of custom knives. He had knives made by such makers as Jimmy Lile, Jim Small, Corbet Sigman, Bo Randall and others. I realized that my knife would be in good company, but that I still had a long way to go."

Franklin says he started to make knives seriously because he wanted more control over his life. He realized that being a teacher meant having many bosses. They were controlling his life, no matter their skills or talents.

"Today," says Franklin, "I spend forty to fifty hours a week in the shop. When a knife show is near, my shop time will increase to fourteen or sixteen hours a day. My customers come from all over the U.S. and many foreign countries, including France, Germany, Holland, Switzerland, Japan and Australia. Customers find me by seeing my knives at shows, on dealers' shelves and through the various articles written about my work. My average waiting period for a knife is now several months.

"I was a member of the Knifemakers' Guild and attended my first Guild show in 1973. I remained a member of the Guild until the early '80s, when I dropped out. I became a voting member again in 1994. For several years, I did not attend any shows. I relied on old customers and word of mouth to sell knives. Later, I realized that there was a generation of knife buyers who did not know who I was.

"Since I added the HAWG! line of working knives, my business has increased many times over. The phone never seems to stop ringing with orders. I have customers who call early and ask about buying knives at shows many months away."

At times, admits Franklin, knifemaking requires a great deal of self-motivation. Only the maker has any control over his time. He is completely responsible for turning out knives. This is especially difficult for Franklin in November during the Ohio whitetail deer season.

"My least-favorite part of knifemaking," says Franklin, "is cutting out the blades and folding-knife liners, cutting my fingers, grinding my fingers, burning my fingers, getting steel and titanium splinters in my fingers, putting a folder together many times over until it works—and putting it together again.

"My favorite times include receiving praise from satisfied customers, attending shows and dealing with customers. I particularly enjoy it when customers and dealers follow me to my table at a show just to see what I have for sale.

"I also like to take the new blade, still warm from the buffer, and run my finger down the sharp edge, and see the action of a butter-smooth folder when it all comes together."

One of Franklin's easiest tasks, he says, is designing new products. Inspiration seems to come in spurts, one idea leading to another. The HAWG! designs have experienced particular

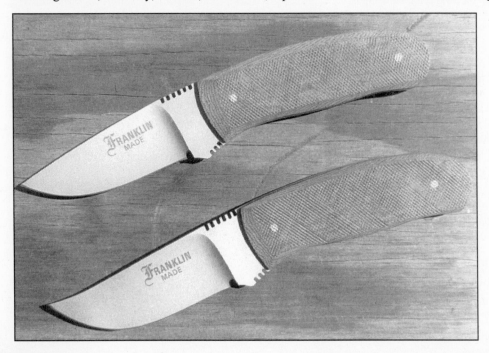

This is a pair of rugged Franklin hunting knives for field-dressing (top) and skinning. The fiber-reinforced handles are hand-checkered for a non-slip grip.

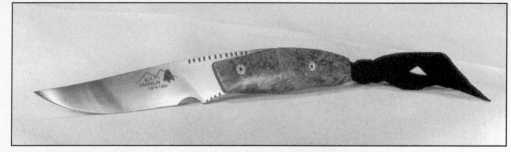

Mike Franklin produced this design on the 20th anniversary of his knifemaking career. Most of these commemoratives were sold to collectors.

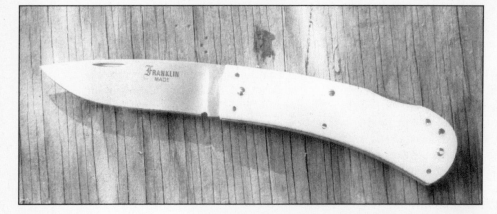

Franklin's lockback folder design sees plenty of use and is very popular.

After years of struggle, Franklin hit upon a design concept that has taken off. The HAWG! knives are simple, lightweight and extremely strong. This tanto blade model has a cord-wrapped grip that is easy on the hand and does not slip. The cord can be any color and can be replaced when worn.

popularity. One customer even called to tell Franklin he thought the design must have been divine. He wanted one of each! Dealers call and tell the maker they will take any and all of his knives—as long as they are the HAWG! models.

Franklin says many people want to know where he got the ideas for the knives and the HAWG! logo. "In January 1995, my hunting buddy (and knife collector) Frank Fulton and I were headed for a hog hunt in Texas. We had the truck loaded down with guns, bows, camo clothing, food, cameras, more gear, and a trailer towing a couple of ATVs.

"My friend was experiencing chest pain, so after I shot a small pig in Texas, we reloaded our gear and headed directly back for Ohio. Fulton's pain increased, so we decided that a hospital was necessary, and I took him to one in Little Rock. He stayed in the hospital and I drove the rig back to Ohio by myself with plenty of time to think.

"I kept thinking about friends who said they wanted one of my knives, but could not afford the prices. They said they preferred something that was easy to sharpen, something they could use without worrying about scratching or damaging the finish. With that thought, I remembered the pig hunt, and a pig with huge teeth and a bad attitude popped into my mind. That became 'HAWG! Knives—Knives With An Attitude.'

"I thought I could bead-blast the blades so they would not show scratches and make them out of tool steel to be inexpensive and easy to sharpen. A simple, inexpensive Kydex sheath would be the final touch. HAWG! Knives took off from there and have sold like crazy.

"My friend, Frank Fulton, was diagnosed with a blood clot in a lung, but he is fine now."

Until the introduction of the HAWG! line, all of Franklin's belt knives had leather sheaths. He and his wife, Marsha, work hard at improving the quality of the leather sheaths they make. Some are carved and dyed with a snap lock to hold the knife in place. The HAWG! line comes with sheaths of Kydex, which is nearly indestructible and safe. The drawback to the Kydex material, however, is that a highly finished knife might be scratched by it.

"Many of my knives," says Franklin, "are tested here at my 89-acre farm and on other hunts in other states. My first

Franklin's HAWG! designs are available as boot knives, fighting knives, skinners, utilities and most other blade shapes.

HAWG! knife was a large hunter I handed to my young son. I told him to do whatever he wanted with it, except for cutting rocks. In time, the knife looked awful, but continued to do its job.

"I have taken a number of nice whitetail bucks on the farm. I have also taken several really large bears and wild hogs with bow and arrow. One boar was more than 600 pounds, and another 450-pounder has record-book-class teeth. All have been dressed with my own knives. I realize most of my knives—especially the expensive folders—will never receive the rough treatment the HAWG! knives do, but they are all built to stand up to hard usage.

"My son, Jerrod, was only eleven when he began making his first knives. He gave his first two knives to a couple of guides on a wild boar hunt. They continue to carry them and say they are satisfied with them. Jerrod designs his own knives, but I help him with heat-treating and sharpening. Naturally, I am proud of his accomplishments."

Mike Franklin does not charge for his product brochures. They are kept up to date with new pages when necessary. New models and designs always are being added. He gets a large percentage of orders from these mailings, he says, so the printing expense is justified.

Drop a line to Franklin to learn about prices and delivery times, but don't expect a quick answer during the November deer rut.

CUSTOM KNIFEMAKERS
Phill Hartsfield

TWO DECADES AGO, Phill Hartsfield was forced for economic reasons to change his occupation and his way of life. At the time, he may not have realized what a major change it was to become a custom knifemaker, but today he has an international reputation for making the sharpest, toughest knives and swords available anywhere. Prices are not cheap, and the wait for an order might be up to two years, but the customers are happy to pay and wait for the product.

There were a few folks who would've forecasted Hartsfield's success upon seeing some of his first efforts at making knives, but most of us had little understanding or appreciation of what he was trying to do. In fact, Hartsfield's first efforts in the knife industry were limited to building and selling what he called Li'l Cranky, a small, hand-powered device for sharpening knife blades. This device was a simple, round sharpening wheel, with a rugged jig to hold the knife at a specific angle while the wheel rotated upward against the blade. The blade was held in place while the slowly rotating, medium-grit wheel did the work. It was contrary to most sharpeners then on the market, and only those who tried it and found how well it worked were sold on it.

Hartsfield no longer makes Li'l Cranky, and most of us wish we had purchased one twenty or so years ago. Selling homemade knife sharpeners is hardly a career with an income to put bread on the table and a car in the garage, however.

Hartsfield had been making knives as a hobby since he was an eleven-year-old child in Baltimore. He was taught grinding on a pedal grinder. Later, he helped pay his college expenses doing leather tooling. Knot tying, too, is a skill that he currently utilizes for his sheaths as well as knife and sword handles. That skill was expanded during his years in the Navy serving aboard destroyers and submarines during the Korean War. His formal training in the Navy was in electronics, and for twenty years after he was discharged, he was self-employed in television servicing. He uses, he says, all these early skills and training in his knifemaking work today.

In 1976, Hartsfield opened a small store in Garden Grove, California, called A Cut Above Knife Shop. He and it are still in the same location. The small, cluttered, efficient little shop sells only Hartsfield knives, although most of the blades on hand are for display purposes only. Hartsfield seldom has knives for sale. Most of his retail work is taking orders for special blades and designs from new and long-time customers who stop by or conduct business by mail.

Hartsfield may be seen working on his designs in the shop or even out front near the sidewalk. He sometimes attracts a crowd of onlookers, especially on weekends or when a well-known martial artist is in the area. Then the shop fills up with knife buyers, martial artists and the curious. All share Hartsfield's enthusiasm and interest in knives and their construction.

Twenty years ago—and some would say it is still true—Hartsfield custom knives looked crude, awkward and unfinished. A typical Hartsfield knife does not feature a mirror finish, fancy filework, engraving, carved exotic handle materials, stainless steel, fantasy blade designs or anything else that might cause it to be considered an art knife or a collector knife.

Hartsfield makes blades, large and small, that are intended to fulfill a specific function. They are meant to be used and used

Phill Hartsfield with one of his earliest knifemaking efforts. He still keeps it on hand as a demonstration. It is big and sharp, but not fancy.

well. They cut things, and their form follows their function. The edges are sharp and stay sharp—sometimes for years, even with heavy usage.

At one time or another, Hartsfield has tried almost all the different tool steels available. He settled upon A2 some time ago and sees no reason to change. He feels A2 is best for his blades and his heat-treating methods. It is reasonably easy to work with when using his heat-treatment, holds an edge better and is stronger than any other steel he has tried.

Hartsfield does all his own heat-treating with a cold quench and a triple-draw procedure. The blades are treated to a Rockwell C reading of 60-61 on the leading edge, while being drawn down a little on the back. The rest of the blade will test out to a C scale reading of 58-59 Rockwell. It is stress-relieved three times to eliminate brittleness. Flexibility is a must, especially for sword blades which could break if too brittle. This provides terrific edge-holding capability with added strength to the blade.

Hartsfield uses the time-tested stock-removal method in fashioning his blades, utilizing a slow-moving, coarse-grit belt. He feels forging the blades would deteriorate the chemical content of the steel. Heat-treating is done by Hartsfield in an atmosphere-controlled oven.

If his blades are so sharp and so popular with those who

When he grinds, Hartsfield sets up the slow-moving belt grinder outside his shop, near the sidewalk. The belt grinder is nothing fancy. He does not use fine-grit belts.

know about such things, why doesn't another maker copy his designs and cash in on what he does? Anybody may see and examine Hartsfield's blades at the several shows he attends a year. One might even take careful measurements of the blade shape, grinds and angles. Then why not head back to the shop and turn out knock-offs?

"I have often been asked that," Hartsfield admits. "And some have tried to copy my designs. But the secret of my knives' edge-holding and cutting abilities is in the heat-treating. And I do not share that information with anyone.

"I do all work myself. I grind the blades, heat-treat the blades, sharpen them; I make the sheaths and do the handles. I test every blade I make. My knives are made entirely by me and I will keep some of the methods to myself."

The handles, too, are deceptively strong, rugged and utilitarian. Hartsfield's earliest knives used various kinds of hardwood with steel or brass pins. He still offers many types of hardwood on some knife handles. They looked crude twenty years ago and still look crude when compared to some of the more popular collector-type knives seen elsewhere. But they are as tough as any and tougher than most.

His most popular handles, especially on larger knives and swords, is a cord-wrap design. He might offer a traditional diamond wrap—tape over cord with polymer epoxy resin, which produces an almost indestructible non-slip grip. With the epoxy over the wrapping, almost nothing, including gasoline, will harm it. There are those who hammer on the cord wrapping—using the knife as some sort of chisel or gouge—without damaging the handle, although Hartsfield does not recommend it. Other variations include tape over copper, cord with no diamond wrap and numerous variations of the cord wrap. When asked what sort of expensive, exotic cord he uses to get such rugged handles, the maker shows a spool of standard, hardware store cotton cord.

Hartsfield makes all his own leather sheaths. He uses a full metal lining, custom formed and pressure fitted for each blade, snug enough to hold the knife upside-down in the sheath against almost any physical activity by the wearer. He uses top-grade leather. A belt sheath may be specified, but a popular option has the sheath suspended around the owner's neck, inside the shirt or jacket, but ready for quick employment. That way, the knife is concealed, inconspicuous and always at hand.

Hartsfield says, "My view on knives and swords always has been the same. I try to make the strongest, sharpest tools available. The way I maintain quality is to try to make each piece better than the last. It also keeps me from getting tired of what I am doing. Each blade is a new challenge."

Japanese-style swords and knives are what Hartsfield has become best known for. Many years of study and reading about the traditional blades have led him to his own expression of this art form.

"The steel of the old blades was absolutely magical for the time," says Hartsfield, "but I feel to ignore the advances of modern technology would be a compromise in producing the best possible blade.

Hartsfield likes to demonstrate the sharpness of his knives and swords with the newspaper cutting test. The paper is a single sheet, rolled into a tube of about 2 inches in diameter. It sits unsupported on any flat surface.

With a single slice, the maker cuts cleanly through the flimsy newspaper.

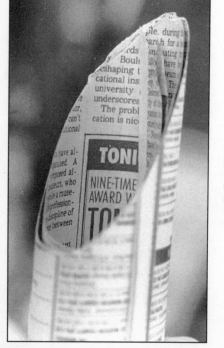

This illustrates how cleanly the newspaper is cut. Keep in mind that the paper cylinder is not supported in any way.

"I am not Japanese, so I do not make a traditional Japanese sword. I make my own version of the old-style blades. The steel in the old blades was developed through trial and error. In some instances, blades of amazing strength and sharpness were created. However, every blade was not a great creation, every swordmaker was not a great artisan! This holds true even today."

Describing some of his knifemaking technique, Hartsfield says he grinds blades in reverse of most others. The grinding wheel or belt moves upward into the steel, rather than away from it. This is a bit more dangerous to the artisan, says Hartsfield, because should the blade happen to catch the grinder, it would be thrown directly into the knifemaker's face or eyes.

Most knives Hartsfield makes these days have a chisel-ground edge; one single side of the edge is sharpened. Most also have a distinctly Oriental look. Many observers have mistakenly called the blades a tanto shape, but the tanto is a distinct Japanese short sword about 12 inches long. Not every large knife with a chiseled edge is a tanto, this maker is quick to point out.

"When I started making knives and was perfecting my design of the Japanese-style Yoroi Toshi blade," recalls Harts-

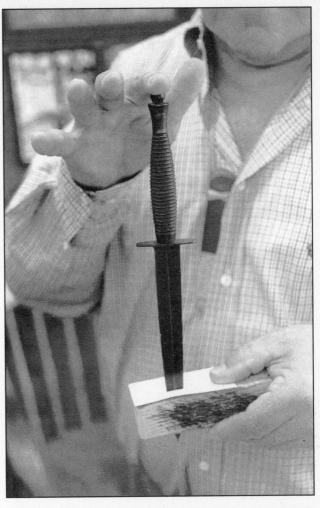

Here's another demonstration of a blade's sharpness. The small block of wood has a hole in it, and a regular business card is placed over the hole. After a start, the Hartsfield knife blade slips down and completely through the paper to the hilt without drag.

Using a typical combat dagger design, the knife must be pushed all the way down to get it to pass through the card to the hilt.

field, "many makers and manufacturers tried and did copy the style. They incorrectly call it a tanto design, which it is not. Having my design copied is a drag, but there is no way to control what others do. In time, I registered my trademark to protect my clients from rip-offs when they bought knives."

Hartsfield has an almost mystical relationship with his craft and with the blades he makes.

"A lot of the things I have tried for the first time seem to be things I have been doing all my life," he says. "Since the beginning, knives and swords always have had their own spirit. Some people understand that; some do not. There are other tools like that, like the hammer. Understanding that fact has nothing to do with its reality.

"The old fellow who taught me to grind so many years ago always said that, if you will grind into the steel, it is a lot like hammering with many tiny hammers. I use heavy belts when I grind. I do not use fine-grit belts. I use 40-grit, coarse belts. That is one of the reasons I use A2 tool steel for all my blades. I can really lean in with the blade against the belt and get a terrific edge on my knives."

Hartsfield's business philosophy is to be of service to all. "My clients are so good about promoting my work and its qual-

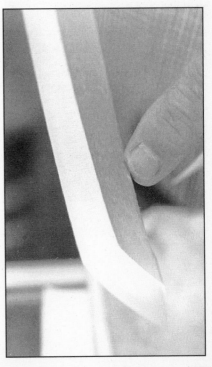

One of the keys to an armor-piercing blade is the design of the tip. Hartsfield calls this his Yoroi Toshi style. The words, in Japanese, mean body armor piercing. When this part of the blade is reached, there is no more drag.

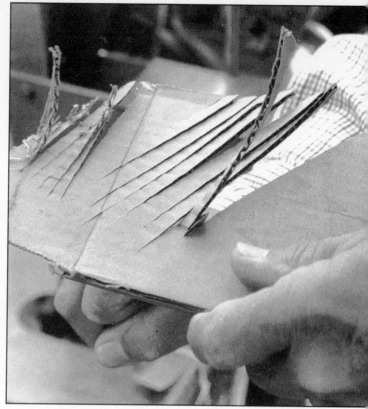

A typical Hartsfield product is not what one might consider an art knife, but is utilitarian to the end.

Slicing through cardboard is not a demonstration of how sharp the blade is. It is the final honing of the edge.

ity, I usually let them speak for me. I really prefer to keep a low profile and make as few waves as possible. That is the reason I don't join with or belong to any group."

Some of his earliest and most loyal customers were and are the riggers and electricians in the Hollywood entertainment industry. They are cutting and rigging hemp rope for scenery

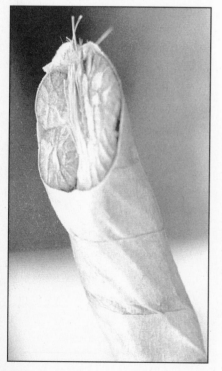

In some circles, much is made of cutting through a free-hanging rope with a single stroke. Using a Hartsfield short Kwaiken knife, a beginner was able to slice cleanly through this 1-inch hemp rope. There was almost no feeling of drag as the blade slipped through.

and sets all night long to be ready for filming the next morning. They would literally carry around boxes of sharpened knives with them on the job, dulling them all with use through the shift.

Other customers include pole climbers and electricians who must cut cleanly and quickly, but without using both hands on the work. Others include businessmen, military and law enforcement personnel, doctors, truckers, as well as martial artists and ordinary people.

For those customers who wish to buy a fighting knife, the maker is careful to point out that a single-edge blade is the most useful. In training or in an actual fight, one would not want to block an opponent with a double-edge blade against the forearm.

For more mundane uses, the single-edge knife lets the user place an extra hand on the back of the blade to cut through really tough material. It is also prudent to remember that in many local or state jurisdictions, a blade with both edges sharpened is considered a dagger and would be illegal to posses or carry.

In the early days, Hartsfield did not consider knife collectors as his customers. He began making and continues to produce the best working knives possible. But along the way, he was reminded by a client that the only way the knifemaker had to protect his customers was to mark the blades, something he was not doing earlier in his career. Many of his first knives were not marked. Collectors are always on the lookout for genuine unmarked Hartsfield blades. With a few exceptions, all of them are marked now.

The proof and the sharpness of the knives is obvious when

one sees some of the videos or actual cutting demonstrations Hartsfield will show. They are incredible. For starters, he has a small piece of wood with a slot cut through it. He holds a standard business card over the slot and begins with any other fighting knife or dagger at hand. A typical Fairbairn-Sykes World War II dagger makes a good comparison. It is started vertically through the business card using as little pressure as possible. In fact, the knife must be pushed down all the way through the card, lightly, but positively.

Then Hartsfield offers the same demonstration using any one of his knives. Once started and held upright, the knife will cut through the card of its own weight. Because of his Yoroi Toshi blade design, there is almost no drag on the blade as it passes through the paper.

The first observer comment might be that the Hartsfield knife is much heavier than the Fairbairn-Sykes. Not true. Each is weighed, and the Hartsfield weighs considerably less than the dagger. It simply has little drag because of the sharpness and design of the blade.

A second demonstration might have the maker slice a paper shaving off the face of the business card. Slicing a piece of paper into strips is passe. Shaving a card is an impressive demonstration.

Another typical sharpness demonstration by some knifemakers is cutting through a hanging piece of heavy hemp rope. At many knife shows, cutting rope is a major exercise for many knifemakers. Hartsfield demonstrates it with his knives, and the authors have emulated the act to confirm the authenticity. Even the shorter blades will cut through a piece of hemp rope nearly without any drag. They pass through almost without feeling it. Without any further sharpening or honing, the same knife will easily slice paper-thin discs of ripe tomato.

Even more impressive is cutting through a sheet of rolled newspaper. A single sheet of paper is rolled into a cylinder and placed on almost any surface about 3 feet high. A countertop or stool is about right. The cylinder is about $1^1/_2$ to 2 inches in diameter. One of Hartsfield's knives, with even a relatively short 8-inch blade, will slice the cylinder as cleanly as a razor or a scissors cut. Little effort is required with a stroke angle of about 35 degrees. A skilled practitioner can make three cuts on the paper cylinder before it topples from the stand. The same blade will cut through the hanging rope before or after the newspaper.

Hartsfield says he prefers to keep his customers' blades sharp, although he includes sharpening instructions with each knife. Local owners bring the knife by the shop and Hartsfield resharpens them at no cost. Others are asked to pay the shipping and insurance costs, but the maker does not charge for the work.

Very little special care of the blades is required, says the maker. During everyday use, he advises the user to wipe the blade clean. The steel is not stainless, so saltwater or other substances will, in time, corrode A2 steel. The maker recommends a light coating of lemon oil for everyday cleaning. Lemon oil is the same stuff many people use on wood furniture. If the blade is to be stored or is used in and around saltwater, he suggests coating it with STP, an engine additive available at most auto parts stores. With STP on the blade, no moisture will penetrate to the steel.

Hartsfield always will say knifemaking is a constant learning process. He knows more than he knew last year, but not as much as he will next year. He likes to tell a story about his first experience at a knife show. Everything was so new to him and his wife, Pat, that it seemed rather difficult at first.

"The first time we went to a knife show in New York," he remembers, "it was at Madison Square Garden. Well, we sold out all the knives in about two hours after the show opened. We didn't know any better, so we just packed up our gear and left

To sharpen his blades, Hartsfield uses a simple wood-block jig to hold the metal against the slow-moving belt.

Final edge sharpening is done on an old grinding wheel. Years of experience have taught Hartsfield the proper angle.

Three types of handles and knives: The knife on the left is called Kwaiken, in the middle is the Strong Boy, while at right is Hartsfield's version of a traditional Bowie design.

Small, useful, sharp and, some would say, ugly, but the knife will cut almost anything.

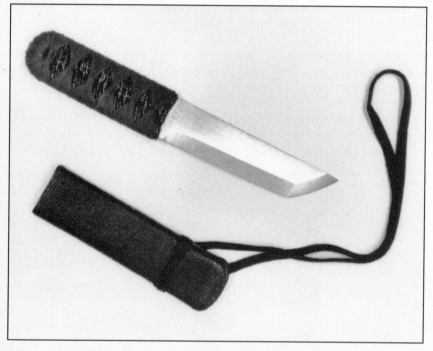

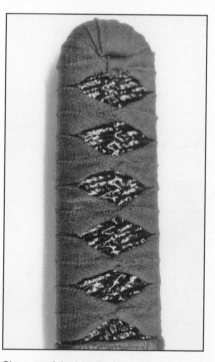

The smaller Hartsfield knife fits into a custom scabbard that holds the blade tight during any activity. It may be worn around the neck, under a shirt.

Close-up of the handle detail. The wrapping in this case is regular shoelace. Hartsfield is not one for unncessary adornments.

the show. We didn't realize we were supposed to stay until the show was over, even though we no longer had anything to show.

"The show management was most kind to us. They let us come back again, even though we'd broken one of the rules.

"My goal always has been to make the strongest, sharpest sword available, for the serious user. I make each blade with that in mind. When I deliver a sword to a client, I remind him that a lot of my spirit goes into the blade. As time passes, the sword will assume the new owner's spirit, too. It will always have its own spirit. When you combine these three elements, the blade must be treated with respect."

There are no two blades alike. Each is unique and a personal experience for Hartsfield. He is most often asked how long it takes to make a sword. His answer is always, "Until it is finished."

CUSTOM KNIFEMAKERS

Chris Reeve

CHRIS REEVE WAS born in Durban, Republic of South Africa, in 1953. In 1975 he was an apprentice tool and die maker, about to be called upon to serve part of his compulsory annual national military service. Reeve noticed then that his army kit did not have a good, all-purpose knife. He decided he had the skills to make a satisfactory field knife to take with him while training in all sorts of terrain and weather conditions.

This early design featured a hidden tang with a rather ordinary wooden handle. It was the best-looking knife in training camp, but the dry semi-desert air quickly dried out the wood and the handle began to crack. The cracked handle set Reeve to thinking about a knife that would not be affected by hot or cold, wet or dry weather. Could he design and make an all-steel knife?

As a trained tool and die maker, Reeve knows about the properties and idiosyncrasies of various types of steel, and he has the training on the machines he needs. In 1983, he designed and built his first one-piece knife, the MK II. Only a year later, Reeve deserted his occupation in toolmaking and became a full-time knifemaker.

Chris Reeve's first custom knife show in the U.S. was the 1986 New York Custom Show; the California Custom Knife Show in October 1987 was next. He had attended several shows in South Africa before that. He found he was well received by the buying public and by fellow knifemakers. Applying for membership in the Knifemakers' Guild, he was made a probationary member in 1988 and has been a voting member since 1990.

While still in South Africa, Reeve and a staff of three full-time employees were able to produce approximately 1600 knives from January 1988 to February 1989.

But in an effort to improve his business opportunities, Reeve made a permanent move to the United States in March 1989, settling in Boise, Idaho.

For any small business, including Chris Reeve Knives, the disadvantages were outweighing the advantages of continuing to do business from South Africa. At that time, there was continuing political strife, a spiraling cost of living, a worldwide threat of trade sanctions, and a general anti-South Africa feeling through most of the world. The sensible thing to do was to move to the United States.

Lengthy and careful considerations were given regarding the choice of locations. Boise was chosen because the city is large enough to provide the services required for the business, yet small enough to allow newcomers to find their place. The beautiful Idaho countryside offers plenty of space for the recreational activities

Knifemaker Chris Reeve is a trained machinist, and that background shows in the precision of his knife designs and their construction.

that Reeve and his wife, Anne, enjoy: hiking, camping and a general appreciation of the wilderness.

Six weeks after their arrival, the Reeves occupied a workshop space and the production of knives had resumed. They attended a dozen knife shows that first year in the U.S., exhausting but beneficial to Reeve. The presence of Chris Reeve Knives was becoming known to buyers and suppliers. The effect of other companies that had been importing the knives from South Africa and misrepresenting the product was soon dispelled.

Growth has been the overall pattern of Reeve's business since he moved to Idaho. By 1991, he had cut the number of large knife shows to six per year. The range of his one-piece

While each knife requires plenty of hand work to complete, Reeve has many machine tools in the shop, and some of it is pretty sophisticated.

Reeve uses a Rockwell hardness tester to determine the RC reading of his blades. Quality control is extremely important to him, and this attention to detail has helped build his reputation.

knives grew to 21 different models, and he was making selected high-dollar custom knives as time permitted. Retail sales and the number of dealers handling the line were growing. In recent years, Reeve has reduced the number of different knife models to concentrate better on current market trends and customer demand.

According to Reeve, "The ideal working knife is a tool that is strong, reliable and impervious to temperature and humidity. Extensive time has been devoted to design, research and development of my knives to improve both the blade designs and the methods used in making the knives."

Each knife is made from a solid billet of A2 tool steel. Reeve contends the stock-removal method results in two distinct advantages: The strength/weight ratio is exceptional and there is no handle-to-blade joint.

"This means," says Reeve, "that there is no area where the blade and handle could come apart, a weakness in the design of other hollow-handle knives. The handle cavity is larger than that of any similar knife. The hollow handle is closed with a buttcap made of 6061 aluminum, which screws into the handle against a neoprene O-ring, ensuring the cavity is sealed from dust and moisture."

All the one-piece knives are hardened to 55-57 RC by Reeve. A random check is made to ensure the accuracy of the treatment. This hardness gives superb toughness and good edge retention, and it makes for efficient sharpening in the field.

Each knife is coated with Kalgard R, originally developed for use in the aerospace industry. This coating offers a durable, long-lasting, non-reflective covering to the steel handle and blade. A handmade leather sheath is included with each one-piece knife.

Reeve's knives are used by hunters, backpackers, SWAT teams, military personnel, firefighters and police all over the world. They also are found in many knife collections. Many customers, says Reeve, own more than one of his knives.

Some feel that once their Reeve knives have been used, they lose their collector value. "Not so," says Reeve. The knife may be returned to the shop where it will be sandblasted, re-coated with Kalgard and resharpened, thus returned in original condition. The charge for the service is nominal.

All the money Chris Reeve Knives makes is reinvested in new machinery. A look into the neat, compact production shop will reveal the validity of that statement. Quality control and customer service are important facets to Reeve, so additional staff members are employed. Continuous attention is placed on refining the knife designs and methods of production as well as making sure the designs offered are what the public wants to buy.

Until a few years ago, all the retail knives from Reeve had been the larger one-piece models. In 1992, his first folder, the Sebenza, was introduced, resulting in rave reviews and strong demand. The first eighty-six production knives were sold to customers sight unseen.

A major step forward in the increased production capabilities required by the popularity of the Sebenza was the addition in September 1992 of a computer-controlled machining center. Reeve was able to increase the quality and the quantity of the components of the folder. A smaller model of the folding knife was introduced in 1993. The knife is available in two sizes, left- or right-handed versions, in many configurations and appearances. The Sebenza features titanium handle slabs and artistic, machined decorations and computer-assisted designs, no two alike.

Reeve has this to say about his Sebenza Integral Lock: "My first impressions of the liner lock-style locking mechanism were very favorable, but when I examined it more closely, I didn't like the flimsiness of the thin liner. After some thought,

The Reeve workshop in Boise, Idaho, measures some 2350 square feet. Note how clean and orderly it is!

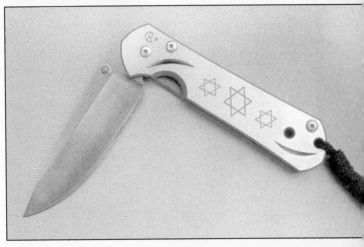

The newest Reeve design is called the Sebenza, a Zulu word from Reeve's native South Africa, meaning "work." Reeve offers a variety of handle decorations.

I redesigned the concept to create the Sebenza Integral Lock, which I believe to be the most rugged folding knife on the market.

"My one-piece knives have achieved popularity as strong, working, fixed-blade knives through simple, effective design. The Sebenza is a folding knife to complement them. I have put a great deal of thought into the different features and know that this is a knife that will work hard, keep a good edge and will be easy to clean.

"Each knife is supplied with an Allen wrench that can be used to dismantle the knife. This allows easy cleaning. The knife also can be cleaned quite safely in a dishwasher. A drop of silicone or Teflon gun oil needs to be applied to the hinge after cleaning."

An examination of the Sebenza will reveal a recess in the

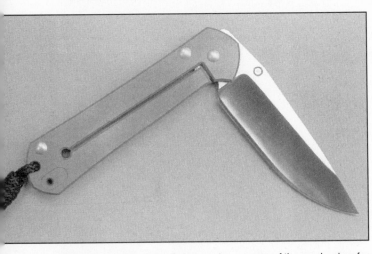

The opposite side of the Sebenza shows some of the mechanism for locking the blade open. Reeve calls the design an Integral Lock, an improvement over most liner locks.

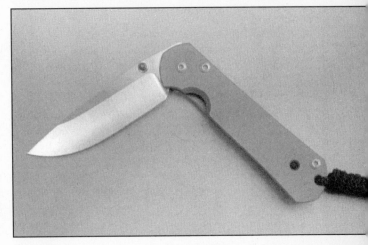

Blade material of the Sebenza is ATS-34 stainless steel, while the handle is made of titanium with 303 stainless steel spacers and pins.

back of the blade that bears onto the stop pin. When the blade is open, this recess provides an increase of area and prevents excessive wear on the stop sleeve that could result in a loose lock. The stop pin has a sleeve around it, which can be rotated, if necessary, to tighten the lock.

The action of the Sebenza is as smooth and strong as any folder to be found anywhere. The pins are large, and the blade movements are silent and silky. The lock is a machined titanium handle slab, cut and formed to snap into the locking position as soon as the blade is fully open. To close the blade, the user pushes on the spring section with the thumb and the blade may swing shut. That locking action is as strong and rugged looking

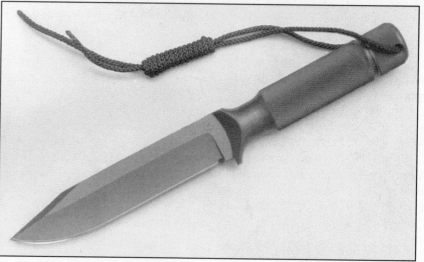

While the Sebenza folding knife has become wildly popular, the original Reeve one-piece knives are still big sellers. Each is machined from a single piece of steel and finished with non-reflective Kalgard.

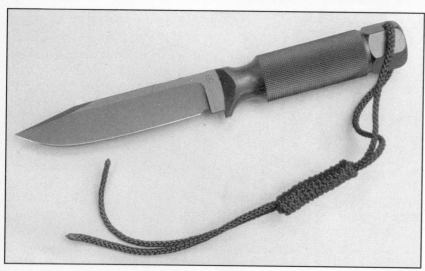

The hexagonal buttcap on this one-piece Reeve knife indicates the blade is 4 inches long.

Larger Reeve knives may have blades ranging up to 7$\frac{1}{2}$ inches long. Some have a serrated edge near the hilt, and all have hollow handles.

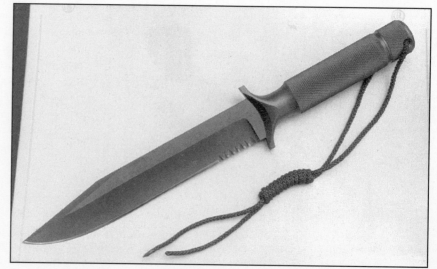

as any knife—stronger than most. The work seems flawless.

To aid in opening the blade, a serrated thumb push-button on top of the blade permits one-hand opening. The large pivot bearing surface provides more area against which to clamp the handle slab. Lateral strength is increased and should ensure a longer life for the pivot bearing. The thrust washers are phosphor-bronze. They are corrosion-resistant, able to withstand heat and are quite slippery, assisting the smooth opening and closing action of the blade.

Often, the machined-in designs in the titanium also are colored. They are clean and simple, yet somehow compelling and exciting to the eye. No doubt, those artistic touches add to the appeal of the knives.

The name of the knife, Sebenza, is from the Zulu word for work. Zulu is the native language of the province in South Africa where Reeve was born and raised.

"The Zulu warrior was one of the most effective of his time," declares Reeve. "This reputation was achieved with strong discipline, simple battle strategies and weapons used with devastating efficiency. Many of the Zulu people still live their lives in a simplistic, no-nonsense way, and maybe some of this has rubbed off on me, resulting in my simple, no-nonsense approach to knifemaking."

In Southern California, one cutlery shop that handles Chris Reeve Knives is South Coast Cutlery, owned by Dan Delavan. Because of the worldwide demand for the Sebenzas, South Coast Cutlery keeps a few of the folders in stock. Dela-

van has no trouble moving as many Reeve knives as he can get. There seems to be no customer hesitation among those who know quality custom knives or those who know about Reeve's reputation.

As this is written, the production of Reeve, Incorporated, Boise, Idaho, has reached 1700 knives annually. His immediate goal is to exceed 2000 knives a year. When time permits, Reeve likes to make one-of-a-kind custom pieces. These are always of his own design, although the influence of Europe or Asia may be seen in some. The knife designs range from folders with unique locking mechanisms to truly elegant table cutlery. Reeve takes pride in the knives, forks and spoons he makes, and that pride is obvious when he shows the pieces at knife shows he attends.

He shows favor to exotic materials and frequently inlays gold, pearl or wood into the titanium or wood handles. These touches present interesting contrasts of color and texture to his designs. Because of his African heritage, Reeve uses indigenous African hardwoods where and when he can. He learned, he says, much of his knowledge of wood from his father. As a young man, his father was collecting stumps and root sections in and around the family home. Many of the exotic pieces Reeve uses for his art knives are considerably older than he.

What sets Reeve's knives apart from most others is his dedication to quality, performance and value, he says. The knives all have been tested extensively and are the result of unique design, top-quality steel, sophisticated machining and hand craftsmanship, as well as old-fashioned hard work. The company is small, but manned by a team of hard workers who strive to produce the best knives at affordable prices.

All Reeve's knives are a combination of modern computer-controlled technology and hard work. Some of the initial stages of handles and blades are prepared on large, expensive machinery.

"Some of the work on both folders and single-piece knives is done for us by an excellent machine shop in Boise," declares Reeve. "All important work is done in-house, blades are ground by hand and all polishing is done with that special ingredient: elbow grease. Heat-treatment is done in-house under my scrutiny. Folders are assembled with total dedication so that the fit of pivot pins and bearings is within the most exacting standards.

"In the past three or four years, I have been experimenting with different methods of sharpening and have now achieved what I believe to be the optimum cutting edge. Our blades are as sharp as or sharper than any others on the market."

Effective sharpening, Reeve believes, depends on several factors working together. The combination of geometry of the hollow grind, the grind right at the cutting edge and the final polishing of that cutting edge all are vital to produce a blade that will cut well.

"In order to keep a knife cutting well, maintain the edge on a set of crock sticks or Spyderco Tri-Angle Sharpmaker. I will regrind and sharpen any knife I have made for a nominal charge. Return it to me and I will restore the cutting edge to original."

It would be hard to turn down an offer like that.

Anne Reeve handles the order-fulfillment and bookkeeping chores for the small company.

Mike Tamboli

WHEN YOU CAN'T find what you want, you make it yourself. And, in the process, you launch yourself into a second career.

If you're Mike Tamboli of Glendale, Arizona, that's how you become a custom knifemaker. Unable to find the skinning knife he wanted for deer and elk hunting, the forty-seven-year-old Navy veteran decided to make his own.

An avid hunter and fisherman whose pleasant home in a Phoenix suburb is decorated with the mounted heads of deer, elk, antelope and javelina he has harvested, Tamboli came to custom knifemaking naturally. He even remembers being impressed with the first real custom-made knife he saw.

"I was probably in my mid-twenties when a friend of mine, who had gotten the knife as a gift for somebody, showed me this fancy, inlaid, engraved knife. I thought, Wow! That's nice looking. I wonder how you make something like that."

With a chuckle, Tamboli also remembers thinking that the $125 price tag was outrageous.

A Phoenix native, this craftmen grew up working during summer vacations in the machine shop where his father was employed. This gave him the basic knowledge of tools and techniques that certainly would stand him in good stead as a knifemaker. And his father, also an avid hunter, had made a few hunting knives for his own use.

"I still have my dad's first knife," Tamboli says. He also has the first one he made himself in 1978. That skinner was the first of many hundreds of knives to come from MT Custom Knives. Today, it is "pretty crude, really, with simple slab handles," in Tamboli's judgment.

But, as with all labors of love, there's more to it than that: "At the time, I felt it was a pretty nice blade and that I'd accomplished something. It's especially true, since it was my first one, and I hadn't known any better."

That first knife was also a learning experience. Starting with a bar of high carbon steel, a drill press, lots of files and a small grinder, Mike Tamboli spent two months of evenings and weekends creating his skinner.

"I learned a lot. Although I had no real problem profiling, the grinding was the hardest part, and that was because I was underpowered." Today, his garage workshop—maintained with meticulous neatness—does not have that problem. He has three grinders for various phases of the process, a wood/metal band saw, buffers for polishing, a drill press and an extensive collection of files.

"I also learned that making a knife was a lot tougher than I thought. So I really learned to appreciate the hard work and

craftsmanship that went into the handmade knives I'd seen over the years."

Over those same years, Mike Tamboli has developed into a knifemaker with two distinct specialties.

He makes hunting and trout knives for friends and friends of friends, what he calls his "blue-collar" clientele. Although some of these blades are one-of-a-kind, he has developed and maintains a standard outdoor line, consisting of a single-design trout knife and two designs for hunting knives. All three have varying blade lengths, depending upon the customer's preference, but the norm is a 3- to 4-inch blade length.

The first step in manufacture is to cut the profiled knife out of the 440C stainless bar. Already Tamboli has spent many hours creating the design on paper and in his mind. Many more will follow for grinding, filing, polishing, and fitting the handle and embellishments.

His other specialty is at the opposite end of the knifemaking spectrum: the ever-expanding world of miniatures. This line is for his "white-collar" clientele—doctors, lawyers, other professionals and overseas customers, including two Japanese men who are avid collectors.

Miniature knives are a growing part of the custom knifemaking industry. Once just a curiosity turned out by a small number of makers, the miniature knife has arrived. They command full-size prices, with $500-$1000 becoming the norm, and a price of $2500 is no longer unusual.

Along with the increase in price and popularity, miniatures also must be virtual works of art. Customers demand something stylish *and* unique. In addition, the miniature must be made of high-quality cutlery steels, tempered to spec and ready to cut. Everything must be in proportion, and the result must be a knife with nice lines and all parts cleanly done. Makers also have to use exotic materials for handles and stylize them in unique ways.

That's fine with Tamboli. Almost all of his miniatures are of Damascus steel, which he buys from Devin Thomas, a full-time Las Vegas, Nevada, knifemaker who also forges the uniquely layered steel into the bars that this maker and others profile, cut, grind, file and polish into a finished knife.

This sander begins the process of polishing the blade to the mirror finish that custom collectors demand.

Tamboli got into miniatures a few years ago because he wanted to see if he could make them. As his expertise, design imagination and reputation have grown in the miniature field, he gradually has come to do more and more of them.

"They're more fun to me, and they sell better. So, I've kind of become known as a miniature guy. You end up in a category whenever you have a popular seller or when you do the same kind of thing back to back for a while. So, miniatures is my category. That's my niche, and I'll stay in it, I expect."

It's a niche this craftman fills with a certain artistic flair. Because all his miniatures are one-of-a-kind, Tamboli's design output has been varied: daggers, fighting knives, hunting knives, belt knives, boot knives, et al.

Once he produced a series of twelve miniature hunting and utility knives in cooperation with knife artisan David Yellowhorse, a Navajo who has designed hilts and handles for Buck Knives. Yellowhorse employs a number of Native American artisans for making custom handles with a Native American and Southwestern look to them.

When working with Yellowhorse, Tamboli made the 440C stainless blades and the handle artisan made the handles from turquoise, corral, jet and aged ironwood.

Nowadays, Tamboli turns out his own handles, almost never using man-made products. His miniature handles have been composed in part or totally of such exotic materials as pearl, snakewood, fossil ivory, ironwood and burls, and particularly redwood. He's even used shittimwood, of which the Ark of the Covenant was made in Biblical times.

Both his miniatures and full-size knives are stamped with his name, city and state. He also offers custom engraving and scrimshaw, but does not do this work himself.

The engraving is done by Pat Holder, wife of D'Alton Holder, the Phoenix knifemaker who was Tamboli's mentor years ago. The scrimshaw is the handiwork of Texas artist Lou McLaran. Most of the stylized scrimshaw is of animals or Western themes.

When the knife requires a sheath, Mike Tamboli turns leather worker and produces his own.

Of the 60 to 100 knives per year that constitute this maker's normal output, 75 percent will be miniatures. Although not a member of the Knifemakers' Guild, he does belong to the Miniature Knifemakers Society.

However, despite his concentration on miniatures, Tamboli still makes full-size knives. With the exception of his "blue-collar" orders, they all are one-of-a-kind for collectors who come to him with a particular design or shape in mind.

After making his first skinner, Tamboli then produced a dagger and a sub-hilt fighter. His main full-size output has been hunting and utility knives. Like most knifemakers, he's produced a Bowie, including a pair of variations on that venerable theme that had 14-inch blades of 440C; sambar stag handles; and top fittings, guard, buttcap and inlays of Damascus.

He's also done a series of twelve African-themed knives whose blade shapes and lengths were derived from traditional

(Below) One of the most time-consuming chores for a knifemaker, especially when he works on a miniature blade, is the seemingly endless filing that follows grinding.

Tamboli uses a drill press in his garage workshop to cut in the broad outline of top fittings on a miniature knife. Several hours of very fine filework and polishing will follow.

Using a magnifying visor to see the fine details, Tamboli uses a scribe to examine the details of the engraving on this miniature knife.

African hunting and utility knives, and whose handles included such exotic elements as various antelope horn and amber.

Over the years, he's made about everything except swords, which he says do not really interest him. Doing what interests him is the key to Tamboli's philosophy of knifemaking.

"I do what I enjoy doing. If it was a full-time profession, I couldn't do it that way. Some of the things I do may not sell all that well, but I enjoy making them. When I retire, I'll have to change my way of thinking, because then I'll make knives full-time," the maker explains.

Currently employed by the U.S. Postal Service, Mike Tamboli still is a few years away from retirement, but he's already making plans for it.

Besides changing his philosophy of knifemaking, he'll travel—partly for pleasure, partly for work.

Currently, he attends only two knife shows a year: the California Knife Expo in Pasadena and the Arizona Knife Collectors Association Show in Phoenix. With more time, he'll attend more shows and travel for pleasure. The love of travel is something engendered in Tamboli by his three years in the U.S. Navy.

He served from 1969 to 1971. Trained as a locksmith and engraver, Tamboli was stationed aboard the aircraft carrier, *U.S.S.*

Kitty Hawk, and spent his time on Yankee Station, the carrier operating area in the Gulf of Tonkin off the coast of Vietnam.

"I remember making port calls to a lot of strange and exotic cities, and I remember how much I enjoyed seeing new places and cultures," he says.

When he attends knife shows in the future, Tamboli will be doing what he does now: selling and looking. Although established in the business, he still finds new clients at the shows. With his steady clientele and the referrals they give him, he has all the orders he can handle in the fifteen to twenty hours per week he can devote currently to knifemaking. Right now, a full schedule means he no longer even has to advertise, though that too could change when he retires and goes into the business on a full-time basis.

Besides the time this craftsman spends selling and talking to prospective clients at the shows, he makes a point of walking the aisles. But, he's not looking for something to buy.

"When I'm at the shows, I study what the other makers are displaying. That gives me a springboard, sparks ideas of my own." He also talks to friends and long-time customers about what they'd like to see, but haven't. And, he reads knife books and magazines.

This research is necessary, because Tamboli admits design is

One of Tamboli's full-size custom knives, this one is a skeletonized, 8-inch hunting blade of 440C with a nickel-silver guard and a camou-flaged Pakkawood handle.

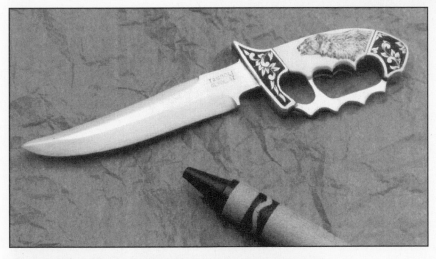

A one-of-a-kind, this miniature by Tamboli is 3 inches in overall length. The blade is 440C with a nickel-silver hilt engraved by Pat Hold-er. The fossil ivory inlay was scrimshawed by Lou McLaran.

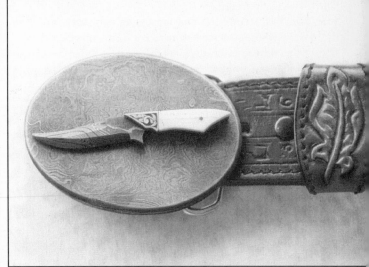

(Above) This MT Custom Knives miniature is a fully functional knife, but is also permanently affixed to the belt buckle. Its Damascus steel blade blends perfectly with the buckle of the same material.

This dagger is a one-of-a-kind MT Custom Knives orig-inal. The blade is double-ground Damascus steel, with a nickel-silver guard and buttcap, and an ivory handle.

These full-size slip-joint folders have 3-inch blades—five of 440C and one of Damascus steel. The handles are of such exotic materials as aged ironwood, redwood, cocobolo and fossil ivory.

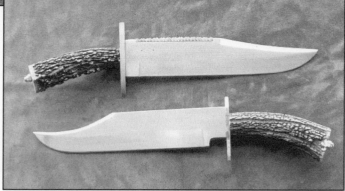

These two variations on the venerable Bowie knife feature 14-inch 440C stainless steel blades with Sambar stag handles. The top fittings, guard, buttcap and inlay are Damascus steel.

always the hardest part of the process for him, especially in an industry whose customers demand constant innovation.

"You have to be creative, but there's only so far you can go or you get too weird. If the design doesn't sell, then it's a waste of time, even when you personally like it. I've come up with lots of them I liked, but I knew they wouldn't sell so I didn't bother with them."

Over the years, he has learned what is worth bothering with. And for those planning to get into the business, he offers this advice:

"Don't plan on making a million dollars overnight. There probably are not five custom knifemakers in the country who can make enough to do this full time. That's tough odds, so plan on keeping another full-time job."

Equally important, he says, is equipment. "Get the right stuff up front, so you can make the knives right from the start.

"And, get tips from someone who's already established. Learn as much as you can from him about the techniques. Spend time with him in his shop and ask lots of questions. Of course, you have to find someone who's willing to do that for you."

A trick of the trade that novices can acquire on their own is Tamboli's old standby—research. He stresses the value of read-

ing and really studying as many books as one can find on knifemaking.

"Not only did the books help me learn how to make knives, but they gave me ideas for my own unique designs."

It is in the uniqueness of design that the future of custom knifemaking is to be found, Tamboli believes.

"I see a bright future for the industry. More and more makers are coming into the industry, doing decent work and selling their designs. The public and the collectors want our products, but you have to come out with something new and different each year."

Like most of the top-notch pros in the custom knifemaking business, this pro prefers not to copy, then just alter existing designs. "It's not as much fun, but that means I have to be creative to come up with something new."

That drive to be creative has brought Mike Tamboli a long way—from a crude skinner in 1978 to the exquisitely and exacting designed miniatures of 1997. He's traveled far, and all without ever leaving his garage workshop.

In the years ahead—with more time to devote to his hobby-cum-career, he'll travel even farther, and who knows where the road will take him?

CUSTOM KNIFEMAKERS

Bob DeFeo

NEVADA CUTLERY CRAFTSMAN Bob DeFeo used to be a dentist. In fact, he maintains his license and still could pursue that career should he choose to do so. His father also is a dentist back in Philadelphia and tends to shake his head over his son's preoccupation with knives.

Dentistry was the first career for Bob DeFoe, and he had his own practice until 1978. That was when he decided he wanted to get involved in what was termed the casino industry.

"It's not that I'm a professional gambler," he explains, "but the business and operational end of the gaming business I found intriguing, and I wanted to get into it." Chances are, that brought another series of shakes of the head from his dentist father.

Bob DeFeo spent nearly a decade in Atlantic City, major home of East Coast gambling. It was in 1988 that he left that seaside gaming capitol, where he had been employed by one of the big casinos, and made his way to Latin America and the gaming houses of Costa Rica. There he spent another year, learning more about the ins and outs of the various games.

In 1990, he arrived in Nevada—specifically, Las Vegas—and found immediate employment at the Golden Nugget, one of the older and best known of the downtown gambling houses.

A floor supervisor for this gaming establishment for a number of years, DeFeo then worked what many would call odd hours. He checked in at 8 p.m. and usually wrapped up his night's work at 4 in the morning.

"Normally, I slept until about noon," the craftsman explains, "then I'd be in my shop for several hours, designing knives or turning them out on my equipment."

In recent months, however, DeFeo has been promoted to pit boss. With this came a change of hours that finds him usually reporting for work at 2:30 a.m., then heading for home just before noon.

"I've had to revise my schedule," he admits. "I try to work at knifemaking soon after I come home as a sort of come-down from my casino job, but that schedule gets complicated by the fact that all three of my sons now are into Little League and other sports, and I spend a lot of my free time getting them to their activities."

Nevertheless, DeFeo's knifemaking still is an everyday thing, laboring in the complete cutlery shop he has set up in his garage and listening to music as he works. He listens to the classics, blues, rock and Cajun music during these sessions.

"The combination of working with my hands and hearing the music I love is a great relaxant from what sometimes tends to be a high pressure career in the gaming industry," he explains.

While still living and working in Atlantic City, Bob DeFeo

Custom knifemaker Bob DeFeo has developed a fully outfitted shop in his garage in Henderson, Nevada. A pit boss at a Las Vegas casino, he finds knifemaking relaxing and productive, spending several hours a day in his efforts.

Bob DeFeo has involved his sons in his knifemaking efforts: (from left) Joey, seven; Mike, eleven; and Daniel, nine. The two older boys hold knives they have ground from rosewood blanks, using their own designs and their father's equipment.

made his first knife, and he made his first sale—a hunting-style blade—two years later.

"Judged by the standards of what I can do today, those early blades probably were somewhat crude," he admits.

It was during this particular era that he began to assemble the array of professional blade-making equipment that is installed in his garage on a quiet residential street in Henderson, far from the bustle of Las Vegas only a few miles away.

"I sold my gun collection so I could buy the equipment I needed," he recalls. "I was mighty proud of that collection, and it was a hard decision to make. In retrospect, it certainly was the right choice, though."

At the time we talked to DeFeo and visited his working digs, he estimated he had completed and sold more than 500 knives. Of the various styles he makes, he favors the classic Bowie knife and has found that he will have an average of 50 hours invested in a big one.

"When I'm making one of those Bowies, I go through a lot of grinding belts, but my work is slow and meticulous. I take a lot of time in finishing, but it's not like real work. Listening to some of my favorite music through my headphones, I feel at peace with the world. I guess you could call it therapy of a sort."

For the Bowie knives, he favors ivory as a handle material. When it comes to other knife styles, this craftsman enjoys working with the various exotic woods. If building a knife to a customer's specifications, he will use whatever material is ordered for the handle. His standard handle materials are cocobolo and micarta, either black or white. At extra cost, he will use ivory, stag or stabilized exotic woods.

The ivory used by Bob Defeo is fossil ivory from mastodons that died thousands upon thousands of years ago. Much of this material has been found in glaciers in Alaska during hydraulic gold mining efforts. The tusks, some of them 10 feet long, have been cleaned up and sold to purveyors of such exotic materials.

As for steel, he uses ATS-34 whenever he can. "It has a great grain structure," Defeo feels, "and takes an edge better than any other material I've used." However, he also works with 440C, D2 and O1 steels as standards. Guards, bolsters, pins, et al, normally are fashioned from 416SS, 304SS, brass, nickel or silver. Each knife is furnished with a custom sheath of 9- to 10-ounce leather. DeFeo also does hand tooling and will produce such a sheath at extra cost. Other extra-cost items are guards, bolsters or pommels that vary in design from his own. He also does scrimshaw at added cost and has engraving done by Bruce Shaw.

"I bought a whole set of engraving tools a year ago, but have not had the time necessary to be become fully adept," the knifemaker adds. "It looks to me as though it'll be a couple of years before I'm good enough to start doing that kind of work."

The Nevada maker also has involved his three sons, Michael, eleven; Danny, nine; and Joey, seven, in the shop work.

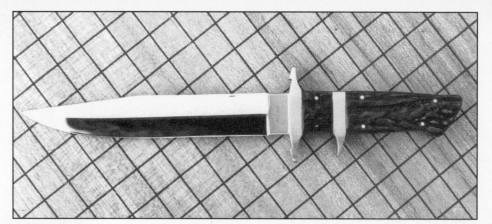

This DeFeo knife is featured on the cover of his brochure. It measures 14$\frac{1}{2}$ inches overall and is ground from ATS-34 stainless steel. The guard and sub-hilt are of 416 steel. The handle slabs are of stag, setting off the mirror-polished blade.

Both of these matched fighters—one measuring 12 inches, the other 9 inches—were ground from ATS-34, Bob DeFeo's favorite blade material. The handles are of desert ironwood and the 416 bolsters were engraved by Bruce Shaw. The blades have a mirror polish.

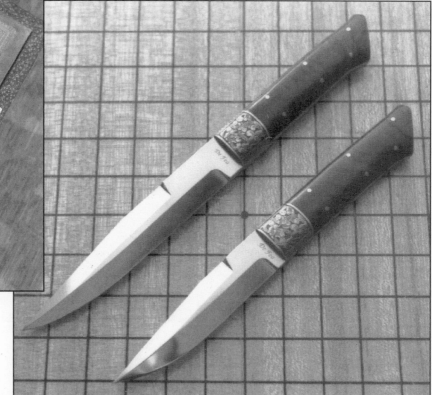

This 12-inch dagger is mentioned in the text. The double-edged blade is of ATS-34 steel, with 416 steel used in the pommel and guard. Buffalo horn is the handle material, which is wrapped in silver wire.

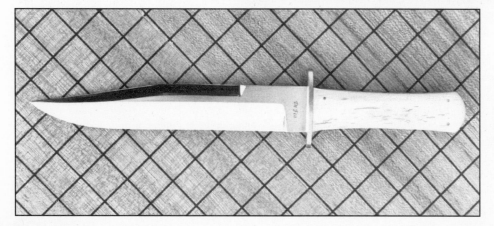

This craftsman's favorite design is the Bowie, as reflected in this 12-inch, hollow-ground example. Bladed of ATS-34 stainless steel, the flats are satin-finished while the ground areas have a mirror polish. The guard is 416 stainless steel, with the handle fashioned from mastadon ivory.

A mirror-polished blade and bolsters engraved by Bruce Shaw are features of this drop-point model by DeFeo. As might be expected, the blade is of ATS-34, the bolsters of 416. Ivory was used for the scales.

This Sheffield-style Bowie is 16 inches overall and has a flat-ground blade of ATS-34, plus a guard and pommel of 416 stainless steel. Engraving is by Bruce Shaw. The ivory handle is from some long dead elephant.

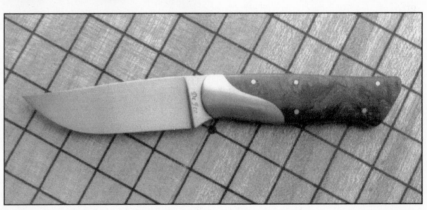

Bob DeFeo agrees with many hunters that little can be better. This flat-ground hunter model measures 8 inches overall, and has a hand-rubbed finish. The blade is of ATS-34, the bolsters of 416. The handle is of burled rosewood.

"It's something we can do together, and it gives us a chance to exchange ideas," the father states. "Michael is my helper in the shop, and one day soon, I want to teach him how to make knives. Danny, though, may have the best hands in the place, including mine. When he decided he wanted to make a knife out of wood, creating his own design, I didn't have to show him a thing! Joey's interested, but is pretty young to show any kind of attention span.

"Actually, with their interest in sports and other things, their interest in knifemaking right now is a sort of sometime time. They're interested for a while, then they're not. It's a sort of cyclic interest at this point." He also is the father of a thirteen-year-old daughter, Alexandra, who "is strictly into girl things. To her, a knife is a kitchen tool!"

While Bob DeFeo favors his Bowies, one of the knives we found of particular interest was a real departure. It was a 12-inch dagger made from the familiar ATS-34 stainless, with the fittings fashioned from 416 stainless.

On this particular knife, the custom cutler used buffalo horn as the handle material, carefully filing a spiral channel which then was inlaid with silver wire.

"I hadn't done much of that kind of work," DeFeo recalls, "and I wanted to see how far I could go with it." From overall appearances, it would seem this craftsman went all the way!

The fact that Bob DeFeo enjoys a challenge is reflected in the fact that he has just begun to delve into the mysteries of making folding knives. When we called a few days ago to clear up a couple of points, he was involved in assembly and was frustrated over the fact that it had taken him four hours to get the knife to "walk and talk."

"This is some challenge," he admitted, adding that, since the Knifemakers' Guild has announced it will be holding its annual meetings in Las Vegas for the next several years, he will be able to participate actively. Thus, the Nevada knifemaker is applying for probationary membership in the organization.

CUSTOM KNIFEMAKERS
Tim Alverson

IT MAY SEEM totally ironic—and there probably are those who will resent the implication—but what has been declared an endangered species, the spotted owl of our Pacific Northwest, has helped Oregon resident Tim Alverson to become a better knifemaker!

Alverson considers himself a full-time knifemaker, but the truth is that he works a regular shift in a lumber mill, then goes back to his home and spends another shift making knives.

During the period of economic upheaval in Oregon, when thousands of acres of timber were put out of bounds for lumbermen in an ecological move to protect the habitat of the allegedly endangered owl, some of the mills closed down and others were forced to cut their production. During this forced hiatus, Alverson had considerably more time to spend at his grinding wheel, improving his techniques and turning out enough knives to help bridge the unexpected gap in his family's cash flow.

Alverson enlisted in the Air Force during the Vietnam unpleasantness, training as a weather service technician. Following completion of training, his first duty station was Klamath Falls, Oregon. In the ensuing years, he also prognosticated the weather in Alaska, Montana and Germany. Upon discharge, though, he came back to Klamath Falls and went to work almost immediately in the lumber industry.

"I didn't even know there was such a thing as a custom knife until about 1980," the Nordic-looking craftsman admits. "At that time, Dave Pitt was running an archery shop here in Klamath Falls, and I became interested in bowhunting. With the number of deer and elk in the area, it was a good way to help out with the food bills, I thought.

"Hanging around Dave Pitt's shop, I saw my first custom-made knife and learned Dave had made it. I was properly intrigued with the fact that he didn't have any other knives around his shop; that he was able to sell all of them he could make."

Alverson began to help the owner of the archery shop in his part-time cutlery projects, and Dave Pitt quickly introduced him to the basics of custom knifemaking. It wasn't long before the lumberman began to assemble his own array of equipment and set it up in his garage.

"I figured I needed something to occupy the hours when I wasn't in the lumber mill and knifemaking seemed a good alternative to watching television," Alverson says.

Today, he makes between forty and fifty knives per year, concentrating largely on Bowies and daggers, although he will take on any kind of knife-building assignment that seems to make sense. He spends about fifty hours a week in his shop, even when carrying a full work schedule in the lumber mill. "I guess that qualifies me to call myself a full-time knifemaker, doesn't it?" he asks, grinning.

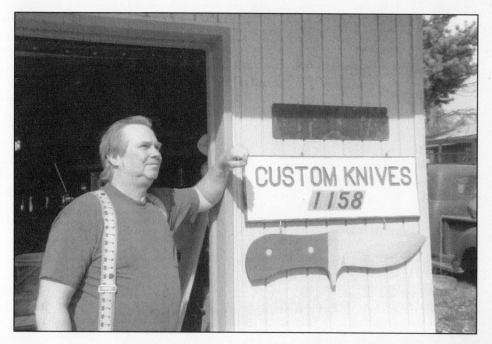

Tim Alverson takes a break from his knifemaking labors, which are conducted in the shop set up in his Oregon garage. This Klamath Falls resident pursues two careers: one as a knifemaker, the other as a lumber mill worker.

Tim Alverson's shop is small and compact, making it easy for him to work with the tools and machinery he has assembled over the years.

Alverson enjoys all facets of knifemaking, but considers profiling one of the more interesting aspects of a trade he has followed for more than a decade.

In recent months, he has started to build folders and has found them quite a challenge. "Building a folding knife involves intricacies that are not found in turning out a fixed-blade type," he admits.

"Remembering to follow each step that is required is part of the challenge. I finally made a list of the needed steps in sequence. That helps. If I get stuck or forgetful, I now have an instant reference."

Today, Tim Alverson works primarily with three types of steel. He has found that ATS-34 and 440C meet most of his needs and are highly acceptable to his customers, but he also is doing some work with Damascus which he purchases from Chris Peterson.

Like most artists, he has his preferences when it comes to handle materials. As a knifemaker, he favors ivory, sambar stag and any of the hardwoods. His absolute favorite—and one largely ignored by other makers—is amber, which he has used in a number of art-quality knives. At the other extreme, if you want a tough using knife, he'll give you micarta or another man-made material.

At the moment, he resides in a rented apartment, where his garage has been turned into his cutlery shop. "Some people would say the place is crowded," Alverson acknowledges. "But to me, it's simply compact. Everything I need is either at hand or within a couple of steps."

Installed in the converted garage are three different grinders, 16-inch drill/mill, table-top drill press, bandsaw, a broad assort-

ment of hand tools including hammers, files and scrapers and, of great importance, a Paragon furnace.

Alverson does his own heat-treating, settling in most instances on a Rockwell hardness of 58 to 60C. "This is the general hardness used by most knifemakers," he has found, "and it's the Rockwell reading recommended by Paul Bos and Bill Holt, who do the heat-treating for a lot of custom cutlers."

Alverson was granted membership in the Knifemakers Guild in 1984 and found that through association with other knifemakers he meets at the annual convention, he has been able to improve his work, taking advantage of the criticism and tips his contemporaries offer.

"I have no formal training in this kind of work," Tim Alverson says, "but I enjoy working with my hands. My greatest source of learning has been by asking questions—lots of them—of other knifemakers. When I go to the annual Guild meeting, I have the chance to exchange information with others, and that is important.

"Out here in the mountains where I live, I'm pretty much by myself," the craftsman explains. "There's no one I can turn to if I come up with a problem. Some of the local Indians make knives, but they are primarily for their own hunting and fishing."

Two highly respected knifemakers Alverson credits with offering encouragement have been Frank Centofante and Mike "Whiskers" Allen, who have helped with design and technique advice. In turn, the Oregon craftsman has counseled a number of newer, less experienced makers, including Eldon Coats.

Here's an Alverson-made Bowie, the type he enjoys making most. This one has a handle made from the antler of a deer the Oregon craftsman killed himself. The knife measures 15 inches overall, with a blade of $^3/_{15}$-inch 440C stainless. Depth of the blade is 2 inches.

As a total departure, Alverson made this wedding-cake serving set as a wedding present. Amber and ebony have been used in the handle capped with engraved silver. The engraving was farmed out.

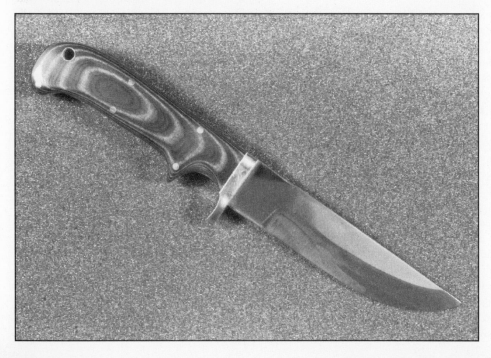

Alverson's Cascade Hunter model is among his most popular sellers. The laminated wood used in the handle gives the knife style and is a selling point.

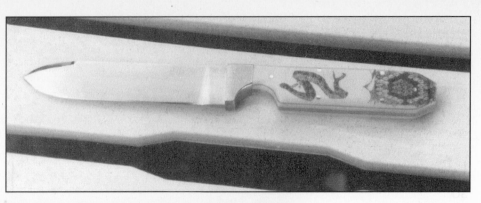

Alverson calls this knife his Best Style Fighter. The handle is of ivory micarta. It measures 9½ inches overall.

This drop-point hunter is listed in Alverson's brochure as the Lee model. It is named after his son, who designed the knife.

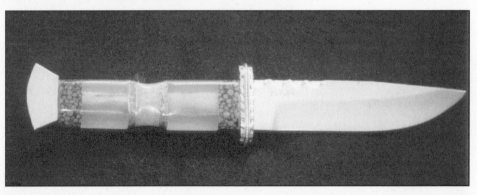

Alverson is one of the few knifemakers using amber as part of his artistry. The handle of this knife is made of amber and turquoise.

When it comes to making a knife, Alverson admits that the toughest part is "just getting started with each blade. Once I'm over that hump, I enjoy working with my hands and get a real joy out of finishing out each blade. The easiest part for me, though, is the handle."

Many of his knives are decorated with scrimshaw and engraving, but he farms this out to professionals in their individual fields of art, using several of them. "But I hope to be doing my own engraving within the next few months," he confides. "I'm practicing as often as I can."

He feels that he could use some more equipment in his shop, but perhaps his greatest need is help on the business level. "I'll take all of that I can get!" he declares. "When I'm shuffling paper, I'm not making knives!"

Obviously, the knifemaker feels that dealing with deliveries, billing and that sort of thing also tend to interfere with the thought processes involved in designs for new knives. He admits that many of his ideas come from his customers or from other knifemakers, but "some just come out of thin air." In addition to his standard designs that sell well, he does a good deal of strictly custom work.

"I don't sell many knives in my own community," he says. "Here, we have mostly hunters and fishermen who are just interested in getting the hide off a deer as fast as possible with a minimum of effort. They aren't interested in a knife's beauty. Too, a custom knife is considered expensive in this locale, which is understandable."

The Klamath Falls maker is a member of the Oregon Knife Collectors Association, and attends this organization's shows, as well as those of the Knifemakers Guild and big custom cutlery shows in Las Vegas, California and other cities. He also has gained some local notoriety by donating custom knives as prizes or awards to various sporting groups.

Today, Tim Alverson's 50-hour knifemaking weeks are full of projects, and one can plan on a wait of ten to twelve weeks for delivery, if ordering one of his knives.

CUSTOM KNIFEMAKERS
Charles Weiss

SOME WOULD SAY Charles Weiss has not lost what might be termed his native-New York accent, despite his years of living in Arizona. Perhaps some of the typical competitiveness of life in the Big Apple still influences his philosophy regarding success.

"When I start something, I cannot give it up. That might be good or bad, but that is the way I am," says Weiss. "Maybe that's why I got into this dendritic steel experimentation business and why I continue to work with it. I want to get it right, and I think I have."

The dendritic steel process is not new nor is Charlie Weiss the first custom knifemaker to use it. It is a common process to produce many metal products ranging from automobile and gun parts to art works, jewelry and other cast components. The word is a derivative of *dendrite*, a Greek term that relates to branches or branching minerals. The dendritic steel process causes a network of mineral branches to form within the molten metal as it cools. The branching network distributes the minerals in what appears to be a fern-like pattern when viewed under a microscope. Speaking unscientifically, the process produces a strong, inexpensive, edge-holding knife blade. Some believe the resulting steel properties are better than other methods commonly used in the industry.

Using this type of steel in knifemaking is considerably less expensive and time-consuming than the standard stock removal or forging methods of producing blades that most custom knifemakers use. Far less time is required because much of the blade formation is done at a casting foundry. Foundries are located in or near most large cities, and some will do the relatively small custom jobs typically required by knifemakers.

Readers may be familiar with the lost wax casting process common to the jewelry business. It has been in use for centuries, using mostly silver and gold as the metal to be cast. Weiss has a background in jewelry design and is familiar with the process. For knives, the first step is to produce a knife blank complete with bolster, guard, butt or other components, as it would be when machined or ground from a single piece of steel. With that as a guide, Weiss machines the hollow mould, two halves made of aluminum. He will make several moulds of the same design so the artist can produce several blade blanks at once; it is more economical that way.

Molten metal access holes and venting outlets are also machined into the moulds. From the aluminum mould, Weiss makes knife blade blanks using a special artist's wax material that has been melted and poured into the moulds. He can make a number of wax knives from a single mould, although that is a

Charlie Weiss explains the design and purpose of the wax knife blank. On the workbench are the aluminum moulds used to make the models.

slower process because of the cooling time required for aluminum. He can pour into several moulds, each alike.

When cool, Weiss carefully breaks open the mould and removes the wax knife blank. He cleans it up, removing the sprues (extra protrusions left from the process of pouring the wax) and sands it to final form. To be economical, he may fashion a dozen or more at a time to be taken to the foundry.

The casting foundry attaches the wax "knives" around a cylinder-like form with all the blades protruding evenly around the form. The resulting "tree" is carefully dipped into a liquid ceramic slurry. After each dip into the slurry, the tree is dipped into silicone sand that sticks to the liquid. The mould tree is re-dipped alternately into the ceramic slurry and sand until it is strong enough to handle the stresses of holding molten steel.

95

Weiss's workshop is equipped with all the essential power tools of his craft, and he is expert at their uses.

(Below) Knives made of the dendritic steel process are the answer to high custom knife prices, believes Weiss. The molten steel is poured into the moulds and results in a one-piece blank ready for finishing.

The foundry people know from experience how many dips and how thick the mould has to be.

The mould is dried and cured for a specified period of time, making sure all the moisture is gone. That done, the tree is put into a high-temperature oven to melt out the wax. The hot mould is then ready to accept the molten steel. All the temperatures are predetermined and matched to the blade steel production. At a specified point, the sand and ceramic mould is broken away to reveal the steel blades. They are straightened if necessary, annealed and trimmed of excess steel. Finally, the lot is delivered to the knifemaker for the finishing touches.

While the process is a bit tedious to describe, it is faster and cheaper than having the knifemaker grinding out each blade from a piece of cold steel. Weiss will grind, polish, sharpen the blank and add the chosen handle material to the dendritic steel as he would a ground or forged blade. It is a custom-designed, hand-made knife with the maker's imprint on it, but it will sell for considerably less than a one-at-a-time custom knife. The dendritic process also produces an extremely sharp blade that will maintain its edge through repeated cuts and slices. Resharpening is not difficult, either, according to those who have used these knives.

Charlie Weiss is no rookie when it comes to making knives. He made his first one in 1948. There were plenty of WWII souvenir knives of all types around then and Weiss saw plenty of them. That first knife was a school project. Were a student to make something similar in school these days, he probably would be expelled at best.

The first custom-made knife Charlie Weiss ever saw was while he was still in the U.S. Army. It was a Randall fighting knife that, at the time, Weiss bought for $12. For an extra $9, Randall put the buyer's name on the knife.

Weiss was into custom firearms work when he finished school. He has designed and made custom or repair parts for guns for years and still consults on shotgun design for some makers from time to time. The process of making gun parts at a foundry is the same as making blades.

He began serious knifemaking in 1973. Today, he specializes in classic knife designs such as Bowies, coffin-handle designs dating back more than a century, collector knives, recreational and hunting knives and other designs he gets from his clients.

Some designs come from inside the maker. "Knifemakers have photographic memories," declares Weiss. "I remember—at least subconsciously—every knife or art design I have ever seen. That memory bears on what I make. No two of my knives are exactly the same. I make changes to each knife I build, even those built to my customers' specifications. No artist can eliminate himself from his work."

Formal machinist and metal-working training comes from his background in firearms. Weiss taught himself to make knives, although he acknowledges the help and influence of other makers such as fellow-Arizonan D'Alton Holder and Fred Carter of Texas.

"Fred Carter is the thinking man's knifemaker," says Weiss. "I would show him my ideas for a knife, and he would make comments and suggest improvements. He has always given his time to any knifemaker who asked for it."

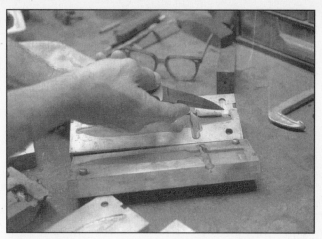

Each dendritic steel knife model has its own mould that may be used over and over.

The dendritic steel moulds are as carefully constructed as the original designs.

This is a finished Charles Weiss dendritic knife, complete with stag handle. The price is affordable and it is an excellent handmade knife.

Custom knives by Charles Weiss may be ordered with various handles, as the buyer wishes.

Two favorites from Weiss: The grind lines on the blades require almost perfect control during construction.

The Weiss collector knives are highly valued by his customers. The maker does his own engraving and supplies the metal sheath.

Charlie Weiss is the current president of the Arizona Knifemakers association. In addition, he has been a member of the Knifemakers Guild for more than twenty years. Most of his customers are successful professional people. Many are serious collectors who appreciate his work and who own several of his knives. His customers, believes Weiss, are good at what they do and will buy the best knives available. Weiss puts himself in that category. He relates well to his customers.

The maker prefers to produce knives of 440C stainless steel, using the dendritic method or the stock-removal method. Such was not always the case. For a few years, Weiss says, the quality of the available 440C steel was inconsistent. Quality control has returned and the better quality steel is again available. He tried knives of ATS stainless for a time, but prefers 440C.

For handles, Weiss prefers natural materials such as stag and exotic woods. He will, however, use tougher man-made handle materials if the customer requests it.

California's Paul Bos does the heat-treating on most of Weiss's blades, and Weiss has high praise for his heat-treating skills. On a few knives, Charlie Weiss will do his own heat-treating. For collectible knives, Weiss specifies a hardness of RC 58 on the 440C blades. For working knives, he calls for an RC reading of 60 to withstand the hard usage the blades must undergo.

Putting in sixty to seventy hours a week in his well-equipped Phoenix shop, Weiss loves to make collectible art knives.

He says, "I like the routine, tedious tasks of knifemaking. I like the repetitive work. Hand-finishing the blade is one of my favorite things to do. I also like to do my own engraving."

Many of his customers like the engraving he does, too. Except for the working knives he makes, most collectors' knives will include engraving by Weiss.

Charlie Weiss's shop is notably clean and neat, at least to the casual observer, and he has a full complement of power machines. A milling machine, drill press, several wheel grinders, belt grinders and sanders, band saw, plus the usual

The art knives are beautifully made, and Weiss does all the work. The price, however, puts these knives out of reach of most knife users.

assortment of clamps, vises, hand tools and files are arranged neatly for easy access and safety. Weiss has each power machine vented with a dust vacuum tube to exhaust the potentially dangerous dust and particles of wood and steel. He has the knowledge and skill derived of more than four decades of experience to operate all his machines with efficiency and skill. To put it simply, he knows what to do to get what he wants.

Most of his collector knives have matching metal sheaths made by Weiss. Frankly, he says, he would rather make knives than sheaths, but his customers demand them and he complies. Depending upon what type of knives he is working on, he figures he produces between twenty and sixty custom knives per year. Most are on order from customers, but he manages to produce some that he shows at the various knife shows he attends.

The artist no longer offers a catalog. They have become too expensive to update, maintain and produce. His regular customers know how to reach him; they see him at shows and know what he can do. Weiss will, however, offer photographs of some of his designs when requested.

CUSTOM KNIFEMAKERS
Bud Nealy

TODAY, BUD NEALY and his wife, Toni, live in a quiet neighborhood in Stroudsburg, Pennsylvania, a far cry from his days—and nights—on the road as the drummer for the Glenn Miller orchestra. His full-time occupation as a custom knifemaker is even further removed from his earlier life of one-night stands in an endless collection of forgotten towns and cities.

Nealy originally headquartered in New York City, but longed for the wide open spaces and began to spend vacations and weekends in the Pennsylvania countryside. Eventually, he and his wife decided to resettle. At that time, Toni Nealy had an executive position with the American Society of Composers, Authors and Publishers in Manhattan. She was about to resign when ASCAP powers suggested that she work three or four days a week, commuting the hour-plus to the city on express buses.

In the beginning, Bud Nealy was playing in night clubs in and around their new home, but the hotels and resort areas eventually gave way to condominiums, leaving fewer places for a musician to make a living.

By that time, he recalls, he didn't care. He had become a knifemaker. He has lost track of the total number of knives he has made over the years, but in 1995 alone he produced and

sold 650 of his creations. Waiting time for a customer ranges from forty-five to sixty days, depending upon the style of the knife ordered.

In the meantime, wife Toni had qualified for retirement with ASCAP and quit the commute to New York City to assume a new role as business manager and administrator for her husband's efforts.

"My first exposure to knives was in New York City, where friend Mike Gugleotti showed me his collection of custom knives," Bud Nealy told us. "Mike was a hard-hat deep-sea diver who later lost his life in a diving accident, but he was the one who fostered my intrigue as to what could be done with a piece of steel.

"That intrigue led to my buying a worn-out circular blade used in sawmill work. I took it to a local machine shop where they cut it into pieces for me. The father and son who ran the shop, Herb and Ed David, were helpful in the beginning,

"Later, Lou Millard, a trumpet-playing gunsmith, took me under his wing," Nealy says, "and began to teach me. At the time, I had no experience with grinders or the drill press and didn't even know where to put a drill bit."

Bud Nealy made his first knife in 1980 and has experiment-

In his well-equipped shop, Bud Nealy throws a lot of sparks, using the stock-removal method of knifemaking. He works both stainless steel and Damascus, his personal choices of materials.

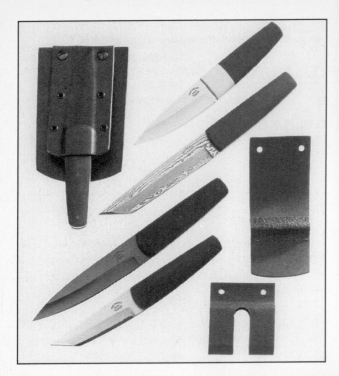

This art piece was a collaboration between Bud Nealy and Shelley Krongard, a New York City jeweler, who did the work in green gold and diamonds, including the accompanying earrings. There are thirty-six grade-D diamonds set in the hilt, the pommel and the earrings. The handle is of ebony. Overall length of the knife is 7 inches, and it has a 3-inch blade.

(Above) Knives of two lengths and two different materials are made for use in Bud Nealy's Multi-Concealment Sheath system. The sheath is made of Kydex and nylon, and it can be worn in a number of positions on the body.

This Nealy fighting knife is in the Persian style which has influenced his work to a degree. The blade is of stainless steel, as are the pins. The handle is ebony.

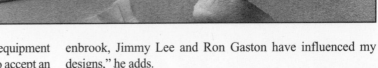

ed over the years with various grinds. He bought the equipment he would need and, in 1988, had a grinder modified to accept an oversized wheel.

"I figured out that a shallow hollow-grind creates a more gradual radius from edge to spine with less resistance," the craftsman explains. "The result is a finer-slicing and better working blade. Space-age technology and sophisticated heat-treating techniques provide hardened steels that hold an edge. The result is a long-lasting edge with ease of sharpening, and an excellent working knife that is restored easily to its original beauty once the job is done."

Nealy joined the Knifemakers Guild in 1988 and qualified for full membership two years later. He also is a member of the Professional Knifemakers Association and credits the members of these organizations for much of his success.

"For the most part, other knifemakers are quick to help each other with information and explanations of technique," he has found. "In the more than fifteen years that I have been making knives, I've only had one maker tell me to take a hike when I asked for help."

Nealy says his designs range somewhere between those of the late Bo Randall and the knives of Bob Loveless. "And maybe on a subconscious basis, the work of the late Jim Hard-

enbrook, Jimmy Lee and Ron Gaston have influenced my designs," he adds.

He will use whatever steel a customer desires, but Nealy personally favors ATS-34 and the titanium-coated Damascus made by Daryl Meier. As for handle materials, he uses neoprene, stag, mother of pearl and some of the exotic woods.

Nealy was making knives in his garage until several years ago when heavy snow caved in the roof. "That was a blessing of sorts," he contends, "because I was able to put up a new garage with a separate area for my shop."

Today, that shop houses a trio of Bader grinders, bandsaws, a buffer and two drill presses, one of them a 1917 four-spindle model. He also has a custom-made shear and kick press that is used in making sheaths of Kydex.

The big item for Nealy today is his patented Multi-Concealment Sheath System. This is made up of a Kydex sheath, plus an array of Kydex and nylon accessories that allow the knife to be carried on the body in a wide range of positions. As a result of lengthy experimentation, Nealy has included in the sheath powerful magnets that retain the knife securely, no matter what the position, including inverted, with the handle suspended in a downward position.

In any of the carrying positions, there is no danger of the

(Below) This Nealy combat knife has a 9½-inch blade made from Damascus twist steel. The handle is of ebony, with the hilt and pins of 416 stainless steel. With the sheath, this set sells for $1200.

(Above) Nealy's Cherry Creek Hunter model is one of his most popular. It is made of Daryl Meier's Damascus, has 416 steel bolsters and a handle of sambar stag. Length of the blade is 3¼ inches. This particular knife was stolen from the maker's table during a New York City knife show.

(Below) The Pennsylvania craftsman calls this knife his Camelback Skinner. Engraving on the hilt is in the French motif, and the handle is fashioned from mother-of-pearl.

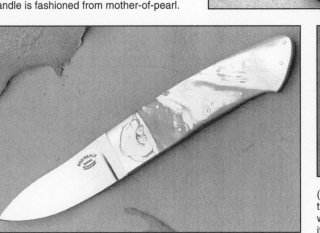

(Above) This knife is named the Deladan. It is made of Daryl Meier's twisted radial Damascus, as is the rosette attached to the handle with an 18k gold pin. Overall length of this art piece is 8 inches, and it has a price tag of $800.

(Left) This is an example of the type of knife Nealy enjoys making. It features a blade of Damascus made by Daryl Meier, who the knifemaker considers a genuine genius in matters of metallurgy.

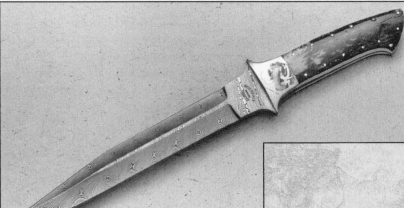

(Right) This is another self-defense knife Nealy spent a good deal of time designing. Light in weight, it is designed to be worn around the neck. Grinding for proper shape on this style is particularly hard, Nealy says, and the finish is everything. Desert ironwood has been used for the perforated handle.

Bud Nealy enjoys grinding and being able to see the knife of the moment take shape. He considers knifemaking a lonely business and likes to collaborate with others on design.

knife falling out of the sheath, which is custom moulded from .080-inch thick Kydex. The key is four gold-plated magnets that hold the blade in place until drawn.

The knife for which this MCS rig is designed is Nealy's Pesh-Kabz or Travel Knife. When we first looked at this knife, it had the appearance of a single-edged boot knife with Persian influences. The designer admits that he has taken the functional facets of the Persian design and used them in a basic fighter. An unusual grind pattern has been used to give the blade strength, cutting quality and balance.

Nealy makes this knife in blade lengths of $3^1/_2$ and 5 inches, using either ATS-34 stainless steel or 100-layer Damascus from Daryl Meier. The ATS-34 blade is black due to a coating of titanium-carbo-nitride. The Damascus knife is of 52100 sandwiched between two layers of 304 stainless steel.

A stainless-steel bolster is topped by a handle of either neoprene or micarta. The craftsman will substitute a handle of exotic wood if the customer demands, but he feels none are as practical as the man-made materials.

Nealy's Multi-Concealment Sheath system—or simply MCS, as he calls it—is protected by patent. Let it be known that at least one other maker who came up with a direct copy found himself faced by an angry lawyer and members of the Knifemakers Guild ethics committee.

"I've helped a lot of other up-and-coming young knifemakers the same as others helped me," Nealy reports, "but when it comes to a direct rip-off of something I spent a lot of time developing and a batch of money in getting a patent, I tend to get irritated."

In fact, Nealy loves to collaborate with other knifemakers or with his customers in designing and making a knife. "I guess that goes back to my origins as a musician," he muses. "Music—at least, the big band music we played—was a team effort. Knifemaking can be a lonely business, and I enjoy working with others on projects of mutual interest."

Lonely or not, Bud Nealy knows he has found his niche in a business he has come to love, and he'll just keep on grinding.

CUSTOM KNIFEMAKERS
Allen Elishewitz

ALLEN ELISHEWITZ IS a young man with plenty of craft experience, as well as a great deal of martial arts and military background. All these show up in his knife designs. His long training in arts and crafts—such as acid etching, printing, drawing, architectural drafting as well as knifemaking—has lead to the outstanding knives he makes that are working tools, as well as pleasant to look at.

Elishewitz made his first knife in 1987. He saw his first custom-made knife, the Rambo model made by Jimmy Lile, not long before that. He burst onto the national custom knife scene in early 1994, at about the time he became a full-time knifemaker, and in 1996, he was the youngest member of the Knifemakers Guild. Before and since that time, he developed a following among martial artists who prefer his designs and skills.

Elishewitz is a native Texan, but is well traveled. He has lived in Indonesia, Taiwan, Singapore and Thailand. That may explain the distinctive Asian appearance evident in many of his knife designs. He has studied martial arts for nearly twenty years of his young life and is a master of several techniques. His martial arts experience includes the Okinawan karate, Thai boxing, northern Shaolin tai chi yang style, tae kwon do and kali. His studies of martial arts are what triggered his interest in the world of knives and knifemaking.

The authors were first drawn to Elishewitz because of some shared Marine Corps backgrounds. Down Texas way, Elishewitz serves with a Marine Corps Reserve Reconnaissance unit. He has had specialized training in the Marine Special Operation Training Group, amphibious reconnaissance, reconnaissance patrolling, as well as the standard combat training all Marines undergo. Elishewitz says the training and military experiences have taught him the value of a good using knife in combat and field environments. Most of his designs seem to reflect those values. The maker produces all kinds of different knives, but he continues to specialize in combat, fighting and specialty knives.

"My designs and ideas come from my experiences and background, as well as from all the knives I have seen over the years," says Elishewitz. "I have my standard designs and I also do plenty of custom work. Most of my customers are professionals in their fields."

Obviously, those same professionals recognize the quality of Elishewitz's work. He puts in plenty of hours in his well equipped shop turning out the knives he sells. He typically works over eighty hours a week during his busiest times, operating in a shop that contains all the standard power tools. He has

Elishewitz at work on one of his knives. He uses the stock-removal method for producing simple but highly useful blades.

several belt sanders, drill presses, a lathe, a mill and heat-treating equipment. He is able to produce about 350 knives a year. Some are standard designs of his own, others are custom designs that come from his clients. He attends up to six knife shows a year, including the annual Knifemakers Guild show which has been held for several years in Florida, but will be moving to Las Vegas in 1997. Perhaps more people will become aware of Allen Elishewitz and his knives at the new location. For now, his estimated delivery time is three to five months.

Elishewitz does all his own work on his knives. He uses the stock-removal method, all freestyle, using no machinist's jigs. Blades may be hollow ground or flat ground, according to the customer's desires.

He says, "All my knives have been designed scientifically and balanced to insure adequate strength, allowing the user to exert minimum effort."

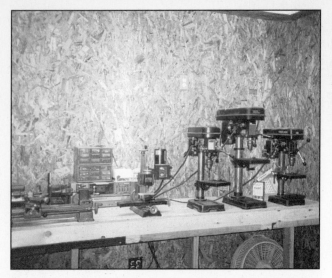

The maker's Texas workshop is well equipped with power tools such as drill presses, a lathe, sanders, and heat-treating equipment.

Hand finishing is an important aspect of Elishewitz's knife production. The knifemaker puts in over eighty hours per week on his craft at the busiest times.

The Elishewitz Combat SERE Attack design has proven a popular knife design for the young but accomplished maker.

He makes his own handles and most of the sheaths, and is one of the few custom knifemakers who also heat treats all his knives. The steels commonly used are ATS-34, D-2 and Meier's 304/52100 laminated steel, sometimes T440V, 440C and Sanvic 12C27.

"I chose ATS-34 over other stainless steels because it holds a keener edge longer. It is also easier to resharpen," declares Elishewitz. "It is heat-treated and double-tempered to a reading of 58-59 on the Rockwell C scale, then sub-zero quenched. That cryogenic quenching increases the toughness of the steel, but does not decrease its flexibility.

"D-2 is a tough semi-stainless steel with 12 percent chrome in it. It holds an edge as well as any high-carbon tool steel. D-2 is heat-treated and double-tempered to a 59-60 RC, then cryogenically treated.

"The Meier 304/52100 is a laminated steel that combines both stainless and tool steel. This gives a knife an unbeatable force in the cutlery world. This steel is heat-treated and double-tempered to a 61-62 RC. I have used other steels in my knives, only on special request.

"If customers have a particular steel in mind, they should feel free to ask for it to be used on a knife they may order."

Elishewitz welcomes customer designs and enjoys making special customer orders, he says. He periodically refines his designs to create a higher-caliber knife for consumers. He believes this maker characteristic indicates an intention to strive for the best knife. He is not stagnant in his work.

"The primary handle materials I use are micarta, exotic woods, stabilized woods and horn," says the young Marine. All Elishewitz knives are guaranteed against flaws in craftsmanship. Exotic woods, horn, antler, bone and the like cannot be guaranteed due to their unpredictable characteristics. I charge a fee for repairing any damage caused by improper use."

The maker shies away from special art work such as scrimshaw and engraving on his knives. He will incorporate some file work on the tang area of some knives, but only if requested by the customer.

"I try to not use any special art work, because I feel it takes away from the knife," is the way he puts it.

He buys pouches and sheaths made of Terylon from a specialty manufacturer, but he makes his own Kydex and leather sheaths.

Like many other Texans, Elishewitz hunts and fishes. He tests out new and different designs and materials in the field. Some of his professional customers are assigned to elite military groups and test other designs in other ways. They understand the designs and appreciate the functionality and beauty of the simple lines.

As required by the rules of the Knifemakers Guild for membership, Elishewitz has a small catalog with photos and descriptions of his standard models.

CUSTOM KNIFEMAKERS
Alex Collins

IT IS NEVER a good idea to say anybody is the oldest, youngest, tallest, shortest, first, last, only one of what the group may be—but Alex Collins may be the only African-American custom knifemaker. It seems indisputable that he is the best known, if not the first, of his race to be recognized as a custom knifemaker.

Alex Collins is a man with a fine sense of humor and irony. His business cards are printed KKK, meaning Kustom Krafted Knives; knives made by a black man. He has, he says, no time for anyone who does not get it.

Collins has been around long enough and makes knives that are good enough that he can be his own man. He is a careful, patient craftsman and will take all the time necessary to educate any potential customer or client to what he does and what he makes. He is quick to appreciate a customer who can see the value in his knives.

Collins is not a black man who makes knives. He is and would rather be known as a knifemaker—a good one—who just happens to be black. He does not seem to seek out and have more customers who are black. At the knife shows where we have encountered him, he attracts hundreds of customers of all skin colors.

Al Collins is no rookie to the knifemaking business. He sold his first knife in 1972, before many of his customers were born. He now is a full-time knifemaker, but has worked for many years as an electrician in the movie and television industry in nearby Hollywood. He knows what qualities a good working knife must have to perform its duties.

Several years ago, Collins shared a workshop with Jody Samson, well known for many of his movie swords, and pioneer custom knifemaker John Nelson Cooper. At the time, the shop was in Burbank, only a long stone's throw from several of the major Hollywood studios. Samson, Cooper and Al Collins counted some of the famous names in entertainment among their customers. Samson and Collins still do; Cooper died in 1987 after 60 years of knifemaking and 30,000 hand-made knives.

Collins and Samson both offer a lot of credit to Cooper and what he taught them about knifemaking. There would seem to be no visual influence of Cooper on Al Collins' knife designs, but the attention to detail and clean lines of his knives—the quality—would seem to be legacies of John Nelson Cooper.

Al Collins is not bound by tradition in the knives he designs. He makes knives in designs no one else seems to make. Each is unique as well as beautiful. Most of his designs are for useful knives, practical knives, but he makes them most attractive, no

Custom knifemaker Alex Collins is a common sight at many of the Southern California knife shows.

matter for what purpose they are intended. The curved, sinewy lines and surprise twists and turns of steel and wood provide delights for the eyes when the knives are examined closely.

And the Al Collins knives should all be closely examined to be appreciated. At knife shows around Southern California, Collins entreats passersby to pick up and look at his designs. When that happens, the maker enjoys the looks of surprise and expressions of delight he sees, as the potential customers realize what they have in their hands. His specialities are what he terms working dress knives. They are attractive as well as practical.

Collins likes to make sets of knives, all with a common theme. He may produce a dozen or so designs that all have, say, the same handle material and general handle shape. A "family" of knives may include a paring knife, butcher knife, fighting knife, boot knife, a couple of push daggers, hunting knife, skinning knife and a couple of fantasy knives. But they have the same general look, no matter the size and blade shape.

He likes to use all sorts of different and unusual materials for handles. He may use the standard and common micartas and woods on some knives, but he also enjoys hafting his knives with such things as man-made kitchen countertop material, some sections of which are dyed to uncommon colors. Pink, purple, red or some brown shades may not be everybody's choice of handle colors, but Collins manages without much difficulty to find customers who favor the unusual.

Some knife handles are attached with the standard two-part epoxy cement and with two or more steel or brass pins. Others, with hidden tangs, rely on the epoxy cement. Still other designs

may use rivets or cutler's bolts to assist the epoxy. Handle designs are straight or curved and fanciful, depending upon the intended use of the knife.

With more than twenty-five years in the business, Collins has seen, tried and worked with most of the typical knife steels available. Today, he prefers to grind his knives from O1, 440C and 154CM steels. He has his large, well equipped workshop in the rear of his street-side retail shop in Los Angeles. It is a working-class neighborhood with video rental shops, restaurants, stereo equipment outlets and auto body shops in the vicinity.

The shop contains the same power machines that are found in most custom knife-making shops or machine shops. He has his share of grinding wheels, belt sanders, band saws, cut-off saws, drill presses and other specialized equipment. To one of

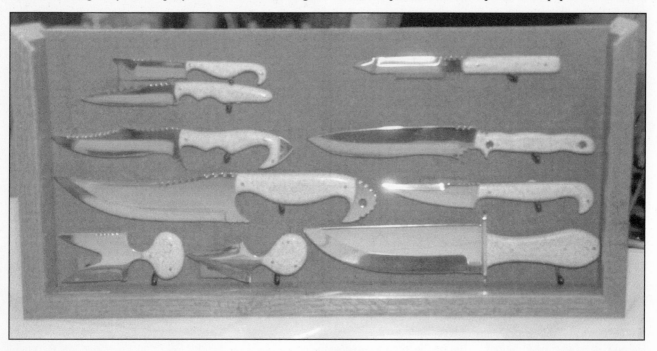

(Above) This set of ten Collins knives carries a common theme through the designs, even though each has a different mission.

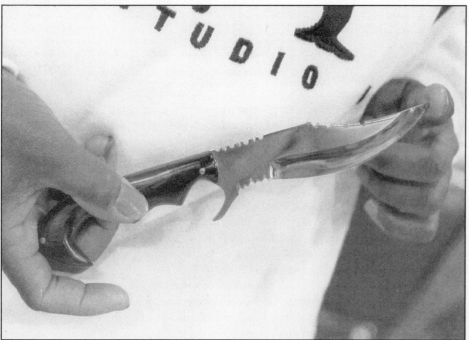

The shape of the handle on this Collins knife ensures a good grip.

his belt sanders, he has added an unusual and expensive speed controller. Slowing the belt speed down considerably permits the maker to grind on blades without dangerously overheating the metal.

Despite his casual public demeanor, Alex Collins is a careful and safe metal worker. He always uses the appropriate hand, eye and lung protection while working with power tools. He often dons a shop coat while working on knives to protect himself and his clothing from dirt, dust and chemicals. The shop floor is swept regularly and the power tools are situated in logical order to best utilize the available space.

Many of Collins' designs feature fancy filework. He likes to put in filed grooves and serrations on the tops of blades, on the bottom just ahead of the choil, around the butt and on the tang, hidden by the handle slabs and visible only directly from the top or bottom of the knife. Blades will be ground with different lines on either side. One side might be hollow-ground, the other straight. The grind lines may be at different heights on opposite sides. One side may have a blood groove while the other does not. Variations are left to Al Collins and the customer, but Collins has ideas that most of us have never seen or even considered before.

At least one of this craftsman's knife designs features a blade with two tips or points. Collins meticulously files and grinds the tip of an untapered blade to produce two points. A knife such as this may not be your standard outdoor knife used to cut campfire kindling, but the buyer will know there are not many others around with the same features.

Because of his long association with the entertainment industry, Al Collins has many customers from the business. They are not necessarily the well-known actors and stars, but rather are the riggers, set decorators, carpenters, electricians, painters and others who work behind the scenes. They are professionals who know the value of a good blade to help them do their jobs. He

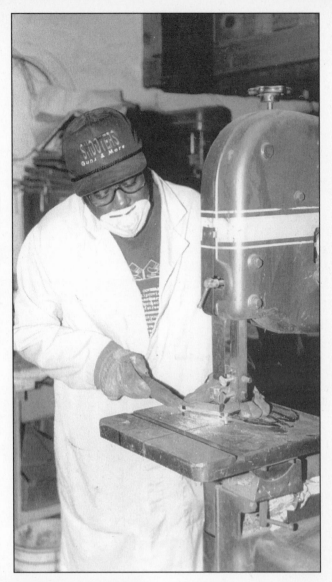

(Above) While working in his shop, Collins always insists on wearing all necessary protective gear. Here, he uses a push stick as a safety measure while cutting out a wooden knife handle on the band saw.

One of the belt sanders Collins uses has a special speed regulator to allow special grinding techniques without overheating the metal.

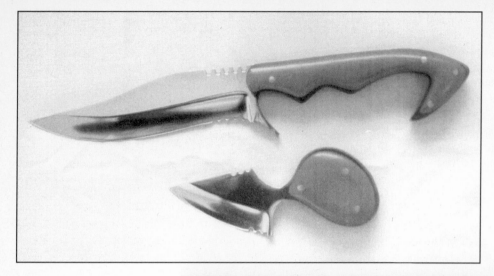

This pair of knives is intended for street defense. The small push dagger is a Collins signature. Both have the same handle material.

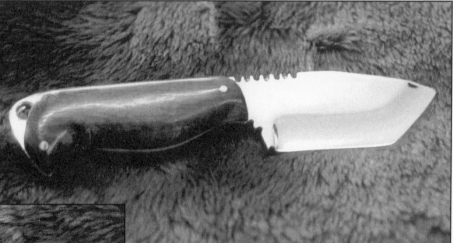

(Below and right) This design reflects a mild Oriental appearance. The right side of the blade is hollow-ground. Below is the opposite side of the same knife. Each side is ground differently. Fancy filework is another feature.

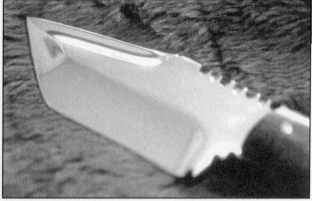

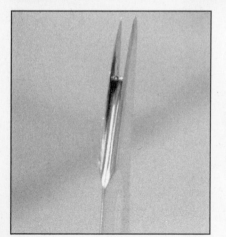

This is the unique double-tip Collins knife. The knives are ground by hand, without jigs, and require considerable skill on the maker's part.

gets some walk-in customers at his retail location. Knives are exhibited in a large display window in front of the store. Dozens more of his knives are shown in a couple of display cases inside the door. Several clients are in law enforcement and the security business; others are martial artists who have heard of the KKK brand knives.

Collins attracts serious collectors at the knife and gun shows he attends. They are collectors of the unusual and rare, rather than high-rollers who seek art knives from the most sought-after makers of the day. Most of Collins' knives are not expensive. Some models start at about $100. Sets and special orders can be considerably more expensive, of course. He makes a satisfactory living selling his knives, but never has been one to keep raising prices on the same designs only to make a buck.

Alex Collins enjoys what he does and is constantly experimenting with new designs and new techniques. He always has something new and interesting to display at every show.

Collins always has an adequate supply of completed knives on display at his retail shop. He prefers to produce what he calls street survival knives, swords and axes.

If appropriate to the design, the maker will supply a sheath or pouch for the knife. He can and will make customer-designed knives, too. He works fast, and his delivery time is usually not long.

CUSTOM KNIFEMAKERS

J.W. McFarlin

LAKE HAVASU CITY, Arizona, is where J.W. McFarlin makes his knives. This is an area in the Mojave Desert where the summer temperatures can reach 128 degrees Fahrenheit. And because of the adjoining lake and the nearby Colorado River, the humidity has been measured on some of the hottest days at 78 percent!

That combination, he feels, gives McFarlin the right to call himself "the world's hottest knifemaker!" But it's not unlike some other areas weather-wise where this craftsman worked in his earlier years as an oil driller. He spent thirty-one years in that occupation, working in such places as Mexico, Canada and even Fiji, in the South Pacific.

"Finally, in 1990, I quit trying to find other people's oil," McFarlin says. "The work had just lost its appeal and it was interfering with my knifemaking."

He made his first knife from an old hacksaw blade, using oak flooring for the scales. This was while he was doing drilling work in Bonanza, Utah. Actually, he made several of the little knives and later gave them to his children, five girls and a son ranging in age from twelve to thirty-two.

To date, this desert dweller figures he has made well over 1000 other knives, although he admits he has kept no truly accurate records.

McFarlin admits he got off to a slow start, making only fifteen to twenty knives a year during his first couple of years of production.

"I didn't really look at it as a true career in that era, I guess" he recalls. "Most of those knives were made for friends and acquaintances. I was having fun making them, and I didn't understand that it's possible to have fun and make a living at the same time!"

However, he went to his first knife show in the late '80s and discovered there was a whole new element of private enterprise that he had missed—or perhaps simply refused to recognize—until then.

McFarlin's favorite knife styles always have been drop-point hunters and daggers. Perhaps it's not surprising that these are the two types in which he specializes. As for the types of steel he favors, first is ATS-34, followed by D2, A2 and 440C.

"If I'm working with Damascus, I prefer the billets turned out by Devin Thomas and Chris Peterson," the craftsman adds.

The Arizona maker's shop is smaller than most. In fact, it measures only 6 by 10 feet. "Actually, I do most of my grinding outside, under my carport because of the temperatures," he says, "then I do the rest of the work inside. I don't have much in the way of equipment, because virtually all of my work is done by hand. All of my blades are hand-finished. It's slow, but there's a lot of therapy involved, too."

Using a Bader grinder set up in his carport, J.W. McFarlin trues up the edge of a blade.

McFarlin hand-draw sands a Bowie that measures 18 inches in overall length. He will go to 400-grit paper before heat-treating.

McFarlin's shop covers only 60 square feet. The drill press beside him is about 60 years old, but is still fully functional and does what the maker requires.

McFarlin did not see his first custom knife until 1985 and that was one made by Harvey McBurnett. He had made his own first knife, because he could not find one he liked. Today, he works forty or more hours a week and turns out forty to sixty knives a year. Customers can count on a wait of about a year before delivery.

McFarlin is not a member of the Knifemakers Guild and thus does not have access to their shows. However, he runs a string of gun shows throughout Arizona and Nevada as weekend endeavors. It is at these shows that he displays his own knives and takes orders. Since he lives only a few hours by vehicle from Las Vegas, he also displays at the major shows in the gambling mecca.

Asked where he gets ideas for some of his unusual designs, McFarlin explains that he has several standard designs that he uses a great deal, but he also is involved in a goodly amount of intricate custom work. "I like to make fluted handles," he explains, "and I research old books for possible design ideas."

Like most of the knifemakers with whom we've talked, J.W.

McFarlin also has his likes and dislikes regarding specific facets of his work.

"For me, at least, the easiest part of making a knife is the handle work. I prefer fossil ivory or natural woods and enjoy working with all of them. I don't use much micarta, but when I do, it's linen micarta. I prefer it for its strength.

"The toughest part of making the knives I'm proud enough to show and offer for sale is fitting the guards so that there are no gaps visible. That takes time and a lot of patience, if it's to be done right."

In spite of the fact that he is not a member of the Knifemakers Guild, McFarlin has received a good deal of help in the way of shop tips from makers who are members, including Arizonans D'Alton Holder and Ken McFall. He also is quick to recognize Tennessee makers Doug and Dianna Casteel for the inspiration they offered and the fact that they seemingly "passed on their can-do attitude."

From these individuals and others, he learned enough that he is able to do his own heat-treating on tool steels, but sends stainless blades to a professional heat-treating shop in Phoenix.

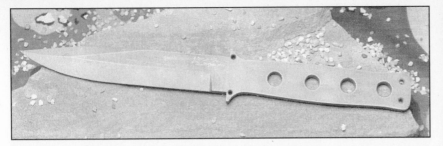

This McFarlin utility fighter has a 6-inch blade, and the handle will be wrapped with parachute cord. The blade is flat-ground and has been sand-blasted to reduce glare.

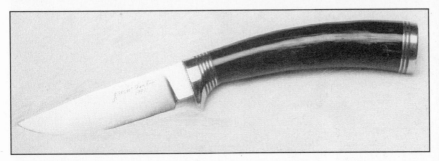

This is J.W. McFarlin's Danger model. The blade is $1/8$-inch thick and measures $2\,1/4$ inches. Overall length is $6\,1/2$ inches, featuring either a hidden or full taper tang. The guard is of nickel-silver bronze or brass, and the buyer has a wide choice of handle materials. The ATS-34 blade is tempered to 58-60 Rockwell C.

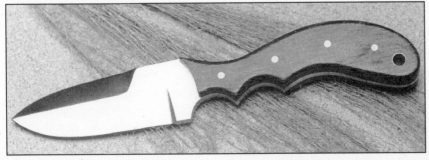

(Above) McFarlin's Scorpion model has an overall length of $7\,3/8$ inches and a $3\,3/4$-inch blade. The full tang is tapered with finger grooves and a lanyard hole. The knife is made with either a single or double edge. Steel is ATS-34 heat-treated to 58-60 RC.

(Right) This is one of the maker's favorites, a drop-point hunter with 4-inch blade of ATS-34. It has a tapered tang and burled maple scales with nickel-silver fittings. Note the flat, hand-finished grind.

A fighter with a blade length of $8\,7/8$ inches, this McFarlin knife has an overall length of $12\,1/4$ inches. The blade has a full double edge, and the guard and skull crusher are of bronze. Stacked leather washers form the handle.

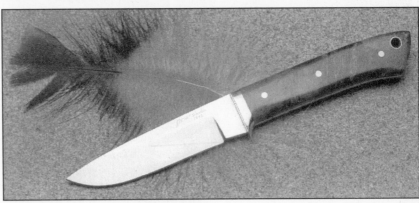

This Damascus Dangler has a $2\,1/4$-inch blade with steel by Chris Peterson. The full tang is tapered, and the knife has nickel-silver fittings. The scales are from a desert bighorn sheep.

111

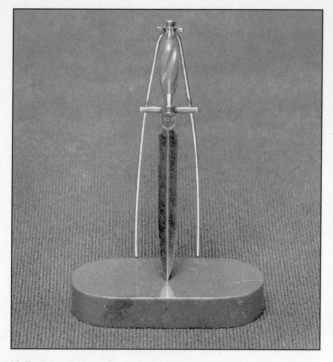

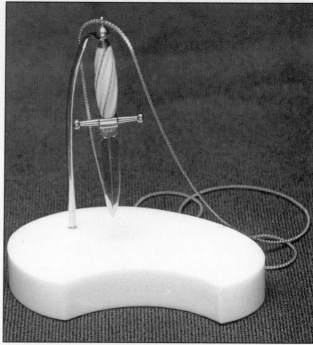

McFarlin's miniature Scottish broadsword measures only 2³/₄ inches in overall length.The four-fluted handle is of *lapis lazuli* with silver fittings. The blade is of Chris Peterson's twisted Damascus.

The overall length of this miniature is 2³/₈ inches with an ATS-34 blade of 1¹/₈ inches. The guard and pommel are of bronze. The handle is of walrus ivory with four flutes on a half twist with a silver wire inlay.

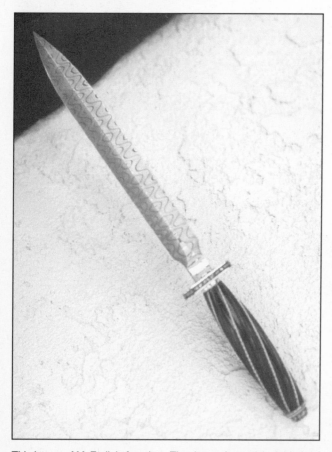

This is one of McFarlin's favorites. The dagger has a 9-inch blade of ladder Damascus from the forge of Devin Thomas. Overall length is 14 inches and the guard and pommel are inlaid with thirty-five gold nuggets. The six-flute handle is of water buffalo horn wrapped with silver wire. All work was done by the maker, who also does all of his own scrimshaw work.

"With the amount of heat we have in summer from natural causes, heating up an oven for heat-treating is not my idea of an afternoon's fun," the knifemaker admits, "but I enjoy the results, because I have been in full control of the knife from start to finish."

His blades are hardened to 57-59 on the Rockwell C scale, which McFarlin considers as offering "a good, standard edge capability." Few of his knives have blades that are mirror polished, since he favors a satin finish, instead.

Some of McFarlin's feelings relative to doing his own heat-treating appear to lapse over into other facets of his work. For example, he makes all of his own sheaths, cutting, fitting and sewing each of them by hand. Since most of his knives are sold to collectors and hunters, he tests his own blades during hunting trips throughout the Western states. He wants to be sure no hunter ever is going to curse a McFarlin blade when field dressing a deer, moose or elk.

J.W. McFarlin has not been smitten with the desire to spend his days turning out lockblade knives. At this writing, at least, he is making only one model, which features a 3¹/₄-inch blade.

"I'd rather spend my time making miniature knives," he says. "I had been making a few and suddenly, they just took off. I probably could make a decent living building nothing but miniatures." Instead, he recognizes the fickle nature of the buying public and prefers to continue to cover all facets of knife-making for which he feels he has the talent.

McFarlin, incidentally, is a member of the board of directors of the Miniature Knifemakers Association. Over the years that he as been making knives, he has had one simple guarantee. If you damage the knife or simply don't like it, send it back.

To date, he never has had a knife returned for refund.

CUSTOM KNIFEMAKERS
Ken Hoy

WHEN ASKED TO whom he feels he owes the most in helping him to become a professional knifemaker, Nevadan Ken Hoy answers, "Don Mount, of course."

Usually, there is laughter in his voice and an amused glint in his eye, but Hoy makes this statement with a seriousness that is downright suspicious due the fact that it is such a departure from his normal personality.

"Why Don Mount?" we asked just as seriously.

"Because he's the one who taught me to grind knives in the nude!"

There may have been a moment of semi-shocked silence on the part of your reporters as this reply soaked in. Then the realization of what Ken Hoy was saying did make some minor degree of practical sense.

Both knifemakers reside in the immediate vicinity of Las Vegas, Nevada, thus both of them live and work in a desert environment where summer temperatures often run higher than 125 degrees Fahrenheit in the shade. Both makers grind knives in their garages which have been turned in to shops. There is no air-conditioning in these garages, so, in the heat of a summer day, the only apparel for either of them is a set of safety goggles and a pair of heavy work shoes!

"It's an art in itself," Hoy declares with straight face. "Dodging all those hot steel sparks calls for special talents."

In recent months, however, Ken Hoy has begun to train his teenage son in the intricacies of custom knife work, and he admits he has become a bit more of a clothes horse than in the past.

"I now wear my swimming trunks to grind," he explains. "Most of the time, at least."

Hoy made his first knife in 1989. His driver's license had been suspended for a period of several months and, as he tells it, "I was going nuts, when Don Mount looked at a drawing I had made of a knife I had dubbed the Bone Breaker. He asked if I was satisfied just with the drawing or would I like to make the actual knife.

"It sounded like a way of filling the temporary hole in my social calendar," Hoy reports, "so I said I'd like to give it a try.

"Don provided the steel and the necessary tools, then talked me through the first knife in his own shop. I took the finished product to work at the atomic test center where I was a security guard and showed it to some of my co-workers. I sold that knife and got orders for seven more just like it. I knew that day that I was hooked!"

Hoy continued to work full-time as a federal security guard at the test center until July, 1994. That was when he turned in his badge and became a full-time custom cutler.

Asked what kind of knives he considers his specialty, Hoy replies, "Anything with a point or an edge," but admits he has tended to concentrate on "rather plain working knives until recently. Now, though, I'm trying some art pieces.

"For working knives, I favor micarta as a handle material. For the more expensive artistic efforts, I have a personal preference for Indian stag and ivory, but I'll use whatever material the customer wants so long as it's legal."

Ken Hoy checks the handle fit on one of his Bone Breakers. This was his first design and the one that got him into the custom cutlery field.

This obviously is a wintertime photo. In the heat of the Nevada desert summer, Hoy often grinds blades in the nude, wearing only safety glasses and work shoes!

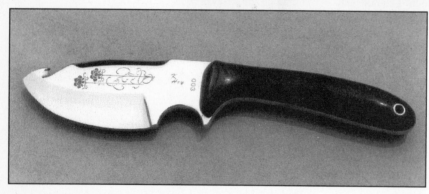

Custom etching is available on all of the knives made by Ken Hoy, but the price is added to the standard cost and should be negotiated at the time the order is placed.

When it comes to the type of steel he uses, Hoy doesn't seem to have any great preference. He will grind O1, ATS-34, 440C or 154 CM with equal aplomb, turning out what has to be considered a better than adequate knife from any of these materials.

"I'm just getting into Damascus," Hoy adds, "learning from Jim Hrisoulas how it's handled best. In a few months, I should be marketing Damascus knives, too."

Hoy does heat-treating in his own shop, which may lead to naked work in this effort as well as grinding, but he isn't ready to discuss that particular facet. His working knives and the more expensive display items he hardens to 58-59C on the Rockwell scale. He also has started to turn out a line of kitchen knives that seems to be catching on among Nevada housewives. These he hardens to 50-52C Rockwell, "because they have to be a bit easier to sharpen."

While Ken Hoy has the usual array of hand tools on his bench, his shop is equipped with a Burr King and a Bador grinder, as well as a milling machine and cut-off.

"Right now, I don't seem to need a great deal more," he explains, "but I have some items on my wish list that I know would make things move a little faster." At this time, he is spending between fifty and sixty hours a week in his shop to meet orders.

As a single parent to young Daniel until recently, Hoy feels, the heavy work schedule has had some definite advantages. "Working at home as I do that means I'm here when he leaves for school in the morning and I'm here when he comes home. "Before I remarried, someone asked whether I really enjoy making knives or whether it's because, in the past, it has given me a chance to be both mother and father.

"The answer is both. I love the creativity and I also love the fact that this type of work gives me the opportunity to be a part of Daniel's life as he grows up.

At present, Hoy makes about 250 knives per year and attempts to keep about thirty of them on hand to fill orders as soon as possible. On a more realistic note, he states that those who submit custom knife orders can expect a wait of about three months for delivery.

Questioned as to the identity of his customers, Hoy identifies them as "anyone who likes knives. They find me through magazine articles, trade shows and my own mailings."

A member of the Knifemakers Guild, he also is a member of the Professional Knifemakers Association and the Montana Knifemakers Association. Reason for the last-named membership is the fact that, in years past, Hoy and son Daniel took off

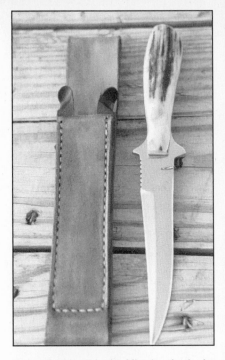

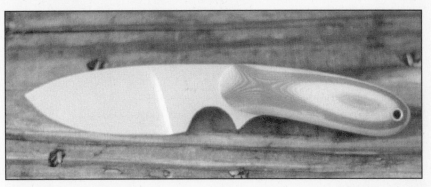

Ken Hoy's Mini-Bone Breaker model has a bead-blasted finish and a handle of black Micarta. Overall length is 6³/₄ inches, with a 2-inch blade.

Hoy calls this style the Mistake. Again, he doesn't tell why it's been named that. The 4¹/₄-inch blade has a high-polish finish. Overall length is 9 inches, and the handle is of matched slabs of Indian stag.

The Ken Hoy Model #4 Hunter has a 3³/₈-inch blade and measures 8³/₈ inches overall. The knife has a tapered tang and a bead-blasted finish.

Hoy's Model II Fighter, a limited-edition knife, has stag handle scales, a false edge atop the blade and a highly polished finish. Blade length is 7¹/₂ inches. Overall, the knife measures 12³/₈ inches.

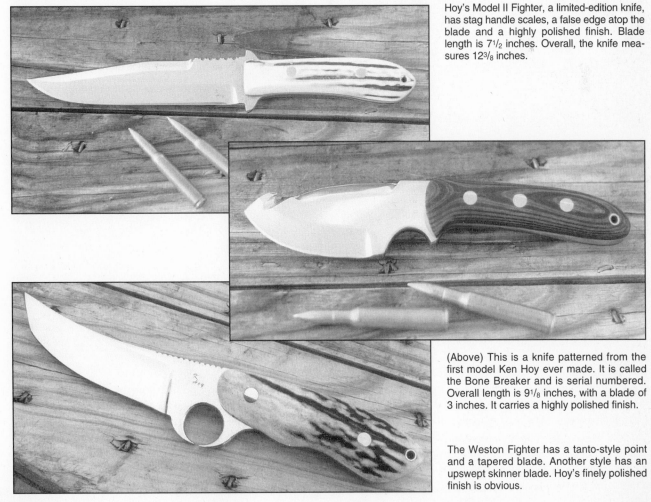

(Above) This is a knife patterned from the first model Ken Hoy ever made. It is called the Bone Breaker and is serial numbered. Overall length is 9¹/₈ inches, with a blade of 3 inches. It carries a highly polished finish.

The Weston Fighter has a tanto-style point and a tapered blade. Another style has an upswept skinner blade. Hoy's finely polished finish is obvious.

Starting with his original Bone Breaker design, Hoy makes knives in sundry designs and with varying specifications. He concentrated on working knives originally, but now is doing more in the way of cutlery art.

Ken Hoy and his wife make all of the sheaths for the knives he makes and sells. Each sheath is designed and made specifically for the blade it is to hold.

each summer to tour knife shows and other outdoor outings in Montana, returning in time for school in the fall.

"When Daniel graduates from school, I'd like to rig a shop in a motor home and the three of us—him, my wife and me—would simply tour the West, making knives as we go and hitting all of the knife shows, big and small, to sell our wares and see what other knifemakers are doing," Hoy declares.

With the help of his wife, Hoy makes all of his own sheaths and pouches. He also hopes to get into scrimshaw in the near future and learn that facet of decoration. He also feels that doing his own engraving is not impossible and will become a reality sometime in the future.

In addition to the means of contacting customers already listed, Don Hoy now is looking into establishing a web sight on the World Wide Web in which to advertise his line of knives.

This craftsman feels he has found a way of life that suits his needs and he shows endless enthusiasm for what he has learned from such custom knifemakers as Don Mount, Jim Hrisoulas, J.W. Townsend and Bill Wolf.

As a result of this help and advice he has received from others, we find that Ken Hoy has been quick to pass on his knowledge to other up-and-coming young cutlers.

"There's plenty of room for the talented," Hoy says.

CUSTOM KNIFEMAKERS

Dr. Lawrence Wilson

THERE ARE TIMES when a knife just doesn't have the weight, strength and cutting ability needed to get the job done.

A number of years ago, Dr. Lawrence Wilson was trying to cut through the pelvic bone on a large nine-point whitetail he had dropped. As often happens with older, larger bucks, the joint had fused and just wouldn't allow him to cut it open with the hunting knife he had made and carries in the field. The doctor said, "Next season I'll have a tool that will get the job done on any old buck."

Wilson has been crafting items from steel for over a decade. He started by making kitchen knives from two-man crosscut saw blades, putting handles on them and etching scenes on the blades.

"These varied from whales to sharks and whatever else he felt like putting on them," reports C.R. Learn, who has followed the doctor's part-time cutlery career. "A set of his creations may consist of five or six knives made for use in the kitchen, and this set might include a cleaver if he feels like making it at the time. The scenes etched into the steel blade are deep enough to last very well."

The next thing Dr. Wilson started making was a series of fixed-blade knives for hunting and camp use. Most of these were normal in size until he got carried away on one project. The knife he created might have been a bit large for that simple description. It had a 14-inch blade and uses a 10-inch length of elk antler as the handle.

Most of the doctor's hunting knives are made from 5160 spring steel. Until recently, these knives were given to family members and friends, but two years ago he decided to see if he could sell them. Selling such creations, he thought, would go a long way in helping to defray the cost of materials. He enjoys making knives and usually takes all his projects to a mirror finish, which he prefers.

However, the big buck problem still was bugging him, so he sat down one evening and sketched out several versions of an axe on a pad. The idea was to make a hunting/camp axe, one that would be large enough and sufficiently heavy to eliminate the problem of the fused pelvic bone, if he should encounter it again. The axe style he ended up with certainly will handle a chore like that.

Here, too, he uses 5160 spring steel. There is a cutting edge of 4 inches and a full-length steel handle, or tang if you prefer, that ends with a semi-wrap-around handle with or without finger grooves.

To start, Dr. Wilson buys a chunk of spring steel that is 4

Dr. Lawrence J. Wilson makes axes, knives and other items when he has the time off from his chiropractic practice in Lakeside, California. He likes to take the metal to a mirror polish, since he feels it looks better.

inches wide and ¼-inch thick. He then transfers his pattern to the flat surface of the steel.

Incidentally, one often can buy 5160 spring steel in spring shops; it is used for making leaf springs for cars and trucks. Asked about using old springs, Dr. Wilson said he tried that, but found it extremely difficult to get the curve out of the formed springs. It is easier, faster and less time-consuming simply to buy flat steel and start with that.

The outline of the axe is cut using a cutting torch, since the thick spring steel is tough on the blade of a bandsaw. After the basic shape is cut, the doctor moves to a belt sander and does the final shaping, using different belt grits to create the desired form. This takes time, of course, but Wilson told C.R. Learn that he truly enjoys making items from steel, and his current

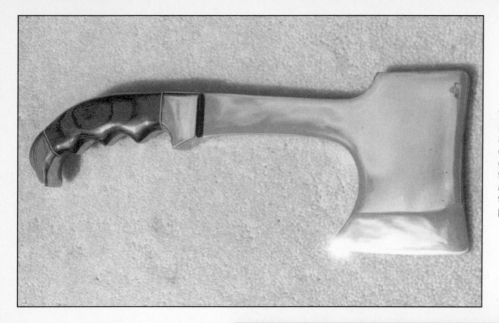

The main difference in the axes Wilson makes is in the handle materials and shapes. This one has a curved grip section with finger grooves. The front and back curve to fit the clenched hand very snugly and will prevent the axe from flying from the user's hand. The mirror polish makes them look good.

The grip is designed to shape to your hand. If you like to wear gloves and use the axe in cold weather, it will be a snug fit, but it is designed to help prevent losing the axe when using it to chop or cut.

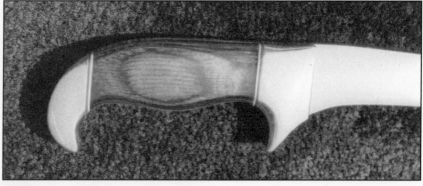

The 5160 spring steel Wilson uses for his axes starts at 4 inches wide by 1/4-inch thick. The finished axe will weigh in at 2 pounds, give or take a few ounces.

This axe blank has been cut using a torch, the edges cleaned up and Dr. Wilson's logo stamped on the handle. Now the work begins to shape and polish to the finished product.

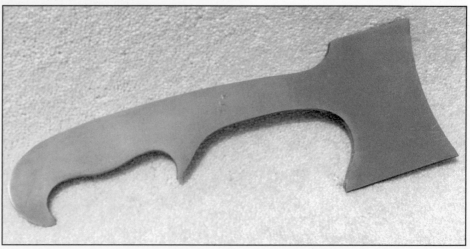

This axe has a different edge grind and no finger grooves in the handle. Wilson makes what pleases him at the time, and this keeps the work interesting. Each of his axes is different in some respect.

passion for making axes has brought no end of ideas he can incorporate.

The handle Dr. Wilson puts on his axe is designed to be hand-fitting to prevent the axe from flying out of his hand when chopping or cutting bone.

"Green bone cuts rather easily," the doctor reports, "and this axe certainly should make the job quite simple."

The handle may be fashioned from a number of materials, but he often uses Pakkawood and sometimes sizable sections of elk or deer antler.

"This isn't a really small axe," Learn reports, "but it's not a timber cutter's axe, either. The head ends with that 4-inch cutting edge, and overall length of the axe—including the handle—is around 12 inches. He often varies the grind on the blade edge for a different appearance and function. The edges of the shank section are smoothed and almost rounded for style, thus varying the profile of each axe. He usually starts with a specific design idea, but may change it as he cuts the steel."

The Wilson hunting/camp axe tips a postal scale at a touch over two pounds. This is mostly solid steel, but the handle section is slabbed and varies with each axe he makes. One wise guy stated that if Wilson missed a deer with his rifle, he could blind it by using the mirror finish to flash the sun into the deer's eyes. The finish is that good, and no scratches or blemishes are visible. The axe is heat treated to a 54 RC hardness by Paul Bos. Dr. Wilson now is considering making a few axes with a matte finish to see whether he likes it as an alternative to his mirror polish.

Dr. Lawrence J. Wilson received his degree as a doctor of chiropractic in 1970. He opened his office in Lakeside, California, and has been there for more than twenty-five years. He takes Thursdays off and pursues his avocation of knife and axe making because, "It gives me a feeling of accomplishment, and since I can make what I want, there is no pressure to get anything finished at a certain time." Wilson is considering selling his axes on a wider scale and feels there is a need for a good hunting axe that could double as a camp axe.

Wilson plans to continue with his knife and axe work, since

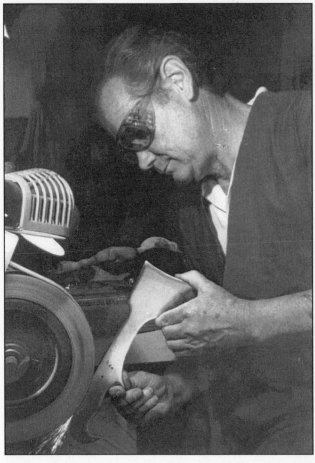

Dr. Wilson spends a lot of time at the grinder. His axes are so well finished that they'd look good hanging on the wall. However, they're meant to be used.

he feels the variations and potential uses are unlimited. He is going to carry one of his 2-pound axes in the field the next time he hunts his home country back in Kentucky. If he drops another big whitetail with a fused pelvic bone, he will be prepared to open it with one blow of his axe. This blade will certainly do the job.

A MATTER
OF COLLECTION

Reasons for cutlery collecting seem to number on a par with the collector population

NINE-YEAR-OLD Calvin Lewis, the grandson of one of your authors, is a knife collector and cutlery trader. In little more than a year, he has amassed some fifty knives, including his grandfather's Marine Corps officer's saber!

To this youngster, numbers are the thing at this point. He is far less interested in the make, age or condition of his pieces than he is in the aggregate number. He probably doesn't yet appreciate the fact that he owns a custom-made Ted Dowell hunter, although he realizes that this particular treasure is worth probably $400 on today's collector market. The youngster considers each of his currently owned knives a treasure, although selectivity probably will flourish in time.

Knife collecting is not new, but worldwide interest has increased in recent years with the growing number of custom cutlers. There are those makers who have their own cadre of followers. Some of these collectors virtually stand in line for the opportunity to add a new style by a specific custom maker to their collections.

Bob Loveless is a prime example of this situation. Some of his early knives now sell for as much as $6,000, and many of today's versions go for $10,000 to twice that amount.

Incidentally, we once asked Loveless which of his models he carried. His answer, accompanied by raised eyebrows, was classic.

"Hell, I can't afford one of my knives," he stated. "I carry an old Schrade folder!"

Phill Hartsfield is another maker whose entire production seems to be spoken for before the knives and short swords come off his grinder. To some of us, his production seems to be somewhat crude, following the Japanese tanto influence, but our personal feelings certainly don't keep them from selling.

As stated, the interests today in cutlery appear to be virtually endless. There are those who collect antique knives, others who specialize in commemorative issues. Still others specialize in military cutlery, Bowie styles or specific types of folders. Name a specific type of knife and you'll find collectors seeking one—or more.

There have been those who have seen the knife-collecting hobby develop and flourish. They also have come to realize that it is possible to develop such a market. One such individual is A.G. Russell, who operates out of Springdale, Arkansas, with his Knife Collectors Club.

Russell was one of the founders of the Knifemakers Guild, although he is not a custom knifemaker as such. He does, however, market the products of a number of custom makers and, several years ago, acquired the designs, patterns and company name of Morseth Knives. Today, he produces the Morseth line based upon the original designs and sells them through his club, which issues several professionally produced and updated four-color catalogs per year.

As A.G. Russell explains it, "In 1969, I found I could not afford all of the knives I wanted to collect and continue to raise my four children. I had to find some way to collect knives and continue to feed my family. I decided that if I could design and have high-quality knives made in limited numbers at fair prices, there would be a market for these knives. I was sure I could find a few thousand people like myself, who could not afford to buy all of the expensive handmade knives they wanted.

"The Knife Collectors Club was established in 1970. In 1971, we issued our first limited edition, the Kentucky Rifle pocketknife. The lowest serial numbers were made with 14-karat gold bolsters and inlays. The next lowest serial numbers

Knife collecting has become entertaining and profitable for many. Those who were able to obtain an older Bob Loveless handmade knife have realized an increase in value many times over the original cost.

(Below) Bob Loveless has appeared at custom knife shows for the past several decades. This photo was taken about twenty years ago.

were engraved and etched. The knives carrying serial numbers over 1000 were sold for $12 each."

Those same knives sell today for a minimum of $135, according to Russell and other collecting experts.

In 1985, the club offered a limited-edition Loveless hunter model at a member price of $495. Today, one of these Loveless knives sells for no less than $1,800. The following year, the club offered a Dietmar Kressler Gentleman's Hunter, whatever that is, for $695. Today, this knife sells for a minimum of $1,700, if you can find one for sale.

Since 1971, the club has offered quality folders from a host of companies, foreign and domestic. Included are Schrade and Camillus, representing the United States; Puma and Hen & Rooster from Germany, and Japan's Shabata.

"The club also offers a lot of new knives, such as those from Morseth and Schatt & Morgan, to members at special discount prices before they are offered to the general public. Knives that are not included in the catalog are offered on an exclusive basis to members," the club founder explains.

As indicated, Russell introduces three or four special knives in limited numbers for members of his Knife Collectors Club. Should some of the production run fail to sell as club issues, it still is considered a collector item and well may find its way into his catalog somewhere down the road.

One example that appeared in the A.G. Russell Catalog of Knives Spring 1996 edition was the CM-12 Split Bolster Jack. This knife was produced for the Knife Collectors Club in 1987 by Cattaraugus, each knife being individually numbered. This was a 3-inch modern locking-blade jackknife with a $2^{1}/_{4}$-inch clip-point blade of flat-ground high-carbon stainless steel. The knife carried jigged bone scales and nickel-silver bolsters, liners and inlay. In advertising this knife, Russell pointed out that all of the serial numbers available were above 1000. The knife sold for $45.

Always on the lookout for the unusual, Russell came up with an exclusive Doctor's Knife in the same catalog edition. We're not privy as to the actual maker, but the design was from the last century, when every horse-and-buggy country doctor carried a knife to use for harness repair as well as medical purposes.

This special knife had a standard clip blade as well as a spat-

ula blade for help in counting pills. This blade had a square end that could be used to split pills when a smaller than normal dose was required.

A number of other manufacturers had issued modern replicas of this antique medical tool, and Russell was fully aware of this. Still, he wanted to list his version as an exclusive. The answer was to add burnt India stag scales and inlay his acorn trademark in nickel silver. The knife had a $2^{3}/_{4}$-inch spatula blade, while the main blade measured three inches in length. Closed, the knife measured $3^{5}/_{8}$ inches. It sold for $85.

Today, there are more than 100 knife collector clubs around the country whose members meet on a regular basis to exchange information, as well as to buy, sell and trade knives. In reviewing the list, there is at least one such club in every state except Hawaii and in some—particularly the Southern states—there are as many as ten clubs meeting. Some of these are limited in interest to specific types of knives or those produced by specific manufacturers, but for the most part, interest in knives is of a general nature.

Some knife collectors specialize in the strange and exotic. These knives and swords are from Southeast Asia.

Taking a leaf from A.G. Russell's notebook, however, are a number of companies that have formed their own collector clubs. Among these are the Buck Collectors Club, the Bulldog Knife Club, the Case Collectors Club, the Ek Commando Knife Collectors Club, the Ka-Bar Knife Collectors Club and the Swiss Army Knife Society.

In nearly all instances, these clubs are located at the company's manufacturing headquarters and are administratively overseen by factory personnel. Each of the clubs, and the closely connected factory marketing arm of each, is involved in producing special issue or commemorative knives that will have collector interest.

Perhaps the least recognized maker of commemorative knives is Buck, which has made well over 100 different models commemorating everything from Alaska's 25th anniversary to the 100th anniversary of *Sports Afield* magazine. As one might suspect, the majority of these were short runs done in the maker's custom shop and were standard models with cosmetic additions. They were not designed nor ordered, in most cases, with the idea that they would increase in value by leaps and bounds. In actuality, only 100 of the *Sports Afield* knives were made, and the original price was $125 each. The value today is about $175 each.

Case offered a scrimshawed John Wayne edition a few years back that has gained little in value, but the knives were not serially numbered and there is no way of knowing how many actually were made.

At the other extreme, the same maker issued a Johnny Cash limited edition of which 1000 were made and serial numbered. It was built on the company's Muskrat pattern and measured $3^7/_8$ inches closed. The scales were of honeycomb bone and the blade carried the country music legend's etched signature. It was marketed in an etched glass and wood display case at $69. Today, the knife, including the case, is trading at roughly twice the original price.

In the years between World War I and World War II, Remington Arms became a leader in the cutlery industry. Thousands of skilled cutlers from both England and Germany, whose products had dominated the U.S. market for centuries, were slain during World War I. This was a blow from which neither country ever recovered fully when it came to knife production.

Remington recognized that with our government having no immediate need for more rifles and bayonets, new markets and products had to be found. The result was that one of their knives to come off the line in the Depression-ridden 1930s was used as a premium for a magazine of the period that offered twelve issues and the free two-blade folder for $2.50! Today, if one can be found in mint condition, the price is $2,500 or more.

The Remington cutlery operation was shut down in 1940, when the approach of war made it more profitable to build mil-

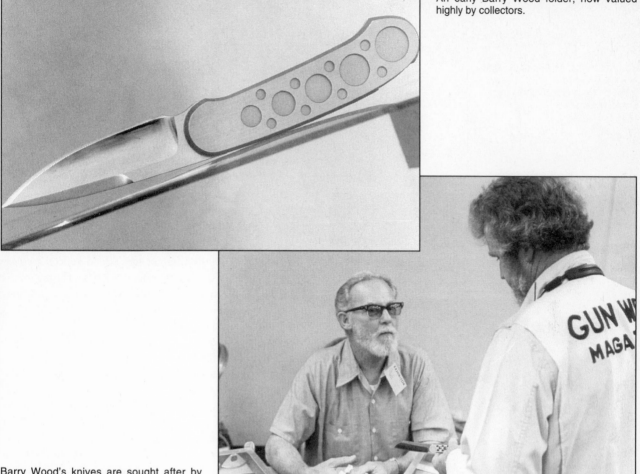

An early Barry Wood folder, now valued highly by collectors.

Barry Wood's knives are sought after by knife users as well as investors.

itary firearms than knives. However, in the years between 1919 and 1940, the Remington Cutlery Division produced an unbelievable 874 different models, ranging from ordinary jackknives to specialty knives for bartenders!

In 1979, however, Remington commissioned Case Cutlery to mark a limited number of the cutler's Cheyenne hunting model with the Remington logo silk-screened in white. These were given away to salesmen at the annual sales meeting.

This proved such a success with sales personnel that Camillus was contacted in 1982 and asked to etch the Remington logo on 100 of their Wildlife lockback model. These again were distributed to sales personnel, but also set the pattern for a new marketing effort.

In that same year, Remington introduced the 1982 Year Knife in a limited run. The first were given to outdoor writers at the annual Remington Firearms Seminar. Remington is listed

A.G. and Goldie Russell operate a profitable mail-order custom and production knife sales company from Arkansas. They feature many collector knives.

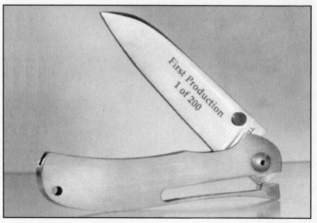

A.G. Russell came up with the design for his One-Hander knife. It still sells well in the production run.

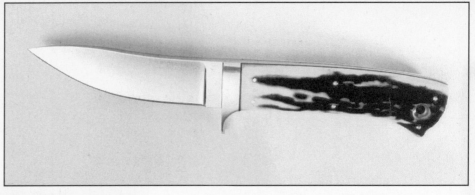

In 1980, the Lloyd Pendleton Bird Knife was sold for $165. Today's collector must identify those makers on the way up.

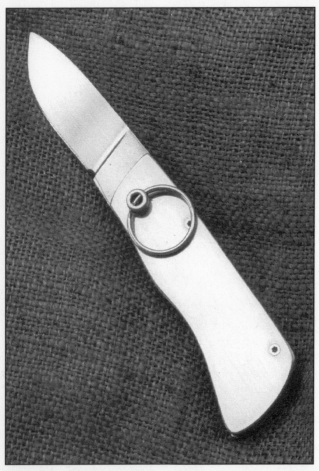

(Above) A couple of decades ago, this Michael Walker folding knife showed the maker's earlier technique. Today, its value has multiplied many times.

Tommy Lee's Bowies are strictly for collectors. He uses 440C stainless steel, ivory handles and nickel-silver furniture. Scrimshaw is by Don Haynes.

as the maker in much literature, but Camillus was the actual manufacturer, using Remington's old 1123 pattern and etching the blade. These knives sold originally for $39.95. Today, they are worth approximately $600 on the collector market.

Each year since, Remington has issued several knives, including a limited edition or commemorative. The early editions have continued to gain in value, while more recent models—all based upon the original Remington patterns—have simply held their value.

Winchester also entered the cutlery business between wars, but was not able to make it a profitable operation in that twenty-plus-year period. The cutlery branch was closed down in favor of weapons of war production.

During the 1970s, a few knives appeared carrying the Winchester logo etched on the blade. However, closer inspection shows that these were made by Buck and used by the arms company as premiums. Knives still are being made that carry the Winchester logo, but this is done on a licensing basis by a company incorporated as Bluegrass Cutlery. This group has gone back in history and culled the early Winchester patterns, selecting a number of original designs and bringing them back to the marketplace.

For the past couple of decades, the Ka-Bar Knives company has developed and supported a collectors club with its own products. It produces several special knife designs per year and offers them to members of the club. Some may argue that these are merely standard knives that have been engraved, renamed or altered slightly. An examination of the products reveals that that is not true.

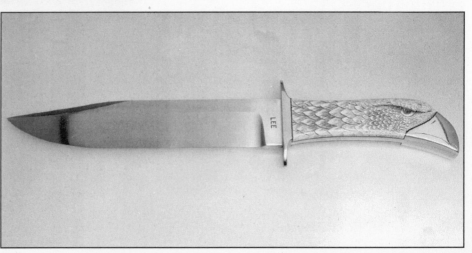

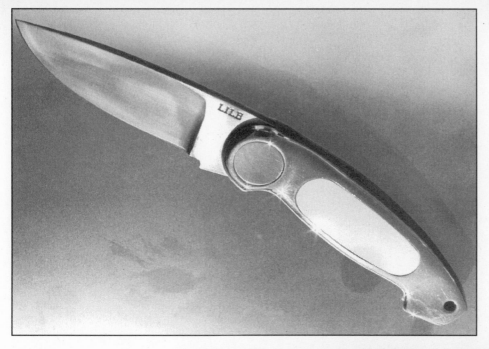

The early Jimmy Lile Folding Hunters were out-and-out collector knives. He made only fifty of these special models, all serialized. Later, he produced many semi-production versions. In 1979, this model went for $350.

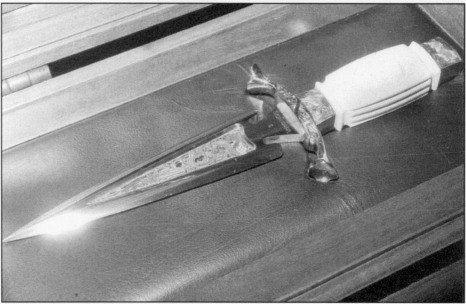

One of the original old masters of custom knifemaking is Herman Schneider, who produced this beautiful dagger for collectors only.

Ka-Bar has looked to its old, sometimes last-century designs to reproduce for its collector club. It has found mostly folders of sizes and blade designs that were marketed in earlier years. They have not increased in value as fast as some other collector models and limited production knives. Some of the club knives were seen to go down in value, but they are all excellent knives that may be used or collected. The most recent Ka-Bar Commemoratives are more expensive than those of several years ago, and some club members continue to accumulate every one announced. The wise buyer will hang on to the knives for the future. They will not appreciate as rapidly as some Bob Loveless or Buster Warenski knives, but they do make a nice collection.

Some folks collect knives with future profitability in mind, just like some collectors of paintings, sculpture, rare automobiles, movie posters and old boats. They buy the thing that is

"in" at the present, hoping and believing prices will soon rise. Many times collector values do go up and the investor makes a killing when he sells. But quite often, the uninformed or unlucky collector buys just at the top of the market and prices can do nothing but go down. At other times, market and world conditions that are far beyond any individual's control dictate where the price of anything collectible will go. But the lure of profits is what drives the price of a Loveless, Horn, Warenski, Lake, Loerchner, Moran, Schneider or Yoshihara knife to be purchased for thousands of dollars. Yes, knives are as much art as rare paintings or sculpture, but it has only been in the past couple of decades that cutlery has risen so high.

Any collectible thing is worth what somebody is willing to pay for it. Rare and fine paintings can sell for millions of dollars and nobody complains. But they do not stay in the stratosphere. Some may remember when Japanese industrialists were willing

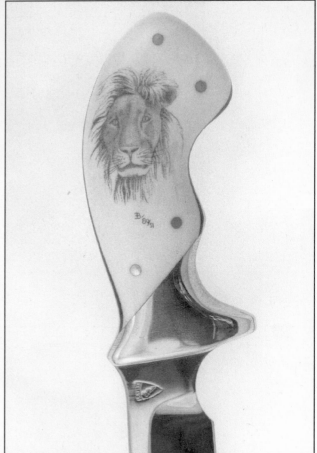

The late Norm Levine made his unique designs for decades before turning to miniatures. The scrimshaw is by Bob Engnath.

Norm Levine was seen at many national and regional knife shows. He enjoyed the trophies he won as well as selling knives.

to pay almost any price for rare oil paintings when at auction. In some recently celebrated cases, those paintings lost more than half of their cost when sold again. Some knives may do that someday, too.

Most collectors, though, collect knives simply because they like them. They may trade, buy and sell some of their collection to fill out a special need or segment, but most of the time, the collection is the end of the activity.

Most old-time collectors we know would answer the question of "Where should I start collecting?" with "Start with knives that you like."

Many if not most of us have had pocketknives since childhood. We may have started with a knife handed down from Grandpa or when we received our official Boy Scout Knife. Do you remember how long ago that was? Scouting is a wonderful organization, but in these days, knives are probably not permitted anymore. Do kids still play Mumbly Peg?

So we trade, buy or find at a local gun show, a knife we remember and cherish. Then comes a couple more for fishing, sharpening pencils at work, a few commemoratives, and before we know it we are collectors.

Perhaps our first knives were not folders. Maybe they were fishing or hunting knives. To those raised on a farm, a sheath knife is no stranger. We might have started a small collection after visiting a gun or knife show and seeing some wonderfully made custom knives by local artisans. It sets off a spark.

A few years pass, and all of a sudden, the person who just liked knives has several dozen or more. He begins to improve the collection. He may specialize in certain types of folders, such as those from the 1920s or 1930s or perhaps wartime knives hold an interest. The best place to improve the collection is to go where there are other collectors: knife shows, gun shows and craft shows. There, the new collector will find others with thousands of knives in his or her area of interest. They are all interested in buying, selling and trading up or down. Some may be giving up collecting. Some may have inherited a collection and are trying to turn the knives into money for other purposes.

There probably will be several professional knife dealers looking for buyers and sellers. There are a few full-time knife dealers around the country, but the number seems to be shrinking as profits go down and supplies dwindle. Custom

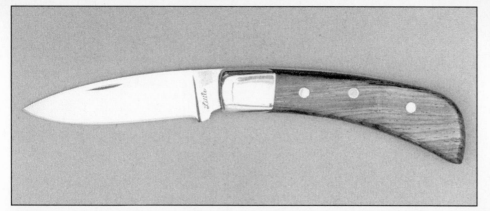

Twenty years ago, Ron Little was producing some fine folding custom knives. His work is difficult to find today.

(Below) Custom knifemaker Charlie Weiss has experimented with miniature knives, shown here with a pocketwatch to show scale.

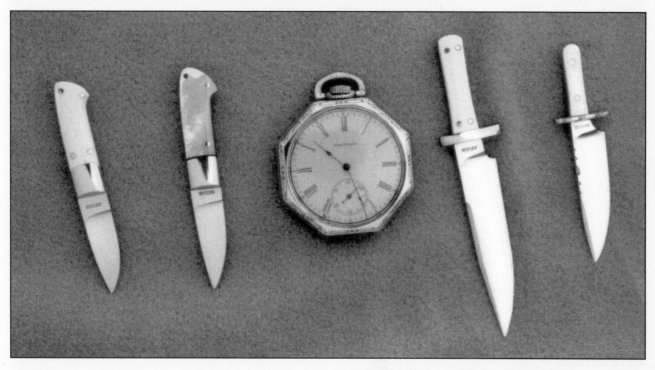

knives are now shown and sold on some television shopping networks.

Swords and long knives also seem popular with some collectors. Most knife and gun shows seem to have a number of exhibits of strange and exotic swords. Most of these collections are not for sale, but are there because their collectors are proud of what they have been able to accumulate in that field. Exotic swords always draw a crowd at shows.

There are plenty of military knife collectors. Most seem to have initiated their interest while serving in the armed forces, equipped with a bayonet, fighting knife or folding utility knife. Did you keep it when you got out? Most such collectors don't seem interested in selling any of their knives. They display them at shows just for the satisfaction of doing so.

Locating some authentic and verifiable military knives might take years of diligent searching. There are too many counterfeits. The collector must become well educated in his area of interest to keep from being defrauded. New collectors will do well to observe and listen closely to veteran collector as a way to save time, embarrassment and money while building up a serious knife collection.

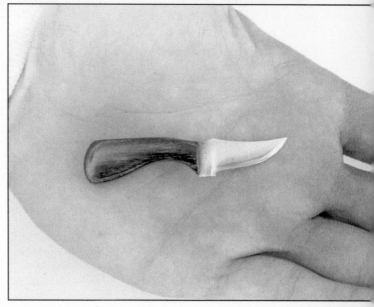

Anza Knives, a small company in Southern California, produces some miniatures, using old files for the blades.

Another champion custom knife-maker is Jess Horn, who has buyers lined up waiting for the chance to buy his work. This fighting folder went for $430 about fifteen years ago. It might be worth ten times that now.

Nineteen years have passed since Travis Winn made this little skinner of D2 steel, stainless steel pins and linen micarta for the handle.

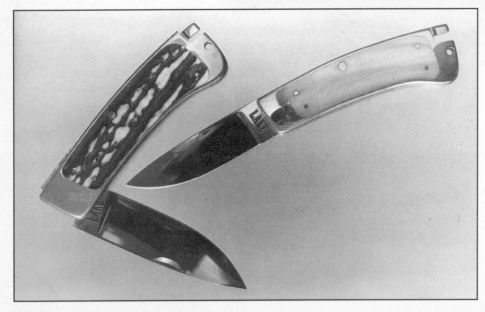

There is no doubt among collectors that the knives of Ron Lake are among the most sought-after in the world.

Another segment of collecting that has aroused interest has resulted in the establishment of the Miniature Knifemakers Association. This is a group of craftsmen who have found a thriving market among collectors of things small. Many of the members of this association also are members of the Knifemakers Guild and make knives of both standard size and miniatures of the same, often selling them as a set. As an obvious example, D'Alton Holder, president of the Knifemakers Guild at this writing, also is a member of the board of directors of the Miniature Knifemakers Association.

The late Norman Levine perhaps set the tone for miniaturization during a conversation we had some time before his death in 1996. It was the last afternoon of a three-day Great Western Gun & Knife Show at the Los Angeles County Fair-

The King Tut replica dagger sold for a king's ransom. It was made by Buster Warenski of Utah, and it caused a considerable stir when first shown.

(Below) Long before he made the King Tut dagger, Buster Warenski, in black hat, had a reputation for producing superb collector knives.

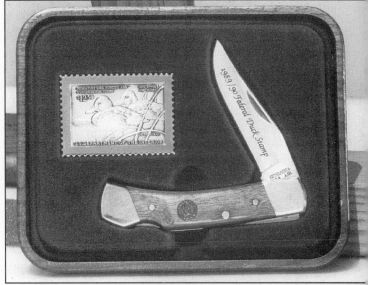

Schrade produced a series of Federal Duck Stamp commemorative knives. They included a handsome display box and replica stamp.

grounds when we slid into chairs in Levine's booth to ask how he had done. There still were a dozen knives on his table and we expected a negative answer.

"I've been doing this wrong all these years," the veteran craftsman declared. "For years, I've been telling people that I have to have $30 per inch of blade for a Bowie knife or $45 an inch for an Arkansas toothpick. Most of them look like I'm crazy and go off to buy a Filipino-made machete."

"Well, it doesn't look like you did so well here," one of us ventured, but Levine shook his head.

"I did great," he declared, grinning. "I sold all miniatures...and at a helluva lot more than 30 bucks per inch!" In short, this show had shown him that he could sell a 2-inch miniature Bowie knife for almost as much as he could one with a 10-inch blade, and have about a third the number of man hours involved in the making.

Another who has taken a different tack in custom knifemaking is Buster Warenski. He began making knives professionally in 1971, favoring fixed-blade styles such as Bowies, boot

knives and daggers, as well as fancy hunter models. He also learned to do his own engraving, fancy file work and scrimshaw, as well as to make his own sheaths.

This was a satisfying business, conducted from his shop in Richfield, Utah, where there isn't much to distract one from the chores at hand. Then Warenski became enamored with the knife that was found in the grave of King Tutankhamen, king of Egypt's 18th Dynasty, who was buried among the pyramids around 1355 B.C.

"At the time, I wanted to go to the Middle East to see the knife which then was on display," the craftsman says, "but that part of the country was too unsettled. I had to be satisfied with a series of good photographs."

In building a recreation of the Tut knife, Warenski started experimenting in 1983. The knife finally was unveiled in 1987. It incorporated 32 troy ounces of 22-karat gold and required "a number of techniques that either have been forgotten or just aren't used anymore by jewelers," the knifemaker says.

"For example, there are a few jewelers who know how to use

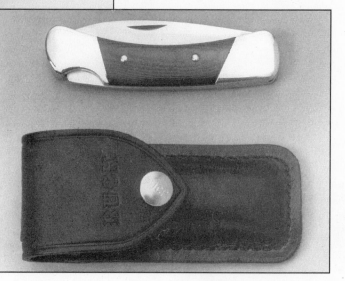

The Ka-Bar collector's club has offered different and interesting knives to its members for many years. This folder is dubbed Diamond Lil, a reproduction of knives of earlier years.

Buck knife collectors are always trying to find older models such as this Buck Duke folder.

a granulation technique with gold, but they aren't telling how they do it. I had to learn to do this by trial and error. I'd get as much information as I could by reading, then try to follow what I thought I had learned. It didn't always work. For example, one day I did something wrong and watched four months of work disintegrate before my eyes! That was a day I was glad I didn't have a sharp knife within reach!"

The four years of work involved in reproducing the Tut knife were not constant, of course. By his own admission, Warenski would take breaks to "get away from it and allow my mind to clear out. And there also was the problem of making and selling knives for living purposes."

The Utah craftsman does not discuss the price he received for the Tut knife, but he does say that the present owner, Phil Lobred of San Diego, California, has refused an offer of $100,000 for the art piece.

Today, Warenski describes his production as "investor-quality knives" and his prices as "upscale."

"Most of what I do today is special order and commission work," he explains, "but I still do three or four shows a year, including one in Japan and occasionally the show in Paris. For those, I do some speculation pieces so I'll have something on my table. It's been so long, though, since I've done a standard drop-point hunter that I'm not certain I'd know how to start."

In recent years, Buster Warenski has found a new market. This is for huge daggers with blades measuring from 16 to 22 inches and highly ornate.

"Most of these, I find, are ending up in Saudi Arabia," the Utahan explains. "My price on these ranges from $12,000 to $26,000 per dagger. These are what might best be called fantasy knives, but I'm finding a ready market in the Middle East."

Boker is an old-line European knifemaker. Many of its folders are sought out by collectors.

That doesn't mean he has given up experimenting along with his regular work. "I made one miniature a year or so ago to see how it would look," he recalls, "and I've turned out a few folders that were made primarily for my own satisfaction."

But when he describes his prices as "upscale," I think we now all understand how that is defined.

This also leads to a conclusion. There are collectors like the nine-year-old mentioned at the beginning of this chapter, and there are those who can own and covet a $100,000 knife of gold. That means, of course, that there is a market for almost anything that has a cutting edge!

CHAPTER 10

FATHERS AND SONS

Knifemaking skills are handed down to the next generation

KNIFEMAKING IS ONE of the older skill crafts that have been handed down from father to son for centuries. The practice probably began long before the Industrial Revolution and continues today.

One of the most prominent generational knife manufacturers is Buck Knives. Here, four generations of the family have been actively involved in knife production on an international scale. The tradition continues today at Buck, resulting in one of the most successful cutlery businesses in the world. Buck knives are known and used everywhere. Elsewhere in this volume, we take a more detailed look at the Buck family and their knife company.

About three decades ago, when the current interest in modern hand-made knives began to blossom, most of those makers involved were in their twenties or thirties. If they had children, the youngsters were mostly of elementary school age. Today, these same children are adults old enough to have children of their own. Growing up in a house of cutlery, many watched their fathers, learned from them and have become custom knifemakers with their own skills and techniques. Fathers, being fathers, all tend to say that their sons make better knives than they do, but the customer must be the judge of that. For sure the sons have many years of experience behind them, even while still young men.

Bob Engnath is well known to custom amateur and professional knifemakers all over the world. As noted in another chapter, he is one of the major producers of custom sword blades in North America. He also turns out hundreds of semi-finished and finished blades of all types and sizes with which many knifemakers gain valuable experience while assembling and finishing fine cutlery.

Engnath started a company called House of Muzzloading in Glendale, California, a couple of decades ago. Recently, he changed the name to Blades 'N' Stuff, reflecting his changing customer base. The new company specializes in knifemaker supplies of all kinds, mostly sold through Engnath's extensive mail-order catalog. The catalog lists semi-finished blades of several steels, more than a hundred designs and sizes from the smallest to the long sword blades, handle materials, pins, rivets, screws, epoxies and labor- and time-saving tools with which to build knives. If a craftsman needs tools, parts or advice on making knives, all will be found in Engnath's catalog.

The catalog contains more than merely knife supplies and tools. It is a source of knifemaking information, techniques and tips unlikely to be found anywhere else. He offers time- and labor-saving tricks learned over his many years of experience that other knifemakers have used successfully. Bob Engnath shares his experience and the experiences of the many knifemakers who frequent his Glendale store.

The senior Engnath really enjoys grinding out knife blades. He claims he does some of his best thinking while at the grinding wheel, and much of that thinking is recorded in his catalog. Bob Engnath's long sword blades—especially the Japanese blade designs—are in great demand by swordmakers everywhere; even by customers in Japan.

Producing long blades that meet the critical demands of martial artists and sword collectors is far from easy. It is a tribute to Engnath and his skills that his blades are in such worldwide demand that he finds it difficult to keep up. Sword blades are of such high quality that they are difficult and time-consuming to make, at best. It requires special skills to grind such long pieces of steel. Heat-treating them with the special Japanese sword

Bob Engnath is a regular exhibitor at knife shows around Southern California, where he retails his Blades 'N' Stuff supplies to amateur and professional knifemakers from around the world.

Kirk Engnath (left) assists his father during the difficult work of heat-treating sword blades. Each step of the process is critical, demanding concentration and skill.

qualities is particularly difficult and physically demanding. In this effort, Engnath relies on help from his son, Kirk.

Kirk Engnath literally grew up among knives and knifemakers. He hung around the shop as a small boy and has helped his mother and father at the retail store and at gun and knife shows throughout California. The Blades 'N' Stuff booth may be seen at most knife shows surrounded by people eager to talk about knives.

Kirk Engnath made his first knife at age eleven.

"I have made knives all my life," he says, "but I got serious when I made the general utility knife I now carry.

"Everything I know about knifemaking has come from my father, Bob Engnath. My dad taught me how to finish blades. Barry Posner helped me figure out some quick techniques to help finish blades, and Jim Mattis gave me some great ideas on wood finishing."

Working at the store, Kirk Engnath talks to new knifemakers and customers all the time. The retail establishment is seldom without several of each.

"My customers are people who want a small utility knife that they can use without worrying about scratching or marring the blade. Keeping my prices reasonable helps me sell, too. I make about forty knives per year at this stage in my career. My delivery time is about two months."

The younger Engnath prefers to make his blades of ATS-34 steel. He has Paul Bos of Alpine, California, and the man in

charge of heat-treatment at Buck Knives heat-treat his blades. He has Bos bring them to 59 on the Rockwell C scale.

"That combination of steel and hardening creates a fantastic edge on the knives," declares Engnath. "My designs are usually one-of-a-kind blades that other customers or my father form on the grinder."

Early on, Kirk Engnath's parents were displaying his knife-making efforts at their tables at knife shows around Southern California. On the days and weekends when he was not in school, the younger maker would be on hand to talk to buyers and makers about his and their knives. It helped his knife education.

He says, "It would be nice if blade polishing was easier, but when I get to the handle, it all pays off. I truly enjoy designing and making a knife handle. I like the way all the angles and lines come together to form a pleasing unit with the blade.

"I try to produce handles that are unusual and multi-faceted, a type of geometric art work that complements the blade."

Those who have seen Kirk Engnath's efforts agree that the young man shows a lot of talent and promise.

Chuck Stapel is another of those makers who has been making knives for more than twenty years. His son, Craig, has been at it since about 1981, no doubt starting at an early age because of the influence of his father and grandfather. Grandfather Charles Stapel is no longer active at making knives, but his first efforts date back to World War II. He still has a few of those

Bob Engnath's long blades have a definite Oriental look. He is adept at heat-treating to obtain the distinctive two-level hardness common to Japanese sword blades.

Kirk Engnath's knife designs have their own distinctive appearance.

Kirk Engnath fashioned these knives of ATS stainless steel and used canvas micarta for the handles.

Three generations of knifemakers: (from left) Charles Stapel, Chuck (Charles, Jr.) and Craig Stapel. Craig's son hangs around his grandfather's shop whenever he can.

early efforts. They have been in use for a half-century and still will hold a sharp edge.

When you count it up, the Stapel family encompasses three generations of custom knifemakers, with the fourth not quite old enough to reach the workbench. But Chuck Stapel's grandson, Craig Stapel's son, spends plenty of time in and around Stapel's workshop, learning about the machines and other tools.

Chuck Stapel has been featured in earlier editions of this book. He has offered encouragement and help to the authors all along the way. He opened his shop and gave his time and knowledge to assist the authors in describing many techniques of knifemaking.

He loves to experiment. He has made standard working knives, tantos, hunters, folders and utility designs, as well as high-dollar art and collector knives. He produces a number of commemorative knives for several annual charity events, including the annual California Paralyzed Veterans Association trap shoot and the Charleton Heston celebrity fundraiser. Chuck Stapel is also an accomplished shotgunner, as well as a recognized custom knifemaker. Today, his knives are seen all over the world.

Stapel makes the official special knife for the Los Angeles County Sheriff's Office bomb squad. More than a decade ago, one of Stapel's knifemaking partners was Glen Hornby, an early member of the bomb disposal group. Hornby also was part of the team assigned to security during the 1984 Olympic Games in Los Angeles.

He advised Stapel on some of the design considerations a knife used by those in that hazardous profession might want and need. The design has been accepted by the L.A. County anti-bombers, and each member is supplied with one. The design has caught on with the general public, too, and Stapel now makes a mini-version of the knife for the rest of us to consider.

Chuck Stapel is one of the fastest knifemakers the authors have seen. Starting with a slab of heat-treated steel, he can shape, grind, drill, glue, clamp, sand, sharpen and complete a simple utility knife in less than two hours. The slowest part is waiting for the two-part epoxy cement to cure.

Always looking for new challenges, Stapel attends the occasional motorcycle gathering where he sets up a small grinding wheel and sharpens the knives of the motorcycle riders. He meets a lot of potential new customers, he says, and makes a few bucks sharpening many knives.

Stapel has experimented with most of the standard knife steels. One of his favorites is AEB-L. He was one of the first to realize the potential properties of this steel and encourages others to try it. He also makes knives of D2 and 440C stainless steel. He enjoys trying new things such as his recent efforts at custom knife-and-fork sets. He never fails to create a stir at a restaurant when he breaks out his own special silverware to eat his steak.

Son Craig Stapel notes that his first knife sale was in 1984. While his father may be better known, Craig is no rookie at the business. He has been hanging around his father's shop most of his life, and remembers seeing his father's custom knives as far back as 1980. He made a knife of his own for the first time in 1981. He still shares the shop and the tools with his father.

The younger Stapel prefers AEB-L steel for his blades; no surprise there. He has Paul Bos harden the blades to 58-60 RC, because he likes the way the knife holds an edge. A typical Craig Stapel knife is a small drop-point hunter of standard design. He finds designing and shaping knife handles the most rewarding part of his hobby.

Craig Stapel manages to turn out about twenty knives a year on a part-time basis. He requires about six months from order to completion and finds most of his customers at local knife and gun shows he attends. All he needs to increase his knife production, he says, is more time.

Across the country, in Florida, we find a long-time maker of custom knives, Zack, which is short for Don Zaccagnino, Sr., and Don Zaccagnino, Jr. To complete the picture, there is a third-generation knife-learner in the shop, Wallace Zaccagnino, thirteen, already familiar with the workings of power tools. A younger brother, Daniel, shows interest in the processes at age eight.

The senior Zaggacnino died in 1994, but not before he had passed along much of his knowledge and experience to his son.

These are early knifemaking efforts by Charles Stapel, Sr., dating back four or five decades. They still are in daily use.

Some of the latest designs from Chuck Stapel include several sets of custom knives and forks. They create quite a stir at the local steak house.

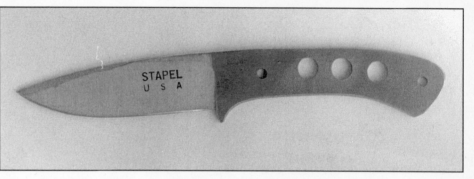

Chuck Stapel makes a simple, basic knife, as well as several art knives for collectors.

This is a Craig Stapel design, similar to his father's. (Photo by Don Fitzgerald Photography.)

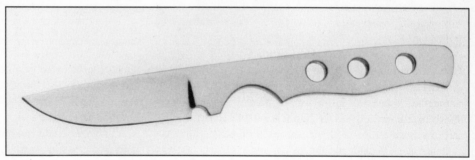

The Stapel eat-out fork has the slightest curve to the tines.

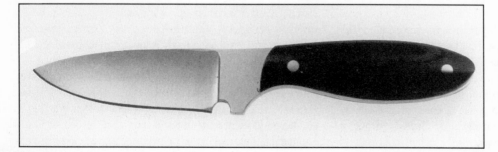

Craig Stapel favors AEB-L stainless steel for the blade and dark micarta for the handle for this purse knife. (Photo by Dan Fitzgerald Photography.)

Don Zaccagnino, Jr. (left) and his late father Don Zaccagnino, Sr., (Zack) examine a ground blade.

Don Zaccagnino, Jr. at the Bader 132-inch grinder.

Another generation learns the business. Don supervises his son Wallace Zaccagnino on the drill press. The father's pride is obvious.

He began teaching and working with knives on a part-time basis in 1969. He taught for eighteen years as a high school biology teacher and vocational instructor in a machine shop. Don Jr. joined his father in the knife business in 1987. His full-time career is as a machinist with the aerospace industry in Florida.

Don Jr. says, "I enjoy making knives, and it is a craft that was handed to me by my father. The little bit of extra money from knife sales is a help, too.

"I usually put in twenty to thirty hours a week working in the shop. Most of my customers are local hunters and people who enjoy finer, hand-crafted products. I have sales in other states as well as internationally. I set up a display at a couple of gun and knife shows each year in addition to the Knifemakers Guild show. I offer knives for sale at a few local stores that specialize in hunting and fishing, and at trap and Skeet clubs."

The Zack Knives shop includes two Bader belt grinders and a machine invented by Zaccagnino called the Zack 132-inch platen grinder. This machine has a four-position turret so it can accommodate a 2- or 3-inch wide belt backed against a soft or hard platen.

Another Zack invention is the Zack Sidewinder, a grinder with five areas to work on plus what is called a Billy Roll, which lets the maker get a 3/4-inch wheel into the cut-out area of a hatchet. Also in the shop are other bench grinders, two Baldor buffers, a Bridgeport milling machine, two lathes, two band saws, two drill presses, a leather sewing machine that dates back to 1925 and plenty of hand tools.

Most Zack knives today are designs from the father. Don Jr. makes only one standard design, which he and his father designed together. He also does some custom work, but prefers working on his standard designs. Most of the custom work he does is from a customer's desired changes to one of those standard designs.

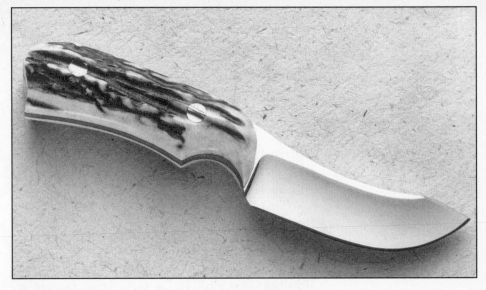

This is the Zack Model 11 Gator III with a 3½-inch blade of 440C stainless steel. The tang is tapered under the Sambar stag handle. (Photo by Weyer of Toledo.)

Two versions of the Zack Model BRH Outdoorsman, honoring writer Billy Ray Hughes. The blades are 440C steel, 5½ inches long. Handles are stag (top) and stabilized wood. (Photo by Weyer of Toledo.)

"I do all my own leather work in the style my father taught me," says Don Jr. "I make regular sheaths for my knives with guards and pouches for the guardless models. I usually use 8- or 9-ounce leather. Most of the time, I double the thickness. Stitching is done by hand when the old machine is not working."

Most of the knife designs are twenty or more years old. Some models, says Don Jr., sell like hotcakes at shows in the Florida area. Most of the knives are lightweight hunting and personal knives, fillet and carving knives, presentation-grade hunters and a lot of large Bowies.

He adds with a wry smile, "A couple of other makers sell all they can copy and make, too. Some do not."

Zack knives are made primarily of 440C stainless steel. Handle materials include Pakkawood, linen micartas, natural and stabilized woods, sambar stag and water buffalo horn. The blades are heat-treated at a local company, Suncoast Heat Treat, to give a reading of RC 58. Hatchets and collector knives have a lower hardness.

"My father passed away in December 1994 after a lengthy illness," recalls Don Jr. "In the fall of 1991, he suffered a stroke that left him paralyzed on the left side. As time passed, he was confined to a wheelchair.

"At the time of Dad's stroke, I took over the day-to-day operation of the shop, filling his orders and trying to build the business back up. Dad started teaching me to make knives when I was about eleven years old. Throughout my life, I spent summers and holidays working in the shop with him. After starting a career with a large aerospace manufacturer, I still put in weekends and after work at the shop. I have all those years' experience in the art of making knives.

"In the tradition of passing down a craft from generation to generation, my father and I began teaching my oldest son, Wallace, the art of knifemaking. At the age of thirteen, he shows great promise for a third-generation knifemaker. Daniel, my youngest son, is also interested in the workings of the system. He has special jobs in the shop to help him on his way to learning this art."

These are but a few samples of the several father-son custom knifemakers we have identified, but there are others. So far, we have not heard of any mother-daughter knifemakers, but it will happen soon, we are sure. No doubt there are also some father-daughter teams that will soon achieve prominence, too.

11

LADY KNIFEMAKERS—
ONLY A FEW

Paula Anzel is a novice who's
as good as her teacher

A FEW YEARS ago, it seemed like a movement or, at least, a trend. Women who were interested in knifemaking, custom knifemaking in particular, seemed to be more in evidence than now. There may be explanations for this, but we are not here to explore that area.

Carolyn Tinker of Pasadena, California, was one of the most prominent and successful knifemakers a decade or more ago, but she is retired and no longer active in the cutlery world. Ms. Tinker was profiled in an earlier edition of this book.

Delores Hayes was featured in the GUN DIGEST BOOK OF KNIVES, Fourth Edition. She still is active in producing art and collector-type knives, and she and her work continue to be seen at local Southern California knife shows. She seems to be specializing in miniature knives these days.

The business of knifemaking and marketing are not restricted only to men by any means. Visit any commercial knife manufacturer in almost any part of the world, and you will see plenty of women on the production floor. In most facilities, women outnumber the men in assembling the components of knives.

No doubt, there are more women who are producing custom cutlery, making knives by hand on their own, but they have not received the publicity they may deserve. They must be hiding their lights under the proverbial bushel baskets.

There are unlimited opportunities for lady knifemakers. Those who have the artistic abilities and ambition can move to the top, if they wish. In our search for such individuals, the authors recently discovered one young woman in Indiana who

Paula Anzel of Batesville, Indiana, is one of the few active lady custom knifemakers in North America, and she really enjoys her work.

seems to be on the right track. Fortunately, she has the help of her mentor who has shown her the way.

Paula Anzel began making knives under the watchful eye of Ken Largin in 1994. She has progressed steadily since that time in skills, experience and ability.

Several years ago, Largin was an employee at Buck Knives' factory in Southern California. He was—and is—an entrepreneur at heart and set out to make knives on his own after learning all he could at Buck. Eventually, he settled in Batesville, Indiana, which could be called Small Town, America. The community is not known for turning out custom knifemakers—not until the arrival of Largin.

Ken Largin is a hard-working, full-time knifemaker. He habitually works at his craft considerably more than eight hours a day. After settling in Batesville, he developed the habit of stopping by the local coffee shop at the end of his long day. Eventually, Largin began talking about his knifemaking with waitress Paula Anzel. She became increasingly interested as she heard and learned more about custom knives. There are plenty of hunters in Indiana and surrounding states. They all use some sort of hunting knives from time to time, but non-hunting waitresses have little contact with most knowledgeable knife people.

Paula Anzel had no previous interest or experience with knives, other than knowing on which side of the plate they are to be placed when serving up lunch or a slice of pie with a cup of coffee.

One thing led to another and, in time, Anzel was spending her days off in Largin's shop, observing how knives are made. She wanted to try it for herself, and it was not long until she was making blades.

Largin says, "She ground her first blades as if she had been doing it for years. She took to it immediately. That was unusual enough, but she showed no fear of the power equipment right from the start. That also came as a bit of a surprise. She is a terrific apprentice and is a fast learner."

Anzel traveled to California to spend her summer vacation at The Gun Shop at Knott's Berry Farm in Buena Park, an amusement park and tourist attraction not far from Disneyland. A local retail knife shop offered her and Largin an opportunity to build custom knives in front of the shop where thousands of tourists from all over the world might observe the operation.

It might be argued that few who saw a knife being built had much understanding of the complexities involved, but Anzel and Largin used every opportunity to explain what they could. And the novelty of a woman seated in front of a belt grinder attracted many curious future knife buyers.

Paula Anzel describes her knifemaking as being broken down into five steps. The first step is to scribe the blade pattern on a slab or bar of steel. Most of her knives are made of 440C stainless. She uses standard designs. Next is the task of profiling the blade from the bar. She reports that she spent many hours at this task in Largin's shop when she began, and it is still a large part of her knifemaking process. Blade profiling is accomplished on a belt sander in Largin's operation.

After the basic outline of the knife has been ground, the next step is to drill appropriate holes in the tang to accept screws, bolts, rivets or pins to hold the handle. That step, according to Anzel, is best done on a drill press, an essential power tool for most knifemakers.

If the blade is to be hollow-ground, that is the next operation. Hollow-grinding is, for most makers, one of the most difficult tasks if it is done well. Anzel admits receiving plenty of help from Largin when it comes to grinding the blade shapes at this point.

"The most difficult part of making a knife for me," says Anzel, "is keeping the grinds straight and level. That is the part I practice the most and the part that will produce a good-looking knife, if done correctly."

After the blade is ground and the tang holes drilled, the steel is hardened and heat-treated. The final step is to attach the handle slabs using steel pins and epoxy. Final edge sharpening and any fancy filework are done after hardening. Most of Anzel's knives are hardened to about 57C on the Rockwell scale. Typical handle slabs might be of jigged bone.

Paula Anzel works on knives full time and no longer waits tables. She works on knives six full days a week at the shop. At first it was taking her about two days to make a knife. Her pro-

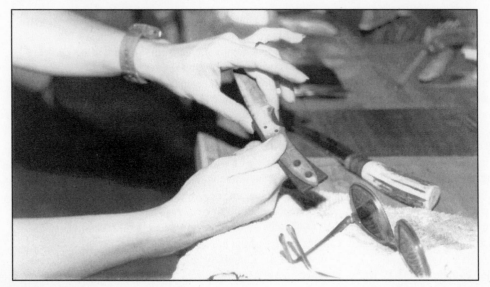

Anzel finds fitting and finishing knife handles, almost the last step in knifemaking, to be among the easier tasks.

Knifemaker Ken Largin is Paula Anzel's mentor and teacher. Anzel works out of Largin's Indiana shop.

Largin says Anzel immediately took to blade grinding. She does the task as if she had been around belt sanders all her life.

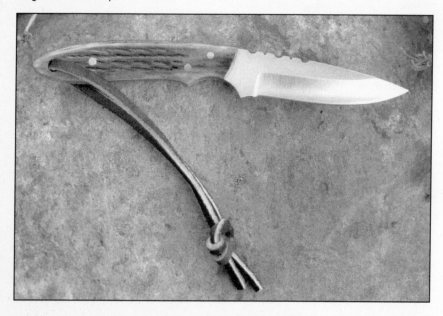

This small utility hunting knife represents an early effort by Anzel. It is made of 440C stainless steel with handle scales of jigged bone.

duction time was soon cut in half and she is working on improving more, as she gains experience.

Her least favorite part of knifemaking is buffing. "I hate it," she declares. "My favorite part of the operation is profiling, but the fancy filework is difficult. I am now able to accomplish all the steps in knifemaking and continue to make my little hunting model. There seems to be a continuous demand for it, I'm happy to say."

In only a short period of time, knifemaking has changed Paula Anzel's life. Before her first trip to Knott's Berry Farm in California, she never had traveled out of Indiana and she never had flown in an airplane. Since that first trip, Largin and Anzel have attended knife shows in California, Florida, Chicago, Pittsburgh, New York City and other locations, as well as displaying their wares at the 1996 Shooting, Hunting, Outdoor Trade (SHOT) Show in Dallas, Texas.

"We had plenty of interest in our knives at the SHOT Show,"

said Anzel. "We had representatives from such well known knife catalog vendors as A.G. Russell and Atlanta Cutlery, as well as several mass-merchandisers. Some will be carrying Largin and Anzel knife designs in their next catalogs.

"We may have trouble keeping up with all the orders, but that is a good problem to have. We are turning out 350 to 500 knives a year at Ken's little shop, and I am sure we can increase that rate if we need to. We have plenty of work to do, but I am thrilled with the prospects.

"Not so long ago, I was a small-town waitress who had never been out of the state. Now I have traveled over much of the United States and seen some of the largest cities. Our next stops are to be Switzerland and France, in addition to more travel in the U.S. I can't wait to see more of the world and more of the country. Knifemaking has been good to me."

As she says, "Ken enjoys making knives after sixteen years in the business. Why shouldn't I, too?"

AMERICAN BLADESMITH SOCIETY

In twenty years, this group has grown from the four founding members to more than 550

MOST MEMBERS OF the American Bladesmith Society like to trace their craftmanship heritage back at least as far as the famous Jim Bowie and the knives he made about 150 years ago. The modern group was founded in 1976 by Bill Moran, B.R. Hughes, Bill Bagwell and Don Hastings. At the time, the ABS founders' membership goals were quite modest. They hoped to reach total membership of about twenty-five bladesmiths in the years to come. In twenty years, the membership has grown to more than 550.

The members of the ABS are all either knifemakers who forge their own blades or those who have "...a sincere interest in the art, science, history, technology and/or romance of forged steel knives, tools, weapons, implements and other objects of art," according to the society's published by-laws. The preponderance of members are those who actually make forged knives.

The bylaws go on to state: "Questions pertaining to membership or the qualification thereof or the eligibility of a person

The first American Bladesmith Society conference was held in Ashokan, New York. The date is in the early 1980s. Bill Moran, one of the founders of the group, is seated on the bench, third from right.

Joseph Cordova, chairman of the board of the ABS, examines one of his finished blades. He has made knives for years by the stock-removal method and recently has become involved with bladesmithing.

A heavy shop vice and blacksmith hammer are basic tools of the forger's trade.

Blades may be forged from almost any steel source, including heavy duty industrial timing chains and motorcycle chains. These can result in some interesting patterns.

applying for membership may be referred by the chairman of the board to a membership committee, which shall report its recommendations in respect thereto directly to the board of directors for the board's consideration and action thereon."

To get the ball rolling to become a member, one must do the following:

"Application for membership shall be on a written form provided by the Society or by a membership committee, signed by the applicant and submitted to the treasurer with the payment of applicable dues.

"All members shall conduct themselves and govern their activities ethically and in accordance with these bylaws so as to preserve and advance the educational and other tax-exempt purposes of the Society."

Obviously, the ABS is interested in promoting the interests of its blade-forging members and reaching more of the general public to tell them of the value of this method of making knives.

The members come from several backgrounds. Some have been—and are—long-time blacksmiths or farriers, making horseshoes, tools and artworks of forged metal. Even in this world of 21st century technology and electronics, there is a need for skilled metal workers to form and repair the tools of industry. Most of this type of work is done with powerful, computer-guided machines, but all of it still requires the skill and training of the smith.

Other members have come from knifemaker backgrounds.

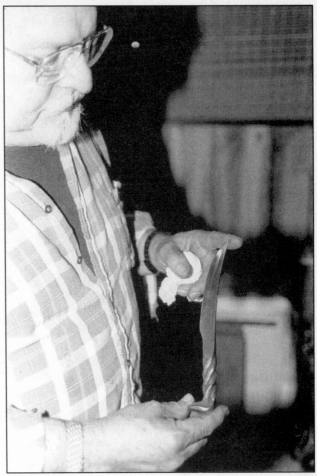

Joe Cordova also makes knives from old railroad spikes, which make simple, straightforward tools.

They may have begun by experimenting with their own heat-treating. Some, as they became better knifemakers and learned more about the various types of steel that might be used to make knives, were attracted by the challenge and intrigue of forging the steel to make their blades. Others are attracted by the popularity, practicality and beauty of Damascus blades.

Many members of this group were and are making hand-made knives using what is known as the stock-removal method to form their blades. Stock-removal means the maker begins with a slab of steel about the thickness of the final blade, say $1/8$- to $1/4$-inch thick, cut about the width and length of the finished blade and tang. The maker merely removes the unneccessary steel stock from the blank by bandsaw, grinder or wheel, until the final blade profile is reached.

Twenty years ago, there were only a few modern knifemakers who had the skill and knowledge to produce Damascus, Wootz or laminated steel knives. Today, there are hundreds who are members of the ABS and probably hundreds more who have experimented with forge-welded steel.

Rather than removing stock from the steel blank until the blade shape is reached, forging a blade means heating a piece of steel until it is soft enough—malleable is the term—to be hammered and pounded into final shape. The process requires considerable skill, knowledge and practice, as well as physical strength, to achieve a level where one might consider membership in the American Bladesmith Society. There are some younger members of the ABS and even, at

this writing, a few women members, but most of the 550 members are older men.

The potential member does not need to labor for years in complete obscurity and isolation, improving his art to the point at which he feels qualified to become a certified member of the society. Among the goals of the ABS are:

"To assist the member bladesmiths in maintaining (and, where appropriate, improving) their standards of work and business.

"To aid and assist its member bladesmiths in respect to technical and aesthetic qualities of their work and to render assistance to members endeavoring to improve and develop knowledge and skill in bladesmithing and related arts."

The current chairman of the ABS board of directors is certainly no rookie knifemaker. Joe Cordova of Peralta, New Mexico, a small community a few miles south of Albuquerque, has been making and selling handmade knives since 1953. He makes several standard designs including fighters, hunters, boot knives and kitchen ware. He has been producing a fighting knife he calls the Gladiator for decades, and it continues to be in demand. His hunting knives are used by serious hunters all over the world. Many of these working knives are ground from such so-called stainless steels as ATS-34, 440C and 154CM. Cordova forges 1095 and 5160 tool steels.

In more recent years, Joe Cordova has gotten into all sorts of steel sources from which to make his knives, both working and fantasy designs. He forges blades from such things as ball bearings, sections of wire rope, roller bearings, used motorcycle chains, timing chains removed from old engines, railroad spikes and other unlikely products. He haunts various motorcycle repair and wrecking yards to find steel chains that will lend themselves to forging. He has, he admits, become somewhat well known among the biker crowd as a guy who will be looking for worn-out chains everywhere in New Mexico.

Most such used chains are covered with old grease and dirt, so the first thing to do is heat them up to the point where most of those impurities will burn off. Motorcycle and industrial chains are made in several sizes; some are huge, others are miniature sizes. The pins, rollers, side plates and other components may be made of diverse metals, presenting a challenge to the craftsman. Depending on the direction or angle at which he hammers the heated chains, all sorts of different and intriguing Damascus-type patterns will result. Cordova might hammer the chain with the pins perpendicular to the anvil, or he may try it with the pins lying at an angle. Each approach provides a different appearance to the finished product.

Several bladesmiths make blades from forged wire rope, large bearings, old saw blades and the like. They may be heated and hammered flat or folded over several times to produce a Damascus effect. In some areas, these materials are plentiful, but scarce in others. Knifemakers are always resourceful and will find available substitutes from which to forge knives.

Forging beautiful and useful blades can be a difficult art. The job is not simply pounding hot metal into a blade shape. Too much hammering, too little, the wrong temperatures, too long, too short, dirty equipment, misjudgments in time and temperature, and improper heat-treatment when the forging is finished can ruin the best steel or produce a faulty blade. Most collectors and critics seem to agree, though, that the most beautiful knife blades to be found anywhere are those that are forged in their construction.

For final finishing, polishing, buffing and sharpening, most bladesmiths turn to the same traditional power tools that the stock-removal knifemakers use. Some will say that greater care must be exercised by the knifemaker at this point, because he or she has a lot of time and effort invested in the blade. Fashioning a forged blade is not easy, physically or emotionally. Heating and reheating, hammering and rehammering a piece of steel over and over requires plenty of strength, skill and patience. The village smith always is depicted with big arms, shoulders and chest for good reason. The work is hard!

Some blade shapes such as curves and tapers are best done by forging. Some steel forms, such as wire rope, rods, spheres and other unusual sources, are impractical for stock-removal. Only the highly skilled bladesmith can turn out a long sword successfully, for instance, from a length of wire rope. Such projects are real challenges for any knifemaker.

The process of forging a knife, whether by hand-hammer or power-hammer, does more than simply form a blade to shape on an anvil. The hammering causes the grains of the hot billet to pack closer together along the blade edge, if done correctly. While much of the grain packing returns to normal after the steel cools,

The ABS offers classes and instructions on the art of forging. This student is heat-treating the back of a blade with a blowtorch. (Photo by RIT Communications.)

Students learn how to bring their forged blades to a razor-sharp edge in the ABS classes. (Photo by RIT Communications.)

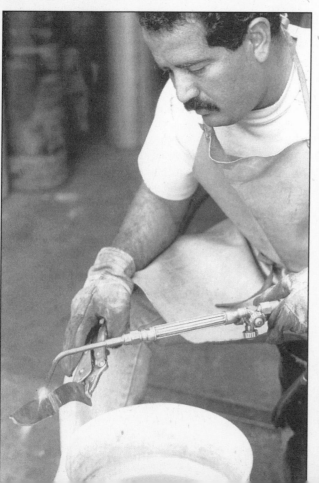

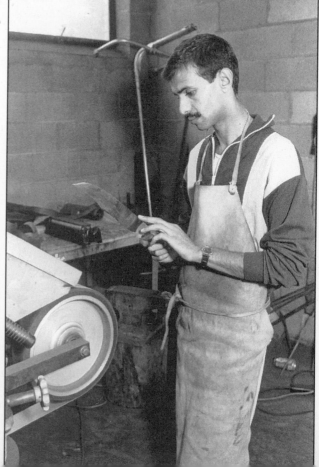

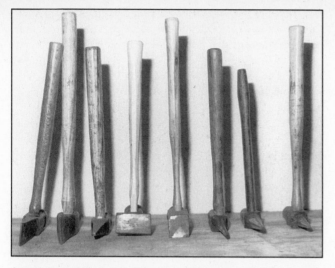

A typical set of blacksmith hammers as found in a bladesmith shop. Each has a specific use for shaping the metal.

some of it remains in the edge area to provide extra strength and hardness along the cutting edge. The experienced bladesmith knows that the forged blade should not be hammered too thin in the edge area before heat treating, because if it is too thin it may cool too rapidly and become brittle instead of tough. Final sharpening and polishing must wait until after heat treatment.

To oversimplify the matter, given enough time, almost anyone can produce a beautiful *looking* knife blade by the stock-removal or forging method. And there is a market for knives that are works of art, never intended to be used to cut anything. But forged knives can be made to be strong, have sharp, useful edges, resist wear, and last for years while they are a joy to behold. Many of the top bladesmiths in the world turn out plenty of hunting, skinning, utility and fighting knives that receive plenty of hard use year after year.

Members of the ABS operate a testing program to certify the qualifications of bladesmiths. They are categorized as Apprentice Bladesmith, Journeyman Bladesmith and Master Bladesmith. The ABS establishes qualifications and testing criteria for the certifications. Broken down, these are the standards from the American Bladesmith Society:

An Apprentice Bladesmith is in a learning stage. The Society imposes no formal requirements for entering the Apprentice

Bladesmith level and imposes no standards of quality for the work of an Apprentice, because during this learning stage quality can vary greatly.

A Journeyman Bladesmith shall have achieved sufficient knowledge, skill and experience to produce a well made forged blade of good quality and workmansip that will be a functional and reliable tool or weapon.

A Master Bladesmith shall have achieved the highest standards of the Society. Master Smith blades must be of exceptional quality both in workmanship and execution of design. A Master Smith must have the necessary level of knowledge, skill and ability to make a true art blade that qualifies not only as an object of great beauty, but shall be a blade of vastly superior quality and merit, whether designed as a weapon or tool. Blades made by a Master Bladesmith, including art blades, shall possess outstanding resiliency and edge retention.

The ABS and its members are urged to eschew so-called stainless steel blades. "The Society recommends the use of traditional carbon steels for forging knife blades. Although it is acceptable for bladesmith members to forge blades of stain-resistant steel and other high-alloy materials for experimental purposes, or to fill an order, the Society discourages the continuous use of stainless steel for forging blades unless and until forged stainless steel blades have been proven to the satisfaction of the Board capable of being forged into quality blades that will consistently pass the standard ABS cutting and bending tests."

The ABS board of directors continues to look at stainless steel and the possibilities of forging developments and alloys that may eventually make it possible to consistently forge quality stainless steel blades capable of passing the cutting and bending tests.

In 1996, judging procedures were established by the ABS to performance-test knives from those makers who were willing to submit their work to the panel. The criteria for Master Bladesmith are more severe than those required by those attempting to be judged as Journeymen. Applicants must keep in mind that only their best work should be submitted for judging. One substandard knife may result in failure. In general, the society's guidelines state that the overall quality for a Journeyman rating is in the range of "very good" to "excellent." The quality for the Master rating is "excellent" to "superlative." This all indicates that any knife offered that was made by a member of the ABS and is marked with the mak-

This is a Jim Ferguson forged Damascus blade art knife. Ferguson uses a Damascus of tool steel and stainless, which is not acceptable to the ABS.

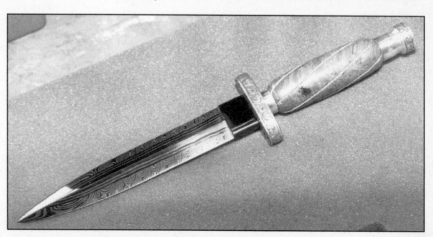

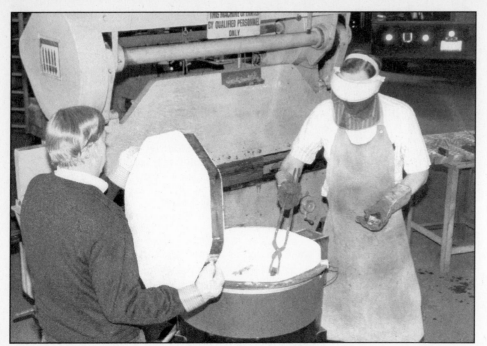

Jim Ferguson uses the most modern equipment available in his knifemaking to produce top-notch quality.

(Below) A powerful machine shop hammer makes quicker work of the red-hot blades, but great skill and strength are still needed for the work.

er's JS or MS stamp must be considered one of the best products of its kind available.

According to the Society's guidlines:

> Design can be very subjective. However, it is the objective of the ABS and the applicant to create well designed knives. A well designed knife will have the proper amount of material in the blade and handle—neither too much nor too little. It is important to design and construct a knife for the intended end use. The applicant should keep in mind that form follows function.
>
> A knife of good design will be more appealing than an equally well made knife of poor design. The objective must be to make a good knife with good design. The following guidelines should be reflected upon and taken into consideration when designing and constructing a forged knife.

Blade Construction:

Flatness, bevels and finishes are to be uniform. Blade surfaces must be free from scratches. Mirror polish, satin or hand-rubbed finishes are acceptable. A distal taper will provide good balance and feel to the completed knife. Damascus blades must be free of faults and pits.

Guard Construction:

The guard must be symmetrical and centered on the blade (side to side). Solder fittings shall be clean and appealing, free from lumps, holes or voids. The guard should be free from scratches and finished uniformly.

Handle Construction:

The handle must be symmetrical and centered on the blade, with even radii on sides and end, clean fit on all matching surfaces with no checks or splits around the pins.

Shape and Form:

A knife is three dimensional. Various lines and shapes show planes of light reflections to the viewer. Convex and concave areas make for exciting shapes. Realistic design should look like a natural object.

Proportions:

Proportion is the relationship of the sections, areas, spacers or parts of the knife to each other as well as to the handle as a whole. Exact mathematical precision and measurement are not essential. The knifemaker's eye for proportions, once acquired, remains the best tool for creating a successfully unified knife design.

Balance:

There is little trouble in achieving balance when symmetry is used. When opposite sides are close to being identical in weight, balance is achieved. The applicant should remember that aesthetic balance is as important as weight balance from a design standpoint. When a knife feels light in the hand, good balance has been achieved.

These guidelines are used when judging any knife, forged or not. They may be used when considering any manmade tool, including mass-produced factory-made knives. One might even argue that any work of art might be so judged.

The first thing a potential supplicant for Journeyman status must remember is that the blade, when tested, will be destroyed. It will be bent or broken—if it breaks, the knife fails—to a 90-degree angle. After that, it is an expensive souvenir. For the Journeyman level, the knife must be forged of standard steel. No laminated or Damascus blades are permitted at that level.

Many of the ABS knifemakers prefer to do it the old-fashioned way, with hammer and anvil and lots of elbow grease.

The Master Bladesmith level tests only a Damscus blade of a different size.

The Journeyman test knife must be 15 inches overall, with a blade width of 2 inches. The blade length can be no longer than 10 inches. The handle may be of any configuration, with or without a guard, bolsters or ferrule, and handle material is irrelevant to the test. As mentioned, steel choice is up to the knifemaker, so long as it is neither Damascus nor stainless.

After a verbal quiz, the knife must pass through four steps, in a prescribed order: rope cutting, wood chopping, shaving hair and bending. All test supplies must be furnished by the applicant.

The purpose of the rope cutting is to test the edge geometry and sharpness of the blade. A 1-inch-diameter sisal or manila rope must hang freely, not touching anything. It must be cut through with the test knife, about 6 inches from the end. The knifemaker is given one attempt. It the rope is not severed, the test judge may authorize two additional attempts. If it appears to him that the maker lacks the strength or skill to cut the rope, the tester may try. The idea is to test the blade, not the maker. If the rope is not cut through, the knife and maker fail.

The next part of the test is wood chopping, designed to test edge toughness. The maker must use the test knife to cut through a 4-foot 2x4 board in two places. After the board is cut twice, the Master Smith conducting the test examines the edge for nicks, chips, flat spots, rolled edges or deformations. If anything shows, the knife fails.

Part three is concerned with shaving hair. No honing or sharpening of the blade is permitted during any part of the testing. The same section of the blade that was used to cut the rope and chop the wood must shave enough hair to demonstrate that the blade edge remains keen and shaving-sharp.

The final test is to bend the blade 90 degrees to prove the heat treatment of the blade. It must have a soft back and a hard edge. The blade is placed in a vise, tip down, and bent to a 90-degree angle. A pipe or other leverage may be placed over the handle to facilitate the bending. At the Master Smith's descretion, some cracking of the blade is permitted, but no more than two-thirds of the width of the blade. Any chips from the blade or any tang breaks will fail the knife.

There are several more administrative and time requirements for final Journeyman membership acceptance in the ABS. Failures may be retested according to a published schedule.

A Journeyman Smith may apply for a Master performance test a year after passing all the criteria above. The same four performance tests, in the same order as for Journeyman, must be passed to become a Master Smith. However, the knife requirements are more stringent.

The test knife must be a hand-forged pattern-welded Damascus blade. The tang must be of the stick type, a hidden tang inside the handle. A full tang is not acceptable for the Master Smith test.

The knife must be 15 inches long overall, with a blade 2 inches wide. Blade length is 10 inches. The blade may be any pattern-welded Damascus steel with more than 300 welded laminations. The combination of steels or the pattern in the billet is irrelevant. The Damascus cannot be laminated to a central core steel piece, such as in a San Mai laminated construction.

Before the maker is declared a Master Smith, the ABS has several other requirements, including the submission to a panel of judges of at least five completed forged knives of various styles. The maker also is required to present the five knives at the annual ABS Show and Meeting within three years of passing the performance test. Verbal testing also is required before final certification.

Most readers would agree that the testing procedures are rather severe. We know of many knives that would not come close to passing some or any the tests. Any number of blades will shave hair off a forearm, but whether they would do it after cutting a rope and chopping through a 2x4 is problematic. Any knife that will accomplish these tasks without noticeable damage must be judged to be among the best.

The ABS has three classes of membership, and one does not have to be an expert knifemaker to fit into the Society. Director members are those who are on the board of directors and who have the rights and powers of members of a non-stock, non-profit corporation under the laws of the state of Maryland.

Non-director members are not members of the board of directors. They have no vote in the affairs of the group. They are further designated as Bladesmith members, those who make knives or tools by forging. Associate members are those who do not forge, but who "are sincerely interested in and support the purposes of the Society." Thus, a person can be a member of the ABS without forging knives.

A final category is that of Honorary member. The board of directors may award honorary membership to any person or persons deemed by the board "to have contributed significantly to bladesmithing."

It is obvious that knives made as described are not sold at low prices. They should be the cream of the crop, and the makers have so many hours in them and the demand for the better makers' output so high, the buyer must pay top dollar. However, the potential investor/user should remember that a

This blade is being cut from the original steel on the anvil, rather than with a bandsaw or sanding belt.

Bladesmiths have been known to haunt equipment auctions to find older machines that are still useful, such as this power hammer.

Perhaps it is not pretty, but a forged hand-made knife such as this one is rugged and useful for many tasks.

couple of decades ago, some of the best forged knives available were on the market for less than $100 each. Needless to say, they are worth many times that today. We cannot predict that today's makers will produce knives worth ten times their current selling price, but good knives always have been in demand.

Potential Bladesmiths need to labor and learn in isolation. The ABS operates and sponsors several schools at various times and places across the country. The ABS secretary, B.R. Hughes, offers a report of a recent Hammer-In class elsewhere in this book. Other schools and training programs are open to beginners and skilled knifemakers, with classes to match their needs.

The training is definitely hands-on and hands-dirty. The Society also offers a couple of Bill Moran instructional videos on the art of forging knives.

The ABS is establishing a museum at the Arkansas Territorial Museum in Little Rock, Arkansas. It's sure to be filled with historical knives, equipment, tools and displays.

In 1991, Bill Moran was elected as chairman emeritus of the ABS. He is the first person to hold that office. At this writing, Joseph Cordova is the chairman of the board of directors for the American Bladesmith Society. Membership and general information may be obtained by writing to American Bladesmith Society.

Teaching the Basics of Forging

FOR THE BENEFIT of the uninitiated, a hammer-in is a sort of gathering of the clan, wherein the aficionados of the forged blade assemble to share information on materials, techniques, tools and tricks of the trade.

"It must be conceded early in the game that any study of hammer-ins should involve a brief history of the impressive growth in the popularity of bladesmithing that has taken place over the past two decades or so, and which is closely tied to the American Bladesmith Society," according to B.R. Hughes, a founding member of the organization.

Until comparatively recent times, the vast majority of quality blades were created by forging—striking metal heated in a forge with a hammer as the glowing steel was held on an anvil. This was hot, dirty, time-consuming work, and it required considerable knowledge on the part of the smith, who had to accurately gauge the temperature of the heated metal by its color.

"By the mid-20th century, advancements in the field of alloyed steel, particularly those of a stain-resistant nature, combined with the popularity of blades made by the stock-removal procedure, seemed to indicate that forging as a practical means of producing knife blades was on its last legs!" Hughes reports.

Simply put, stock-removal means a knifemaker takes a bar of steel, fresh from the mills, and using a metal-cutting bandsaw and a power grinder, removes everything that doesn't look like the desired blade. Next, the blade will be heat-treated in a vacuum oven—sometimes in the maker's shop, sometimes at a commercial heat-treating firm—to bring the metal to the desired hardness level. The steel then will receive its final grinding and polishing.

So it was that by 1971 there were less than a dozen smiths in the United States actively forging blades for sale to the public. In alphabetical order, these hearty souls seemed to represent at that time the last of a dying breed: Bill Bagwell, Clyde Fischer, Wayne Goddard, Don Hastings, C.M. "Pete" Heath, Jon Kirk, Jimmy Lile, Joe Martin, W.F. "Bill" Moran, W.D. "Bo" Randall, and R.H. "Rudy" Ruana. Just for the record, a bit later, because of health problems, Lile ceased forging his blades, although he remained active as a stock-removal knifemaker.

"Then, in 1973, Moran gave bladesmithing a much-needed shot of adrenaline when he unveiled the first hammer-welded Damascus steel blades to be made in America in modern times. This beautiful, patterned material had achieved almost legendary proportions, and while swords in museums of the world attested to the fact that it was not mere myth, the secret of how it was made seemed to have been lost along the way. Moran had been trying to produce this material for several years, and

Master bladesmith Charles Ochs demonstrates how to produce a Damascus billet with stress on heat control, using a gas forge and a power hammer.

on more than one occasion he gave up the quest," B.R. Hughes recalls.

"Like a siren's song, though, the allure was too strong to resist. Once the key was found, he produced several finished knives and displayed them at the Knifemakers Guild Show in Kansas City that year. This captured the imaginations of knifemakers and buyers alike, and once it was discovered that this material could only be made at the forge, several makers vowed on the spot to become bladesmiths."

During this same span of time, Moran began to converse with Hughes concerning his idea of forming an organization that would be dedicated solely to the preservation and advancement of the forged blade. Many letters were exchanged, and after the 1976 Guild Show, held that year in Dallas, Texas, Bill Bagwell, Don Hastings and Moran—the only three bladesmiths forging Damascus at that time—met in Bagwell's shop near

Roger Green explains how he achieves the flawless hand-rubbed finish on his blades. The secret involves as much as ten hours of dedicated work on a single blade.

James Crowell explains the tricks of the trade when using a flat grinder with a wide, 8-inch belt. He received his rating as a master bladesmith from the American Bladesmith Society in 1986.

Vivian, Louisiana. They invited Hughes to share the day with them.

On that hot July afternoon, the seeds of the American Bladesmith Society were planted, and this ultimately led to the formal creation of the society in December 1976, with the four listed serving as founding fathers. Moran was named chairman, a post he was to hold for the next fifteen years. He quickly projected the concept that the only hope of having bladesmithing in America was to educate not only aspiring smiths, but the general public as well, so knife buyers could learn to appreciate the differences between a forged blade and one made by stock removal.

In 1983, with the assistance of Leon Borgman of the University of Wyoming, the first ABS hammer-in was held in DuBois, Wyoming, with Bagwell, Hastings and Moran serving as instructors for fourteen students. Pleased with the success of this initial undertaking, another hammer-in was held in Washington, Arkansas, in the spring of 1984, cosponsored by the ABS and Texarkana College, where Hughes then was dean of students.

This event attracted eighteen students, who met in the reconstruction of James Black's smithy, where that worthy forged a knife for James Bowie in the winter of 1830-31. While the Wyoming hammer-in was later dropped, the Washington seminar proved so popular that by 1986, James Powell, the director of continuing education at Texarkana College, had to turn away prospective students due to the limitations of the facility!

Moran was not satisfied with simply sponsoring weekend seminars on forging, and he expressed his dream of seeing a school of bladesmithing established where would-be smiths could spend several days learning how to forge, how to fit handles and guards, and even how to make Damascus steel. The ABS board of directors supported this idea, and in the late summer of 1986, Moran and Hughes met with the Pioneer Washington Restoration Foundation to explain the quest of preserving an ancient art form. During the course of the meeting, this group agreed to build a suitable facility in the old town.

The instructors would come from the ever-growing ranks of ABS master bladesmiths. At the same time, Texarkana College would provide supervision of the classes, plus all of the required materials and supplies. The college, a state-supported institution, is located about thirty-five miles from Washington. All of this was made possible in large measure by a generous grant provided for this purpose by St. Louis businessman and knife collector Jeffrey Harris, who had attended a hammer-in and was favorably impressed with what he had seen and heard.

The bladesmithing school officially opened in late April 1988, and the excellent facilities included a large shop area containing six forging stations, two power hammers, and work benches with six power grinders and a number of vises. Only a few feet away was a large classroom that would hold up to twenty-five students.

This provided not only a splendid environment for teaching students how to forge and make knives, it also made it possible to increase the number of individuals who could attend the hammer-ins and to expand the offerings at these events. So, it was now a rather simple matter to handle seventy-five to eighty students. However, much quicker than anyone might have anticipated, even this expansion failed to keep up with the ever-increasing number who wanted to enroll.

Encouraged by the success of the ABS/TC hammer-ins, other seminars were created, with the one sponsored by the

Master bladesmith Greg Neely prepares his coal forge for a demonstration on hand-forging a blade during a session of the hammer-in conducted in Washington, Arkansas.

Greg Neely uses a firm but not heavy hammer blow to shape the heated metal into the desired blade shape. This steel in this case is 5160, which lends itself well to forging.

Alabama Forge Council being one of the more popular. Under the leadership of Dr. James Bastion, an ABS master bladesmith, the AFC annually attracts some 100 to 125 participants to its April conclave.

In 1992, James Powell was promoted to associate dean of instruction at Texarkana College, and Scotty Hayes was named to head the institution's non-credit division, which included the school of bladesmithing. One of Hayes' first innovations was to launch a fall hammer-in, which, in theory at least, should double the number of individuals who could attend, although in practice it must be said that a great many—perhaps even a majority—attend both! Scotty Hayes also instigated the practice of having large tents erected on the grounds of the school so that as many as three activities could occur at the same time.

With that preamble out of the way, let's take a look at a recent hammer-in held in the historic little hamlet of Washington. The event was blessed by clear skies and cool temperatures, with some sixty-five participants in attendance. In alphabetical order, here's the all-star cast of instructors who taught during the busy two days:

James Crowell, Mountain View, Arkansas, received his ABS master's stamp in 1986, making him one of the real veterans of this august group. Crowell was the recipient of the first W. F. Moran Award, presented for the best knife exhibited by an ABS member at the society's national show.

Freddy Duvall, Benton, Arkansas, is a maker of folding knives who has established an enviable reputation for himself since turning out his first folder in 1981.

Jerry Fisk, Lockesburg, Arkansas, earned his master's stamp in 1993, and since that time has won more national and international honors than any other smith. He is the only man to have won the W.F. Moran Award twice.

Freddy Duvall shows students the proper alignment for construction of a lockback folding knife. This craftsman from Benton, Arkansas, is noted for good work at modest prices.

Joe Flournoy, El Dorado, Arkansas, was awarded his MS in 1992, and the next year won *The Blade Magazine* Award for the best forged knife at the International Blade Show and Cutlery Fair. He is also a past winner of the W.F. Moran Award.

Bert Gaston, North Little Rock, Arkansas, has won critical acclaim for his meticulous workmanship and his careful attention to detail. He received his master's rating in 1993 and is a product of the School of Bladesmithing.

Roger Green, Joshua, Texas, is a protege of the late legendary knifemaker Ed Henry, and since 1991 he has carved a worldwide reputation for himself among collectors and makers alike! He is particularly noted for his immaculate hand-rubbed blades.

Al Lawrence, DeQueen, Arkansas, not only provides blade and handle materials for many of today's knifemakers, he is also an active supporter of the ABS and the Arkansas Knifemakers Association.

Greg Neely, Houston, Texas, another product of the school,

earned his master's in 1993, and while his knife output is extremely limited due to his full-time work as a homicide lieutenant with the Houston Police Department, he has found time to produce some truly outstanding pieces.

Charles Ochs, Largo, Florida, was the 1989 recipient of the W.F. Moran Award. That was a big year for him, because he also received his master's stamp at the same show. Knife buffs greatly admire his renditions of Bill Scagel classics.

Timothy Potier, Oberlin, Louisiana, won *The Blade Magazine's* 1994 award for Best Forged Knife, and he also received his Master's Stamp from the ABS that same year. Potier has received almost as many kudos for his tomahawks as for his knives.

Kenny Rowe, Hope, Arkansas, is a leatherworker whose artistry has quickly won him a national following. A second-generation sheath and holster maker, he is also an active writer whose prose has been featured in several knife journals.

A.A. Sanders, Oklahoma City, Oklahoma, is a well-known maker of lockback folders that feature clean lines, excellent workmanship and attractive prices. This hammer-in marked his first appearance as an instructor in Washington.

Next, let's consider the various topics covered at the '95 fall seminar: Air Hammer Operation; Fitting Guards and Butt Caps; Hand Forging; Inlaying an Escutcheon Plate; How to Make a Wrist Axe; Lock-Back Folders; Point and Clip Grinding; Rubbed Blade Finishes; Slip-Back Folders; Temperature Control; and Wrapped Ferrules. But equally important is the constant give and take between those attending the conference. At almost any time, it was possible to spot some aspiring smith asking a question of one of the many masters in attendance, including David Anders, Michael Connor, James Ray Cook, Steve Dunn and Roger Massey. They came to learn, but they were never too busy to lend a helping hand.

Obviously, hammer-ins have come a long way since the one held in 1983, which consisted primarily of demonstrating how a blade was forged. Of course, not too many folks knew how to forge back in those days! Now, these meetings offer basic information as well as lore for the advanced smiths. Crowell has

attended almost every hammer-in either as an instructor or a student and once stated he had never been to one at which he did not pick up at least one tip that was more than worth the cost of attendance, which is about $100.

A recent addition to the school, demonstrated for the first time at this hammer-in, is an air-hammer donated by The Order of the Mystic Brotherhood, a fraternal, non-profit organization dedicated to the advancement of bladesmithing. At a cost of about $9,000, not every smith will be able to add one to his or her shop, but all who saw it in use were impressed with this new piece of equipment.

Following Neely's session on forging, he was asked what he considered to be the single most important aspect of producing a blade in this manner. "Keep the heat of the steel 'just right'!" he replied. "Don't try to forge the metal if it's a bit too cool or a little too hot." Queried on his choice of blade materials for non-Damascus blades, he quickly responded, "I like a good spring steel such as 5160 or a high-carbon steel like 1084. The latter possesses an almost ideal manganese content, which permits deep hardening." Then he quickly added, "But it's not the steel so much as it is proper techniques on the part of the smith. A good bladesmith can turn out a superior blade from a wide variety of steels."

That represents just one example of the type of information that is available for the asking at a typical hammer-in. And

Timothy Potier teaches the art of making a small hand axe. This session was conducted in a tent outside the main shop of the bladesmith school.

Greg Neely uses one of the bladesmith school's power hammers to demonstrate its function to a group of interested students.

Timothy Potier (right) points out an area on a knife that needs improvement by J.T. Gorenflo. This type of personal exchange of techniques is one of the strong points of the hammer-ins.

Joe Flournoy, a past winner of the W.F. Moran Award, uses one of the school's Bader belt sanders to grind the clip area of a large Bowie.

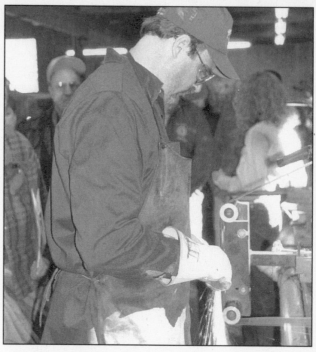

don't think you're ever too advanced to learn! Master smith Michael Connor, Winters, Texas, has taught at the school many times, but he was enrolled as a student at this particular seminar. A protege of the late Don Hastings, one of ABS's founders, Connor's work is greatly admired by advanced collectors, and when he executes an escutcheon plate, it appears that it literally grew out of the handle material. But after Green's section on such plates, Connor reported he had learned a new technique and could hardly wait to get back to his shop and put it into practice.

The key element of Green's inlaying style is to first make the hole in the knife handle, then fit the escutcheon plate into the cavity. Most makers execute the plate first, then try to create the proper-sized hollow in the handle.

"If I mess up," Roger Green said with a smile, "all I have to do is make a new escutcheon plate. But if you try it the other way, you may have to construct another handle!"

The key to a flawless inlay is not technique, according to this affable Texan, it's patience. "That sounds too pat," Green acknowledged, "but it is the truth. I've been doing this type of work for years, and while I can now fit a plate in about 15 minutes, when I started, it would take two to three hours. Devote whatever time it requires to do it right. Trying and fitting is the name of this game."

The matter of practicality must always be maintained when teaching in a hammer-in. Kenny Rowe has a well-equipped shop and can handle any leather chore up to and including saddle-making. But during his demonstrations at the school, Rowe shows how it is possible to make attractive and functional sheaths using nothing more than a few hand tools.

"It would be a disservice to those attending," he explains, "to suggest they should go out and buy several thousand dollars worth of equipment to make a few sheaths. If you're in the leatherworking business, you must be set up to make hundreds of items, but most of these men and women simply want to

know how to make a decent sheath from time to time, and I'm pleased to show them."

Steve Dunn, another master, also attended as a student and, when asked about those who maintained they could not afford to attend activities in Washington, mused, "If you're serious about wanting to be a good bladesmith, you can't afford not to attend!"

Dunn, from Smiths Grove, Kentucky, added that students should enroll in the regular classes to gain hands-on experience, but pointed out that the hammer-ins provide information on many different topics, so all have their place in the scheme of things.

What do non-masters think of the programs offered at Washington? Mickey Ames, a journeyman smith from Lebo, Kansas, stated that he hated to miss any hammer-in. "I pick up valuable information that is available nowhere else, and perhaps even more important is the camaraderie so obvious between the bladesmiths. It's almost as if you are a member of a fraternity, and the generous spirit that prevails is something that must be experienced to be fully appreciated."

Some of those who attend are not practicing smiths. One such person at the fall affair was Jerome Smith, a beginning collector from Texarkana, Texas, who wanted to meet some of the smiths about whom he'd heard and read. It turned out well for all concerned, because Smith met a number of makers and ordered some knives!

It is traditional for the second day to begin with a "BYOB" early-morning gathering. That's "Bring your own Bowie," in case you're wondering. All of the participants—students and teachers alike—gather to show off their craftsmanship, and many knives were the objects of admiration as the group clustered around several display tables. The most frequently asked question was "How'd you do that?" And answers were forthcoming.

It seems that each hammer-in features new topics, such as

Jerry Fisk demonstrates the school's new air-hammer, using a length of wood to show how the hammer, properly controlled, can merely "touch" the wood without crushing it.

Bert Gaston tries his hand with the air-hammer. This new addition to the school's equipment was a contribution by the Order of the Mystic Brotherhood, a fraternal, non-profit organization that is dedicated to the advancement of the forged blade.

Bert Gaston explains to a class how to achieve an airtight fit between the guard and the blade. With the shop, the classroom and a tent, as many as three activities can take place at the same time.

Joe Flournoy shows students how to set up a machine safely before it is used to turn down a brass guard. Shop safety is stressed constantly at the school during regular classes as well as hammer-in sessions.

those on the operation of the air-hammer and inlaying escutcheon plates. Both the ABS and Texarkana College are looking into other possibilities for the future, but the emphasis will always be on proper forging, the heart and the spirit of the bladesmithing school.

"If we ever lose sight of that," admitted Scotty Hayes, the director, "we're in big trouble!"

Contact Texarkana College if you'd like more information on forthcoming hammer-ins or the regular bladesmithing classes.

Emil Morgan's Railroad Spikes

WHEN EMIL MORGAN fires up his forge in his backyard patio, most of his neighbors have no idea what he is doing. Morgan is a private, unassuming man who likes to make knives, and he likes to do it in what many might believe is the hard way.

Morgan has reached an age where he is eligible to receive a full Social Security retirement check. He has worked hard all his life at difficult, demanding, labor-intensive work, yet he shows no signs of slowing down.

Morgan is not new to knifemaking, having been at it for more than fifty years. He made his first knife in 1944, and his first knife for sale in 1978. Most of his knives are produced by the stock-removal method. He cuts and grinds out a blade shape from steel bar stock, the method common with many custom knifemakers.

Most of the time, he prefers to make knives of the popular 440C stainless steel, like many other knifemakers, and he produces some excellent hunting knives, fighters and fillet knives. Successful hunters who use the Morgan knives swear by their edge-holding ability, utilitarian shape and practical application. Although his knives are in demand by hunters and others, they sell in the low-to-medium price range.

The stock-removal stainless steel knives by Morgan all are heat-treated by the well-known Paul Bos of California. Bos sub-zero quenches blades that have nickel or chromium in their alloy, thus ensuring the grain structure is transformed and that stain-resistance is optimum. Knives made of high carbon content are heat-treated by Morgan in his shop. He uses a blow-torch to heat the metal to what he considers the proper temperature, judging the heat level by the color of the blade. It is a skill he has developed in his decades of experience.

Morgan has a well equipped workshop in his converted garage in Thousand Oaks, California, about an hour north of Los Angeles. The weather is usually pleasant and beyond most of the big-city smog. Over the years, he has acquired and modified all the power and hand tools he might need for his art. He works hard at his craft, and it shows in his knives.

Knifemaker Emil Morgan fires up his backyard coal forge before heating railroad spikes.

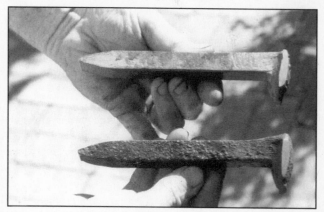

New or used spikes may be used by Morgan to forge knives. The metal is similar.

A code is usually found on the spike head. The HC here designates the spike as having high carbon steel.

With the coal fire at the proper level, the spike is heated to just the right temperature, as the maker's experience indicates.

With the spike glowing bright orange, it is locked in a bench vise. This is where the muscle power comes in. Morgan grips the spike with a heavy wrench and twists 180 degrees.

In more recent years, Emil Morgan has begun experimenting with forging techniques in his home workshop. He now makes knives from old—and new—railroad spikes. The technique is simple, logical and fast. Starting with a spike, he can turn out a finished knife in about half a day. Using several spikes and working a mini production line, Morgan can produce ten to twelve simple knives a day, finished, sharpened and ready to use. The only thing needed to take the knife to the hunting camp is a simple leather belt sheath, which Morgan supplies with each knife.

Most of us may not know that there is a difference between old railroad spikes and new ones; it's not much, but there definitely is some difference. Morgan says, however, that the techniques of forging and sharpening them into knives is the same for both types. But aside from the appearance of the spikes—old ones look old, used and mostly rusty—there is a slight difference in the steel alloys. In modern track building, the spikes are driven in by power hammers. The spikes need to be a bit harder than they were in the old days when they were driven into the wood ties by human-powered sledge hammers.

The heads of the spikes, old and new, are marked with a code. The letters HC indicate high-carbon steel. Additional numbers and letters have a meaning to railroad maintenance workers, but are insignificant to knifemakers.

There is some demand for used spikes from collectors, but on most railroad tracks, they are replaced on a regular schedule. There is no shortage of used railroad spikes, as yet. Unless an old spike is rusted more than halfway through, there is enough metal in the body to forge a useful knife from almost any of them.

Before he starts to forge, Morgan grinds down the outer shape of the spike head somewhat to reduce the width of the butt. He leaves most the head codes alone to add to the charm of the finished knife. A few customers prefer to have everything clean and shiny, and Morgan will accommodate them. Otherwise, no more grinding is done on the metal until after it has been forged.

Emil Morgan uses a simple coal-fired forge that looks like an open barbecue, only with heavier metal bottom and sides. The bottom is filled with concrete to prevent the metal from burning out too soon. He uses a variable-speed electric blower to regulate the amount of oxygen reaching the coal fire.

Now the blade end is heated bright red to orange, and the spike is placed on the anvil, ready for the hammer.

Skill, rather than brute force, is the key to forging a knife blade by hand.

Experience determines how hot the fire needs to be. Basically, the coal should be glowing orange to yellow across an area large enough to encompass the entire blade or blades to be forged. Most forgers—blacksmiths— prefer to work outdoors if the weather permits, but under deep shade so a judgment on the color of the coals and steel is easier to make. Morgan works under his outdoor patio cover.

He pushes the rail spike into the coals after the fire has been burning for about fifteen minutes, occasionally shifting and turning the steel and the coals to maintain even heat. When what will be the handle portion of the spike has reached the optimum color and temperature, he grabs it with a pair of blacksmith tongs and clamps the butt end in a heavy shop vise. Once fixed, he grabs the protruding end of the spike with a large, strong wrench and twists the metal 180 degrees. The twisted metal will be the handle of the knife. We have seen other knifemakers using this technique to put a 360-degree twist to the handle. It is a matter to be determined by the artist and/or the customer.

With the twist done, the knife blank goes back into the forge while the blade portion is heated to orange-yellow. The glowing spike/almost-knife then goes to the anvil to be hammered into blade shape.

This is where the skill and experience of the forger shows. Physical strength plays a part in the forging process, but the correctly placed hammer does the real work. The blade must be reheated and hammered several times until it reaches the approximate shape of the intended blade. While the blade is being forged to shape, the grains of the steel are being packed tighter along the edge for a tougher knife.

Eventually, the spike will assume the desired knife shape, and it is set aside to air cool enough that it may be safely handled. The shape is only approximate and there is plenty of grinding and shaping yet to be done. The blade is ground down to its final outline on a belt sander. It needs to be thinned somewhat and may be flat-ground or hollow-ground in its final form. Some customers prefer that Morgan leave the corrosion pits and other imperfections in an old-spike knife. They contribute a unique appearance to the finish.

Morgan likes to leave the handle in rather rough form. However, some customers prefer a smoother handle surface. This step is done on a belt sander and buffing wheel. The handle por-

After the knife has cooled enough to handle, it must be ground to final shape on a belt sander.

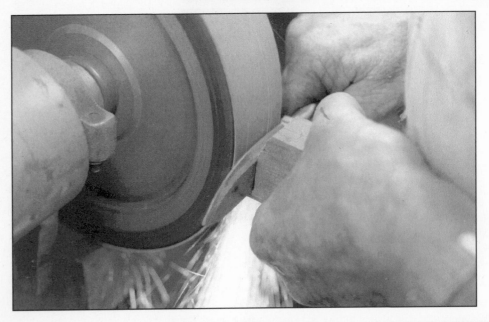

Morgan uses a simple wood jig to sand the hollow-grind on the blade.

A blowtorch is used to reheat the blade for heat-treating. The cherry-red blade is then plunged into a bucket of water for final quenching.

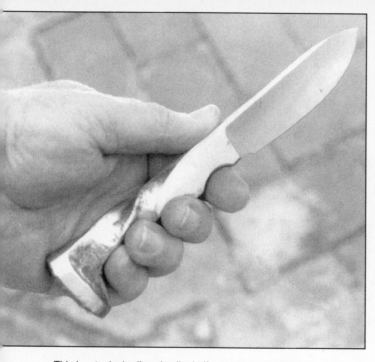

This is a typical railroad spike knife, ready for the field.

These are the three phases of creating a simple knife from a common railroad spike.

tion may be smoothed and sanded as much as the blade, if the customer wants it.

On his forged blades, Morgan does his own heat-treating. He uses a propane blow torch to heat the blade to cherry red. This step is best done inside the workshop for color/heat uniformity. When the blade has reached the proper color, it is plunged into a water quench.

After the knife is quenched and cooled, all that remains for finishing is sanding, polishing and edge-sharpening. There is no other handle to apply because the twisted spike creates a natural finger-grip handle.

Morgan puts a light coat of machine oil on his spike knives before they are delivered. Rail spikes are not made of stainless steel, and they will rust if not cared for properly. If kept away from excess moisture, the amount of care is minimal. The edge is extremely sharp, favorably commented on by those who have used any of these knives. The knives are heat-treated to be not too hard, so they can be easily resharpened when necessary. All are hand-forged, shaped and finished, so no two are alike. Each will twist differently, have a different thickness, blade shape and size.

The railroad spike knives can be delivered in about a week. Other popular designs may take up to four months for delivery. Emil Morgan makes his own leather sheaths for all his knives, as required.

KNIFEMAKERS GUILD

More than a quarter of a century ago, these custom craftsmen had a meeting of the minds

"IN THE LATE 1960s, I had a dozen or more knifemaker friends, all of whom I thought were great fellows, but they all despised one another and seemed to feel any other knifemaker would be taking business away from them."

Those are the words of A.G. Russell, dating back nearly thirty years to the time when custom knifemaking was being recognized by outdoorsmen and collectors as an art and worthy of support.

At that time, Russell was on the edge of the custom knife business, if it could be called that, for he was engaged in selling Arkansas sharpening stones from his home base in Springdale, Arkansas. Due to the nature of his business, he soon came to know a number of custom makers across the nation and could not understand the continuing animosity that existed among them.

"I knew that if I could just get these people together, they would like each other as much as I liked each of them," Russell recalls today. "I also believed it would be possible to get a great deal more publicity for an organized group of knifemakers than for each of them, one at a time.

"Yes, I was certainly young and naive," the Arkansas native admits, "but it really worked in the end. There were a few who saw no reason for not joining together in some sort of mutual effort. R.W. Loveless and Dan Dennehy both were fast becoming well-known makers at the time and I talked over my idea with them.

"Then I bought twenty tables at the Sahara Antique Gun Show in Las Vegas and invited knifemakers to come and display their knives. Come they did and most of them found they could learn from each other." Russell adds, though, that "a few of them were so sure of their own superiority that they knew no one could match them.

A.G. Russell is probably most responsible for founding the Knifemakers Guild. After discussing the possibilities with Bob Loveless and Dan Dennehy, he rented tables at a gun show and invited knifemakers to display and meet.

"The ones who felt they could learn and benefit from associating with other knifemakers were interested in forming some sort of a guild."

A number of those displaying at the Las Vegas show agreed to meet that summer at the antique gun show to be held in Tulsa, Oklahoma.

At that time, A.G. Russell was running a newsletter for his customers, the knifemakers who used his Russell Sharpening Stones. R.W. Loveless said during this initial meeting that he had some ideas on paper about forming a guild. Russell agreed to circulate the ideas with his periodic newsletter.

In June 1970, A.G. Russell again reserved a block of tables, and in off hours from the show, he and a dozen knifemakers sat down and formed the Knifemakers Guild.

When Dan Dennehy isn't making knives or tending to Guild business, he offers instruction in knife-throwing techniques. He was one of those who felt a professional organization should be formed.

Bob Loveless was the first secretary of the Guild, serving several terms in that post. A pioneer in custom knifemaking, he also was a founding member of the Guild.

"Actually, there were eleven founding members, and I was voted honorary president. The twelfth knifemaker walked out of the meeting when he was told he would have to give up using the commercially made Indian Ridge Trader blades and start hand-making the blades for his knives," Russell recalls now, more than a quarter-century after that eventful meeting.

In that first meeting, it was determined that the focus of the infant Guild would be to help each other with the technical aspects of knifemaking and to encourage ethical behavior between the knifemaker and his customers.

Up to that point there had been instances of some makers accepting deposits for handmade knives, but failing to deliver or even disappearing from the scene. It was generally agreed among members of the founding body that such practices reflected upon all of them, and that efforts should be made to bring a halt to such conduct.

R.W. (Bob) Loveless was elected Guild secretary—actually, the organization's chief executive officer—and it was decided to hold the new Knifemakers Guild's first show in conjunction with the Texas Gun Collectors show in Houston in July 1971.

During those early days, much was being written about custom knives and their makers, but according to Bob Loveless, a good deal of misinformation was being disbursed.

"We thought it was a good idea to set the record straight," Loveless tells us. "The purpose of the guild was purely and simply to promote knives and knifemakers.

"For most of us, knifemaking was then and is now a serious thing. It is the way we make our living and support our families. And we began the collective effort we call the Knifemakers Guild to bring our work in front of a larger audience and a broader marketplace.

"Beyond that," Loveless stated as long ago as 1974, "knifemaking is a singular craft and trade, and knifemakers are a proud bunch of men. We strive to do a simple job extremely well, and we felt the need, four years ago, to let the world know of us and our work."

That effort continues today and the annual Guild directory reflects the number of custom cutlers who have joined in that effort.

"Only a few years ago, knifemakers were a lonely bunch. We worked in isolation, making our mistakes and learning our lessons the hard way. And the best thing we took away from that first Las Vegas meeting was the sense that we were no longer alone," Loveless states. "We could get together to compare notes and get help on our problems.

"In those early days of the Guild, we seemed ready to share our hard-won knowledge and to pool our skills. This sense of fraternity influenced all of us in Tulsa at that founders' meeting and continues today as more and more new makers come to join us."

The founding members of the Knifemakers Guild who attended that 1970 Tulsa gathering were John Applebaugh of Blackwell, Oklahoma; Walter "Blackie" Collins of Atlanta, Georgia; John Nelson Cooper of Burbank, California; Dan Dennehy of Yuma, Arizona; T.M. Dowell of Bend, Oregon;

A past president of the Knifemakers Guild, Jim Nolan joined early in the life of the organization. He passed away in 1980, leaving his brother to carry on the business.

Mike Franklin was a Guild member from 1973 until 1982, then rejoined the organization in 1994 after an extended illness.

Chubby Hueske of Bellaire, Texas; John Kirk of Fayetteville, Arkansas; R.W. Loveless of Riverside, California; John Owens of Miami, Florida; Jim Pugh of Azle, Texas; and G.W. Stone of Richardson, Texas.

The charter for the Knifemakers Guild stated that members would meet once a year to exchange information and to display their wares. The original eleven members were at the guild's second formal meeting in Houston, and they were joined by what Loveless describes as "a whole bunch of knifemakers. The guild grew by twenty-one new members, almost tripling in size."

In 1972, the annual meeting was held in Kansas City, where ten new members joined the Guild. "We got around to agreeing on a set of bylaws, which were distributed by our new secretary, Bill Moran," Loveless recalls.

"We felt welcome in Kansas City," he says, "and liked the way the Missouri Valley Arms Collectors' Association ran their show. We voted to return in 1973.

"Houston had been the seed show," Loveless adds, "where we learned how many of us there were. Kansas City showed us what fine work really was, as new knives and new designs seemed to come out of the woodwork. We all began to feel a strong sense of pride in what we were accomplishing."

By the time the second Kansas City show came about in August 1973, Bob Loveless had had a full year to think up what A.G. Russell describes as "more trouble." Loveless contended the organization was large enough and strong enough by this time to publish its own membership directory. The membership agreed about the need for such a project, and plans were made. Today, more than two decades later, the Knifemakers Guild Directory is an annual publication. Instead of the some sixty names that appeared in that first edition, however, the pages

An early custom knifemaker, R.D. Nolan joined the Guild in 1978, working with his now deceased brother in a shop near Pike's Peak in the Colorado wilds.

now contain the names and locations of literally hundreds of members.

It was at this 1973 meeting that the Guild named its first honorary life member. The person so honored was one of the original founders of the Guild, John Applebaugh. He had gone suddenly blind in the midst of an active knifemaking career.

"We missed his quiet composure and calm humor," A.G. Russell states today, "and he is remembered by the many friends he made among us."

That second Kansas City show for the members of the Knife-makers Guild more than suggested that the organization had arrived on the national scene and no longer was considered an experiment.

Prominent collectors came from across the country to acquire new knives from a broad variety of designs and materials. And

it was there that Bill Moran introduced his beautiful, authentic reproductions of Damascus blades. According to Loveless, "These blades were the hit of the show and knifemakers suddenly were scrambling for information on how to relearn what amounted to a lost art at that time: the forging of Damascus blades!"

Returning to Kansas City for the 1974 gathering, Loveless, reelected the previous year as secretary, pointed out to the membership that the bylaws of the organization provided for a class of membership composed of people who are not knife-makers.

"They are the associate members," Loveless reminded, "those many people who have given uncommon support to knifemakers everywhere.

"Some of them are authors who have told the story of knife-making in just the last few years to an ever-growing readership. Some are advanced collectors, who have supported us with their purchases of our work and have assembled collections that they are proud to display in our annual show.

"Some of them have taken an interest in the technical side of knifemaking and have helped us with their investigations into esoteric points of metallurgy and materials," Loveless continued. "To all our associate members, we owe our gratitude and appreciation for their support, and we take this opportunity to acknowledge them publicly."

The Knifemakers Guild announced its first list of associate members at that Kansas City meeting. Included were Harry Archer, Richard Barney, John Bats, Jim Schippers, Billy Ray Hughes, Sid Latham, Shaw-Leibowitz, Jack Lewis, Phil Lobred, Dr. Gerard F. Lukaszewics, Al Mar, Dr. Harry November, Bob Schrimsher, Ken Warner, Dr. Richard J. Wever, George and Rita Winter and John Wootters. Dr. Wever, incidentally, was designated as the Guild physician, and he has treated many ills at the annual shows.

Since that meeting of the founding members in Tulsa in 1970, several of those original members have passed on: John Applebaugh, John Nelson Cooper, Chubby Hueske, John Kirk and G.W. Stone.

The growth of custom knifemaking, in general, has gone beyond anyone's expectations. The late W.D. "Bo" Randall, in 1979, wrote to Roger Combs: "When I started in 1938, there were only Scagel, Ruana and myself, as I recall. Now there are 580."

There probably are a great deal more custom knifemakers than that number in the nation today, but not all of them are members of the Knifemakers Guild. In fact, at this writing in late 1996, Guild membership stands at 349, with between forty and fifty probationaries, according to D'Alton Holder, the 1996-1997 president.

The probationary member program was set up early in the Guild's life and allows such membership to be granted by the board of directors. However, such status has some rather stringent rules and requirements:

Probationary member applicants:
1. Must apply in writing to the Guild president.
2. Must be engaged in the making of benchmade knives for

All members of the Knifemakers Guild mark their knives in one way or another, usually on the blade. However, Ted Dowell, a founding member, usually inserts a medallion bearing his initials in the handle as seen here.

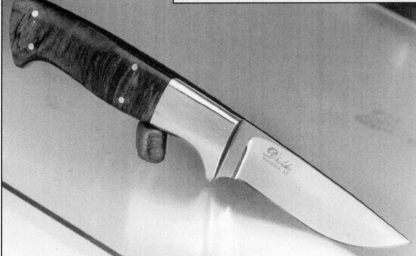

This knife by D'Alton Holder meets all of the requirements for workmanship demanded by the Guild. A member since 1973, he has held Guild offices since then and, at this writing, is the president.

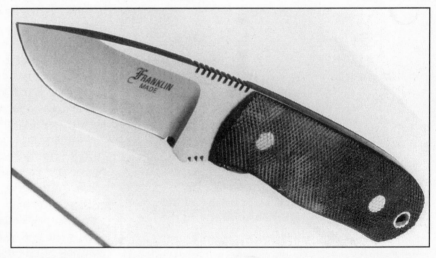

Makers generally mark their knives on the blade with their name, a logo or some other means of identification. This knife by Mike Franklin illustrates the point.

sale to the public, including the grinding and/or forging of his own knives.

3. Must offer a printed catalog of his knives.

4. Must submit an official recommendation list, signed and dated by four voting members in good standing.

5. Must attend the annual business meeting and show following his application for membership on a first-come, first-served, space-available basis at the discretion of the board of directors and display such number of knives as deemed proper by the directors or their designee(s). At the meeting, he will be considered for probationary membership.

6. Must attend and display knives for inspection by the technical committee at the second annual business meeting and show following election to probationary membership in order to be considered for voting membership. Failure to attend and display knives for inspection by the technical committee or to meet the criteria set forth by the technical committee will result in a one-year extension of probationary membership.

Failure to attend and display knives for inspection by the technical committee or to meet the criteria set forth by the committee at the third annual business meeting and show following election to probationary membership will result in immediate and automatic termination of membership.

7. Must not claim in his advertising to be a Guild member.

There also are rules for expulsion from the organization, most of them dealing with business ethics. As Bob Loveless told us long ago, "As I see it, the purpose of the Knifemakers Guild is to establish respect and status for our members. Anyone who violates that purpose shouldn't be a member."

DECORATING KNIVES

A beautiful knife can be made more attractive with the right artwork

PLAIN OR FANCY, a knife has a single purpose: to cut! In its simplest form, a knife is a piece of steel with a sharp edge along one side, a sharp point on the end and a wrapping or covering as a handle so the user can grip the tool.

But we always seem to want to improve on simplicity. We want our tools to look good as well as to do an efficient job. We have all seen many of the typical decorations and embellishments commonly found on knives: engraving, etching, carving, scrimshaw, coloring, plating, decorative pins and other artwork. Some artisans specialize in doing only the artwork on a knife made by someone else, much as an engraver might do on an expensive shotgun. Other knifemakers are able and willing to do all sorts of things to their own knives to make them more appealing to the eye.

Knife artwork might be divided into two categories: doing something to the metal blade and doing something to the handle material, whatever it might be. For centuries, the most common art decoration added to knife handles has been scrimshaw, an art that originated during the days of sailing vessels. Sailors would scratch pictures and designs in pieces of whale teeth and bones to while away idle hours aboard ship. It is an art form that is still practiced by numerous artists and now commonly seen on knife handles.

Natural materials such as elephant ivory, whale teeth and walrus tusks are sometimes scrimmed, but most of the new supplies of these materials are protected and may not be possessed, even by well-meaning artists. Only such material that can be proven as antique or from much older sources may be used for such things as knife handles. Many artists feel the amount of paperwork and red tape necessary to obtain these things are just not worth the effort.

Today, most knife handles suitable for scrimshaw work are made of plastic, white or ivory micarta, plus some other colored substances that will stand up well to hard usage. A cost factor is involved, too. The man-made materials are far less expensive than, say, old ivory.

One of the best practitioners of the scrimshaw art is Bob Engnath, also well known around the world for his sword blades. Engnath has been an artist all his life and has the background and talent to produce realistic animal and human figures that feature accurate depictions of anatomy. Much of his work is astonishingly realistic.

"My work consists almost entirely of very small dots on the material I use," said Engnath, during our visit to his Southern California workshop and studio. "This technique requires from four to six times as much time as line-type scrimshaw. But creating a piece of art that is nearly photographic in detail and shading is my goal, and the time is worth the effort.

"I have had considerable success in doing various animals, nudes or pin-up-type figures, American Indian portraits and character studies such as John Wayne in some of his roles. The dot-type scrimshaw does not lend itself to subjects with a lot of lines such as birds or sailing ships. I generally prefer to convince my clients to avoid those subjects."

Bob Engnath's research library is extensive enough that it is relatively easy to locate a photo of almost any animal, usually in a variety of poses.

"The big predatory cats are my favorites," says the artist, "particularly tigers.

"Work can be done using a client's photos, too. For those who enjoy the female form, I will do classic or full frontal

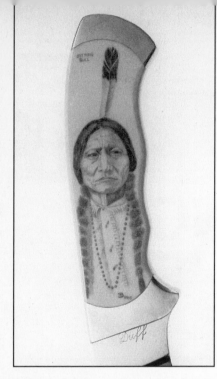

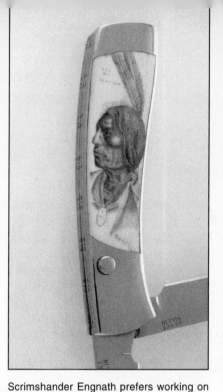

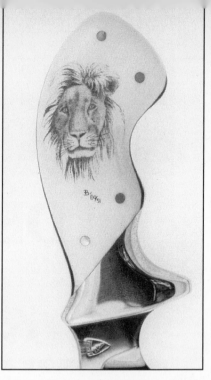

Historic Indian figures seem to be a favorite of the scrimshaw artists. This rendition of Sitting Bull was done by Bob Engnath on a Bill Duff custom knife.

Scrimshander Engnath prefers working on elephant ivory whenever available. This portrait of Sioux Indian Slow Bull was done on a Sawby-Mullen folder several years ago.

The late Norm Levine made the knife, and Engnath did the scrimshaw of the king of beasts. The grips are ivory micarta.

nudes, but I prefer that they be in good taste, not some raunchy shot from a nudie magazine."

Engnath charges hourly rates for most work, such as on knife handles. He is able to provide the customer with a reasonable estimate of how many hours the job will take, before beginning any work. In fact, he is able to guarantee that the price will be within fifteen percent of the original estimate. Larger collector pieces will be more expensive. For a piece of ivory about 2½ by 5 inches oval, the price would include a display box. The customer may supply the ivory or other material to be scrimshawed, or Engnath often has a supply of materials.

Prices also are based upon the difficulty of the work. A flat knife handle is easier to work than one on which the design must wrap around a curve. A design on a semi-automatic pistol grip, relatively flat, costs far less than the same pattern on a rounded knife handle or on a single-action revolver grip. The rounded version will cost twice as much as one on a flat surface.

Says Engnath, "If you take a John Wayne image with a gray hat instead of a black hat, you save yourself a third of the cost. The black hat can take a couple of days work. It will also make me mumble unpleasant things about your ancestry while I work."

The scrimshander sometimes uses old photos to guide his efforts, as in this likeness of Bear Bull on a Davis boot knife.

The opposite side of the Davis boot knife features the face of Red Wing.

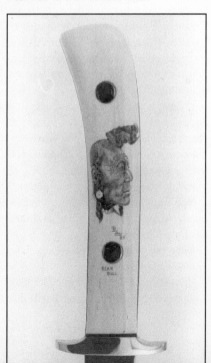

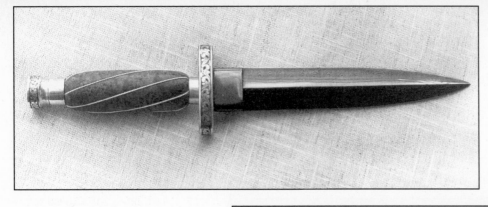

A beautiful custom-made knife by Jim Ferguson is embellished with cast silver engraving by Bruce Shaw and a burl maple handle with wire inlay. The Damascus blade was etched to bring out the pattern. (Photo by Bill Herndon.)

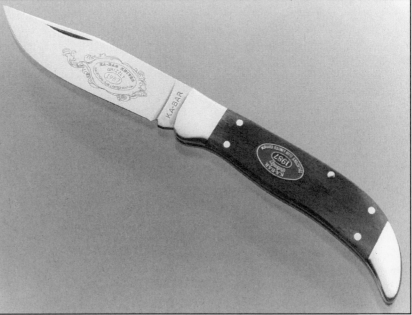

This is the Ka-Bar Grizzly folder made as a 1987 knife collectors' club selection. It is engraved and marked with limited-edition information.

That might be called artistic license.

According to Bob Engnath, scrimshaw works well on paper-based micarta—black, white, blue or brown—using contrasting ink for the design. Ivory produces the best work and is his favorite medium. Workable materials include elephant ivory, hippo, walrus, whale and boar's teeth, as well as polished stag, cow or buffalo horn.

Scrimshaw is a simple form of illustration. The design or picture is scratched, carved or dotted with a needle into the material, and ink—sometimes several colors—is rubbed across the dots and lines. The ink penetrates the lines and dots and is left there by the artist. Excess ink is removed from the surface and the image remains. The skill of accomplishing a beautiful picture is much more difficult than this description, however.

Dark areas mean the dots must be closer together. Shaded details require a clear understanding of how such images are formed by means of dots and scratches. A piece of ancient elephant ivory or walrus tooth can be worth thousands of dollars, and the artist knows that he must use care to not botch the job. A good job of scrimshaw on the handle will enhance the value of any knife, but it probably is not something to be added to a favorite hunting or skinning knife.

We shall discuss Bob Engnath further and some of the work he does with swords in another chapter.

Scrimshaw is artwork for only relatively soft materials. It cannot be done on steel. Steel can be etched, engraved, ground, machined, colored, anodized, plated, polished, blued, cut, sanded and otherwise changed. Somewhere at this moment, some custom knifemaker is thinking up something else that might be done to a knife blade to make it different and more appealing.

Most of us have seen etched blades. Patterns, illustrations and designs can be etched on steel. Etching Damascus steel, however, serves a somewhat different purpose. The acid etching is done to enhance the Damascus pattern that has been forged into the blade. Each inch of Damascus will change in appearance, which gives it that exotic look, while it remains an excellent cutting tool.

The etching process on a Damascus blade will depend on how the blade is forged. Most layered Damascus blades are fashioned from tool steel, but some are made from a variety of stainless steels, sometimes intermixed with tool steel and/or high-nickel-content alloys. The acid etching system works best on the oil-hardened tool steel, because most stainless materials do not really lend themselves to the process. That's why they call it stainless steel.

There are two methods a knifemaker might use for etching. The preferred one is to do the etching before the handle is installed on the knife. However, if the blade already has a han-

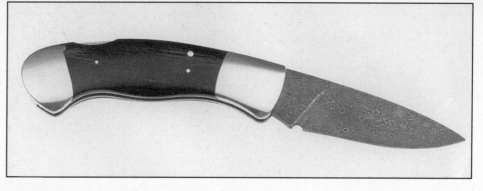

Folders, too, may be made with Damascus blades. This handsome version is from Damascus USA. (Photo by Weyer of Toledo.)

(Left) Bruce Shaw did the beautiful engraving on this Jim Ferguson Damascus dagger.

(Below) Lance Kelly specializes in daggers and does it well. Extensive fine engraving enhances their beauty. (Photo by Weyer of Toledo.)

dle attached, it still can be etched, although the job will be a bit more difficult.

For the bare blade with no handle, all that is required is to immerse the blade in an acid bath to etch the steel. Various simple acids such as swimming pool acid (hydrochloric) or plain battery acid (sulfuric) may be used. Both will work, and they are weak enough to not work too fast for the beginner. A mild-strength acid might take longer to etch the steel, but it is simpler and safer. A powerful or concentrated acid should be the knife-maker's last choice, because it works fast and could easily ruin the blade.

Another liquid that etches well, is safer than an acid and which can be bought in electronic shops is ferric chloride. It is used for etching electronic PC boards. It is dark yellow in color and works fast enough to offer adequate control of the depth of the etch and still not move too far, too fast.

Regardless of the type or strength used, the craftsman must use commonsense safety precautions. It is best to work outdoors with plenty of moving air around to prevent fumes from causing breathing problems. Rubber gloves must be worn to prevent burns to the hands. Experienced etchers will wear a smock or apron to protect their clothes and, as an absolute minimum, safety glasses to protect the eyes. A face shield is a better choice. Most of us have thrown away clothing damaged by battery acid while working around the car. The danger is not to be taken lightly. One drop of any of these chemicals splashed into the eyes could cause permanent damage.

We asked C.R. Learn to look into the specifics of etching, particularly for Damascus blades. He did some experimenting and came up with the following processes.

For the knife blades on hand, Learn chose to use ferric chloride because it is a bit safer to work with. It is possible to

Before the etching process commences on a Damascus or any other type of blade, the handle must be protected with heavy-duty tape.

After the blade has been acid etched, the action must be neutralized with a baking soda paste applied to the metal.

buy ferric chloride at any Radio Shack or other electronics store.

Use a heavy-duty plastic dish or bowl large enough to allow the blade to be covered with the solution, suggests Learn. Before immersion, though, *thoroughly* clean the blade of oil or other foreign matter. Place it in the plastic dish and pour in the ferric chloride until it completely covers the blade. Move the blade around in the solution with plastic tongs or a stick. Move it slowly so as not to spill or splash the liquid, until all parts are covered. Cover the dish with a rag to prevent fumes from entering the workplace, open all the windows if working indoors, and let the blade sit in the solution.

This requires a minimum amount of monitoring. The blade and acid should be examined every once in a while to see how the etching is progressing. How long will it take? Learn says the time element depends partly on the number of layers that have been folded together to form the blade, and the freshness of the ferric chloride.

After about an hour in the solution, the blade should be removed using a pair of tongs and wearing rubber gloves. Rinse the blade in a can of water. At this point the blade looks terrible, says Learn, "...a yucky black thing, but that is merely the chemical solution doing its work."

The blade should be rinsed and rubbed with a brush or rag. Rubber gloves and a face shield must be worn for this operation.

The pattern of the Damascus layers will begin to show up as the black goop is removed from the blade. The layered structure of the steel will appear. If it is what you like, stop and finish out the blade. If you feel the pattern is not deep enough, the blade should be returned to the solution for further etching.

The Damascus blade pattern is brought out by etching, bluing and fine polishing.

One of the blades Learn was working with took about an hour and a half to etch. Another blade with finer layers required three hours to bring out the pattern.

When a satisfactory pattern is reached, the etching solution is rubbed off the blade with more water and a soft brush. Experienced knifemakers suggest the use of additional chemicals to neutralize the acid and stop any further etching. Baking soda from the kitchen is excellent for this. Mix the soda into a paste, cover the blade with it, and let it stand for a short time.

Clean the soda from the blade using water and a brush to get into the layers of steel. Several fresh-water rinses and more brushing will do the job. At this point, Learn reports, the etching pattern is visible, but is not very clear.

The blade surface can now be gently rubbed with 400- or 600-grit wet/dry sandpaper. With the blade in the water, gently rub the surface with the sandpaper. The high spots of the steel will show up brighter and the low areas will be dark.

Continue cleaning the blade in this manner until the desired color and pattern are achieved. If you go too far, go back and re-etch the blade to change the appearance.

This work is only the first phase of the etching process. The next step is to darken the more recessed layers of steel which will provide a greater contrast. With the blade thoroughly dry, cover the entire surface with a gun bluing solution, available at most gunsmithing shops or gun dealers. There also are other antiquing solutions on the market.

Once again, says Learn, the blade will become totally black and look terrible. Allow the bluing to dry, then lightly rub the surface with 400-grit emery paper. With the bluing removed from the higher layers, the lower layers will remain darker,

achieving the desired contrast. The more you rub with the emery paper, says our experimenter, the deeper the polish will go. A blade with only a few Damascus layers will result in a high-contrast pattern much more quickly than a blade with 100 folds of steel.

The final phase is to saturate the blade with a high-quality gun oil to set the bluing. This also brightens up the pattern. Instead of gun oil, some blades are treated with a good grade of wax to produce a slightly duller appearance.

Some knifemakers might complete a Damascus knife, but not etch it right away. The process is the same as used for the bare blade, but the handle section must be sealed to prevent the etching solution from coloring or damaging it. Clear nail polish works well for this. In addition, use a tough masking tape to wrap the handle to prevent etching fumes from doing any damage.

Perhaps the easiest method, according to Learn, is to suspend the blade over the ferric chloride and immerse only the blade in the solution. It works well and is just as fast. The project knife etched, blued and finished by Learn using this procedure had a deer antler handle. No damage was visible to the handle after the etching process. The baking soda will prevent any of the etching solution from creeping up into the handle base in later years.

Not all Damascus blade makers agree that acid etching is the thing to do to their blades. They prefer the appearance of the forged Damascus as it comes off the anvil.

Etching is a simple, fun project that does not require the training of a chemist to get right. It should enhance the looks of almost any Damascus knife.

DECORATING KNIVES

A Horn-Handled Damascus Knife

THERE ARE NOT many among us who can make a knife from the raw steel to the finished cutting product, but almost all of us can make a unique handle to fit a knife blade. This isn't too difficult with normal shop tools, and if it doesn't work out the way you like, you can remove that handle and put on another style.

When C.R. Learn, a practiced tinkerer, travels through the West, the bumper sticker on his truck reads: "I STOP AT ALL TRADING POSTS."

While rambling through southern Wyoming a few years back, he noticed a good-looking skinning blade in a trading post in Lander, Wyoming. On examination, it turned out to be a hand-made Damascus blade made by a custom knifemaker located a bit south of Lander.

"I purchased that blade for a fraction of what it would bring at a knife show. This blade had a good, sweeping curve for skinning game of any size. All it needed was a good handle," Learn recalls.

This particular knife blade had a slip-over tang—a skinny rod-like thing that extends back from the blade itself. It would require a solid handle to make it look right. Learn felt it might be easier to make a slab-style handle. For this, though, the steel is the full width of the blade and one merely adds two slabs of whatever is chosen for a handle, one on each side of the tang.

"About two years after obtaining the blade, I was still looking for the right handle. I had some stag antler in the shop, but it just didn't look right, so I kept looking,"Learn tells us. "The right material almost tripped me up while bowhunting in the high Arizona desert—a winter-shed antler from a desert mule deer. These are seldom found, since mice and other critters love

to chew them for the calcium, and they are demolished in perhaps one season."

This particular horn was a unique three-point tine. One of the tines was straight to about three inches from the tip, then it curled in a sharp right angle that was different from most horn tips Learn had encountered over the years. "There was my Damascus knife handle already formed and almost ready for the blade," he says.

After several days of deliberation, a hacksaw was used to cut the curved tine tip to provide a flat handle section of four inches.

"Most sheath knives have a handle length of about 4½ inches, depending on the blade size and length. I taped off a section with masking tape and cut the horn, allowing a half-inch to make adjustments for a straight knife handle," Learn reports.

"This horn has a slight spine down the inside of the tip that made a perfect register for the hand while cutting. I planed and sanded to make that spine angle match the angle of the blade," we were told.

When installing a handle on a knife, it helps to put a finger guard in back of the blade, between the handle and back edge of the blade. This prevents the hand from sliding forward while working with a slippery handle when field dressing a deer.

"I thought of using the crown section, the part of the horn that attaches to the skull, but it was too big.

"After cutting the handle to length, an angle was cut to make the finger guard. The horn wasn't large enough for a straight cut, so an angle cut was made, and another cut was made allowing ³/₈-inch for the finger guard. This gave me an angled cut of the same horn for a longer section to make a good-looking

A nice Damascus blade requires a special handle. This unusual piece of desert mule deer antler will provide the basic material.

Hollowing out the antler to accept the knife tang can be a tricky proposition, especially if the horn is curved. By working slowly, it can be easily done.

An additional piece of antler section becomes the finger guard or hilt for the knife. It, too, must be drilled out for the tang.

guard that matched the tone and color of the main handle, since it was from the same antler," the craftsman explains.

Now the tricky part began. Slip-over handles do just that: Once a hole is drilled, they slip over the tang of the blade and slide up to the base of the cutting section.

The simple way to do this is with a drill press and drill press vise.

"Any size drill bit will do since you are only aligning the horn to the drill at this point. Once you have the handle aligned to make a vertical hole in the horn, you probably will have to shift the horn in the vise to get the proper angle, since the horn is curved. You then are ready to select the correct size drill bit."

Use the thickness of the blade as your minimum drill bit size. Select the longest bit that is just a bit oversized for the blade.

The tang is seldom round, and in this case it was wider on one side than on the other but the same width for the full length. Drill one hole in the horn just off center, then move the vise the width of the bit and drill another hole alongside the first one. If you have a vise that goes in both directions, you can crank it forward or backward and sideways using different controls. They work great for this project.

"The tricky part here is to have alignment and depth set so you don't drill through the side of the horn. When you are satisfied with your alignment, turn on the drill and lower the bit into the horn section. I always get nervous at this point, but after an hour of fussing with the alignment, I had two holes side by side

for putting the tang and horn handle together the way I wanted," Learn says.

Place the tang into the hole and check for fit. This one needed a bit of round rat-tail file work to open up a few spots where the drill obviously drifted on the hard horn. Take it slow, check it often and you will have no problem.

You also can cut some of the length from the tang if you don't have enough handle material. A skinning knife is a light-duty unit and if you can get $3^1/_2$ inches into the handle, you will have no problem. The more tang you can put inside the handle, the stronger it will be, of course.

The tang and horn handle fit great, but it is a bit too long, and there is a gap between the horn and tang. Don't worry, you still need to add the finger guard, and that gap will be covered when you put the guard on the front of the handle. Take the guard slab you cut earlier and polish one side on a sander or use a small hand tool such as a Dremel to clean up the hacksaw kerfs.

Check the fit of the guard to the handle to make certain there is no gap. When you are satisfied with that fit, clean up the other side, using the same technique, except this will be facing the blade and it doesn't have to be square with the handle section.

When you slice the guard from the horn, you will have the horn rim at an angle. Learn used that to make it fit with the angle forward and polished that, too. It is easier to clean and polish the guard before you put it on the handle and tang.

The hilt fit should be as tight as possible before it is epoxied to the knife tang. Excess epoxy cement will fill the gaps.

The finished knife offers a friendly grip. The antler can be sanded and polished to produce good color and tone.

The blade is now cleaned up and fits inside the guard and handle section properly. The hole you drilled and filed for fit is a bit oversized and that is the way it should be, because some room is needed for the epoxy to cement.

The hooked section of the horn for our project knife was the tip of the handle. The horn wasn't round but had that slight ridge on the inside, as mentioned earlier. Learn twisted the blade in the horn until the ridge fit his right hand to give him a straight line on the blade when holding the handle with the blade down. This would be the skinning position. When he turned the blade up as for field dressing, it curved around the base of his hand for a good, solid hold.

All that was left was to apply epoxy to the handle. There are two basic types of epoxy, the five-minute type and the longer-curing systems. Some feel the longer-curing type makes a stronger finished product, feeling the short-cure epoxies can become brittle as they get older.

"I used a two-solution, five-minute epoxy, since that is what I had in the shop. If you use this, work rapidly because it can set at the wrong time and this often causes problems. Mix a sufficient amount of epoxy in a container, since that hole drilled in the horn must be fully filled to make it strong."

Put the mixture in the hole, insert a stick and push the epoxy to the bottom. Add more and make certain as you add that you shove it down the hole. It won't flow down by itself, and you can get an air bubble that won't allow the epoxy to fill the hole.

It might be best to remove the finger guard, push in epoxy, then insert the tang and push it down until the mixture oozes out the top.

When you have it full, remove the blade/tang and place the guard on the tang, slide the tang down the hole and line up the guard, tang and blade to the desired position. Learn clamped the handle blade in a vise, and taped the blade to make certain it cured in the desired angle. Wait at least overnight for the epoxy to cure.

If everything went right, you will have a clean line between the guard and handle, and the hole in the guard will be filled with epoxy and look clean and solid. The final phase is to clean the knife of any spilled epoxy. You can use some light sandpaper to polish up the horn and the guard, but if overdone, it will look more like plastic than a natural horn.

"The finished handle is a touch long, since I kept the full curl of the tip and made the handle section to fit the hand without using the tip length," Learn reports.

The blade was cleaned up using some 0000 steel wool. All that remained was to make a sheath to carry it in. The blade is unique in the Damascus steel and the handle is one of a kind to match the blade.

"This desert horn material has no soft center as does most deer horn. I attribute this to the high mineral content found in the desert. It makes a beautiful knife handle, since it all polishes to a good color and tone," our craftsman states.

SHEATHS AND POUCHES

The right container protects and carries—and has the knife always ready for use

WITH THE POSSIBLE exception of folding pocketknives and some special art knives, almost every knife has to be carried someplace on the body, safe and handy. In most cases, that will mean some sort of sheath or pouch worn on the belt. True, there are some miniature knives that have sheaths, but these are really too small to be worn on a belt.

The most common and traditional sheath/pouch material is leather, and has been for centuries. One of the advantages of leather is that it is readily available and easy to work. It can be formed into almost any shape, even by beginners. Leather—or animal skin, at least—has been used to carry things by humans for at least as long ago as the Stone Age. It is still one of the best materials ever developed in which to carry a knife.

Leather sheaths can be long or short, curved or straight, thin or wide. They may be tanned, dyed or bleached to almost any desired color. The leather may be left in its natural finish, boned smooth or turned rough side out. Leather may be carved, engraved or stamped to produce simple or complicated patterns, names and pictures. Buttons, pins, rivets, gems, and other types of decorations have been added to leather products for a distinctive appearance, much as is done with handgun holsters. Leather is popular because there are many things that can be done with it. With the right tanning techniques and the proper care, a good leather sheath or pouch will last a lifetime or two.

Other traditional sheath materials included wood, horn, copper, bronze, sheepskin, banana leaves, bamboo and anything else that would safely carry the blade. The best will do the job without causing rust or other chemical reactions with the blade.

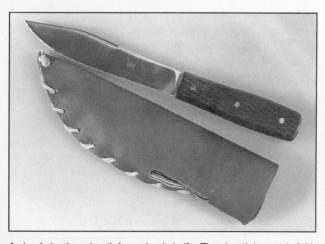

A simple leather sheath for a simple knife. The sheath is merely folded over and laced with thong, and the belt loops are slit in the leather near the top.

This Browning Model 1886 knife was a limited-edition model that included a stiff leather belt sheath.

Custom knifemaker Dennis Brooker made a fine wooden sheath out of the same log from which he stocked the knife.

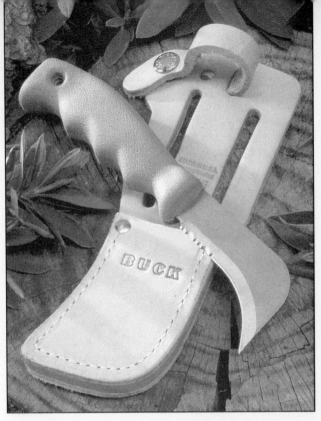

Leather sheaths may be of almost any color and shape. This curved-blade Buck was intended as a gardening or shop knife.

In the movies, most of us have seen pirates and others carrying the bare blade thrust into a sash or belt, ready for use. This may or may not have happened in real life, but think of the corrosion that would beset an unprotected sword blade on a ship surrounded by salt water for months or years at a time.

The sheath for most modern ceremonial military swords is most commonly of stainless steel with brass, silver or even gold ornamentation. That means the sword may be stored safely, withdrawn and returned to the sheath hundreds of times in practice or on parade without harm to the blade. Military students are required to spend many hours learning the sword manual, drawing and returning the sword many times, all without looking. For some of today's fine display and art knives, a handful of artisan knifemakers are including engraving, precious metals and gems to the sheath. Gold is used to enhance the knives and daggers of royalty, but the metal is too soft to be used by itself. It usually is added to silver or other metal sheaths as an embellishment.

It was not uncommon in the past—and is still true today—that many leather sheaths were reinforced with metal, plastic, wood or some other hard material. In another chapter, we talked to Phill Hartsfield, who lines his knife sheaths with thin aluminum. This serves to keep the leather, which may soften after years of use, from collapsing inward so the that blade no longer will slip into the sheath easily. The metal liner also grips the blade to keep it from accidentally sliding out. Most of us have come across older leather sheaths that showed slits and cuts from the blade being thrust in, and the tip poked out through the side or end.

This protection is more important as the blade gets longer or if it has a curved shape, such as is found on a skinner or a fish-filleting knife. These days, most fillet knives are notably thin, curved and long. Most of the sheaths for them are made of heavier plastic that resists penetration and will not lose its shape or stiffness after years of use near and in the water.

In more recent times, newer products have been used for sheaths and pouches. For the typical military knife or bayonet, a couple of wars or so ago, brass-reinforced canvas was the mate-

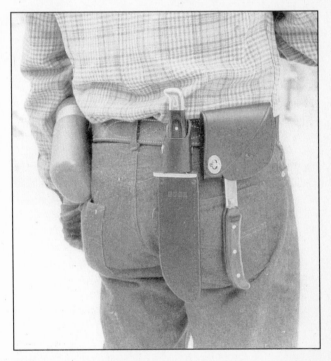

Campers appreciate the matching field knife and small axe, both carried in smooth leather sheaths.

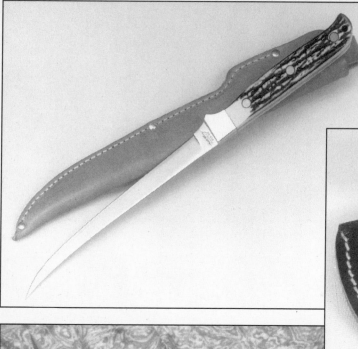

Most fish fillet knives have long, slender, flexible blades, and the sheath must accommodate the shape. This one by Schrade has a leather sheath.

Custom maker Bill Duff decided on a leather sheath for his special blade.

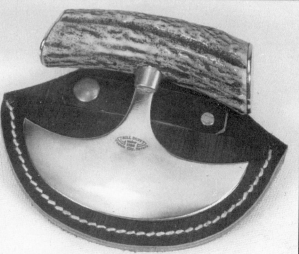

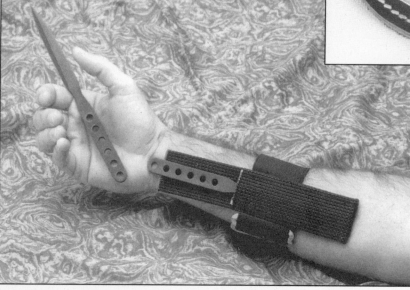

This sleeve dagger from Blackjack Knives uses a simple nylon sheath wrapped around the forearm.

rial of choice. It might last for years in some climates, but cotton canvas will rot quickly in warm, wet weather, such as in the jungles of Pacific islands, Central America or Southeast Asia. Soldiers quickly learned that the life of canvas sheaths, packs, leggings, straps and cartridge belts was short in this climate. It would happen to canvas rifle slings as fast as it happened to knife sheaths.

The same weather was unkind to leather goods, too. American troops who served in the Southeast Asia area in the early and mid-'60s soon realized a pair of leather combat boots would fall apart in a couple of months of slogging through rice paddies, jungle streams and muddy roads. The same was true for leather or canvas sheaths and other gear.

It was about this time that manufacturers began experimenting with synthetic materials for jungle combat. Nylon in varying combinations was added to the familiar green canvas equipment. Nylon is unaffected by heat and water, and was often used as a thread to stitch the various components together.

The amount of nylon added to the canvas soon increased until many all-nylon sheaths, belts, straps, bags, boots and pouches were commonplace. Manufacturers were quick to realize the value of such materials, and they adapted the nylon material to civilian uses.

A further advantage to the nylon pouches and sheaths is that they do not fade after several washings or immersions in water, even salt water. This feature is essential to military web gear, but also a positive marketing tool for civilian uses. Some makers use a nylon fabric that is heavy and thick enough to maintain shape after years of rough usage. Other products rely on some sort of plastic liner, perhaps sandwiched between two layers of the nylon, to help maintain shape and rigidity required of knife sheaths.

There is also the factor of how easy or how difficult it is to return the knife to the sheath. The best knife sheath will be of a shape, position and location that the user may return the knife quickly and safely without the need to look. An old, soft leather sheath, collapsing in on itself, can make the task much more difficult.

Modern plastics have found their way to the world of sheaths and pouches. Ideal for a long, flexible fish-filleting knife is a sheath made of relatively hard plastic. The stuff is impervious to salt water damage and is hard enough that the curved blade will not penetrate as it is being inserted. Any fish flesh or scales left on the blade will not cause damage to the plastic material.

The hard plastic is not for every use though, because it may not be soft and flexible enough. In some military applications, the plastic would make too much noise as the wearer passed through jungles, brush and trees.

Hard plastic is used for sheaths for even tiny knives. Several manufacturers offer small fixed-blade knives with sheaths that attach to a key ring or clip onto a purse. Schrade recently came

out with a small knife and sheath that clips to a belt loop so the knife hangs down into the hip pocket, mostly out of sight, but ready for use. The little plastic sheath locks the knife in and releases only when a safety button is pressed.

A belt pouch for a larger folding knife has somewhat different design requirements than does a fixed-blade sheath. Generally, the pouch will be smaller and more compact. Of course, the blade is folded into the handle, so there are no sharp edges to cut through the material.

In many cases, leather belt sheaths will be formed to the particular fixed-blade knife, fitting rather tightly. That means a more snug fit for the knife than a belt pouch might provide.

A standard-size belt pouch often will accommodate any number of sizes, brands and types of folding knives. Several companies make a sort of universal knife pouch, and the knife

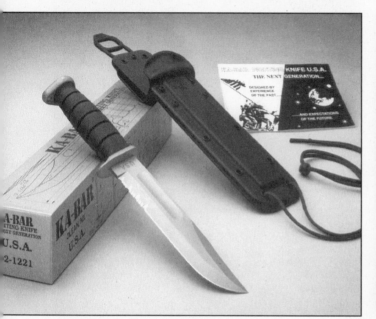

This Ka-Bar knife design extends back to early WWII. The sheath is modern hard plastic, which holds up well under hard use.

Charlie Weiss of Arizona made this unabashed collector knife with an engraved, gold-detailed steel sheath.

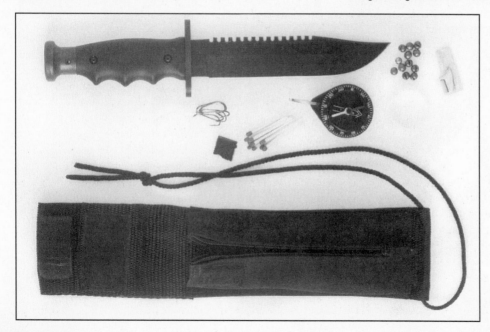

A heavy-duty nylon sheath in black or camouflage pattern is ideal for the Western Cutlery survival knife.

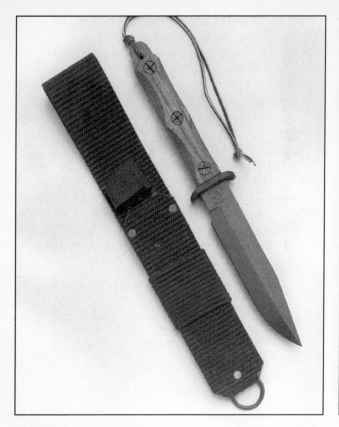

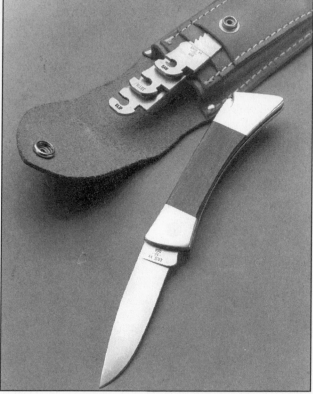

The Ek Woodstalker knife is at home in a heavy nylon belt sheath. It's a simple and rugged design.

The Case XX-Changer blades are carried in a multi-slot leather sheath to keep them handy. Each blade type is labeled.

Martial arts trainer Laci Szabo uses a Kydex sheath worn cross-draw for his special fighting knife.

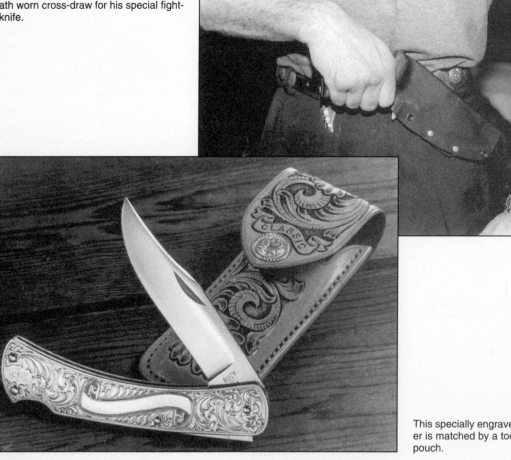

This specially engraved Buck lockblade folder is matched by a tooled brown leather belt pouch.

Cold Steel Cutlery calls this knife Hai Hocho. It is intended for concealed carrying under the shirt, at the chest. The sheath locks the knife in the handle-down position.

manufacturers need only stamp their brand name on it. The folder should not fit in too tightly, as it then becomes difficult to withdraw the knife when it is needed. In fact, that might be an argument against carrying a folder and in favor of a fixed-blade knife. The straight knife is always more quickly employed in an emergency situation.

Carrying a large fixed-blade knife is impractical in many situations, but necessary in others. A sheath knife is mighty uncomfortable on the belt while riding in a car or truck. But when walking through the woods on the way to your deer hunting tree stand, you would hardly know it is there. A folder in a pouch can be worn on the side with no problem while in a vehicle. Each has its use and place.

Wearing any knife on the belt is not the only option available. Some prefer to have the knife in a cross-draw position, feeling that is a quicker way to employ a knife. A sheath knife can sometimes be worn comfortably cross-draw style while driving, assuming one is a right-handed person. It makes for fast action for those trained to use it.

For some military applications, the sheath knife may be worn on a pack shoulder strap, handle down. For this, the sheath must hold the knife safely and firmly. It cannot fall out on the run or when jumping from aircraft or vehicles. Most often, the sheath design will include some sort of safety strap across the hilt to hold the knife in. Other designs rely on fit and friction to hold the knife in place. When silence is required, a metal snap or hook-and-loop closure will make too much noise when the knife is to be used.

The sheath may be sewn to the shoulder strap, glued or taped in place. It can also be worn tied down on the thigh, well below the belt line. Some military or martial arts users wear the knife at the small of the back, inside the trousers in a semi-concealed, but easily accessible location. Another place may

be the upper back, with the knife handle protruding behind the head or neck. The old bayonet location used to be on the left rear of the pack, to be drawn and attached to the rifle in a smooth, single motion.

A defensive sheath knife can be strapped to the wearer's forearm as a sleeve dagger. Another location might be the lower leg or calf area, inside the trouser leg. This is similar to a boot-knife sheath which might have a metal clip attached to the back so it can slip over the boot top. Another way to carry a smaller sheath knife is to suspend it from a soft cord or shoelace around the neck. The knife hangs down the wearer's shirt, against the chest, hidden, but still is readily available. None of these applications are really suitable for folding knives, but no doubt somebody, somewhere, has tried it.

A long-time custom knifemaker named Jim Barbee, from down Texas way, used to specialize in a knife sheath with a horizontal belt loop, rather than vertical. His reasoning was that wearing a good hunting knife that hung straight down while riding in a pickup or on a horse might become at least uncomfortable or at worst dangerous. His sheath had to be fitted carefully to each knife so it could not work itself out while riding, but it did make for quick, easy access when needed. Barbee is not the only cutler ever to think of this design. A number of factory sheaths and pouches are available in a horizontal carry mode.

A belt sheath sometimes carries more than a single knife. Several makers offer a combination knife and camp ax carrying system. When making camp, it is really handy to have both a knife and small ax close at hand. Other designs might hold two or more knives, perhaps a utility style and a skinner or fish knife. Several have been designed to carry interchangeable blades that attach to a single handle. A number of these change-blade designs have been marketed over the years, but none has shown great acceptance by the public.

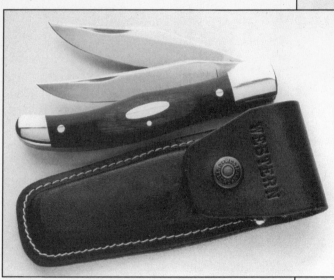

A moulded leather sheath carries this Western two-blade folder in nice style.

The Schrade LB3 folder comes with a heavy leather pouch.

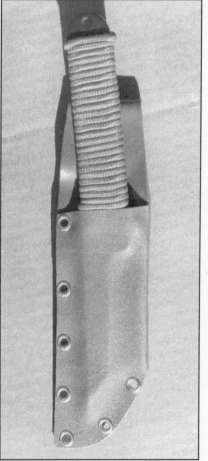

Mike Franklin puts his HAWG! knife in a tough, one-piece Kydex sheath. It's simple and easy to use.

A currently popular material used for knife sheaths is a plastic called Kydex. We have not been able to determine the original use of the material, but Kydex has proven ideal for sheaths. At room temperature, it is rigid enough to take and maintain its shape and will not soften or collapse unless heated. It can be formed around the knife to hold it with friction only, not requiring a safety strap. The material is not expensive, and is impervious to most corrosive substances. It is seen mostly in black, but other colors are available. Custom knifemaker Mike Franklin, for instance, often markets his HAWG! line of knives with a bright red Kydex belt sheath.

A Kydex sheath may be made by the average handy person at home. The material is available in sheets and can be cut with tin snips or a large pair of scissors. A thin cardboard or heavy paper pattern should be drawn and cut first, wrapping it around the chosen knife. It is trimmed until the pattern is about a half-inch larger than the knife all the way around.

The Kydex can be heated to about 350 degrees in the kitchen oven until it becomes soft and pliable. While in that state, it is formed around the knife and pressed hard with, say, two heavy blocks of wood covered with some sort of soft material such as pieces of wool blanket. It does not take long for the Kydex to cool, and when it does, it will retain the moulded shape. You then have a custom-fitted sheath.

The only fastening methods we have seen for closing the Kydex is rivets or cutler's screws, but most knifemakers use rivets. The open edge of the Kydex pattern is riveted shut, and a belt loop also may be riveted onto the sheath. It is a clever, quick way to make a working sheath for any knife.

NEW DEVELOPMENTS IN FOLDING TOOLS

Folding knives, blades and locking systems are changing

WE DO NOT know when and by whom the first knife was made. We do not know when and by whom the first folding knife blade was developed. What we do know is that there have been hundreds of styles and folding mechanisms tried and used the past couple of centuries. Early examples of folding knives are to be found dating back to the late 19th century. Some designs have remained or been refined for manufacture to this day. Others are known only to collectors.

The idea of the folding-blade knife was that it could be carried concealed and in a pocket—thus the term pocketknife. At first, only the friction of the pin and pivot mechanism was used to hold the blade closed or open. These systems are still common with smaller pocketknives.

But, as the blades became longer and heavier, makers tried all kinds of devices to lock the blade open during use; sometimes when the blade is closed, too. When subjecting any larger knife to a difficult task requiring considerable pressure, one does not want the blade to close on the fingers accidentally!

Mechanical locking devices have been placed on the front, middle and rear portion of the folder. Buttons, levers, slides and pins have been used with varying degrees of success. A common method of locking the blade open is to use a steel lever that bears against the back part of the blade. The design is such that the more pressure that is placed on the edge of the blade, the more firm the locking mechanism. Unless the metal actually should break, the blade cannot become unlocked in use. To unlock and close the blade, pressure is exerted to the back end of the lever, unlocking the blade, which then can be swiveled back into the handle.

A mechanism that gained some popularity after World War II and again during and after the Vietnam War is the Bali-Song

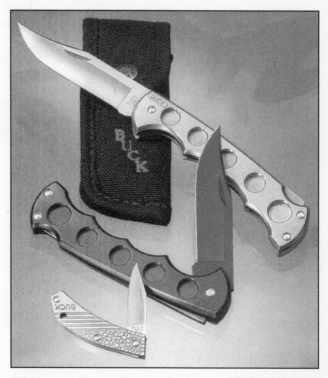

A few years back, Buck Knives introduced a set of lightweight titanium folding knives. They have the standard rear locking mechanism for the larger blades.

or swing blade. These knives reached America in the kits of returning servicemen.

For a while, several cheap imitations of the precision-made knives flooded the U.S. market, but today, only a couple of reputable manufacturers still produce them. The blade is contained

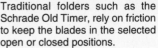

Traditional folders such as the Schrade Old Timer, rely on friction to keep the blades in the selected open or closed positions.

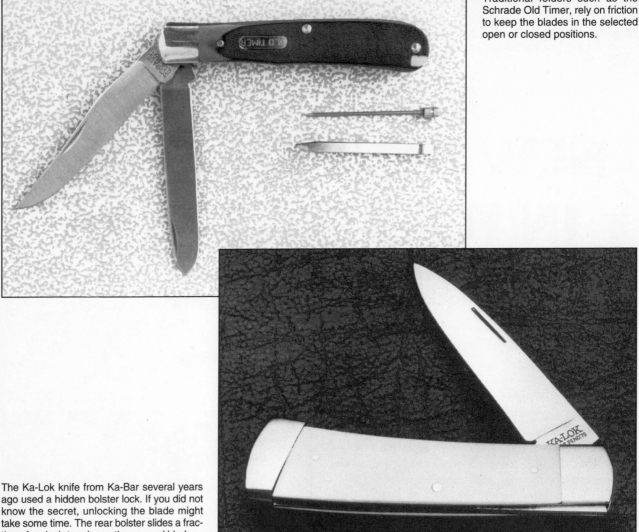

The Ka-Lok knife from Ka-Bar several years ago used a hidden bolster lock. If you did not know the secret, unlocking the blade might take some time. The rear bolster slides a fraction of an inch to release the opened blade.

in two swiveling sides of the handle. The practiced martial artist can loose the blade and swing it out to the open position in a fraction of a second.

The Bali-Song design fell into ill-repute with law enforcement agencies for a time. The knives are outlawed in certain jurisdictions, as are switchblades and gravity knives. Perhaps other designs are faster to employ and cheaper to manufacture, and the marketplace has solved that problem.

More and more of the modern locking folders are being made so the blade can be opened with the use of one hand. These are not spring-loaded switchblades or gravity knives that require the press of a button to shoot the blade open. There is no spring action that forces the blade open. The knife is opened by placing the thumb on some part of the closed blade and swiveling it open while holding the knife body with the same hand.

The trend probably was initiated by Spyderco. There have been others before, but the Spyderco design has achieved great popularity—and greater imitation.

It started with a wide blade that has a hole drilled through the top into which the thumb tip could fit to open the blade with one hand. Since then, all sorts of opening buttons, pins, plates, bolts

and hole shapes have been used to swivel open the blade. It is a simple concept. Anything that allows the user to get a purchase on the closed blade to swing it out has worked. It may take a bit of practice by the user to get the action smooth and fast, but this has become the most popular type of folder in recent years. Almost every large knife company and many custom knife-makers offer one-hand-opening knives.

The second popular development from Spyderco is the pocket clip folder. As the one-hand opener was developed, the pocket clip made it that much faster to get a knife out and ready for use. Instead of carrying the large folder in the pocket or in a belt pouch, it is held inside the front or rear trouser pocket at the top of the seam by a metal or plastic clip a couple of inches long. This knife may be left- or right-handed, and can be clipped to a jacket pocket, purse flap, notebook or other handy object. With practice, the knife is ready for use in a second, using only one hand.

Another old/new locking mechanism that has gained wide acceptance is the liner lock. The design is seen on knives dating back to the early part of the 20th century, but has enjoyed a surge of popularity recently. The concept is simple. Most folding knives have copper or steel linings inside the handle slabs, surrounding the blade. Copper is really too soft to lock the

When this Bali-Song butterfly knife was made, the manufacturer was known as Pacific Cutlery. Today, the firm is in Oregon and called Benchmade. The blade opens and closes with a practiced snap of the wrist.

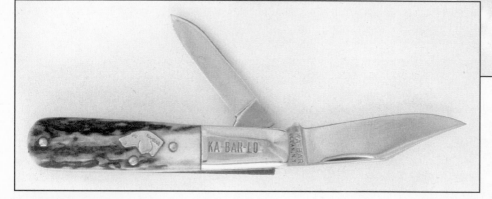

(Below) The Ka-Bar Dog's Head folder is a replica of an old favorite that uses friction and a cam design to lock the blades in place.

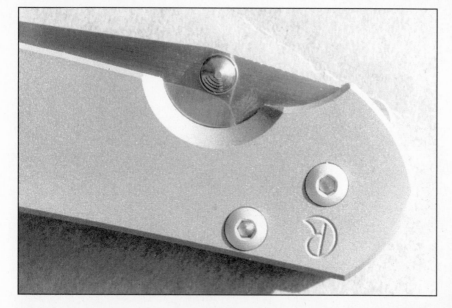

(Left) Custom knifemaker Chris Reeve refines the button opener for his folding knife. All components are precision made and operate flawlessly.

(Below) The Chris Reeve locking liner is an excellent design, making this one of the most rugged of any knife today.

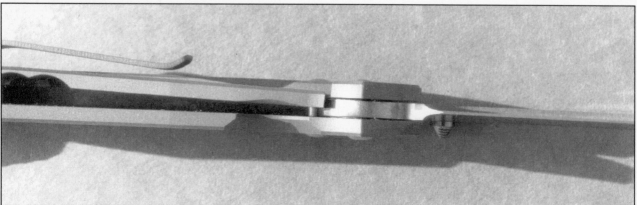

Benchmade specializes in rugged, well-designed folders. This one-hand-opener uses a liner locking mechanism.

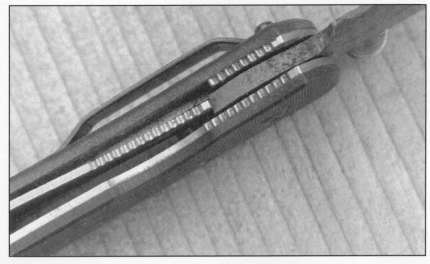

On the Benchmade folder, the spring liner is rugged and stiff. Serrations offer a firm grip.

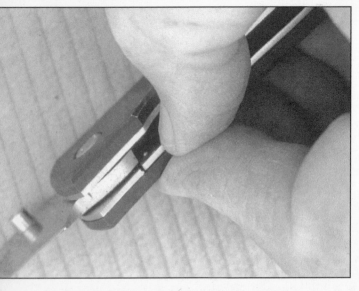

To close the blade on a liner lock blade, the spring liner is pushed aside to release the blade tang.

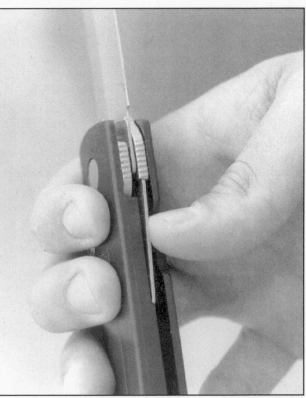

The liner on the new Buck folder is thinner, but the operation is the same.

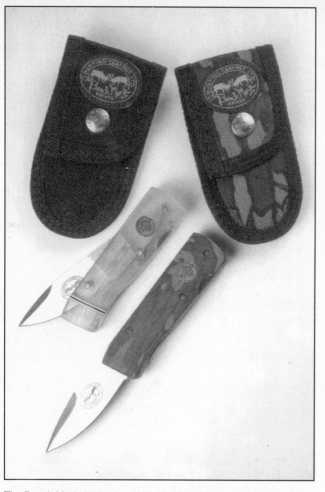

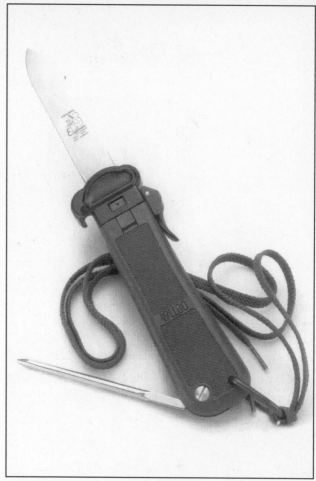

The Bench Mark design is a kind of sliding/folder. It has been around for a couple of decades, but has not achieved great popularity.

This sliding-blade knife, imported from Germany, is said to be used by German paratroopers. That's questionable, but it's an interesting design.

blade, so one side of the steel liner is cut and shaped so that as the blade is opened, it springs over a fraction of an inch to lock the blade open.

The designer's skill determines how much, if any, play is left when the blade is fully open and how strong the spring lock is. If the lever is too flimsy, a blow to the back of the blade will permit the closing mechanism to override the liner lock and the blade will swing shut, perhaps on the user's knuckles. Some mechanisms are designed so that the more pressure placed on the blade to close it without unlocking, the more firm the lock.

To close the blade, the user pushes the liner over against the inside of the handle until the blade releases. That action puts the user's fingers in line with the blade edge, so all such knives must be closed with care. Only a little pressure should be exerted against the back of the blade as the liner is pushed aside. Then the thumb or finger may be moved safely out of the way of the closing blade.

Design of the locking liner mechanism requires precision fitting, if the blade is to lock open with no play, snapping into place as the blade is opened. Repeated hard openings will result in some wear on the mechanism over time, so the steel must be hardened properly to take the abuse. Some designs permit the mechanism to be adjusted to remove the play, if and when it develops.

Leroy Remer of Lakeside, California, is a custom knifemaker who is enjoying the popularity of liner locks. Not too long ago, Remer stopped by to show author C.R. Learn his new liner lock folding knife. Remer pointed out that his execution of the locking system uses Space Age materials and, better yet, it is simple to make in comparison to others. He is able to use just about any hard material to make it.

The blade from the end of the front bolster to tip is 2³/₄ inches long, and is big enough to work over a downed deer nicely. The total length, with the blade open, is 6¹/₂ inches. Closed, the knife is 3³/₄ inches long, which is just right for a denim pocket, but not too big to carry without a belt sheath.

The locking system is different from what usually is found, but it is not new. The knife can be opened with one hand by a flick of the thumb on what Remer calls the thumb bob, located toward the front end of the handle section. This is a small screw that threads into the back of the blade. To open, place your thumb on the bob and move the blade up and forward until the liner lock engages at the forward position, locking the blade in the open position. The thumb bob can go on either side of the blade to accommodate right- or left-handers.

Remer has made this style of folding knife in many materials. The bolsters and the blade are of Damascus steel with the beautiful swirling patterns in the visible metal. The cutting edge eas-

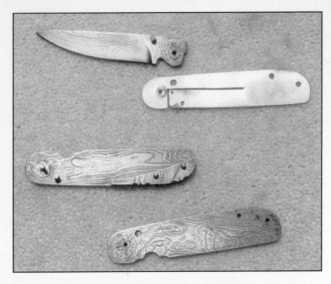

The heart of Remer's folder is the titanium liner. It is cut and slotted to form a powerful spring.

Custom knifemaker Leroy Remer makes a titanium and Damascus steel folder that also utilizes his version of a locking liner to keep the blade open during use.

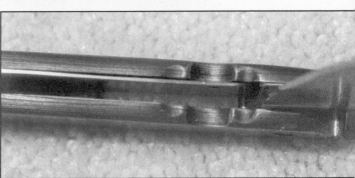

(Above) As the blade pivots open, the titanium spring liner is held back, not interfering with the blade.

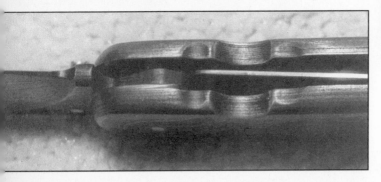

(Left) When the blade reaches its full open position, the liner springs across the cam to lock the blade open. If this is not precision made, the blade will have unwanted movement.

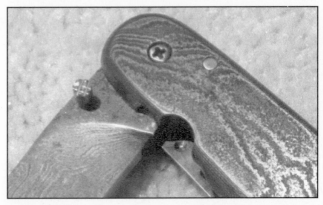

A small dimple is formed into the liner to hold the blade in its closed position, a feature not commonly found in folding knives.

ily takes a shaving sharpness, and the layered steel works almost like a mini-serrated edge. In a test, the blade cut easily through a piece of electrical wire without any damage to the edge.

Remer makes this style of folding lock-blade knife on order. He likes working with 440C, ATS-34, Damascus and many of the other blade materials. When he makes a new style, it is usually in 440C. This steel has proved itself in the blade industry to be tough, reliable and easily obtainable.

Remer does not advocate taking the liner lock knife apart. However, there are few pieces to the design. There are two bolsters of hard material, a razor-sharp blade of your choice and a funny-looking piece of shiny metal that is shaped the same as the bolsters but seems to have no function.

That is actually the heart of this liner lock system. That .030- to .050-inch shiny piece of metal is titanium. This is really tough stuff to work. Remer selected titanium because of its resistance to wear, plus it has memory. If you bend a piece of titanium, it always will return to its original shape, just the thing for this mechanism.

Another interesting part of Remer's design is the thumb bob attached to the back top edge of the blade. This is a short section of stainless steel rod screwed into the blade and it has a slight rounded protrusion on the other side. This is a stop for the blade when it is closed. Remer peens a dimple at a specified point on the titanium lock to fit this rounded section.

When you close the blade, the rounded section of the thumb bob engages the dimple on the liner and helps to keep the blade in the closed position.

To close the blade for carrying, place your thumb at the slight indent in the bolsters, and you'll find the edge of the titanium liner lock. Push this to the side and the blade is released. Move the blade closed a bit with the first finger until you can reach the thumb bob with your thumb. Now swing it down, keeping your fingers out of the way until it closes. The dimple will engage the rounded section on the thumb bob, making it is a safe knife to put in your pocket or a sheath.

NEW DEVELOPMENTS IN FOLDING TOOLS

Year of the Multi-Tool

PERHAPS THE FIRST successful multi-tool is the now-famous Swiss Army knife. More than a simple blade and handle, the Swiss Army knife has become a do-all, multi-task tool with dozens of functions. Its development dates back more than 100 years. The folding blades are limited in their use only by the necessity to make them small enough to fit into the knife handle, and tough enough to withstand the stress and pressures required. As a demonstration of the art, large and small folders have been built with literally hundreds of blades and tools. Obviously, though, these make quite a bulge in your trousers pocket.

In more recent years, the multi-tool in the shape and form of a pair of pliers has found a large following. One thing the buying public insists upon is that the tools be rugged and well made. Tools that break or do not fit the task are soon off the market.

To qualify within this category, a tool must have at least one knife blade. It might have two or three. Some Swiss Army knives have more than that. The other built-in tools are a matter for the manufacturer to decide. They may be based on experience, market research or be particularly appropriate to the customer. An electrician's knife or fishing knife might be examples of narrow markets with special needs.

The original, genuine Swiss Army knives, by definition, are manufactured by one of two Swiss knifemakers: Victorinox and Wenger. These two makers have been designated officially by the Swiss government to make knives for the army.

Readers will be aware that any number of others, particularly some manufacturers in the Orient, have attempted to replicate the design and quality of the real Swiss Army knives, but all are soon off the market from a combination of lack of demand and legal pressure in Switzerland. The real thing must have the Swiss cross on it, and others may not use the symbol at the risk of legal action because of patent and trademark violations.

Aside from the legal aspects, the characteristics of genuine Swiss Army knives are obvious as they are picked up and used. There is no requirement that the handles be red, but most are. The blades and other tools, which number from one to thirty or more, all are made of high-quality stainless steel. Each moves in and out of the liner smoothly and easily.

Some of you may be familiar with copies made in other countries that have blades guaranteed to break even the strongest fingernail. When extended for use, all the tools of a real Swiss Army are tight; there is little or no play at the pivot point. Knife blades open and close with a firm snap, what is known in the trade as "walk and talk."

Most pocket knives have at least a pen blade. There are many specialty tools that may be added, but a partial list of commonly found Swiss Army knife tools includes such

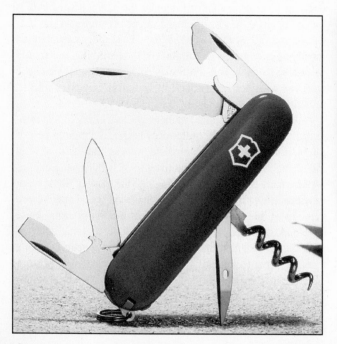

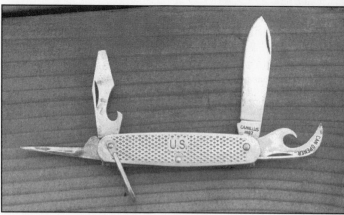

Camillus Cutlery makes a multi-use knife designed for military work. The tools include the can opener and cap lifter, as well as a screwdriver, knife blade and the ever-useful awl.

A typical variety of blades in a Swiss Army knife may include a bottle cap lifter, can opener, screwdrivers and a couple of knife blades.

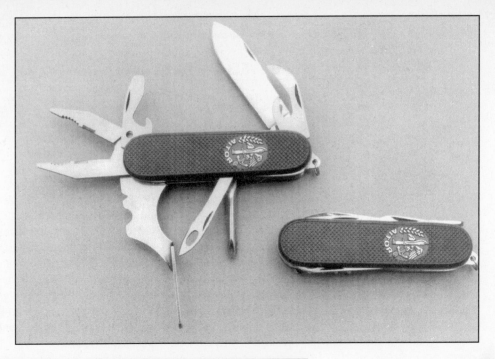

The Aitor Al-Ligator is made in Spain. It looks like a large folding knife at first, but opens up into several useful tools, including a powerful set of pliers.

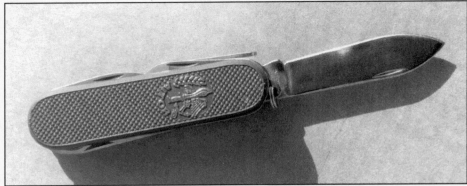

things as a lanyard ring and short chain on the end, a pair of small scissors, metal file, metal saw, shotgun choke-tube tool, can opener, ski wax scraper, tweezers, golf or track shoe spike wrench, Posi-drive screwdriver, pointer, international wrench, corkscrew, awl, Phillips screwdriver, groove cleaner, fingernail file/nail cleaner, combination screwdriver, can opener and cap lifter, wire stripper, divot repair tool, magnifier for reading small print and topographic maps, hook disgorger, fish scaler, line guide, diamond-coated fish hook sharpener, toothpick, flat Phillips screwdriver, reamer, compass, ruler, slip-joint pliers, wire crimper, wire cutter—and any of a number of larger knife blades. Victorinox, for instance, makes several knives with special pruning and grafting blades for gardeners.

Special tools for bicycle riders, truck drivers, golfers, mountain climbers, anglers, archers and electricians will have different needs. Some knives may include a small ball-point pen that slides in and out of the handle. As more and more tools are housed in the handle, the knife becomes wider, and there is a point after which the thing no longer can be considered a pocket knife. Many of the largest, most versatile Swiss Army knives must be carried in a belt sheath or pouch.

While the tools are handy to have along in an emergency,

caution is advised while using such things as screwdrivers. A knife blade is used in the open position, pressing against the opening lock or mechanism. Unless the screwdriver blade is locked open, it may snap closed under pressure and the user can be injured when that happens. These tools are intended mostly as emergency substitutes for the real thing and should be treated as such. But if a Swiss Army knife is all you have with you when the need arises, it can be a lifesaver or, at least, save the day.

A decade or so ago, the Leatherman Tool Group, Inc., introduced a new concept in multi-tools designed around a pair of pliers. It was an almost immediate success and led to several modifications, refinements and new models by Leatherman as well as many competitors jumping into the market. Some manufacturers, Leatherman included, have designed specialized versions of their basic model, much as the Swiss Army knife developed. The concept of a single, compact tool that will perform many tasks has appealed to consumers for years. Today's manufacturing techniques and materials have moved the product closer to the ideal. Let's take a look at some of the products available as this is written.

The Aitor Al-Ligator multi-tool is made in Spain for the North American market. The blades and other tools are all

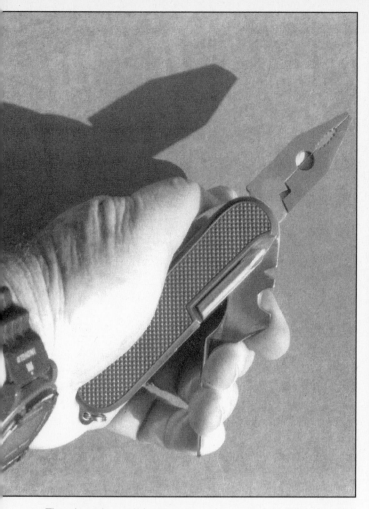

The wire stripper and cutter are cut into one of the pliers handles. One side of the pliers handles swivels out of the knife handle. The other side is the knife handle itself. They offer plenty of leverage.

The strong Aitor Al-Ligator pliers jaws will function as a small adjustable wrench when needed. The tool is ideal for the truck glove compartment.

made of 440B stainless steel and a machine-checkered man-made Macrolon composite material serves as the handle. It looks like a large folder, a bit bulky for most trouser pockets, but should ride well in jackets, coats or briefcases. The primary knife blade is large enough for serious cutting work, but it does not lock open.

The pliers operation is different from most of the others we have seen. This tool is folded entirely inside the handle and is invisible. To open, one pulls out a large lever from the pivot pin end of the knife. This lever has two wire strippers in it. It comes to a soft stop about half-way out. As you continue to rotate the spring-loaded action outward, the pliers emerges from inside the handle. The opening lever becomes one handle of the pliers, and the knife handle body is the other. The pliers has the precision appearance of a well made tool. It has two wire-cutters and the usual two pair of serrations inside the jaws. The jaws close together evenly and with enough leverage in the handles to do some real work. When tested on some tightened-down nuts, they took a good grip and had plenty of bite and leverage.

Aside from the 3-inch knife blade, the Aitor contains a standard blade screwdriver with a bottle-cap opener and a lever-type can opener on the other end. Opening from the back side

are the Phillips-head screwdriver and an awl with an eyelet for sewing really heavy canvas or leather.

None of the multiple tools are locked when open, so extra care must be exercised when using them, but with that in mind, this a tough, rugged set of tools to carry. It might be ideal for the glove compartment, just for emergency repairs or other work. The Aitor products are imported to North America by Catoctin Cutlery.

In addition to Aitor products, Catoctin imports and markets dozens of knife brand names from around the world, including Spain, England, Germany, Italy and the Philippines.

Coast Cutlery is offering their rugged Sport Mechanic multi-tool, with at least ten functions folded within its checkered Zytel handle. This model is based on a pair of pliers and all the tools are of stainless steel. A nylon belt pouch is included that, for longest life, should have the Sport Mechanic inserted pliers-up. It makes a compact package for the truck or the workshop.

The Sport Mechanic is rather an ingenious design. The single handle is also a combination pry bar, and it looks strong enough to do some serious prying. We did not stress it to the breaking point, but we tested it at prying some heavy carton staples—the tough, sharp brass kind—and it made short work

189

Coast Cutlery's Sport Mechanic features twelve different tools all folding into the handle. Folded down, the Sport Mechanic is carried in a nylon pouch.

of what is sometimes a difficult task. The other half of the pliers handle is the knife body itself. The pliers jaws come together precisely and the bottom of the jaws are sharpened to serve as wire cutters.

A Phillips screwdriver folds to the outside of the knife on the same side as the pliers handle/pry bar. The first tool on the other folding handle is a medium-size pair of scissors. They are sharp, with a spring to keep the jaws open for easier use. Next is a 2½-inch spear blade, reasonably well sharpened as it comes from the factory. Next out is what is billed a fishing tool. It has a 3-inch measuring scale on the back, a hook disgorger on the tip and scaler serrations on the concave inside edge. The last blade is a combination serrated-blade with a large flat screwdriver on the tip. It forms a wire stripper near the pivot and there is a metal file on the reverse surface.

We tried the knife blades, pliers, both screwdrivers, wire cutter and the scissors during our testing, and they all worked as tools should. We did not catch any fish to try that aspect of the Sport Mechanic. The tool has a solid feel to it, and the sharp checkering on the Zytel handle should keep it from slipping, even when wet. One might wear the tool in the belt pouch or store it in the glove compartment or in your bicycle tool bag to take care of most mechanical emergencies when they arise.

Coast Cutlery, the importer, guarantees the Sport Mechanic to be free of defects in materials and workmanship for the life of the original purchaser. Misuse, normal wear and tear and neglect are not covered.

As we mentioned, Leatherman was the pioneer of the multi-tool concept in recent times. Folded, their version is 4 inches long and resembles a Bali-Song folding knife. However, the Leatherman is more than a knife. The original design contains twelve tools, including strong needle-nose pliers with a wire cutter at the base, a 2½-inch knife blade, a ruler on the folding body, standard bottle-cap and openers, large screwdriver, small screwdriver, medium screwdriver, Phillips screwdriver, a file for metal or wood, an awl and a punch.

Everything, including the handle, is made precisely of stainless steel. All folding tools are a tight fit. One interesting feature on the Leatherman Pocket Survival Tool is what is known as a Posi-Stop. None of the various tools lock open for use, but once a particular blade or tool is opened from the handle, the handles should be closed. The blades cannot now accidentally be closed, although there is a little movement in them. The Posi-Stop will keep any of the blades from closing on unwary fingers under hard use.

The ruler is marked off in inches and centimeters when fully extended. To use, the pliers handles are opened about half-way, leaving the pliers jaws together. The ruler-marked handles are pushed close together for the full 8-inch or 20 centimeter ruler. Leatherman includes a compact leather belt pouch with the original model.

For a smaller, less obtrusive package, the Leatherman Mini-Tool will do a lot of things. When folded, it is only about 2½ inches long, and its black nylon pouch is no larger than a pager. Also made of all stainless steel, the Mini-Tool contains needle-nose and regular pliers with wire cutter, a small knife blade, bottle and can openers, flat-blade screwdriver, metal file and a 5-inch/13-centimeter ruler when open.

Because of the compact size, greater care must be exercised when using the Mini-Tool. Big fingers and hands can be pinched. To open and use the pliers, Leatherman has designed-in handle extensions. It might be possible to use the pliers without the extensions, but there would be considerably less leverage. As the handles swing open, the user finds two small nail nicks up near the base of the pliers jaws. With a bit of practice, we could use both index fingers to open the two extensions at the same time. These extensions also contain the can and bottle openers.

The original Leatherman Pocket Survival Tool is the model that caught the public's fancy, leading to several improvements and plenty of competition. It weighs 5 ounces and packs at least twelve different tools, all made of stainless steel and carried in a leather belt sheath. The individual tools include needle-nose pli-

One of the pliers handles also functions as a pry bar. The pliers jaws open wide and offer a good grip.

ers, regular pliers, wire cutter, knife blade, ruler, can and bottle opener, large, medium, small and Phillips screwdrivers, metal file, wood file, awl and punch. Several of these fold-outs have multiple uses. Our tests show the pliers and wire cutters have plenty of leverage to do the job of several individual tools.

The 2½-inch knife blade, awl, medium and large screwdrivers are enclosed in one side of the handle, and the file, can and bottle opener, small and Phillips head screwdrivers are in the other side.

The Pocket Survival Tool is guaranteed for 25 years against defects in material or workmanship. Although the product is made of stainless steel, no steel is truly stainless. A more correct description would be corrosion resistant. The company warns that all its tools should be cleaned, dried and oiled from time to time, especially after use in a wet environment. A light penetrating oil should be used to lubricate the pivoting areas.

These tools are made in the U.S. and are the products of Leatherman Tool Group.

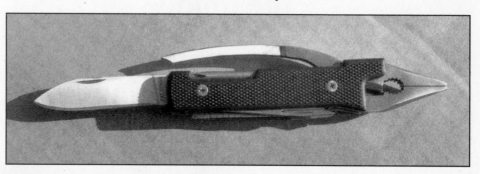

The large spear-point knife blade handles cutting chores very nicely and seems to hold an edge.

The large screwdriver tip really works. The serrated blade has a metal file on the reverse side.

Leatherman got the multi-tool movement going not so long ago. The tool has all the essentials for a survival/emergency situation.

A.G. Russell has made many contributions to the world of knives. He has a multi-tool design called the A.G. Russell Pocket Tool box, an update of a German-patented tool made about eighty years ago. Russell redid the tooling, using modern methods and materials. He replaced the leather punch with a Phillips-head screwdriver and added a serrated edge to one side of the screwdriver blade. That blade also has a fine file on one surface. The Phillips screwdriver does not lock open, but it has a mild

detent in the mechanism that tends to hold it in place in use. It works at right angles to the knife handle, offering plenty of leverage to turn stubborn screws in or out.

The tool is compact, lightweight and is made of stainless steel. Closed, the unit is 4⅝ inches long, and it weighs only 4½ ounces. It is less than a half-inch thick, so it actually can be carried in a pocket or purse with no problem. A nylon belt pouch is optional. The pliers, which also include the mandatory wire cut-

The Unique BuckTool

As with every product, the marketplace will decide whether or not the BuckTool is a success. For a first look, though, what follows is writer C.R. Learn's evaluation of the newest tool from Buck Knives.

BUCK KNIVES' BUCKTOOL is a compact unit that fits into a moulded Cordura belt pouch. It might be a good idea to buy several of these tools and put them in different locations such as the truck, the shop, your bike's tool pouch, briefcase and so on.

The tool weighs in on a postal scale at 7 ounces; pretty light considering it is made entirely of stainless steel. With the tool folded inside, the pouch measures 4¼ inches in length. To open the tool, the handle at the bottom rotates outward and the pliers appear out of the folded unit. Continue rotating away from you and the pliers move to the fully extended position, the unit rotating on the left pliers handle. The tool is now fully open and ready to use, and measures 6½ inches in length.

At this point, the BuckTool looks like a fancy pair of pliers with unique handles. The jaws have coarse and fine grooves for gripping. At their widest opening, they span 1 inch.

The wire cutter opens to ⅜-inch and works by the jaws passing each other for a fast, clean cut. Most wire cutters on

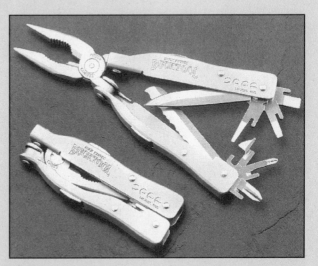

Buck Knives is the latest to get into the multi-tool business. The BuckTool features a unique locking system for each of the ten tools in the handles.

pliers merely mash the wire on the cutting jaws. A rubber-coated 16/3 extension cord was cut easily.

The wire cutters overlap by .070-inch and are made of the same stainless steel as the jaws and hardened to the same 54RC. A test was done by cutting a simple wire clothes

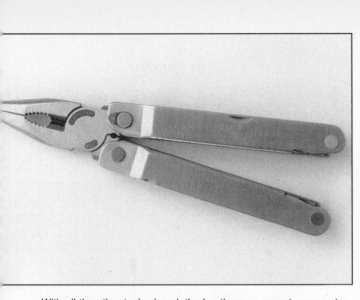

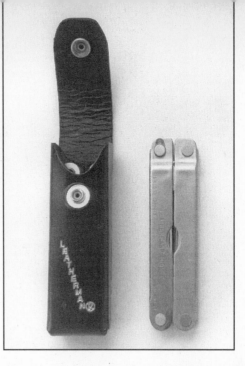

With all the other tools closed, the Leatherman operates as a standard pair of pliers with an efficient wire cutter. It folds to a compact size and comes with this leather belt pouch.

ter at the rear of the jaws, has a spring-loaded handle. The handle is held locked within the handle slabs. When that lock is rotated open, the single handle springs out, ready for use. It makes the pliers easier to use and lessens the chances of pinching fingers or your hand during use.

The primary knife blade is $2\frac{1}{4}$ inches long and is marked Seki, Japan, an area long known for its quality cutlery products. The Pocket Toolbox does not have the number of individual

tools of some of those we have encountered, but each is precision made and offers easy access. All in all, it is a typical A.G. Russell quality product.

Spencer Frazier has his knife business in Washington state now, but is a transplanted Californian. Perhaps that has nothing to do with his company's success, but since he made the move a decade or so ago, SOG Specialty Knives has flourished. Frazier, like Russell, is a brilliant designer and innovator. He mar-

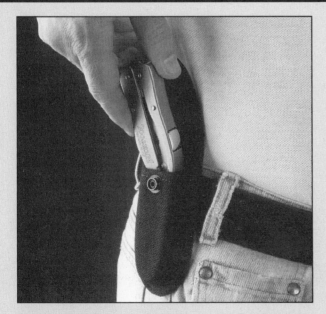

A nylon belt pouch is a handy place to carry the BuckTool or any other multi-blade folder.

hanger. Ever try cutting one of these? They are tougher than you think. The BuckTool cutters cut a section easily time after time.

The handles are made from 410 high-carbon (HC) stainless steel. The jaws are 420HC stainless hardened to 54 RC.

The rivets that hold the unit together are of stainless steel with a high shear strength that withstands 1000 pounds of pressure.

The pliers are just the beginning of the gadgets stored in this unit. Perhaps the easiest way to check out the tools available is to rotate one of the handles. At the rear, you will find little icons or symbols that indicate the tools stored in that handle.

The BuckTool has two knife blades, one in each handle section. One side holds a sheepsfoot blade, $2\frac{1}{2}$ inches long, fully serrated. It looks mean and is extremely sharp. This is a great cutting blade for rope, nylon cord, fishing line and other slippery, hard-to-cut materials.

For safety's sake, close each blade back into the handle before opening another. Three more tools in the handle include a can cutter and large and small Phillips-head screwdriver blades. Instead of the fingernail-ripping slot found on most blades in a folding system, there is an extended prong that you can get a fingernail under and lift one or both of the blades from the handle storage.

The can opener is a bit touchy to get used to, but is great for cutting holes in juice cans. It is quite sharp and has a holder that grips the can lid, allowing you to cut quickly. The Phillips screwdrivers work well, even though they look weird. We are used to standard items and most screwdrivers are round. This is only half a driver. When put to the test on large, small and in-between screws, they did a great job.

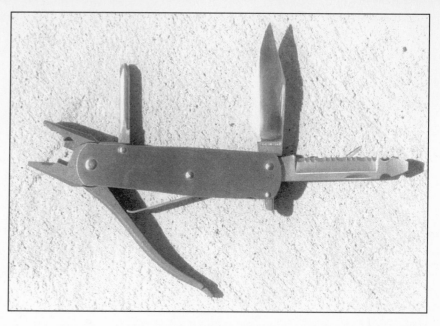

The A.G. Russell Pocket Toolbox easily lives up to its name. It's an update of a German patent from the World War I period.

kets several multi-tools, the Power Plier being one of the most interesting.

Using an ingenious lever and gear design, the pliers, gripper and wire-cutting components use compound leverage to really get a grip on things. When everything is closed, the Power Plier is 4½ inches long. Rotated open, with the pliers ready for use, the tool is 6¾ inches long, offering plenty of length for extra power. The jaws are almost 2 inches long, opening wide enough to grip all but the largest nuts, pipes, rods or wires. SOG warns that all other tool blades must be closed before using the pliers. The additional tools within the handle include a double-tooth saw blade; a 3-inch knife blade that is serrated for half its edge; fine, medium and coarse blade screwdrivers; Phillips screwdriver; a combination can and bottle opener; an awl; chisel; square drive; fine and coarse files; and 1-inch knife blade. For emergency repairs of firearms, bicycles, autos or household gadgets,

At the back of the group of tools is another razor-sharp knife blade of 2¾ inches, the back ¾-inch serrated. This gives you the normal cutting edge of the straight-blade knife with the added advantage of a tough line-cutting serrated section. There are three more levers that allow you to bring up three flat-head screwdriver blades. These are hollow-ground blades of #4, #6 and #8 sizes.

All the tools except the knife blades are made from 420LC (low-carbon) stainless steel. A twisting tool of hardened high-carbon steel will snap off when stressed, but softer steel accommodates the twisting action and will not be too brittle.

To close the pliers, fully rotate the two handles and you are back to the basic folded configuration. When you open the tools from the handles, you feel a bump or pause as you reach the half-open position. Apply a bit more pressure and a wide spring holds that tool or blade in the open position and you can't move it. This is the same locking principle of the famous Buck 110 Folding Hunter they came out with years ago. The Buck designers used much of the engineering from the Buck 110 when working up the BuckTool. The spring in the handle also is of 410 high-carbon stainless steel and it takes a bit of pressure to open the spring to release the tool.

The Buck design includes polypropylene washers on all moving parts. This makes the action smooth and easy on fingernails. There are twenty-three components assembled to

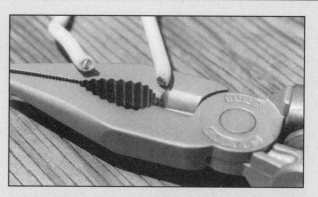

The pliers feature a wire cutter near the pivot point. The cutting blades actually overlap for a clean, easy cut.

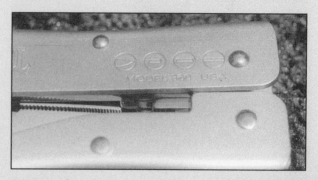

Buck has stamped each handle with icons to indicate what tools are contained therein. The knife blade and three screwdrivers are indicated here.

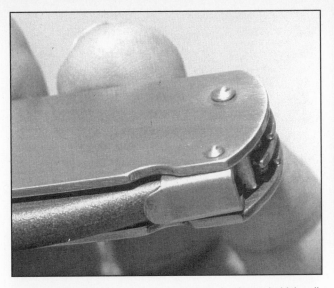

The Pocket Toolbox has a unique locking mechanism to hold the pliers handles closed.

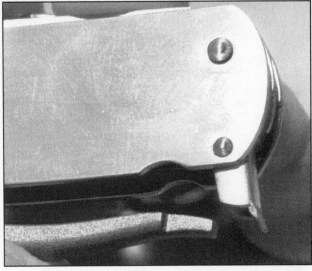

The handle lock is flipped open and the spring-loaded handle swings out for use.

the SOG Power Plier ought to get the job done. Also, the handle is marked with scales in metric or English measurements.

As with all mechanical devices, care must be exercised to prevent accidents, especially when opening or closing any of the blades. All the tool blades have nail nicks and nail slots to help get them open, but most of the time more than one wants to come out at once. The unwanted blades should be pushed back into the handle before using the selected tool. Further, the two

handles must be closed together, back to back, to prevent the unwanted closing of the blade in use. Some, especially the smaller knife and screwdriver blade, may be more difficult to close. The instructions contained with the Power Plier suggest the possibility of pressing against a table or workbench to help get them closed. All the blades are sharp where they are supposed to be, and extra care is called for when opening or closing them.

The SOG tool is made of stainless steel. Some breaking-in

A tough test for any blade is cutting through a nylon-reinforced hose. The serrated sheepsfoot blade really shines.

make one BuckTool. The tools and blades are shaped, hollow-ground, then polished in a tumble polisher. The handles and jaws are not tumbled, but bead-blasted to give them a satin finish.

One thing I found missing from the BuckTool is a traditional leather punch. If you work with leather you need a

punch or awl. Looking it over, it seemed the small flat-head screwdriver might do the job. A piece of 5-ounce, medium-weight leather was placed on a board and the small screwdriver blade twisted and turned into it, making a round hole. That hole could be enlarged by twisting it up the blade section, if necessary.

When driving a tough screw, you can move one handle to a right-angle position to the other handle, hold the working handle to prevent the screwdriver from slipping off the screw and obtain maximum torque. This technique removed a rusted, almost headless wood screw easily.

The BuckTool is just like any other in that the more you use it, the more use you will find for it. The tools often will do more than they were designed for, with some imagination.

Based on extensive research and field testing, the Buck-Tool has been ergonomically designed for maximum comfort. It is smooth and rounded, it will not pinch nor gouge your hand, no matter how much pressure you apply.

BuckTool's unique open/close pivoting system offers a variety of in-use configurations for extra versatility. For example, in the 180-degree configuration, the extended handles offer greater reach. The 90-degree configuration provides extra leverage and torque when used as a screwdriver.

The BuckTool is made in the U.S. and backed by Buck's lifetime guarantee. Every Buck product is guaranteed for the life of the purchaser against defects in materials or workmanship.

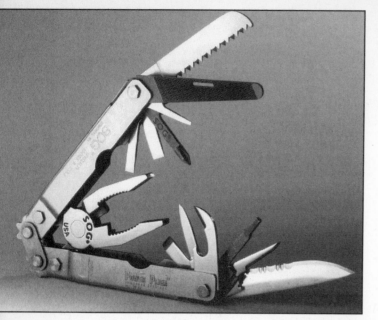

(Left) The SOG Power Plier boasts at least twenty tools in a compact package.

(Right) The SOG Power Plier uses a compound leverage system to generate plenty of gripping and wire-cutting ability.

The SOG line includes a smaller, compact ToolClip model that has lots of handy tools.

period and a bit of lubrication will help eliminate most of the stiffness in the action. Under some conditions, even the best stainless steel will rust. The smaller blades should be examined from time to time, but especially after contact with water, to prevent rust from starting. A little oil and fine steel wool will take care of any signs of corrosion. A lightweight nylon carrying pouch is included with the Power Plier. It is from SOG Specialty Knives.

There are other multi-tools on the market. Gerber has a couple of models, but we have not had a chance to work with them. We also had reports that Schrade, too, was developing one of these multiple-use tools, but none was available for evaluation.

Buck Knives has been working on a multi-tool design for more than a year. Buck's version is called the BuckTool, and was first shown at the 1996 Shooting, Hunting, Outdoor Trade Show in Dallas, Texas. Production got underway in mid-1996. Writer C.R. Learn has had a long, close relationship with the

Buck family and business. He was able to get his hands on one of the first production models to roll off the assembly line.

Chuck Buck, third generation of the knifemaking family and president of the company, says, "The BuckTool was designed by popular complaint."

He explains that their research and development team spent months in the field ferreting out what consumers liked and, more importantly, what they did not like about existing multi-tools.

"We found they really liked the basic concept of a compact tool and its versatility," Buck says. "But they were equally emphatic about the things they disliked.

"The tools they had used were not comfortable to grip; they pinched your hand; they did not lock open; the knife blades were not sharp; and it was hard to find the implement you wanted," he explained. "Our R&D people came up with answers to every one of those complaints. That's why we are convinced we have made a better tool."

The Gentleman's Pocketknife

THERE IS NO universal agreement about what constitutes a "gentleman's" pocketknife. By most definitions, any knife that folds small enough to be carried in a pocket is a pocketknife. It would follow that if it is carried by a gentleman, it must be what the title says. But a gentleman's pocketknife is something more than simply a small folder.

These little folders were—and still are—handy for sharpening pencils, snipping off wayward thread, cutting string and tape, opening letters and packages, slicing cardboard, cleaning pipes, trimming cigars—even slicing off a bite of apple, if the blade is kept clean.

The history of pocketknives dates back a couple hundred years. Bernard Levine, in his excellent series of books, *Levine's Guide To Knives And Their Values*, traces the beginnings of German, English and American knifemaking, especially the making of small folders, as far back as the late 18th century, particularly in the U.S. At that time, most of the cutlery production in the United States was being done in New England and the northeastern part of the country, where the streams and rivers furnished waterwheel power, then later steam and, even later, hydroelectric power.

The point is, pocketknives have been around for at least a couple of centuries. Methods of locking the blades open and closed, types of steel, various handle materials and decorations have changed over the centuries, but not the basic knife design.

Generally, we shall define the gentleman's pocketknife as a small folder, thin enough so as not to produce an unsightly bulge in the wearer's pocket, with one or two blades that may or may not lock open. Furthermore, our definition shall insist that the knife present an attractive appearance. On that last part, beauty is in the eye of the beholder, so what may be attractive to one of us may not be to another.

Most of the gentleman's pocketknives we have had a chance to inspect are single-blade folders, but some have two blades, usually swiveling out from opposite ends of the handle. Perhaps the most common blade found in such knives is called the pen blade. The pen blade is small, perhaps an $1^1/2$, but less than 2 inches long. It has an almost equal curve to the edge and back, coming to a point in the center. It is always supposed to be quite sharp.

The original purpose, as one might suppose, was to trim the tip of a writing quill when such instruments of communication were still in style. The little blade proved to have many more uses over the years, so the shape lives on. One of the two blades will be a pen blade.

As a matter fact, our gentleman's pocketknife does not have

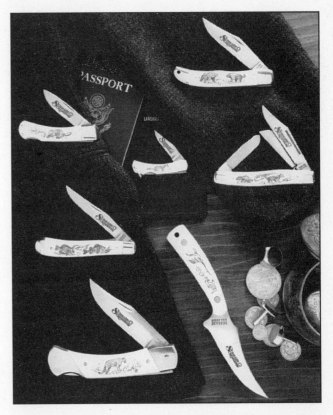

Some of the knives in Schrade's Scrimshaw Series may be termed gentleman's pocketknives, others not. The smaller folder at the top center fits the definition.

to have any particular type, number or shape of blade. It may have one, two or three blades, opening from either end. To qualify, though, it must not be too thick or too long.

There are hundreds of small pocketknife styles that millions of people carry and use every day, but some are too thick for this category. They make an unsightly bulge in the pocket of a business suit. And if the gentleman wears Levis, there will soon be in evidence a lighter-colored outline of the little folder on the outside of the pocket. The outline might be OK in the hip pocket, left from a can of chewing tobacco, but a gentleman should not reveal the location and size of his pocketknife.

Another issue that must be considered is travel with a pocketknife. Anyone who travels with even the smallest folder knows the perils and difficulties that may be encountered at airport security check stations. In most airports, getting aboard with a small, non-locking folder is no problem—just place it in the little tray with your coins and pen, and most security per-

These lightweight MiniBucks are small enough to be termed pocketknives with locking blades.

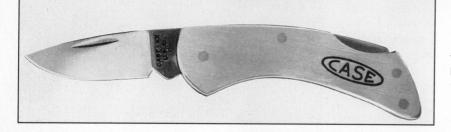

This simple little Case folder has a single locking blade and is carried unobtrusively.

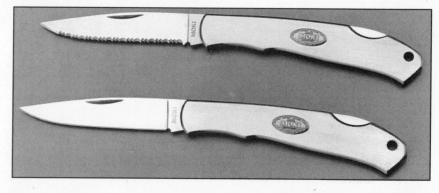

Spyderco's Moki 520 is designed to be thin and comfortable in the pocket. The blade is 2½ inches long, stainless steel, available with plain edge or serrated. It does not have the familiar Spyderco pocket clip.

sonnel will not give it a second thought. However, as the knife grows larger and when it has a locking blade, some guards at some airports will question it. We offer no guarantees, but most so-called pen knives and gentleman's folders cause no delays in boarding.

This brings us to the issue of to lock or not to lock. There is a degree of argument among some knife people as to whether the definition of a gentleman's pocketknife would include some sort of locking blade. Some say no; some say yes. There are dozens of factory production and custom-made knives on the market today that meet the other criteria for small pocketknives and have locking blades. If the folded knife is shorter than, say, 3 inches with an unobtrusive locking mechanism, it will carry without leaving its spoor.

Locks and their releases are to be found in various locations and positions on small knives. Some are up near the blade; others are at the rear or bottom of the handle. To qualify as a gentleman's pocketknife, we will arbitrarily restrict the acceptable locks to those that feature flush locking buttons or levers. Large protrusions and button openers, the kind that permit the blade to be opened with one hand, need not apply. The buttons or bolts make too obvious a bulge.

A folder without a locking mechanism actually does have a blade "lock." The design relies on friction to hold the blade open or closed. The typical small pocketknife has a friction lock. Otherwise, the blade would flop closed when held with the edge down and ready to cut. After a great deal of wear, such a design might become too loose and need tightening; not a job

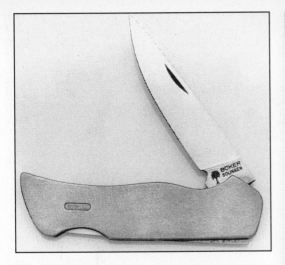

The little Boker Model 2009 was designed as a gentleman's pocketknife.

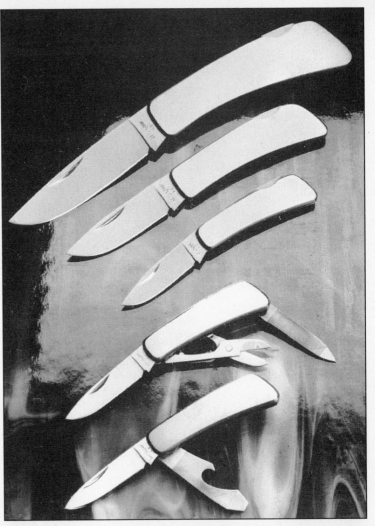

Out of the five knives in Kershaw's Cascade Series, only the smallest two may qualify.

A fine example of a gentleman's pocketknife is this engraved folder, produced by Al Mar a few years ago.

for an amateur, but it can be done. On the other hand, even a blade mechanism made of stainless steel can become dirty or experience some corrosion or damage. All folders should be kept clean.

The typical pocketknife will attract all kinds of pocket lint, sand, thread and other dirt problems. The little knives must be cleaned from time to time. Start by carefully and slowly opening and closing the blade. In everyday use, you may not notice any sticking or hesitation that has developed over time. Many small folders rely on a simple spring on the back of the folder to keep the blade open or closed. The spring may be seen moving slightly out of the handle slabs when the blade is opened and closed. The folding blade cams on the spring, and those surfaces are critical to the smooth functioning of the blade action. They must be clean and free of corrosion.

After watching and feeling the blade(s) open and close, the next step is simply to look down into the blade cavity. It probably will be dirty. The opening may be quite small, so a wooden toothpick or small sliver of wood may be all that will fit into it. Most small pocketknives do not have the room to accept a cotton-tipped stick, although they are ideal for larger models. After loosening the lint and fuzz, blow hard to remove it. Push the toothpick along the slot to remove as much dirt as possible, although it may be difficult to get it as clean as new. Use care to not break off the toothpick in the knife handle.

If the knife is extra dirty, the only thing to do is soak it in a bath of thin machine oil, remove it and let it drain for a day or

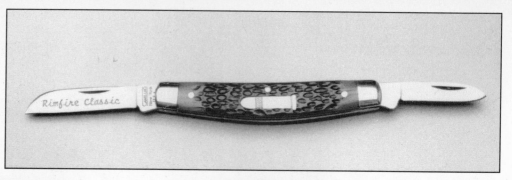

The Camillus Rimfire Classic features a 1³/₄-inch etched sheepfoot blade and a 1¹/₄-inch pen blade. It fits the bill.

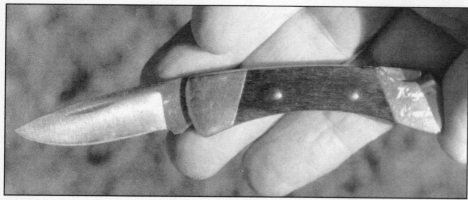

(Left) Buck has produced thousands of these little locking pocketknives, ideal for a gentleman's pocket or lady's purse.

(Below) The Boker ceramic-blade folder was plenty sharp, but expensive and breakable.

two on a thick pad of paper towels or a shop towel. Hopefully, all the foreign matter will drain out with the excess oil. Run a layer or two of tissue through the slot to clean out any more loosened dirt and oil.

If you have used an oil soak, no further lubrication is necessary. In theory, an all-stainless steel folder should need no oil, but a tiny drop of the thinnest oil at the pivot pin and locking mechanism may be appropriate for most folders. If you use too much, the oil eventually will leak out and could stain your good suit. Most women would not welcome even a little oil leaking into their purse. It won't matter much on an old pair of jeans, though. No matter, drain out and soak up as much excess as possible before slipping the knife back in your pocket. If you don't, excess oil will tend to attract more dirt and lint, and you'll have to clean it again.

There is no rule as to what sort of steel is appropriate for a gentleman's pocketknife. Most modern pocketknives will use stainless steel. In a pocket or purse, most small knives are subject to moisture invasion damage from perspiration, condensation or wet hands, so stainless is appropriate. Blades of 2 or 3 inches long are more difficult to forge from Damascus steel, but some makers are doing it, and it makes an expensive pocketknife. Also, there have been plenty of small pocketknives made with tool steel over the years, steel that will rust and stain. With proper care, though, they will give good service for decades.

In recent years, other materials have been incorporated into folding blades. Not so long ago, Boker experimented with ceramic for folding blades. It is lightweight, non-magnetic and non-conductive to electricity. Ceramic is hard and extremely sharp. The bad news is that it is relatively brittle and will break if mishandled. Ceramic blades did not experience a mass acceptance in the marketplace.

The latest trend is to experiment with titanium blades. Titani-um is extremely lightweight and strong when compared to steel, but it is difficult to work and requires special machines, techniques and different heat treating. It is also many times as expensive as steel. People and companies from the aerospace industry have experience with titanium, but only a few are experimenting with the metal for knives. Its promise may lay in the future.

BIRD HUNTER BLADES

There are subtle design variations that make the difference

MUCH IN THE way of knife making is pointed toward the big game hunter. Designs like the drop-point, skinner and caper are obvious examples of such specialized cutlery. Although it is possible for a guide or hunter to use just one knife for everything afield, the various jobs of field dressing, skinning, butchering and removing the cape for mounting are more efficiently done with a blade refined for each purpose.

The same concept of blade specialization and overall knife design also can apply to small game hunting. Indeed, as the knife industry has progressed, there are new folders that jibe nicely with a clay target shooter's needs; these aren't necessar-

ily important for the cutting they do, but rather for the fold-out accessories they carry. However, that's getting somewhat ahead of the story. Field applications are the first subject.

"The term bird knife is actually somewhat generic. There can be subtle differences between knives for upland game and waterfowl" according to Don Zutz, a noted shotgun writer and researcher. "For example, upland game is processed easily, and the joints of such birds as quail, doves, grouse and even pheasants are not as tough as those of waterfowl. Thus, the cutting blade need not be massive. A blade of 2½ to 3 inches is perfectly adequate. All that's needed is some tightness and stabili-

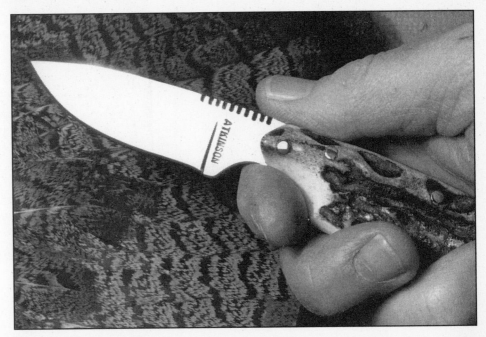

A custom-made small game drop-point by Dick Atkinson works well on most of the larger game birds. The groove for the trigger finger and the pressure point for thumb placement give leverage and control when needed.

ty at the hinge point for strength and security.

"A clip-style blade is fine and seems to be a favorite with designers who conjure up bird hunting folders. The sharp point can help expedite skinning and drawing, and there generally is enough backbone to sever joints.

"Maneuverability is a greater asset in bird knives than cutting blade length. On an upland knife, where the blade is used to sever joints, a blade of 2 1/2 to 2 3/4 inches often works best, because one can exert pressure more efficiently than he can through a longer blade."

When it comes to waterfowl knives, there can be some subtle variations in blade and accessory features. The larger, tougher joints of waterfowl, especially geese, are handled more easily by a serrated blade, which functions like a saw. One popular folder that carries a serrated blade for this specialty is Remington's Waterfowl model.

"Because a lot of duck and goose hunters skin their birds, the blade takes on a new task," Zutz reports. "For this reason, the waterfowl knife can have some length and a curve for skinning."

Skinning can dull a cutting edge rapidly, of course, and one requirement is having a finely tapered cutting edge so it can be touched up quickly while one is at the cleaning table.

"Those big game knives with their ultra-hard steels, thick blades and abrupt edges are sheer frustration for working on even the largest goose, because their edges are purposely thick for a different kind of job, and they seem to take forever to sharpen. Likewise, a long, limber blade isn't efficient on waterfowl, since it can wobble when pressure is applied. It may be a 12-pound goose, but a 2 1/2- to 3-inch blade is adequate."

The point to remember is that for the heavier work, a serrated blade is best for cartilage and neck/wing use. The straight cutting blade isn't always right, and relatively short blades of 3 inches or less are the most efficient, as one can apply hand pressure more directly to the blade.

As mentioned, the evolving designs of bird knives include accessories that can be considered as important to an outing as the blades themselves. One of the main features of a true bird knife, for instance, is the gutting hook. This member of a folder's features is, in some respects, an enlarged knitting needle and is an aid if one chooses to cut open the bird for field dressing.

"Because so few stateside hunters understand the gutting hook, not many knifemakers have had success with the product," Zutz reports. "It is, therefore, often difficult to find such a model in many shops. The most readily available folder of this sort is Remington's Upland folder, which not only has an excellent gutting hook but also a 3-inch blade, plus a choke tube tool.

"Hunters who fillet bird breasts are best served by a truly thin blade. The 3-inch clip blades found on many bird knife folders can do the job. However, it is interesting to note how efficiently a fish fillet knife can function here. These are thin-bladed specialties that either retain a sharp edge or are quickly touched up, and they slice neatly along bone. They are also good in the kitchen for cutting small game into serving-sized pieces. The shortest possible blade is recommended, however, whenever the fish fillet knife crosses over into bird preparation."

Bird hunters aren't the only ones who frequent the uplands, of course. Many people still enjoy the pleasures of rabbit and squirrel hunting, too. Beagles make the swamps ring with their merry music, while a quiet squirrel woods is soothing to one's frazzled nerves. Both are hunting challenges.

The knife market doesn't have a model designated precisely for rabbit and squirrel hunters, but there are some folders that do the job nicely. One of these is known variously as the muskrat knife, muskrat skinner or just plain trapper's blade. Whatever its moniker, it has a long, sharply pointed clip blade and an equally lengthy, curved-tip spey blade, which combine to handle the dressing and skinning of small, furred animals.

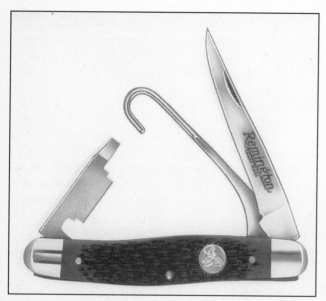

This Remington Upland knife from the Sportsman Series features a gutting hook, one of the very few American-made knives to do so.

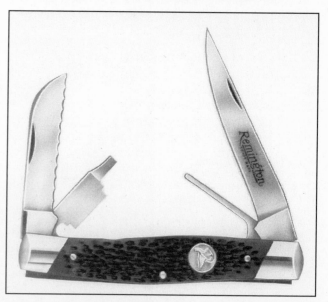

Another useful specialty knife of the Remington Sportsman Series is the Waterfowl model with a serrated blade for severing tough joints. There is also a punch for removing trigger units and a choke-tube changing blade for 12- and 20-gauge shotguns.

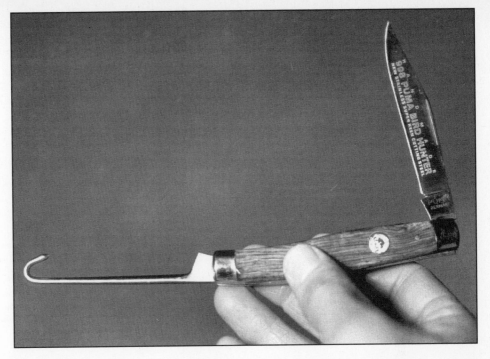

The Bird Hunter in Gutmann Cutlery's Puma line is an effective bird knife with its gutting hook and saber-point blade.

"If one thinks in terms of all-round capabilities for a folder on small game, both furred and feathered, he might find it in the so-called stockman model," Zutz says.

This design is often seen in a 3⅞-inch length, and it has three useful blades: a long clip blade, a shorter spey blade and a moderate-length sheepsfoot blade. A sheepsfoot blade often has a little more backbone than other blades, and it can be effective on bird joints or other places where a relatively short blade with a sharp point is useful.

A growing trend in folder design is the utilization of extensive accessories beyond the realm of cutting blades. Perhaps this was started by the Swiss Army knives from Victorinox, which have everything on them from corkscrews and orange peelers to scissors and toothpicks. Unfortunately, however, the Swiss Army models have little to recommend them as small game specialties. Indeed, the least important points on these Swiss Army knives seem to be the cutting blades, which are of no noteworthy geometry.

But other manufacturers have gone a step further to attach folding accessories that are helpful to shotgunners.

As mentioned, the Remington Upland has a choke tube tool for both 12- and 20- gauges. The Waterfowl model has this feature, too, but includes a fourth appendage to facilitate the removal of a repeater's fire control mechanism, the trigger plate. It is a stubby punch dimensioned to fit the drift pin holes in the Remington Model 870, 1100, and 11-87 and SP-10, as well as those in other repeaters with similar takedown features.

The Remington Turkey Hunter knife also has the punch and 3-inch clip blade. The choke tube tool on the knife, however, is for 10- and 12-gauge guns rather than the 20. The 10-gauge is a more common turkey piece than the 20.

Browning is another gunmaker with good knife ideas for hunters and shotgunners. In the Featherweight lineup, Browning offers a 3½-inch folding Fish & Bird model with a 2½-inch main clip blade and a shorter spey-type member. The same

basic concept is also made in Browning's Traditional line with stag grip. And for those who might like to use a fish fillet knife on game as well as trout and panfish, Browning's 4½-inch-blade fillet knife will give easy maneuverability plus surgical sharpness.

Fixed-blade knives always have been equated mainly with big game hunting, and few bird models have ever appeared. But with the state of the art in custom knifemaking, it wouldn't be impossible for a skilled artisan to fashion fixed-blade concepts scaled to small game. Custom maker Dick Atkinson made a pair of scaled-down designs for Zutz, who is primarily a bird hunter. One was a small game drop-point with a blade little longer than a 20-gauge field load; the other was a sway-back skinner with a well defined point. Both have been used extensively on game from woodcock to Canada geese with satisfying results. The small game drop-point is especially handy. From the standpoint of portability, however, the sheathed folder is a premier item, toted almost unnoticed as opposed to the length and bulk of a sheathed fixed blade.

"If there is any problem with current hunting knives, it is that they frequently contain ultra-hard steels and are difficult to sharpen afield," Zutz opines. "Once an edge is gone, it takes time to put a new one on. This is especially true for knives with thick blades and abruptly tapered edges; those with thinner blades and longer tapers will sharpen more quickly. However, the use of softer steels will accommodate an active hunter's field needs; he'll be able to touch up the edge quickly with just a few strokes on a steel or stone. Hopefully, manufacturers and designers will take that to heart."

Meanwhile, shotgunners have things going their way in the knife business. With people like Remington and Browning selling knives, stylings are being turned out to suit their specialties rather than merely being built according to traditional concepts. Bird hunters and clay target shooters can easily find specialty blades to fit their needs.

CHAPTER 18

KNIVES FOR SALE

Cutlery is made and sold by large and small businesses everywhere

OPERATING A BUSINESS is never easy, no matter what type of enterprise or where it may be located. A small business that is able to stay solvent and operating for at least a decade is a rarity. And when that small business is selling knives, successfully, it becomes all that more impressive.

Part of the explanation is that the cutlery business is relatively small; the industry never has been much of a giant compared to, say, General Electric or General Motors. Competition is tough in the knife business. Nearly every hardware store, department store, mail-order catalog, county fair, gun show and swap meet has knives for sale. Overall, the public is mostly uninformed and uneducated about better cutlery and where to find it. Every businessman specializing in edged tools knows that more than half of his or her time is spent educating prospective buyers. It can be a tough sell to some, but providing a ready purchase to others. Not every consumer can appreciate the work and talent that goes into a $250 factory-made knife, let alone that of a $1500 handmade knife.

One successful retail knife outlet is owned and operated by Dan and Pam Delavan in Southern California. The store is called Plaza Cutlery, primarily because it is located in one of the larger shopping malls of the nation, South Coast Plaza. The names may be familiar to many readers outside California, because Dan Delavan is the man who put on the California Custom Knife Show from 1981 to 1995, until he sold the show to Krause Publications and *The Blade Magazine*.

When the show was first held, the public's awareness of custom knifemakers and their art, as well as the number of custom makers, was far less than today. The number of custom makers, the number of exhibitors and the number of show-goers has greatly multiplied in the life of this and other knife shows.

The Delavans built the show from a couple dozen exhibitors, mostly from the Southern California area, and a few hundred attendees, to the large, successful show it is—one that's on the approved list by the Knifemakers Guild. When the show was sold, knifemakers, commercial exhibitors and collectors were coming from all over the world, eager for the exposure and for the chance to see some of the best cutlery products anywhere.

At the start, the show seemed a natural adjunct to the Delavans' retail cutlery store. While most of the factory-made knives, scissors, razors, darts and other edged tools are familiar to customers, the concept of a handmade, custom-built knife selling for several hundred dollars needed considerable explanation. In time, the knife show took on a life of its own, and the retail store has also thrived and expanded.

Even as a young man, Dan Delavan was no stranger to the world of knives. For many years, his father was the premier Case Cutlery salesman in North America. I.A. Delavan traveled the country and knew many of the sellers and buyers of cutlery in the days after WW II. The younger Delavan learned the knife business through his father and mother; he grew up in the business, as the saying goes.

Plaza Cutlery sells the production of several nationally known and/or local custom knifemakers. Over the years, Delavan has developed a pleasant relationship with several makers, and these folks know their knives will be offered and displayed with care and consideration. The store sells a large number of custom knives each year, some to regular customers who add to their collections every chance they get. The shop also carries the full product line of most of the factory knife manufacturers, including, of course, Case.

Dan Delavan has a heritage in the knife business, because his father was a top salesman for Case Cutlery for many years. Now Delavan operates the popular Plaza Cutlery retail outlet in California.

Delavan displays all types of knives, ranging from the smallest pocket folders to the largest survival knives. The shop is a bit unusual with its display of dozens of swords. Swords, Delavan says, are popular in his shop, and he sells a good many per year. Most, he believes, are sold to collectors or home decorators who want to display a long blade over the fireplace or in the den.

The knives are displayed in the many lighted glass cases in the store, arranged by size and by maker. The customer can easily locate a favorite brand and find the size, price and style knife he or she prefers. There is also a wide assortment of sharpening tools, plus scissors, darts, razors, watches, clocks, pen and pencil sets, some beer steins and other items.

There are dozens of variety, specialty and department stores in the mall that may be offering similar products, but Delavan's philosophy is that he will carry whatever he can sell, with the major emphasis on knives and other cutting tools.

The store also includes blade sharpening and repair services for customers. Delavan does the knife and scissors sharpening after store hours, often at home. He has found that customers appreciate the sharpening service and it brings more customers into the store. He employs his wife and mother, as well as a couple of part-time workers, in the shop. At certain times of the year, especially near the holiday season, the store is crowded with customers and shoppers and the cash register rings steadily with gift purchases. Weekdays, after school, there are usually plenty of young people on the floor checking out the knives, especially the larger models and those featured in recent popular films.

Because of its location, the California Custom Knife Show

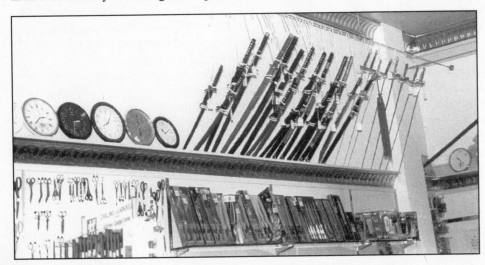

Swords, foils and sabers are on display at Delavan's Plaza Cutlery, as well as most other cutlery items.

Many of the smaller knife dealers are husband-and-wife teams seen at many knife shows across the country. Carol and Ray Smith are typical examples.

always has attracted many of Hollywood's celebrities, past, present and future. Some have become regular customers of Plaza Cutlery and many are seen attending the knife show each year. Many of the knives on display at either location have appeared in films and on television in the hands of actors who seem to know a great deal about the knives they use.

Many entertainment industry workers, other than actors, are avid collectors, too. They appreciate and use all types of knives in their work and while performing. Over the years, well-known and little-known actors such as Sylvester Stallone, Jameson Parker, Sonny Landham, Richard Chaves and many of those who work behind the scenes have patronized the show and Delavan's shop.

Cutlery shops may be found in many shopping malls around the country, but the most common methods of marketing cutlery are through mail order and direct to the customer by dealers at gun or knife shows. In and around many metropolitan areas, the interested buyer might find four or five custom knife shows per year, and at least fifty gun shows within driving distance.

The more expensive handmade, collectible knives usually are found at knife shows, while there are plenty of less expensive knives for sale at most gun shows. Typically, there may be a half-dozen part-time cutlery dealers at a gun show, with hundreds of inexpensive folders and sheath knives for sale. Most of these dealers are not dependent on the sale of a dozen pocket knives a month for a major part of their income, but they present a vast source of interesting knives for most of us.

Longtime, well established knife dealers such as Ray and Carol Smith (R&C Knives & Such) are to be seen at a dozen or more knife shows per year. They maintain a successful business selling knives. Many small businesses like this are run by a husband and wife, with no other employees.

The Smith's business is conducted with a combination of knife and gun show attendance, and through a mail-order product catalog they have developed. Through more than two decades of the cutlery business, the Smiths have welcomed a large following of loyal customers. They collect names of potential customers at the shows, too, to add to the mailing list.

With the cost of postage and paper rising each year, the catalog becomes more expensive to produce and mail, but it is a major income producer for the small company.

The Smiths sell a good portion of their knife stock at shows, as might be expected. Many customers wait to make their purchases directly from them at these shows. Seeing, feeling and picking up a knife is a better way to learn about a specific offering than looking at a picture of it in a catalog.

Another good reason for attending knife shows, say the Smiths, is the chance to locate and buy knives from other dealers and knifemakers. Through the years, they have learned who makes the handmade knives their customers want, who is reliable, who makes good knives. There may be several opportunities for a small retailer to pick up some products from casual show attendees who happen to pass by the exhibitor's table. They know their customers and what they want, and try to obtain and catalog knives that will sell.

A large percentage of knives sold throughout the world is by mail order through catalogs. One of the largest such operations is Catoctin Cutlery, operating out of Smithsburg, Maryland. They are wholesale distributors and importers of thousands of knives, swords and other cutlery items from and to most of the world.

Catoctin imports such brands as Aitor from Spain; A. Wright & Son, Sheffield, England; David Knives, Fox brand and MKM knives from Italy; Hirschkrone from Germany; Neito of Spain; and Vaciacraft from the Philippines.

In addition to distributing those products, the company catalogs most of the other small, medium and large knife manufacturers. Brands include Al Mar, Apex, Bear MGC, Blackjack, Boker, Cold Steel, Doskocil, Estwing, Executive Edge, Pro-Cut, Puma, Queen, Ranger, Chris Reeve, Schrade, Smith & Wesson, SOG, Spyderco, Timberline, Valor and Wyoming. They also stock knives from Buck, Gerber and Victorinox Swiss Army Knives.

Catoctin acts as jobbers for Safesport, Valor, Fury and Compass products.

In addition to police and law enforcement equipment, flashlights and knife pouches and sheaths, Catoctin carries sharpen-

Atlanta Cutlery's plain exterior does not reveal the worldwide business it houses.

(Below) Damascus knife blade blanks are also offered by Atlanta Cutlery.

ing products from Creative Sales, EZ Lap, Lansky, Spyderco and Washita Mountain Whetstone.

If that is not enough, they also list all types of boot knives, butterfly knives, martial arts equipment, machetes, military surplus knives, swords, tomahawks, push daggers, police supplies and throwing knives.

Most of the products the company distributes are available through retail outlets and not directly from Catoctin.

Atlanta Cutlery is another catalog company specializing in strange and unusual knives from all over the world. The company was founded by Bill Adams more than twenty-five years ago, and today mails thousands of copies of its catalog to prospective buyers several times a year. The catalog averages eighty pages and has hundreds of color illustrations. Many of the knives in the catalog are offered exclusively by Atlanta Cutlery.

Among the unusual recent offerings are the Chinese Police Knife, Shanghai Stiletto and what are said to be genuine military-issue Polish paratrooper knives.

There are many American brands represented, as well as knives from Spain, England, India, Italy, Brazil, Taiwan, Poland, Sweden, Austria, Philippines, Germany, Pakistan, Norway, Russia, Switzerland, China, Mexico, Canada, Finland, Japan and the Czech Republic. In all, Adams says the company offers products from twenty-two countries, ranging from the smallest pocket knives to several large, impressive swords, sabers, bayonets and daggers.

Sharpening stones and kits also are listed in the catalog, as are Civil War figures and miniature cannons. There is a section dedicated to blade blanks and knifemaking supplies for those who want to try their hand at the art of custom knifemaking.

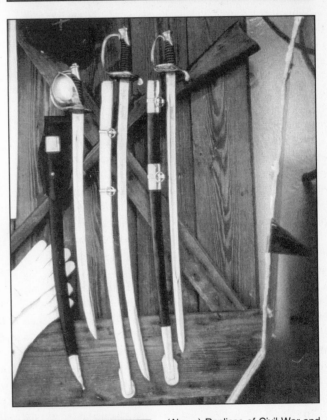

(Above) Replicas of Civil War and earlier conflicts are part of the mail-order mix from Atlanta Cutlery.

Strictly a mail-order operation, Atlanta Cutlery has found a big market for Samurai swords.

Most knife shows feature collector exhibitions. These knives not for sale.

Several sizes and shapes of blade blanks, knife kits, handle supplies, hilts, epoxy cement, polish, solder, rivets and bolts are available for the rookie or the skilled home craftsman to try.

While researching long knives and swords, the authors found that Bob Engnath is considered one of the premier modern swordmakers in the country. He turns out a prodigious number of long blades for customers all over the world.

A large part of Engnath's production goes to the Bugei Trading Company. This small outfit sells Japanese martial arts books, video tapes, artwork, clothing, paintings, woodcuts, swords and knives. Most of their business is generated through a slick catalog, but they have an office and showroom in the small university town of San Marcos, California.

Bugei fills a growing demand from martial artists around the world, but mostly in the U.S. for its Japanese-style swords. These are constructed using blades from Bob Engnath. As pricey as the Bugei swords may be, they are less expensive and more readily available than authentic made-in-Japan swords. Those who know these things claim the Engnath blades are as good as any made in Japan.

To quote the current catalog, "Bugei Trading Company was founded out of the love for the ancient Samurai military arts and of the attributes that the classical-era warrior personified. There has been a trend in modern *budo* to disparage this violent time and to discount the knowledge that we have received from these warriors. Knowledge that was learned was frequently at the cost of their lives. This knowledge, which has been passed down for generations, is a sacred trust.

"At Bugei, we believe that what we have today would not exist without the contributions made by so many and we are grateful. Those individuals under the greatest duress most often are the ones who exhibit these attributes to the highest degree."

The catalog introduction goes on to say, "We don't view the power gained through military skills as a personal power to be used in our own self interest. The trend toward self-aggrandizement, while common in much of modern 'martial arts,' is con-

trary to the ideals of *bushido*. The power and ability that is gained through the military arts is a sacred trust to be used for just purpose, not for personal desire.

"The sword is not admired for its ability to bring death, but because of its ability to give life. This ideal is called *Katsujin-ken*. The sword that strikes down those who do evil, in turn, gives life to those upon whom evil would prey. In our modern society, as in ancient Japan, there are those who through fear and violence prey upon society. The need for warriors and the warrior spirit is as great now as it was for our ancestors."

Bugei can provide fully functional replicas of most types and styles of antique blades used by the Samurai. They strive for historical authenticity in shape, weight, balance and performance in their blades. Each blade is individually made and no two are the same.

The price for a completed katana is $2200 (1997 prices). This includes your choice of furniture, color of *saya* and *tsuka-ito*. All sword orders are dealt with on a custom basis. These blades are designed to be used and are beautiful as well as functional. Please do not confuse them with the gaudy caricatures found in other catalogs.

"Our blades are dangerous weapons and must be treated with respect. They should be used only after proper training and with competent supervision to avoid injury. Bugei will not accept responsibility for negligence or improper use," officers proclaim.

Make no mistake about it, these are real swords for a real purpose. We have seen them under construction and watched them being shaped, ground, polished and sharpened. All of the several designs, shapes and types are as authentic as can be, using furniture and fittings imported from Japan.

"Our blades," declares John Williams, one of the founding partners of Bugei Trading, "are made in the United States of 1050 steel, similar to the steel composition of antique Japanese swords. The shape, size and weight matches those of antique blades. They are tempered in the traditional manner and the

Exotic edged weapons from various parts of the world draw interested spectators at most knife shows. Interest in the exotic, especially Oriental knives and martial arts, has increased in recent years, leading to business opportunities for some small dealers.

yakiba, or fired edge, shows its *hamon* (a visible difference between the heat treatment of the edge and the rest of the blade) clearly when polished.

"The edge is tempered to 57-58 on the Rockwell C hardness scale, while the body of the blade is about 46 on the same scale. This means the yakiba will take and hold a keen edge for cutting while the body of the blade remains ductile to absorb shock. Each hamon—firing line—is unique. Blades may be ordered in specific design and length, but orders take from 90 to 120 days to fill. The blades are shipped unpolished with instructions on how to accomplish this task. All blades are magnafluxed to make sure that there are no cracks caused by the tempering process.

"These are real swords and cut very well. They will stand the stress of actual use when handled properly. Unlike the swords offered in most martial arts catalogs, our swords are real weapons and need to be handled with skill and caution. They are capable of cutting through large-diameter bamboo and will easily do the same to body parts if not handled with caution and respect.

"The type and design of blade runs the basic range and variety of feudal-era edged weapons. We strive for authentic weight, balance and feel in quality antique replicas."

People who have an interest in such weapons often learn about sources for swords and long knives by word of mouth. They hear about them in their *dojo*, or the training center. The

Bob Hajovsky (Bob-Sky Knives) and Bill Herndon discuss the knife business during a Knifemakers Guild-authorized show.

A well-run knife show will draw customers from all over the world seeking knife bargains.

(Below) Custom knifemaker Chris Reeve is one who knows the business value of attending several shows a year.

Bugei catalog has plenty of research and related material listed, as well as details for ordering one of their swords. John Williams is always willing to talk edged weapons and martial arts, too.

A.G. Russell is another catalog vendor of knives. He has several distinctions to his credit. As you read elsewhere in this volume, he was one of those instrumental in founding the Knifemakers Guild, the trade group of custom knifemakers, almost three decades ago. The guild has grown from a few dozen members in the early years to several hundred today. Russell has been in the business of marketing handmade and factory-produced knives even longer. He has helped bring fame and fortune to many of the cutlery stars of today, makers nobody had heard of before their wares were shown in the Russell catalogs.

He produces a beautiful, full-color catalog that is mailed out to customers several times a year, always with new material and photos inside. A.G. Russell never fails to offer a bit of philosophy in his catalog, just to keep things interesting.

The catalogs are so beautifully done that they are almost works of art in themselves. He offers knives of his own design and manufacture, knives from some of the better-known custom makers and several special limited-production factory knives. Often, Russell will buy out the entire production run of a particular design or model in order to offer the knives exclusively in his catalog.

A.G. Russell began it all in the early 1970s, and he had no competition then in the knife catalog business. Back then, a large percentage of his business was in Arkansas sharpening stones, called noviculite.

Noviculite is a natural, soft stone mined from mountains near Russell's headquarters. For years, he was the supplier to the world of these natural Arkansas sharpening stones, and they are still some of the best things available to sharpen and hone knives. However, Russell no longer catalogs them. He apparently sold out the last of the supplies he had a few years ago.

Now he offers other man-made sharpening stones and systems in his catalog.

A.G. Russell has hundreds of products passing through his catalog system to thousands of customers all over the world, yet he is able to maintain the personal touch in his communications and in the catalog presentations. He has done a lot for knifemakers and for the knife business over the years. He continues to locate unusual and unique products to bring to our attention.

KNIVES FOR SALE

Buck Knives

THERE ARE NOT many companies of any kind in the United States today that are run by the same family after four generations. Buck Knives is one of the major exceptions, with C.J. Buck—son of Chuck Buck, grandson of Al Buck and great-grandson of Hoyt Buck—active in the operations.

Hoyt Buck was the man who started it all, when he began an apprenticeship in blacksmithing shortly after the turn of the 20th century. To be sure, the thirteen-year-old Hoyt Buck was not making knives in 1902. He was fixing wagons, shoeing horses and repairing equipment used to harvest Kansas wheat.

But he also was sharpening grub-hoes and reapers used on the farms nearby. Hoyt Buck began to experiment with new and different ways to temper the steel used in the tools. He and others soon noted that his tools held an edge better than before. There were plenty of used files around the shop, so Hoyt Buck began to make knife blades that held an edge. He discovered the secret to a good knife edge was to ensure that the entire blade was at the same temperature before it was plunged into the quenching oil. He also discovered that the task was not so easy. Done right, the technique would eliminate the so-called dead spots in any blade.

These early attempts at knifemaking were not a first step in an unbroken line leading directly to the Buck Knife corporation of today. In 1907, at age eighteen, Hoyt Buck packed his bags and headed for the state of Washington and the opportunities in the Pacific Northwest he had heard about. He worked a number of jobs, including serving as a crew member on a Puget Sound boat, and soon met and became determined to marry Daisy Green, the daughter of a sailing ship captain. They were wed in 1909. Daisy Buck died in 1947, after thirty-eight years of marriage.

Their first child, Alfred Charles Buck, was born in 1910, just before the family moved to western Washington near the lumber industry. They had six more children over the next twelve years.

Life was not easy for the lumber industry and its workers. In 1927, at age sixteen, Al Buck persuaded his mother to sign enlistment papers and Al reported to the Naval Training Center, San Diego, California. He soon came to appreciate the warm winters and mild summers of Southern California. He had learned Morse code and semaphore in the Boy Scouts and soon became a signalman aboard a submarine tender in San Diego. He served aboard submarines until his enlistment was up in 1931.

At that time, the Great Depression was across the land and Al Buck was trying his hand at sawmill work back up in Washington. In time, he joined the Coast Guard and was sent to New York harbor for duty. There, he met and soon married Ida Shapter. They met at the Armed Services YMCA in December 1933, and married in February 1934. The Coast Guard sent the Bucks back to San Diego, and they decided to stay there when the Coast Guard enlistment was finished.

Al Buck was discharged from the Coast Guard in 1935 and

Chuck Buck, the third generation of his family in the knife business, checks out a display carton about to leave the plant for a major discount store.

Buck knives are shipped to and sold in retail outlets all over the world. Here, Chuck Buck examines one of the new Buck Cross-Lock folders.

opened a small laundry service in his garage in San Diego. Two years later, he took a job at the Cudahy meat packing plant near the bay. He purchased a small house on Morena Boulevard, a significant address in the Buck Knife company's early history. Buck's hand was severely damaged in an accident at Cudahy, although he recovered most of its use. However, it kept him out of WWII and he spent most of the war years driving a bus for the San Diego Transit Company. He was driving a bus on VJ Day, 1945.

Meanwhile, his father, Hoyt Buck, was in Idaho when the Japanese attacked Pearl Harbor, December 7, 1941. A call had gone out from the armed forces for fighting knives. Hoyt Buck purchased a forge, anvil and a grinding mandrel and opened a small blacksmith shop in a church basement.

He began making knives and in a short time his reputation began to spread. Hoyt Buck used his special tempering process to produce blades that were sharp, as well as long-lasting. He made many knives, and by the end of WWII, Buck had a waiting list from soldiers who wanted one of his knives.

The good news in 1945 was that the war was over. The bad news was that all the businesses in the little town of Mountain Home, Idaho, that had depended upon the military for most of their work, soon had to close. The local military base closed, and soon most of the townspeople began to leave. Hoyt and Daisy Buck were among those departing, on their way to San Diego where their oldest son, Al, was living.

Hoyt Buck set up a 10x12-foot lean-to alongside Al's small garage on Morena Boulevard and began making knives. Hoyt would make the rounds of butcher shops, restaurants and sporting goods stores, taking orders for his knives, and he would return to the shop in the afternoon to fill the orders he had taken.

At that time, the Buck knives were made from worn-out metal files that had been discarded by some of the huge aircraft plants nearby. The old files had a high carbon content, ideal for the toughness and edge-holding abilities Buck wanted to

achieve. In fact, Buck Knives used worn-out files to make most of their knives for many years.

Soon, father Hoyt was urging son Al to quit the bus company and join him in the knifemaking business. In 1947, they came to an agreement, and H.H. Buck & Son was formed.

In later years, Al Buck admitted he had a lot to learn about making knives. He started by learning how to laminate the thin strips of lucite plastic for the handles, and how to drill the blades for handle attachment. He also had to learn the process of blade tempering.

"It was tricky," he recalled, "but if you did it just right, the entire blade would turn a light tan color just before turning red, and at just that moment you plunged it into oil. Our tempering process was a little bit different than the one used by other knifemakers, and it was one of the keys to our success."

While Al Buck had succeeded in learning the art of blade grinding, Hoyt was diagnosed as having cancer. Hoyt moved back to Tacoma, Washington, in 1948 and died there a year later. He was fifty-nine.

For a while, the company was turning out only twenty-five knives a week. That made them quite expensive. Until 1961, second-hand files continued to be the primary source of blade material. Handles were made from scraps of lignum vitae and rosewood from the Sullivan Hardwood Co. From the nearby McPherson Leathergoods, Buck obtained scraps of leather to make sheaths. As a matter of fact, Al Buck recalled that during this era he was making more money sharpening saws and lawnmower blades than at making knives.

By 1960, on the verge of bankruptcy, it was clear that the little company would have to incorporate and sell shares to raise the capital to expand. Mass production of knives was the only way to survive. The company was incorporated on April 7, 1961. The process generated about $35,000 in working capital, enough to move into a new production facility, a Quonset hut in San Diego's Old Town area. The 3200-square-foot building was renting for little money because, in a few years, the area

Automated, computer-controlled machines are Buck's answer to some of the global competition in the knife business.

Once the machine has been programmed, it automatically places the rivets and pins on this lightweight folding knife. The machines make it possible to turn out thousands of knives a day.

Buck likes to show off the factory's Automated Riveting and Transport operation, called the Dog Track. Many small folder models are produced with the machine.

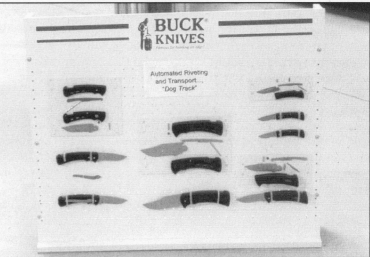

Large folders are still a major part of the Buck knife business and are a big reason for the company's success.

was to be razed to make way for the interstate highway system slated to run through the city.

First production from that location was six models of hunting knives, all fixed-blade knives with black handles. They were priced much higher than competing brands and sales were hard to come by at first. Eventually, their reputation and the hard work of Al and Ida Buck was to pay off. By then, Buck Knives also were being nationally advertised in some outdoor magazines. Orders began to come in, and the first profits were listed.

Perhaps the best known Buck knife all over the world is the Model 110 Folding Hunter. In some uninformed circles, any large folding knife has become known, mistakenly, as a Buck knife. Development was begun on a 4-inch-blade folding knife in early 1963. The design used features from several competitors and from Buck's own design engineer. Many of the concepts had not been used or seen in a folding knife before. Production began in late 1964, and the public accepted the design of the Model 110 with open arms. Within two years, it was the largest selling sports knife in the world.

The price of the big folder was higher than many of its competitors and Buck admits that bugs in the design were being worked out for the next few years. Sales increased in 1966 by 63 percent. They jumped another 60 percent in 1967. The popularity of the Model 110 Folding Hunter helped establish Buck Knives as a leader in the sports knife industry all over the world. By 1991, Buck had sold more than eleven million of the folders, and it continues to be the company's leading seller. Those who bought and held their early Buck corporation stock saw increases of more than 900 percent!

It soon became apparent that the growing company had to expand its facilities again. In 1968, the board of directors autho-

rized the purchase of land and the building of a new plant in nearby El Cajon, California. The building covered 30,000 square feet, large by past standards, but tiny by today's requirements. The company was able to produce better knives faster, and in 1971 they were filling as many orders per day as in a month five years earlier.

Chuck Buck, Al's oldest son, was born in San Diego in 1936. He followed the family tradition and, after completing his Navy enlistment in 1961, joined the knife business with his father and brother. Chuck's main contributions have been steady business knowledge and experience, plus a vision of mass production for Buck Knives. The company was moving from being a small operation to becoming a medium-size knife manufacturer. Between 1973 and 1978, growth surged by 121 percent.

Toward the end of the '70s, the need to again expand the production and administrative facilities became obvious. Buck located 10.87 acres of undeveloped land in what eventually became part of El Cajon, California. After years spent in overcoming obstacles from various quarters, the plant was completed and accepted equipment and personnel in mid-1980. The building is 200,000 square feet, or about $4^1/_2$ acres under one roof. It is known to be one of the most advanced knife production facilities in the world.

Chuck and Lori Buck's first son, Charles Brian Buck, was born in 1960. At about the time of the move into the new facility, C.J., as he is known, began working part-time, making him the fourth generation of the knifemaking Buck family. C.J. has a son, Josh, who already has expressed an interest in the knives of his father and grandfather, and he may become the fifth generation of active Buck Knives participants.

Not long after the move to the new plant, a national reces-

214

Yes, machines are important to the manufacturing process, but the requirement for hand operations continues at the factory.

sion hit all business, including Buck. Sales and profits plummeted. Workers had to be laid off, something the Buck family decried and regretted. Buck fought back with tighter controls, greater efficiencies and several new knife models. Lightweight folders and sheath knives hit the marketplace with great success. The BuckLite series of folders, for

instance, sold more than 400,000 units within a few years of introduction.

Larger survival/military knives and bayonets were produced and have sold well. The BuckMaster was first and the new M9 military bayonet has sold more than a half-million.

Not every attempt at diversification has been a success. In

One of the latest automated machines at the Buck plant is a laser steel-cutting machine. This profiles precision blade blanks from thick sheets of steel.

The Buck CrossLock knife has proved to be a popular seller. It features a spring liner locking system. Both 3¼-inch blades are stainless steel and are quickly accessible when needed.

1987, Buck tried to market a line of outdoor clothing. The experiment was abandoned a year later. An entry into the kitchen cutlery market did not do well, and also was abandoned. However, a move into the international market looks good. The SwissBuck line is the result of a partnership with Wenger, one of the manufacturers of Swiss Army knives. The line includes several multiple-blade folders, intended for the less-expensive market.

Today, this modern facility runs with hundreds of dedicated employees, many of whom have been with the company for several decades. However, these workers are skilled in the use of the most modern machines, computers and equipment in any industry. Chuck Buck is obviously dedicated to producing traditional and modern products using the most advanced means he can find. He is aware of the past and what it means to a knife manufacturer, but he is not afraid to be a pioneer.

Elsewhere in this book, the reader will discover some of the features of the latest development from El Cajon, the BuckTool. It a multi-tool with each folding blade or tool locking open for safety and convenience. It is a compact, precision set of tools in one package, typical of many of Buck designs. Today, Buck Knives lists dozens of designs and variations in its catalog, although many of the standard designs, including the Model 110 Folding Hunter, remain virtually unchanged, and still sell well.

Al Buck died in 1991, but not before he met his great-grandson, Josh Buck, born in 1986.

During our research with Al, Chuck and C.J. Buck, we learned of yet another use of a Buck knife.

Owners of Buck knives have found a multitude of uses through the years, but perhaps none quite the equal of that discovered by E.C. Nash, of San Diego, California. And his "special use" wasn't planned. Nash was standing at an automated teller machine, when two bank robbers ran past. Suddenly, one of them turned and fired at a security guard in pursuit, and a bullet struck Nash in the right hip.

The bullet punctured Nash's checkbook, which was in his back pocket, and came to a halt when it hit his Buck knife. He knew he had been shot, but was surprised to find he wasn't bleeding. Other than the shock of the event, Nash suffered only a quarter-size bruise.

"I feel very lucky," Nash said during a tour of the Buck Knives plant in El Cajon. And he *was* lucky, as police said the smashed bullet was from either a 38 or 357 revolver.

Nash said he had been carrying his Buck knife for thirty years. He bought it aboard a Navy ship and had carried it in his pocket nearly every day since. The old knife, now in FBI custody as evidence, may be shattered beyond repair, but Chuck Buck made a special example of the company's lifetime guarantee by presenting Nash with a new BuckLock Model 531. His new knife bears this inscription: "E.C. Nash, from your friends at Buck."

As Nash admired his new 3-inch lockblade, Buck pointed out that it is wider than the older model. "To give you better protection," he said with a smile.

"We have heard quite a few stories about our knives helping to save someone's life," Chuck Buck said, "but I don't remember any others that actually stopped a bullet."

To be sure, Buck knives are available everywhere through hundreds of retail outlets, from the largest mass retailer to the small mom-and-pop store at the crossroads. Catalogs are available from retail dealers or from Buck Knives.

KNIVES FOR SALE

Imperial Schrade Cutlery

WHEN THE AVERAGE individual purchases a knife, whether it's as a daily pocket companion, for work or hunting, or as a piece of equipment for the kitchen, he or she may select a specific piece because of the name and the trademark. However, it's a known fact that most buyers don't know much about the company that made the knife.

This lack of interest is rather a pity, since much of our nation's history is involved with our commercial background. The Imperial Schrade Corporation is a prime example and illustrates the point being made.

In June of 1997, Imperial Schrade Corporation will begin its ninety-fourth year of operation. The rich history of one of the world's largest manufacturers of quality cutlery has become a keystone of industry legend. The corporation's world headquarters in Ellenville, New York, has more than 548,000 square feet of manufacturing space dedicated to producing the world's finest pocket and hunting knives. Today, Schrade has more than 600 employees at the Ellenville site. Additionally, they have a manufacturing facility in Listowel, Ireland, which currently employs 120 people.

The Schrade Cutlery Company was founded in 1904 in Walden, New York. The quality of the cutlery they produced

was unique to the industry at that time. The Imperial Knife Company, established in Providence, Rhode Island, in 1916, grew to manufacture a full range of value-priced folding pocketknives. The quality of the products of both companies was such that customers were many and the businesses thrived in a society in which a simple pocketknife was considered a tool for every man and boy and more than a few women of the time.

In 1941, Albert M. Baer, whose vision has guided ISC, purchased the Ulster Knife Company, founded in Ellenville, New York, in the 1870s. In 1942, the Ulster Knife Company and the Imperial Knife Company joined forces to become Imperial Knife Associated Companies. With that union, they committed themselves to producing knives for the military throughout World War II.

A significant part of the Baer family history—and the history of the company—developed when Albert's brother, Henry, joined him in 1942. Through the use of his name and photograph in advertising and promotion, Henry Baer become the most identifiable figure in the public growth of the company, while brother Albert preferred to remain behind the scenes, directing his vision. Incidentally, it is unique in the cutlery industry that these two brothers both have been inducted into

The mammoth factory complex of Imperial Schrade in Ellenville, New York, is all under one roof. The company owns sufficient adjoining land for for further expansion.

the Cutlery Hall of Fame. Uncle Henry, as he came to be known, was inducted in 1983, and Albert M. Baer in 1992.

Albert M. Baer purchased Schrade Cutlery Company in 1946 and renamed it the Schrade Walden Cutlery Corporation, which became a division of the Imperial Knife Associated Companies group. The Schrade Walden division was moved from Walden to Ellenville in 1958.

Imperial Knife experienced extremely strong growth through the late '70s, and as the corporation entered the '80s, a consolidation took place and the company divested itself of various holdings. In 1983, Albert M. Baer purchased the stock of all shareholders in the Imperial Knife Associated Companies and became the sole owner of this privately held cutlery giant.

In 1985, the name of the company was changed from Imperial Knife Associated Companies to Imperial Schrade Corp., and all aspects of the company's operations were combined under one roof in Ellenville.

Imperial Schrade's strengths as a knifemaker are those strong craftsmen who boast among their number many third- and fourth-generation employees. Many learned their trade from parents and grandparents who passed along the valuable knowl-

edge, skills and pride necessary for the consistent production of quality knives.

Today's Schrade has blended the decades of hand craftsmanship with some of the most modern technology available to produce quality knives. It is obvious that the company has made tremendous strides in its ability to design and develop new products, produce prototypes and ensure accuracy of tooling with their Auto-CAD and Master CAM, which design both product and tooling.

Prototypes, tooling and production fixtures are produced on four-axis CNC machining centers and wire EDM machines. The semi-automatic and fully-automatic CNC equipment has had a great impact on Schrade's ability to improve quality, reduce inventory and meet customer delivery schedules. These computer-controlled machines have made work safer as well as a great deal easier.

In 1986, Walter A. "Wally" Gardiner was named president of ISC. It is generally admitted in the cutlery trade that Gardiner possesses a working knowledge of this particular industry that is second to none. His vitality, his passion for knives and his instinctive feel for the industry combine to make him what is considered to be an exceptionally strong corporate leader. In building a viable global corporation, Gardiner and his management team obviously are committed to Schrade's ninety-three-year history and continuing standard of excellence.

Joe Hufnagel, senior vice president, Jim Stathis, vice president of sales, and Jeff Ahearn, the director of marketing, handle the sales and marketing end of Schrade's business, while the venerable Dave Swinden, executive vice president with more than forty-five years devoted to ISC, and vice president Jim Economos run the manufacturing and operations aspects of Schrade's thriving cutlery business.

It seems important that we should take a closer look at a couple of the individuals who head up this mammoth operation.

Wally Gardiner joined the firm in 1976. A graduate of the

(Above) Backgrounded by a giant reproduction of a Schrade knife, Wally Gardiner (right), president of Imperial Schrade, and senior vice president Joe Hufnagel discuss an upcoming project.

Dave Swinden (right) tells spokesperson Dave Staples about some of the awards received by the company. They are on display in a quiet corner of the work area, where they can be viewed by employees.

In spite of electronically controlled equipment, there still is a great deal of human effort required in the Ellenville plant. More than 600 workers are employed, and most of them have been there for decades.

(Below) Hand grinding continues to be a demanding art that brings Schrade knives to their top degree of production.

University of Florida with a degree in journalism, he was a pitcher for the Chicago White Sox AA team and subsequently a sales manager for Union Carbide. Among his many activities, Gardiner is a board member of the National FFA Foundation, which strives to make a positive difference in the lives of students by developing their potential for premier leadership, personal growth and career success.

In addition to the presidency of Imperial Schrade, Gardiner also is on the board of directors of Imperial Schrade (Europe), Ltd., and Imperial Stag, Ltd.

Backing up Wally Gardiner is Joe Hufnagel as senior vice president. He joined the corporation in 1987 as director of marketing and was promoted to his present post in 1989. He also came from Union Carbide, where he had been marketing director for the Eveready Battery Division's Pan-American market area.

According to Wally Gardiner, through its Old Timer, Uncle Henry and Schrade Cutlery brands, Imperial Schrade holds an ongoing commitment to the outdoors and to the future generations of Americans with whom it will be entrusted. Through sales of these knives, Schrade donates a percentage of the profits to programs that will assist in the protection and preservation of the environment.

As an example, Schrade Cutlery is closely allied with the Federal Duck Stamp Program and, for the past nine years, has produced a special numbered edition of the Federal Duck Stamp commemorative knife. In 1996, in cooperation with the U.S. Department of the Interior and the Federal Duck Stamp Office, the company brought out a scrimshaw version of the knife that is priced to allow more Americans the opportunity to assist in funding this wildlife program. The program, which

(Above) The work areas at the Ellenville knife factory are well organized and clean, offering a pleasant place to work. The factory encompasses more than a half-milllion square feet of space.

The CNC equipment now used at Schrade requires constant monitoring during its operation. Such machines can produce large numbers of knives, but handwork still is required in finishing.

began more than six decades ago in 1934, raises money to purchase and protect waterfowl habitat areas.

The first scrimshaw version of the Duck Stamp commemorative has been designated as the DS1SC. It houses a stainless steel blade featuring a commemorative etch. The ivory-colored Delrin handles depict artwork of wetlands with ducks in flight. This model measures $3^7/_8$ inches closed, and each knife is clamshell-packed with a Federal Duck Stamp Collector's patch.

This issue probably will be sold out by the time you read this, but don't panic. Imperial Schrade no doubt will be part of a similar program each year through the foreseeable future.

In a similar program, the corporation has produced a special two-bladed knife for the National Reining Horse Association, whose members number in several thousands. This cooperative effort, of course, also is designed as a fund-raising device for the reining organization.

Close inspection of each knife is conducted on the factory floor before it is accepted for packaging and later shipment to customers.

As far as new hardware is concerned, Schrade has their Cliphanger System which incorporates a quick-release fastener that is adaptable to carry not only a knife, but multi-task accessories.

Two new Cliphanger models have been introduced, with four knife models available as the cornerstone of this system. Included are the CH3S Silhouette, a compact folder that measures 3¹/₄ inches closed. The larger CH7S Viper has handles of tough Zytel and measures 4¹/₂ inches closed.

At this writing, the two newest members of the Cliphanger family are the CH4 Shadow, at 3¹/₄ inches closed, and the CH8 Viper CFS, measuring 4¹/₂ inches closed. All of these models feature a liner lock that is designed to offer safety and convenience.

The patented Schrade Cliphanger incorporates a two-sided release mechanism set into the handles of the knives. This mechanism allows the knife to be detached easily with either hand, freeing it from the tether for immediate use. The user can carry the knife and have it readily accessible without the need for a sheath.

The complete system features a rugged nylon strap that can clip the knife to a belt, fishing vest, backpack or a hunting coat. The strap and a black anodized split ring component allow full utilization of such accessories as a compass, flashlight, sharpener or whistle. The accessories thus are within easy reach, with easy availability of the knife.

In keeping with its policy of producing practical using knives, Schrade designers have come up with a pair of fish fillet knives for the angler's tackle box. Equipped with non-slip Safe-T-Grip handles, the Maximum Flex (246OT) and the Minimum Flex (146OT) vary in the degree of blade stiffness and were designed to accommodate personal preferences, filleting techniques and the differences encountered in filleting the various species of game fish.

These models feature 6-inch blades and join the Pro Fisherman (147OT), with its 7-inch blade, which is designed for larger fish. All of these models have blades made from Schrade + stainless steel, which was developed for its edge-holding qualities and rust resistance. The latter quality, of course, is important to saltwater anglers.

All three of the knives feature ergonomically designed grips moulded from soft, thermoplastic rubber to provide a cushioned, non-slip, positive grip for controlled cutting. Each knife, incidentally, is fitted with a rugged, ballistic cloth sheath.

Although the earlier corporations which now make up Imperial Schrade produced combat knives under U.S. government contract during World War II, the company's approach to cutlery has been on the conservative side over the decades. The normal design and production has been toward knives that can be used in everyday life or in outdoor recreational pursuits. In other words, one doesn't check a Schrade Cutlery catalog to find a combat knife; it just isn't there.

However, the marketing thinkers at the Ellenville headquarters have long realized the fact that their customers number thousands upon thousands of outdoorsmen: hunters, bowhunters, hikers, backpackers, campers, et al. The Schrade team recognized the need for a heavy-duty knife that could be used for every type of chore from carving tent stakes to survival needs. The answer to this broad spectrum of needs now is being sold as the Schrade Extreme Survival knife.

According to Dave Staples, spokesperson for the knife works, "The craftsmen at Schrade, working with federal, state and local law enforcement agencies, designed and have vigorously field tested this tool under the most demanding conditions available around the globe. The Extreme Survival knife passed all of the tests and then some."

The knife measures 12¹/₄ inches overall, and has a forged stainless steel blade for both strength and durability. Width of the blade is 1¹/₈ inches, while thickness is ³/₁₆-inch. Weight of the knife alone is 13 ounces; with the ballistic nylon sheath, it weighs 18 ounces. One side of the blade carries a fine edge for precision cutting, while the topside offers the user a file and a

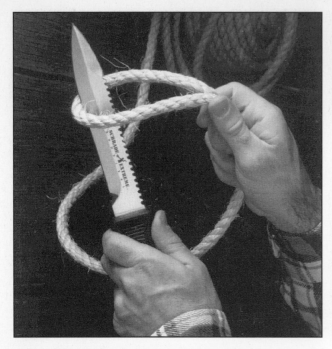

Imperial Schrade has entered the big knife business with its Extreme Survival model, which is designed to serve many functions.

The Roadie model from the Uncle Henry line has been described by its makers as "a gentleman's pocketknife." It is small enough to be attached to a key ring.

rugged 5-inch saw section that will cut thin metal, PVC piping and wood. There also is a wire stripper positioned where the blade joins the textured TPR non-slip handle. The butt end of this tool can be used as a hammer and claw-type nail-puller.

During the heyday of the so-called survival knife of about two decades back, buyers wanted to be able to pack survival items into the hollow handle of the "continued existence daggers" being produced in mammoth numbers back then.

The Extreme Survival version takes a slightly different approach, with two pouches being situated on the face of the sheath. These appear to be considerably more roomy than the hollow handles of yore, which means one can pack more survival items. Such supplies might include a small compass, some type of fire starter kit, a sharpener and proper fishing gear.

We tested all of the advertised facets of the knife and found that it functioned as stated, within reason. We felt the nail puller to be a bit small, and if you are going to use the butt end as hammer, it might be a good idea to keep track of the sharpened sections of the blade. Grab that wrong and you'll be sorry!

In designing the company's line of multi-purpose Schrade STC adventure knives, the aim has been to offer the "ultimate knife specifically crafted for the most rugged outdoor activities," according to Dave Stapels.

"With features that make it adaptable for everything from a trek through the wilderness, a wild whitewater ride or a weekend camping trip, this knife is designed to be a must companion for all forms of wilderness travel."

Overall length of the STC is $7^1/_4$ inches with a $3^3/_8$-inch stainless steel Schrade + blade. Weight is only 6 ounces. The blunt tip on the fixed blade is great for prying and probing, while thumb grooves on the top side are meant to afford the user grip stability and comfort. The serrated edge is designed for heavy-

duty cutting, while the fine edge is for precision cutting. The handle is water resistant and features a textured grip. There is a provision for attaching a lanyard or thong to help prevent loss. The STC is available in black, blue and easy-to-find orange. It comes with a choice of sheath options.

Most knife fanciers, we find, carry a folding knife of one kind or another in their daily lives. In fact, your authors find they are downright uncomfortable should they leave home without that knife in a pocket.

The Schrade folks have come to recognize this need and have introduced a model called the Roadie, which they describe as "a gentleman's pocket knife."

The Roadie (12UH) measures only $2^3/_4$ inches closed and has a modified clip blade of rust-resistant Schrade + stainless steel. Equipped with a shackle, it can be attached to a key ring or a lanyard. The Roadie has durable Staglon handles and is guaranteed against loss for a full year.

Discussed here are only a few of the newer items coming out of the Ellenville factory. By the time this book is in print, there will be a whole new line-up available.

One facet of production we found of particular interest is what would have to be called a "semi-custom shop."

Established right in the middle of the big plant is a production line that makes special-order knives. Production knives are passed to this section for special embellishment such as handles of exotic materials, gold plating on metal parts, etching or engraving for that rich, custom look. Such knives are available to the public at times, but often are produced for customer companies as promotional items or as prizes. This operation is overseen by Dave Swinden, who has been with Imperial Schrade and its predecessor companies for some forty-five years.

Located in a semi-secluded area of the plant is an alcove that

The 1996 Duck Stamp Commemorative knife is one example of the cooperative work Schrade does with conservation programs.

The Old Timer fillet knives feature variations in stiffness as well as Safe-T-Grip handles.

This Schrade knife was produced for the National Reining Horse Association. The company continues to seek out similar projects.

serves as what might be called the organization's trophy room. Displayed there are historic photos as well as an array of awards received by the company. Instead of being tucked away in the office of one of the company executives, these award plaques have been put on display as a means of expressing to the employees the fact that their efforts are appreciated and that the management recognizes the value of each individual involved in producing and marketing a knife.

At this writing, the latest award to be received by the Imperial Schrade Corporation is the prestigious Golden Teal Award from Ducks Unlimited. The award is presented to individuals,

corporations and organizations who contribute goods, services, merchandise or cash to Ducks Unlimited regional and national fund-raising programs. This award was presented to ISC for the company's high level of participation in fund raising for Ducks Unlimited.

It becomes obvious during a tour of the giant manufacturing facility that old-time values such as honest effort, hard work and even respect for the work one does have been coupled successfully with modern computer-oriented technologies. This seems to be a hard combination to create these days, but in the pastoral environs of Ellenville, New York, it works.

KNIVES FOR SALE

GT Knives' Two-Man Team

NEW IDEAS FOR knives—and people who develop them— seem to be appearing more and more often. One such group, operating under the simple title of GT Knives, started operations about five years ago. The two owners/operators of this enterprise are Greg Bark and Todd Jones.

An interesting piece of background regarding this young company is the fact that neither Bark nor James ever had made a knife before venturing into this field of endeavor. Together they have over three decades of tooling design and making injection moulding units for a wide variety of applications. This is their first venture into knifemaking, and they have some unique ideas that really work well.

Jones recalls that one evening he was browsing through a knife magazine, looking at the many blades and variations ranging from simple to exotic, and decided he and Bark would be able to make knives. They had the experience in designing exotic moulds, and it would only require a change of their system to make a knife using their knowledge and the available tooling.

After a few discarded ideas, they settled on a large folding knife that incorporated their new ideas. The actual principle of a button-lock folding knife isn't new, but their approach and final product is. This is perhaps the only button-lock-blade knife that not only locks in the open position, but in the closed position as well. This makes a solid and safe knife to carry, since the blade can't come open inadvertently.

We sent C.R. Learn to take a look at their operation in San Diego, California. Here's what he observed:

"The pair first designed the lock, the handle and finally the blade. The button-lock incorporates several parts for operation. There is a round piece with a hole in the center and two slots in

Greg Bark checks one of the machines in the shop. Bark is the "G" in GT Knives.

Todd Jones is the "T" in the company name. He is setting up a milling machine to turn out small components.

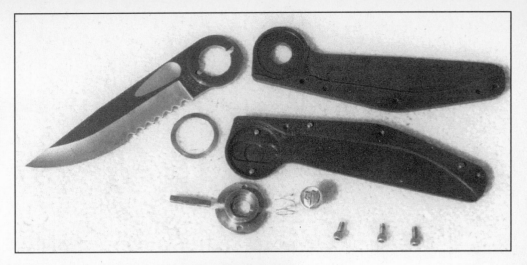

Here are the components of a GT knife, laid out and ready for assembly. All parts are precision made at the factory.

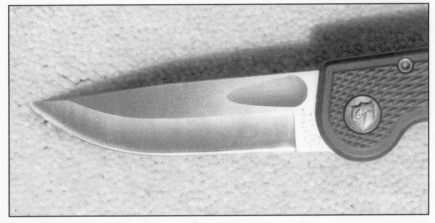

The GT knife features a blade of ATS-34 stainless steel. The teardrop-shaped depression near the pivot point is milled out to provide easy one-hand opening.

it. They call this the biscuit, and it does the locking. A square pin fits into a slot in the biscuit. Other elements include the spring under the brass button that is used to release the lock. This fits into the biscuit and is held in place by the milled rod that slides through a hole in the unit. The ends of the rod fit into the slots on the biscuit, allowing it to be pressed down so the blade can rotate.

"To unlock the blade for closing, one depresses the button on top, and this, in turn, depresses the rod and allows the blade to swing to the closed position, where the pin again drops into the slot, locking the blade closed. Operation is actually simpler than trying to describe this locking and unlocking action. The best part is that the blade is locked solidly in either position," Learn reports.

The handles are CNC-milled, as are all parts for the GT knife. Once set up, the machines do the work, producing each unit to extremely close tolerances.

The handles are made from aircraft-grade 6061 T6 aluminum alloy and are anodized to add color and durability. They are available in gray, green or black. When assembled, the two handle sections are held together with three stainless steel socket-head screws.

The checkered handle has been ergonomically designed to fit the hand with the blade edge up, as for field dressing, or edge down for normal knife use.

"The handle without the blade is interesting enough, but they also went to top-of-the-line ATS-34 material for the blade. The blade on the GT ONE is shaped on the CNC machines and is

hardened to Rockwell 60C. This makes a sharp, durable cutting edge that will last longer than blades made of other steels. The ATS-34 was chosen for this reason."

The blade is $3\frac{5}{8}$ inches long by $\frac{1}{8}$-inch thick with full hollow-grind. The makers offer two blade styles, one with a full-length cutting edge that is sharper than a razor, and another of the same length with a half-serrated edge at the base section and the standard smooth edge on the front. If you have tried to cut some of the new poly and nylon ropes with a smooth-edged blade, you will appreciate this serrated section. It also is excellent for cutting monofilament fishing line.

When the blade is milled, two teardrop shapes are cut into the blade on both sides. This indent is used for one-handed opening and closing of the blade. Hold the knife in one hand, depress the button, find the teardrop and move the blade to release the cross pin. It will swing easily to the fully open position and lock in place. To close, depress the brass lock button, fold the blade into the handle until it locks closed.

Another unique feature is the blade doesn't end with a flat section where it goes into the handle. This blade has a round hole that goes into the handle and over the biscuit piece, perhaps the strongest of all design features. Ask an engineer as to what is the strongest way to form a system, and you will find a circle is the strongest pattern to use. The makers knew this and made the blade unit in the strongest manner they could design.

When you hold a GT knife you'll like the way it fits your hand, whether the blade is up or down. As opposed to a straight,

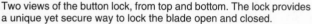

Two views of the button lock, from top and bottom. The lock provides a unique yet secure way to lock the blade open and closed.

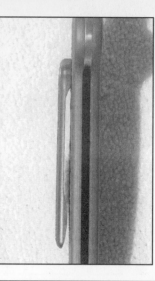

The optional pocket clip is milled from 6061 T6 aluminum and held to the knife body by two stainless steel screws.

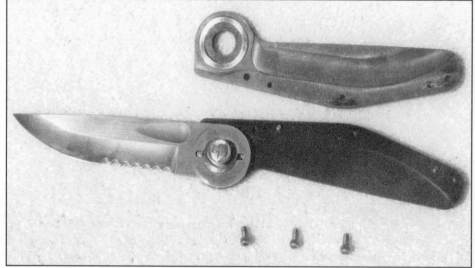

Here are the knife components before final assembly. The button locking system is in place at the pivot point. Even the handle sections are precision machined with tight tolerances.

flat handle, this design makes the blade work faster and easier since it fits properly.

At this point, GT Knives does not offer a sheath for their product, but they have a great idea for carrying the knife. Some knives have a spring-style clip that fits over a pocket edge or your belt. These can ride up or slip out. Bark and Jones use an innovative pocket clip that firmly attaches to the right side handle section with two stainless steel cap screws. It is designed to fit over the edge that is formed on the pockets of denims and other pants. The knife slides into the pocket part way and stays there.

The pocket clip is made from 6061 aluminum and anodized to look the same as the handles. It isn't springy like most, but it will fit snugly over the pocket edge.

"These have never worked for me," claims Learn, "but I accepted the challenge and wore one of the GT knives inside my front pocket at the side. The knife never moved after finally getting it into my pocket. It is made to fit tight on insertion in the pocket, and it never came off, even when I made some erratic moves.

"One place I always lose my billfold and often a knife is when flying in light aircraft. The seat position and the motions required when controlling a plane are far different from every-

day movements. During a test, my wallet dropped out as usual, but my GT stayed in my pocket. This old problem is now solved," Learn tells us.

"A simple test of blade sharpness is to slice a piece of paper with it. A piece of 20-pound-stock typewriter paper was held at the top, the point of the smooth-edged blade inserted below my hand with ease, and by holding the knife lightly at the back section, it sliced down the length of the paper with no tears or stopping. That is dangerously sharp!"

How long that edge will hold will take time to determine, but if you have worked with steel at all, you know the good properties of ATS-34.

Right now you might have a bit of a problem locating one of the GT knives, although they are distributed nationally by reps and are in some stores. Todd Jones and Greg Bark sell the two styles of blades and the handle with and without the clip direct from their factory at present.

What is next from GT Knives? They plan to continue production of the GT ONE, but are in the design stages of a smaller knife. How small hasn't been decided, but it is sure to be made with the same precision as the GT ONE. This will be another unique one-hand-opener with an excellent blade. Several styles will be introduced, with more to follow.

ART KNIFE INTERNATIONAL

**A sophisticated and profitable way
to market high-value knives**

ONE OF THE most unusual collector knife shows and sales is put on by an organization called Art Knife International. As of late 1995, there have been four shows/sales put on for and by the makers and buyers. Another such event is scheduled for October 1997. The show is not an auction; all knives are marked with prices and each is for sale, and nothing can be held back by any maker. The organizer/promoter of these events is Phil Lobred, a well-known Southern California knife collector.

Invited to the 1995 event in San Diego, California, were twenty-five of, arguably, some of the best knifemakers to be found anywhere. The names included Ray Appleton, Byers, Colorado; Fred Carter, Wichita Falls, Texas; T.M. Dowell,

Bend, Oregon; Jim Ence, Richfield, Utah; Virgil England, Anchorage, Alaska; H.H. Frank, Whitefish, Montana; Tim Herman, Overland Park, Texas; Gil Hibben, La Grange, Kentucky; Richard Hodgson, Boulder, Colorado; Steve Hoel, Pine, Arizona; Steve Johnson, Manti, Utah; Jim Kelso, Worcester, Vermont; D. F. Kressler, Bavaria, Germany; Ron Lake, Eugene, Oregon; Wolfgang Loerchner, Bayfield, Ontario, Canada; R.W. Loveless, Riverside, California; Bill Moran, Braddock Heights, Maryland; Willie Rigney, Bronston, Kentucky; James Schmidt, Ballston Lake, New York; H.J. Schneider, Pittsburg, Texas; Gray Taylor, Kingsport, Tennessee; Dwight Towell, Midvale, Idaho; Michael Walker and Patricia Walker, Taos, New Mexico; Buster Warenski,

A group of internationally known custom knifemakers and collectors gathers at the San Diego Marriott Hotel to discuss knives. At far left is impresario/promoter Phil Lobred.

Richfield, Utah; Yoshindo Yoshihara, Tokyo, Japan. Billy Mace Imel was invited, but a conflict in schedules forced him to withdraw. As a result, the member-makers voted to invite Japanese sword-maker Yoshindo Yoshihara, adding to the international flavor of the show.

Potential buyers and collectors, too, were admitted by invitation only. Art knife collectors from around the world were present for the event, conducted and produced by Phil Lobred. The display and sale took no more than four hours, but Lobred worked on the event, from invitations, mailings, promotions, establishing a satisfactory location and hundreds of other details for more than a year. He seemed to enjoy every minute of it. Lobred has plans already underway for another show in 1997, and invitations to buyers and sellers are in the mail.

Maker membership in the group is voted on by all the twenty-five current members. As time passes, a maker may retire or die, and another maker may apply for membership. All the members must agree to the new name.

Sales such as this are not open to the public. The events are intended to provide a private, relaxed marketplace where buyers and collectors may meet with and perhaps get to know some of their favorite knife artists; perhaps get acquainted with some makers with whom they were not previously familiar.

The Art Knife Invitational show operates as follows:

Sometime before 10:00 a.m. of the appointed day, the knife makers gather in the room of the hotel with their wares. Each is assigned a table, arranged alphabetically in fairness to all. On the table, the maker displays three to eight art knives in numbered sequence. Behind each knife is a numbered and maker-labeled slotted box. Thus, each knife is identified on the table according to its maker who is present.

The same listing is printed on "intent to purchase" tickets handed out to the invited buyers. Each buyer has an assigned purchase number with only one ticket per knife on it. The potential buyer may make only one bid per knife, but may bid on as many knives as he or she wishes. Or a buyer may elect to bid on only one knife by one maker, or may decide to not attempt to buy any knife at the show.

The knives and the makers remain near their displays to meet with the buyers and discuss their knives from 10:00 until about 1:00 p.m. During this time, the buyers examine each knife on display. When a decision is made, a buyer will place one of the numbered and identified tickets in the box near the selected knife. A single knife may have none, a few or dozens of tickets in its box as offers to buy. It has happened, so the lore goes, that a specific knifemaker had no tickets in a box—no buyers were interested at the listed price. The individual knife makers must be ready for almost any eventuality and have the courage to face a no-bid situation. Other popular makers might have fifty tickets in a box.

At a signal, each maker reaches into each of his three to eight boxes and withdraws two numbered and named tickets, if there are that many inside. These are numbered one and two, and placed beside or under the particular knife. Bid tickets are drawn for each knife on display. Then the interested buyers pass by the tables searching for their names beside their favorite knives. If one is interested in only a single knifemaker and a single knife, the drama is over in a second, one way or the other.

The selected first ticket holder/buyer has 15 minutes to locate his or her name at a favorite knife. If drawn, he pays for the knife on the spot and takes delivery. Payment is made directly to the artist. If a collector has put a bid ticket on every knife at the show and is drawn several times, he might select one or two favorites, and buy no more. In that case, courtesy demands that he notify the other makers that he is giving up his rights to their knives. After 15 minutes, the person drawn as number two has the option or the opportunity to buy a knife if number one ticket holder has passed it up. The process continues until all the bid tickets have been drawn from the box or all the knives by a given maker have been sold.

Knives for sale are displayed before the sealed buy requests are opened and announced.

Chuck Buck (left) and his son C.J. Buck (second from left) of El Cajon, California, discuss knife designs with H.H. Frank of Whitefish, Montana, who offered four of his total output of seven knives for the year.

The theme knife for the Art Knife International show in 1995 was the Buster Warenski replica King Tut dagger, produced several years earlier.

During that first 15 minutes, shouts of joy and relief and groans of disappointment can be heard around the room. There is no dickering or bargaining allowed during the show. What may take place among collectors and makers after the show has ended is nobody else's business. Presumably, additional trading or selling may take place privately.

At each maker's option, one of his knives may be available on open bid. It is a silent bid by special ticket and there is no reserve. The bidders print the amount they are willing to pay on the ticket and place it in the maker's box.

Prices on open-bid knives are unknown and private. Prices for all other knives are printed in the booklet each buyer gets at registration. Prices at the 1995 show ranged from $950 for a Gentleman's Hunter, up to $17,000 for a Japanese Wakizashi short sword. Many other works fell into the range of $3000 to $8000. Never one to go along with the crowd, Bob Loveless priced each of his six knives on display at $1950. Those who purchased one of the Loveless knives at that price, felt as if he or she had a bargain. One may also presume that Loveless's bid boxes contained several bid tickets.

Altogether, we are told, the twenty-four makers present displayed 129 knives. The average asking price, if that figure is meaningful, was $3996. At the 1995 show, 115 knives were sold, bringing a total of almost a half-million dollars to the makers. Some makers made out better than others. Sixteen of them, including Loveless, sold out. That left eight others who had a knife or knives left on the table when the show closed. The $17,000 short sword did not sell during the show.

Not every knifemaker is in favor of this sort of invitational show. True, those who are invited stand to sell some of their better knives at what might be considered high prices. But the main criticism of the arrangement is that it tends to concentrate the best-heeled buyers in one place at one time, leaving those beginning and mid-ability makers out of the loop. How will serious buyers ever encounter the next level, the next stars of the knifemaking world, if the only work they see is that from the already-successful? There is a certain elitism involved with shows of this nature, from the makers and from the buyers. The custom knifemaker who presents half of his yearly output at this type of show may lengthen his delivery times to his regular customers who may not have an invitation.

Phil Lobred says this method of marketing art works is typically found in other venues, such as those for fine paintings, sculptures and so on. He believes the art of making beautiful knives has matured to the point that those makers participating deserve and will support the concept. So will the collectors.

These invitational shows are not free to the knifemakers, either. In some cases, they are asked to pay a rather hefty fee to the organizer to be included in the show. The money goes to pay for the hotel conference center or display room, food and drink and other expenses the show manager has to incur. The maker must also pay his own travel expenses, perhaps from overseas, room and food expenses, in addition to factoring in the cost of time lost in not making knives for several days. On the other hand, the knifemaker who sells five knives at an average of $8000 each might not begrudge the cost of participation. The concept of the Art Knife Invitational sale seems to have caught on. More are scheduled in other parts of the world. For the time being, they will be on an irregular basis. Those makers who have reached the skill levels and who have their work in such demand will be scheduling their knife production to be ready for such shows. The only limitation may be on the number of qualified buyers who wish to be added to the list of those receiving invitations.

KNIFE RESTORATION

Some old knives just need help to live longer lives

It is always amazing how some people can abuse a tough, stainless steel knife blade. Sometimes this can be an accident, but other times the damage seems deliberate. Ever the tinkerer and fixer, C.R. Learn has done more than his share of knife restoration. He offers the following advice:

WHEN YOU GO to a gun show, a knife show or even a yard or garage sale, you may come across knives in bad condition. The tools vary from large camp/field knives to single-blade folders. You can have fun, save money and rework these damaged tools into good-looking, hard-working knives with just a few shop tools and a bit of time.

With sheath knives there is only one blade, so it is relatively simple to figure out how to restore it. Since these fixed-blade knives seem to be the easiest to restore, let's take a look at this procedure.

Most of the damage seems to occur on the blade tip, while the cutting edge might have "half-moons" or chips on it. The tip damage is simple to restore by using a belt sander to shape a new tip. It's simple, fast and rewarding.

The half-moon on a cutting edge can be caused by a couple of errors. The most common is by trying to pry with the knife edge, such as trying to open the pelvic bone when dressing out a deer. That bone can be cut with a downward pressure, but what often happens is that the knife wielder makes a twisting motion after getting the blade started in the joint. Knives are not intended for this type of stress. With the blade in the bone, the hunter tweaks the blade to one side and breaks out a half-moon-shaped piece of the steel. Almost any blade will do this with the wrong application of pressure.

When you find a blade with a half-moon out of the cutting

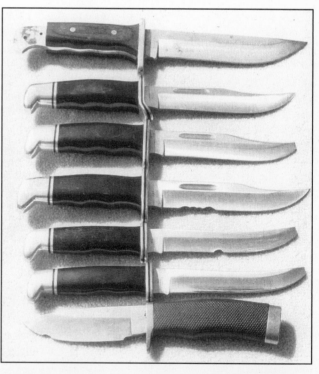

It's difficult to imagine what sort of abuse these knives endured, to end up with blades broken out as they are. They certainly are candidates for restoration.

edge, it may be salvaged with a little time and effort. One blade I picked up at a garage sale had a series of four moons, one right after the other, on the blade edge. This was not an accident; it was knife abuse. Basic knife theory is simple: A knife is made for cutting only. If you want to pry, use a pry bar; if you want to

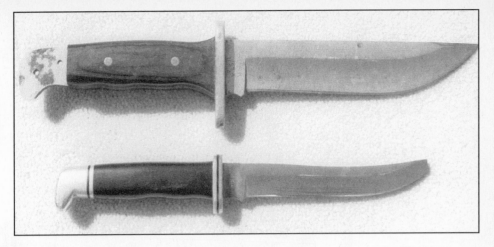

These two old Buck knives have been badly abused, but a bit of shop time and a few materials will have them in great shape for more years of service.

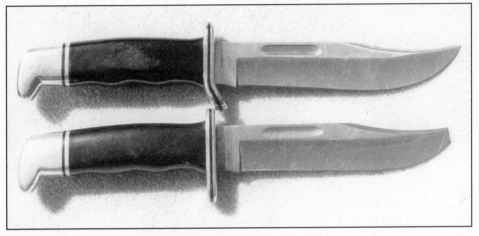

The guard on the upper knife was badly bent, but the blade is in good shape. The lower Buck knife's tip is broken and needs major reshaping to be useful.

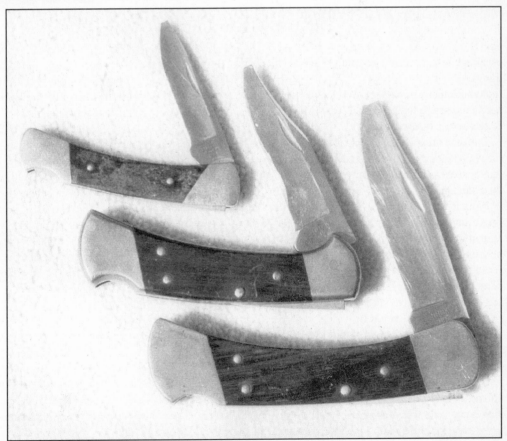

Typical damage to these Buck folders indicates they were being used as screwdrivers. Each has its blade tip broken off, but repair is relatively easy.

The Buck Frontiersman (top) has a new handle made of mesquite wood, picked up in the desert. Mesquite is an attractive wood with interesting grain. The Buck Vanguard has a new handle of antler with a black spacer next to the finger guard.

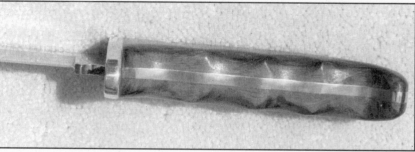

The new mesquite handle slabs have been polished down for a tight fit with the tang. With care, the wood will last as long as the blade.

break something, use a hammer. Save the knife for cutting things.

Perhaps the reason so many blade tips are broken off is that people try to use the knife as a screwdriver. You can count on breaking a tip that way.

One large hunting/camp blade I acquired had the butt cap of the handle—originally epoxied and pinned aluminum—removed for some reason. It was simple to fix after I bought it for a bargain price at a garage sale. The seller did not know how or did not want to repair it. One medium-blade knife had the finger guard twisted up at an odd angle, extending a half-inch. How it was done is a mystery.

When browsing down the aisle of a gun show, one often finds boxes of "stuff" under a table. These are pieces and parts brought to be sold at bargain prices. One box I located at a show yielded two damaged fixed-blade knives and three folding knives that would be simple to repair. The price for all five? Five bucks seemed about right, and a deal was made. The prices on damaged knives can be that low, if you look for them.

You do not need knifemaking equipment to repair most knives. It might be handy if you know a knifemaker in your area, because he'll have the proper tools and equipment. Repairing knives is simple for those with experience and equipment.

For the average shop, you could do nicely with a small belt sander, such as a 1x40-inch belt. All you need to add is a few 120-grit sanding belts and you have the basic equipment needed for refinishing most knives.

A disc sander is usually a part of this particular tool. It comes in handy for surfacing wood handle scales replaced on some knives to give them a "different" look. A Dremel tool with some polishing pads works well, but a homemade buffer and polishing system is even better. These can be made by using a stand, a mandrel and an electric washing machine motor.

Lay out the various blades or knives you plan to rework. The simplest is the broken tip, then the half-mooned blades. After that, one usually gets into handle work. If you do several blades all at once in a system you can get more done faster.

There are some shop tools you should forget you own. Forget the grinder stones used for rough-shaping and cleaning metal parts. These are highly aggressive when it comes to removing steel and often cut too fast to control. They also may cause the steel to overheat, and you can ruin a good blade quickly.

Set up your belt sander with a new 120-grit belt and merely pass the knife tip across the belt. Use a rolling pass to form a rounded tip, for example. You can change a trailing-point blade to a drop-point blade when forming the new tip, if the blade is large enough.

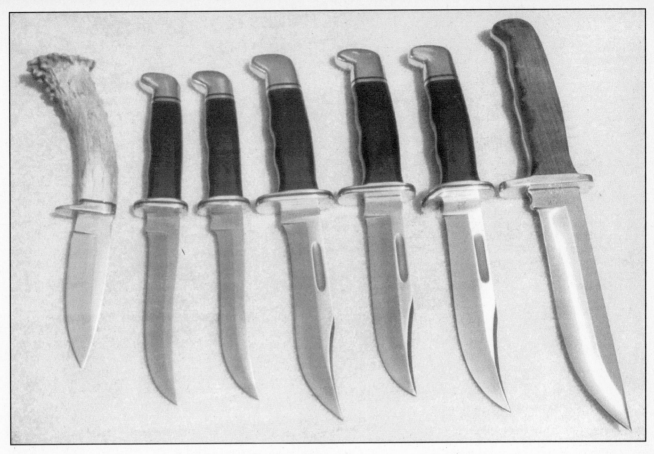

This set of Buck fixed-blade knives is ready for more years of hunting camps or to give as low-cost gifts.

The primary requirement is to work slowly. Do not try to hog off all the blade point material in one pass. Make several passes, removing a bit at a time. When the tip is to your liking, turn the blade to the belt and lightly sand in the cutting edge where the new point is. This is a light pass. You can finish the cutting edge on buffing wheels or with a Dremel tool.

Half-moons take a bit more work, so move from the handle to the blade tip, removing a bit of blade steel to reshape the cutting edge. Work slowly until you have the blade shape you want. Stop before you go too far and end up with nothing but a boning blade.

When my single-mooned blade was belt sanded, it developed a slight upward curve on the blade at the moon section. It still cuts fine, but looks different. The multi-mooned blade needed more sanding and was dubbed the sway-backed blade when finished. Damaged blades rarely look like the originals, but the edge still will cut hide and meat, as it was designed to do.

The two sway-back blades often become conversation pieces in the field. When you prepare to field-dress the deer you just downed, you can tell your hunting partners you have dressed so much game and sharpened this knife so many times it has become sway-backed.

Handle work on damaged knives is also simple. This effort falls into two categories. One is the slip-over handle style, where the tang of the knife is smaller than the blade section. You must drill a hole in the new handle material to accept the tang. The other style is full tang, where the tang comes back from the blade in the same width to make an extremely strong knife.

The big camp/field knife without the aluminum cap was chosen for a new full-length handle. Mesquite wood has great color, fantastic patterns and produces a tough knife handle.

The old handle was removed by grinding off the two rivets on the handle and hitting the hard handle material with a *big* hammer.

The set of mesquite wood slabs for the full-tang handle was rough-shaped on a disc sander, then epoxied to the knife tang. When the epoxy was set, all you need to finish the handle is a bit of time on the belt sander. If you do not have a belt sander, you can use the old rasp removal system; it still works well. Sand and shape the handle until you have the style you want.

One of the slip-over tang knives was selected to be fitted with a deer antler crown handle. This is the butt of the antler that fits close to the skull of a deer. It has a rosette that makes for a great-looking knife handle. The one in use has a curve to the left from the horn growth that fits the right hand nicely.

When working with handle positioning, you should try the fit with the blade up, as you'd use a knife for gutting, as well as edge down, as the knife is held for skinning. It might fit well one way but not the other, so try it first.

The deer antler section was drilled to open the core of hard bone to accept the knife tang. The operation is simple, but be careful to not go too far and drill through the antler itself. If you

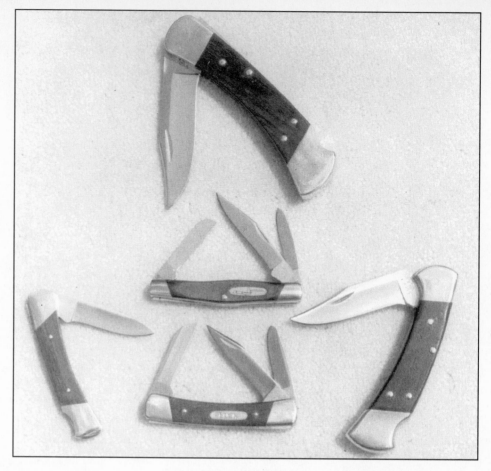

These Buck folding knives were all damaged and then bought at low prices. With the blades restored, there is plenty of metal left to give more years of service.

do that, find another section and start over. The blade tang is placed in the drilled antler piece, epoxy is flowed in around and below the tang, then set aside to cure. When the epoxy has set, all you need to do is polish the antler a bit for a great-looking knife.

There are so many design and material variations you can use to make a great looking knife out of an ordinary blade. There is no end to what you can do. However, if you accidentally get the blade too hot, you can change the temper of the steel, ruining the knife. Use caution while regrinding blades and quench the steel in a bucket of cold water frequently while working.

Folding knives present different problems. Most of those encountered have one damaged or broken blade, but the others are usually in good shape. The popular lock-blade styles have only one blade, so the only thing you can do is to reshape a damaged point or edge. Unless you have access to factory parts, there is not much more you can do. To repair them to original might cost more than buying a new knife.

You are the one to determine whether a knife is worth the expense of renovation. If it belonged to a family member, you can justify it. Grandad's knife might have sentimental value, and you would like to repair it and hand it down to your son. In this case, you really do not care about the price of rework—within reason, of course.

There is not much more to do on folding knives beyond reshaping a blade, cleaning up and polishing the handles. If it started as a three-blade knife and has two good blades left, use

it as a two-bladed knife. Keep the rework simple and enjoy the unit as it turns out.

There is another item to consider while you are browsing through garage sales, gun shows and other places where people sell items for a good price. Before you start grinding, sanding and changing a knife you have found, check to see if you have a collector item. An old knife *could* be valuable. You should find someone who knows this field before you start reworking a knife, because reworking can ruin the collector value.

Damaged knives are a lot of fun to rework. Changing components such as the handles can make them look different from the original. That's part of the fun.

People ask what to do with knives that have been reworked. When hunting or fishing out of state, take a few extra knives along. If a friendly rancher grants access for hunting, dig into the tackle box and give him a choice of knives. Most do not expect this and appreciate the gesture. Ranchers and farmers use knives of one type or another every day. Giving reworked knives as gifts is a great way to make friends. Since you have little money involved, the landowner will not feel you are trying to "buy" access to his land.

One rancher friend has been doing the same thing for several years. He says it gives him something to do when the snow flies too deep to get into town.

Scout your area for broken or damaged knives. They can be purchased for a fraction of the normal price, and you will have fun with the challenge of making a good-looking knife out of a disaster case.

A MATTER OF DESIGN

It took nearly four decades for Rex Applegate's and William Fairbairn's thoughts to crystallize into reality

FOR MORE THAN a half-century, Colonel Rex Applegate, United States Army (Retired), has lived by the time-worn adage that "new ain't necessarily better." In fact, that motto has led to what amounts to a career for the old soldier.

Back in World War II, this Oregon native joined with William Fairbairn, an officer with the British Commandos and a former Shanghai police officer, to design a combat knife that was meant to be the successor to the Fairbairn-Sykes Commando knife.

The Commando knife was designed by Fairbairn and E.A. Sykes, also a former Shanghai police officer, but the former had come to recognize that the original, designed as a double-edged stiletto, was too brittle and lacked proper balance, among other faults.

The resulting Applegate-Fairbairn was designed by the pair as a knife for U.S. members of the OSS. However, due to the fact that the war came to an end before all of the usual military red tape could be cleared and testing evaluated, the design never went into production.

This OSS training group, circa 1943, was located in what now is the site of the presidential retreat, Camp David. William Fairbairn is in the green British battle dress, second from right in the front row. Rex Applegate is fourth from left in the back row. This photo was classified for many years.

This is the custom-made Applegate-Fairbairn fighting knife now being made by William Harsey of Creswell, Oregon. The production version was introduced to the sporting goods trade in early 1997 and is being made in Germany by Boker.

The Applegate-Fairbairn custom fighting knife is shown with the Applegate Folder currently being made by Gerber. During 1996, more than 70,000 of the folders were made and shipped from Gerber's Oregon factory.

Here are two versions of the Mini-Smatchet currently being made on a custom basis by William Harsey. This version and the larger Combat Smatchet will be produced in Germany by Boker in late 1997 for worldwide distribution.

The Mini-Smatchet currently is marketed with a pancake-type Kydex sheath.

That, however, gave us the basic design that has occupied Rex Applegate's mind for the past half-century. It has been produced both on a custom basis by several knifemakers and as a production item by several companies. In some cases, there have been modifications, but the royalties still were paid to the colonel.

But all of this didn't just happen. Colonel Applegate had to have some authentic background for his thoughts on knife design. That background began about the time this descendant of Oregon pioneers was graduated from the University of Oregon in 1939, receiving a reserve Army commission through the university's ROTC program. With Selective Service in force and a war under way in Europe, he was called to active duty immediately and was assigned to a military police unit.

Lieutenant Applegate soon came to the attention of "Wild Bill" Donovan, who had been assigned to form the Office of Strategic Services. Familiarly known then simply as the OSS, this was the forerunner of today's CIA. The young officer was assigned to the new outfit and ordered to "learn all there is about close combat."

President rested at Camp David, which adjoined the OSS training center. He also served as bodyguard to Winston Churchill, when the British prime minister visited Roosevelt at Camp David.

From 1943 until the war ended in 1945, Applegate served at the Military Intelligence Training Center at Camp Ritchie, Maryland, doing roughly the same job he had done for the OSS, adding to his knowledge of close combat and the weapons and tactics involved.

In 1946, he was retired from the Army due to a service-related injury, which led to a new career as an arms dealer in Mexico, where he spent seventeen years learning about riot control on a first-hand observer basis.

The retired colonel returned to the U.S. in 1964 to get serious about writing such books as *Kill Or Be Killed*, which has gone through nearly thirty printings and now is a textbook at the Marine Corps Schools at Quantico, Virginia.

During their joint tenure at the OSS training center, Fairbairn and Applegate had the opportunity to talk to a great number of students who had used the Fairbairn-Sykes knife in actual com-

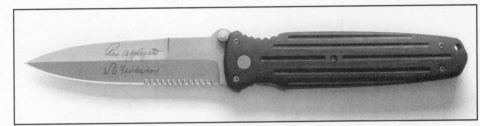

The prototype of Rex Applegate's Mini-Folder featured a bead-blasted, dull-colored blade. The handle design was drawn from the original Applegate-Fairbairn fighting knife.

The production Mini-Folder being produced by Gerber has been sleeked up a bit from the prototype for purposes of more efficient production. The signatures of Applegate and Fairbairn have been retained on the blade.

Applegate went to England and trained with the British Commandos and British intelligence, taking part in raids in Nazi-controlled stretches of Europe. It was during this time that he met E.A. Sykes, who reportedly told him the design of the Fairbairn-Sykes knife had been adopted from medieval daggers on display in the museum in the Tower of London.

Returning to the U.S., Applegate—by then a captain—found himself working closely with William Fairbairn, who was an exchange officer with OSS. Both were assigned to oversee construction of the OSS training center. Off hours, though, were devoted to developing the original Applegate-Fairbairn combat knife, as well as redesigning the Smatchet, essentially a double-bladed knife/hand axe developed originally for British forces. The Applegate-Fairbairn Smatchet also was doomed to remain a prototype and stack of blueprints for several decades, however.

Regular duties no doubt interfered with knife designs for both soldiers during this period, for Applegate had caught the eye of President Roosevelt and found himself serving as a bodyguard to his commander-in-chief on weekends, when the

bat situations. There were reports of the blade snapping off either at the point or the tang, and most of those interviewed didn't like the handle. It might have looked nice on a dagger in the Tower of London, but it was too small in circumference for a good grip by a man with even average hands.

In their revised design of the original, the American and British officers provided a wider tang, came up with a thicker, more hand-filling handle and developed a wider blade with a spear point rather than the stiletto shape of the original.

It was during this period that the pair redeveloped the British-made Smatchet. According to Rex Applegate, the original apparently was an adaptation of the Filipino bolo and boasted a broad double-edged blade that was leaf-like in shape. The versions made in England, and later in the U.S. by Case Cutlery, had blades approximately 11 inches in length.

During the Vietnam War, combat knives once again became a matter of interest not only among service personnel, but with cutlery fanciers and collectors as well. Instead of the appeal dying with the end of hostilities, as seems to have been the case after World War II, interested tended to increase.

The Combat Smatchet originally was produced by Buck Knives, then 300 were made by the late Al Mar. This is one of the Mar-made knives with the sheath of black ballistic nylon.

Said interest led Applegate to dig into his trunks and find the Applegate-Fairbairn-developed prototypes and blueprints, which had begun to fade.

With the development of superior stain-resistant steels for cutlery, it was only natural, Applegate felt, that such gains should be utilized. Thus, 154CM was chosen for the blade, since the edge-holding capability and overall toughness of this material were being touted by custom cutlers. After reviewing the available man-made materials, Applegate settled on Lexan for his handles.

But it was here that he decided to gild the sharp-edged lily, so to speak. He and Fairbairn came up with a removable handle that allowed one to mount lead weights along the knife's tang to alter balance. These weights, Applegate explains, could be positioned by the knife's user for a custom, one-of-a-kind balance.

At that time, T.J. Yancey had retired from the business world to make knives in Estes Park, Colorado. He was contacted in 1980 and agreed to make the knives. Thus, the Applegate-Fairbairn combat knife went into production after a delay of nearly four decades.

Yancey turned out knives for Applegate for several years, but illness ultimately was affecting production. The colonel started looking for another maker, finally approaching Bill Harsey, an Oregon custom knifemaker. Harsey found that a hollow grind would increase the capabilities without weakening any part of the knife. This development went into effect in 1987.

From its inception as a custom knife, the Applegate-Fairbairn combat knife had experienced respectable sales to members of such elite military units as the Army's Green Berets and Rangers, as well as Britain's Special Air Service and other top-rated foreign military forces. The knife then was being sold from his own Wells Creek Knife and Gun Works, which he still operates in Scottsburg, Oregon. However, Rex Applegate came to realize there was a far greater market waiting out there, but not at a price of $250 per knife!

The late Al Mar had left Gerber Legendary Blades some years earlier and started his own Oregon company in a suburb of Portland, designing knives that he then had produced in Japan. Applegate and Mar came to an agreement and a production version of the knife was adopted.

Called the AMK A-F version, this model featured a green rather than black Lexan handle, the lead weights in the handle no longer were included, and there was no metal liner in the lanyard hole. Also, an exclusive Al Mar stainless steel, AM6, replaced the original 154CM.

Applegate's original concept, and that seen in the custom knives, calls for a dull, bead-blasted finish on the blade. The Al Mar version, introduced in 1987, retains the same grind lines as the custom knife, but boasts a high polish. Applegate refers to it as "a Christmas tree appearance."

Al Mar passed away a few years ago, but his family continues to market about 300 of this version per year. The colonel feels the embellishments added by Mar keep this style from being a "true" Applegate-Fairbairn knife. Instead of Lexan, later versions have carried a handle made of plastic-laminated wood. The colonel continues to receive royalties on each sale.

The next production of the combat knife was undertaken by Blackjack Knives in 1993. For this, the manufacturers deep-sixed the polished finish and came up with a flat gray tone that Colonel Applegate felt was more in keeping with any combat mission. The Blackjack blades were being made from 440A stainless steel, with tempering to a hardness of 56-58 on the Rockwell C scale. There also were improvements in the scabbard and the lead weights went back into the handle. However, they were glued in place and could not be removed all that readily.

This particular version of the Applegate-Fairbairn knife was made to retail at about $80 per copy. It sold well until the colonel came to feel that quality control was slipping, and the agreement between him and the company came to an end.

However, that certainly is not the end of the Applegate-Fairbairn combat knife. Colonel Applegate has signed a new contract, and the knife now is set to be produced by Boker in Germany, with sales to be handled in this country by Boker USA, which is headquartered in Golden, Colorado.

Meantime, there have been further developments on the custom level. Bill Harsey has developed two boot knife versions of the knife, which now are being marketed by the colonel's Wells Creek outfit. One version is simply a scaled-down combat knife with a 4½-inch blade, but the second has a hollow in the back of the blade that is said to add to penetration and cutting capabilities. There also is a boot knife version of the Smatchet being marketed.

All of which brings us full-circle back to the original Applegate-Fairbairn Smatchet. Using the old blueprints, the colonel put the revised version into custom production in 1988, with Bill Harsey again being chosen to make it.

The Applegate-Fairbairn Smatchet differs from the original British issue combat tool in several ways. Blades are 10 inches long and the profile of new and old are primarily the same. The WWII version out of England, however, had only one edge totally sharpened, while the top of the blade was sharpened approximately one-third of its length from the point. The current custom version has both edges of the blade sharpened from point to ricasso.

On the versions being made by Harsey, the blades are fashioned from used-up circular saw blades coming out of Oregon and Washington lumber mills. According to Applegate, the Smatchet blades are cut from the sawmill rejects, then annealed and cooled for no less than 12 hours.

While the steel is still in a soft state, the blades are ground to just slightly more than their finished thickness, then they are shaped and the necessary holes drilled. Once shaped to satisfaction, the blades are heat-treated to a Rockwell hardness of 59-60C.

"We designed the Smatchet for rough use in the field, often serving as a hatchet more than as a knife," Applegate explains. "We chose the blades from sawmills because they are proven as a tough steel that can meet the kind of punishment we see the Smatchet receiving."

A good deal of thought and dialog between Applegate and Harsey took place before they settled on a new design for the handle. The circumference has been reduced from the original, making it easier to grip. Dark slabs of micarta provide a positive grip.

In this custom version, the early Smatchet came with a heavy leather sheath with a wide belt loop and a heavy keeper strap. Each knife is individually numbered and priced about $675.

Buck Knives manufactured the Smatchet for a season or so, experiencing excellent sales with the limited run of 500. However, Chuck Buck and his staff decided the big battle blade did not fit the corporate image they sought to maintain, and they declined to continue production.

Prior to his death, Al Mar also agreed to produce a 300-unit version of what was termed the Combat Smatchet. While the name speaks of blood and gore, much of the selling effort was as a utility knife, the literature explaining that the double

edge—like that on a logger's axe—means double the service before sharpening is needed.

Produced in Japan like other Al Mar products, his version improved upon the grind lines that had caused trouble for Buck. Zytel handle slabs also were fitted perfectly, and sharpness edged on perfection, no pun intended.

Sheaths on the production model were of black ballistic

(Above) Applegate introduced the Gerber-made model of his folder at the 1996 SHOT Show. It since has been entered in the GSA catalog and thus is authorized for government purchase.

At a Soldier of Fortune convention, Colonel Applegate evaluates a prototype developed by another knife enthusiast.

Applegate conducts his own business, Wells Creek Gun and Knife Works in Oregon, selling guns, knives and copies of the books he has written. He also makes appearances at numerous gun shows around the nation.

nylon with a plastic liner to protect the double edge of the blade. A large pocket with a Velcro closer held a sharpening stone or a folder-type knife. According to Colonel Applegate, the Smatchet probably will be produced in Germany by Boker as part of his program.

The Model AFMS Applegate-Fairbairn Mini-Smatchet boot knife has the same blade shape and design of its larger contemporary. It has micarta handles with deep finger grooves, a forward thumb-fitting cross guard and a three-quarter tang. Length of the bead-blasted blade is 4³/₄ inches and is of ATS-34 steel. The blade is hardened to Rockwell 61C, and overall length of the knife is 8¹/₂ inches. It comes with a Kydex pancake-type sheath for belt carry, with built-in retaining and thumb-release features.

All of which brings us back to the Applegate-Fairbairn Combat Knife—but now as a folder!

Using the same general blade and handle design as found on the original combat knife, Colonel Applegate worked on the idea of a folder, then turned his notes over to well respected custom knifemakers Bill Harsey and Butch Vallotton. It was they who co-designed the Applegate-Fairbairn Combat Folder, or AFCF, as it has come to be called.

The knife was introduced at the April 1994 Oregon Knife Collectors Association show held in Eugene and was termed an instant hit.

The knife is unique in several respects, but perhaps most unique is the fact that the edition was limited to 200 serial-numbered knives and priced at $475 per copy. If the buyer wanted an inch of saw teeth on the blade, add another $25. The deal also called for a fifty-percent advance with order, the colonel's Wells Creek Knife and Gun Works guaranteeing a delivery time of 60 to 90 days.

Overall length of the knife, with the 4¹/₄-inch blade open, is 10 inches. The blade is of ATS-34 stain-resistant steel, tempered to a Rockwell hardness of 61C and is bead-blasted, double-edged and hollow-ground. Weight of this model is only 6

ounces, and it has a handle frame and spring made from aircraft-grade titanium alloy 6AL4V. Incorporated is a liner locking mechanism that is designed for what Harsey and Vallotton call "maximum dependability and strength." The scales are of black linen micarta and carry deep longitudinal grooves in the same general style as the original fixed-blade contemporary.

One might wonder, with a double-edged blade, how the knife is opened for business. One side of the blade carries the replica signatures of Applegate and Fairbairn, plus a thumb push that extends through the blade close to the handle. Thus the knife is fitted for one-hand opening with either hand.

With the custom model limited in number, it wasn't long before Colonel Applegate found requests and orders outnumbering the supply. Armed with such numbers, he approached Gerber Legendary Blades and soon came home with a contract whereby they would produce and market the same basic knife at a suggested retail price of $135. However, it was being renamed the Applegate Folding Survival Knife.

The first of these knives were shipped to retail outlets in the fall of 1995. Since then, some 70,000 units have been sold. The knife has been accepted by the Government Purchasing Office and is being stocked in the armed forces' post exchange system, with Rex Applegate drawing a royalty on each one sold.

Now, Applegate tells us, he is readying a mini version of the same knife that will have the dimensions of a pocketknife. At the time of this writing, he is negotiating with Gerber to handle sales of this mini version.

Consider the fact that this entire chain of events, covering more than a half-century began with a bull session in which two spies—one English, the other American—made some drawings on a few pieces of paper that led to then unacceptable prototypes.

Do you get the feeling that all this could be incorporated into another sequel to the *Back To The Future* movie series? The possibility of Michael J. Fox playing a young Rex Applegate may be more likely than we think!

LONG KNIVES, SWORDS AND SABERS

For some cutlery forms, big is considered the best

LONG BLADES OF one type or another have been around for as long as there have been knives. Probably, some cave-dweller realized that a broken rock lashed to a long, stout stick gave him an advantage over his opponent because it gave him a longer reach. A spear might be considered a form of sword, when employed in a slashing, stabbing manner.

With the Iron Age, knives and swords became the weapon of choice for those engaged in the business of war. In most parts of the world, only the wealthier—the ruling classes—could afford the cost of a sword or saber. Clubs, axes, sticks, spears and the like were for the common soldier. For the most part, the common citizen was not trusted with swords and long knives because they might provide the means to revolt against the oppressive rulers. That ruling-class philosophy in Western

Europe may be one of the reasons our own founding fathers made sure they included the Second Amendment right to keep and bear arms in the Constitution.

Most of us have seen enough movies and read enough history to realize the importance of a large sword, saber or dagger in the hands of a trained knight, horseman, soldier or sailor. A man with proper strength and the right training could cut down dozens of opponents in a single battle. He could cut an enemy ship's rigging or steering gear so it could not sail, while fending off the defending sailors' own weapons. Horses can fall to a well-placed blade edge, and most early leather, bamboo and even bronze armor could not withstand a blow from a long, sharp blade.

Generally speaking, a saber (also spelled *sabre* in some

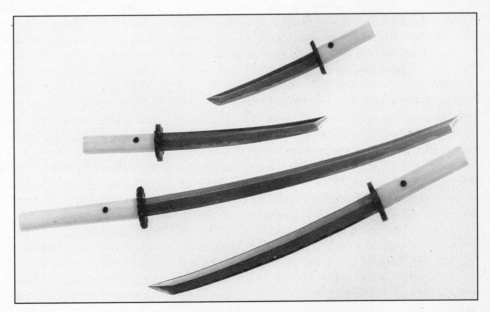

Swords and long knives come in several sizes. The Japanese-style blades are in demand from collectors and martial artists. (Photo by Dan Fitzgerald.)

A Japanese-style sword, complete with display stand, may sell for thousands of dollars.

The hilt of a Japanese sword may be adorned with gold in precise designs.

usage) is a weapon carried by the cavalry. It is defined as a "light sword for fencing, a cavalry sword with a long, one-edged, slightly curved blade."

A sword is defined as, "a weapon with a long, pointed blade having one or two sharp edges and set in a handle or hilt."

In their execution, these definitions have been somewhat blurred by many makers over the years. Certainly, Japanese, Chinese and other Oriental edged weapons do not fit neatly into these two categories. The Indonesian and Filipino kris, for instance, has a long, wavy blade, sharpened on both edges, and some have sharp points. The typical Japanese samurai sword is long, slightly curved and is sharpened on one side, but was not a cavalry weapon when the sword was in its heyday. Horses were not introduced to Japan until more recent periods, although when they were, the feudal Samurai and other soldiers were quick to appreciate how the animals could be utilized for warfare.

When does a long knife or a dagger become a sword or saber? Is a big Bowie knife a short sword? Perhaps it is not important to answer these questions. For the purposes of this chapter, strict definitions are unnecessary. What we will explore are some examples of swords and long knives—where they come from, their uses and their makers. You may call them whatever you wish. In the interest of simplicity, we will refer to these longer-blade tools as swords or long knives.

People buy, have, trade, display and use swords for various reasons. Some wish to have a sword over the mantelpiece as a decorator item. Some of us still may have our officer's or non-commissioned officer's swords or sabers from our military days and proudly display them in our homes. In some countries and some cultures, a knife or sword in the home is as natural as family portraits on the wall.

In another chapter in this volume, we discuss knife collecting and investing. Long knives and swords are a part of the collecting world, with many collectors specializing in these long blades. Such cutlery may present a bit of a problem in matters of storage or in displaying the collection. However, there almost always are a number of sword collections on display at most knife and gun shows around the country.

Many sword collectors specialize in certain historical periods or countries, such as originals or replicas of the Crusades, historic battles or wars. Others specialize in those of Arabia, Britain, Indonesia, China or Japan. Originals can be expensive to the extreme, and there are plenty of fakes around. Most of us opt for modern replicas.

Another market for modern-made swords is the entertainment industry. There continue to be new historically based movies in theaters and on video tape ready to entertain us. While it is true that many of the swords seen in these movies are made of wood, plastic or aluminum, many others are made with great care by skilled knifemakers who specialize in the long blades. Many knifemakers are headquartered in and around the Southern California area and are in close, continuous contact with the movie industry.

Still other consumers—certain martial artists, for instance—acquire long blades for use in their training and practice. By the time a martial artist gets to the level of training in which edged weapons become a part of the curriculum, he or she has a firm idea of what sort of blade it must be. There are several custom knifemakers around the world who specialize in providing these special weapons to students of particular schools of martial arts. Several Japanese- and Chinese-based arts may come to mind.

One thing all swords and long knives have in common is their relatively high price. Part of that is due to the large amount of steel contained in a single sword. Many have blades that are two to three feet long and at least a quarter-inch in thickness, and carry distinctive and ornate handles, hilts and decorations. That much of steel is expensive, but the amount of work a bladesmith must put into a fine sword is staggering. There is no economy of scale when handling such a long piece of steel. A special grind on a 5-inch blade might be relatively easy to accomplish, but will require tremendous skill and time on a 30-inch blade.

We talked over the difficulties and the techniques of swordmaking with two of the premier long-blade makers we know: Bob Engnath and Jody Samson. We have had a look at another sword maker, Phill Hartsfield, in a previous section of this book. All have loyal and enthusiastic followings among their respective customers from around the world. These makers have been kind and patient enough to share some of their thoughts and discuss their skills with us.

Bob Engnath makes a large number of Japanese-type swords and long knives for sale to martial artists and others who know about his work. Grinding a Japanese blade is difficult enough, says Engnath, but the real challenge is in the heat-treatment. Hours and hours of cutting and grinding can be lost through a mistake or a wrong step while treating the blade.

To achieve the typical Japanese blade look and feel, with its distinctive tempering lines visible along the length of the sword, the steel must be specially heat-treated. The blade edge must be hardened more than the back or spine of the blade.

Japanese sword makers studied and worked for years to perfect the technique. They preferred to keep the technique a secret, but the information has spread. The best swords produced in Japan were, for centuries, in great demand by the top Samurai warriors of the time. They are still sought out by collectors. Engnath, with his usual sense of humor, offers the following observations on how he, a Westerner, has been able to produce his highly regarded swords:

"Clay and other refractory glops must be used in tempering—hardening—the Japanese-style blade edge. The use of the material may be the most confusing part of the entire process. Drop a bit on the floor while you are working and you will understand why I use the term 'glop.'"

The refractory clay, says Engnath, has a two-fold purpose in the process. It keeps the quenching medium, be it oil or water, from contacting the main body of the blade, thus preventing that portion of the blade from hardening too much. The clay also helps hold some of the heat in the main body of the blade so that it will cool slowly and not become shocked into hardening.

"Steel has a discouraging tendency built into the process of undergoing selective hardening—it bends. By that, I do not mean the steel simply warps; I mean the steel bends, curving upward from the cutting edge. The maker has to heat a carbon-steel blade to around 1500 degrees F to make it harden. In so doing, the entire blade expands. This is one of those scientific facts of life and elemental physics that one cannot escape.

"When steel is converted into martensite—the hard stuff—it is frozen in the expanded size. The back of the blade does not harden. It slowly shrinks back to the original dimension. This happening will induce plenty of heartburn and ulcers for most knifemakers.

"Water-quenching produces the most desirable-looking temper line, close to duplicating some of the ancient sword types. Water-quenching also produces the most extreme differential between the size of the hardened edge and the soft back. One will find a perfectly straight sword hardening into a cutlass shape, with more than $1\frac{1}{2}$ inches of curvature. The steels 1045 and 1050 move slightly more than an inch, while W-2 steel might approach two inches. Oil-quenching a Bowie made of 5160 with a hardened edge will produce about $\frac{1}{8}$-inch of curvature throughout a foot of blade length."

In 10 seconds of quenching, says Engnath, the blade goes through an incredible combination of cooling and stress.

"You will hear it creak while seeming to sing in your hand. When conditions are a bit too much, it goes *ping*. You do not want to hear that sound. When it pings, it is the sound of the spine shrinking to such a degree that it literally pulls the cutting edge apart!

"When this happens, one hurries over to the steel distributor's manual, flipping pages and searching. It says this stuff can be water-quenched, right there in black and white, plain as day. To make a long story short, the distributors and manufacturers are not thinking about the cross-section of a blade when they discuss this type of hardening. They are thinking about axles, ball bearings and other items with a nice, even cross-section and

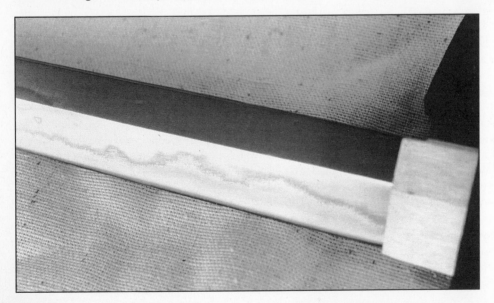

The Japanese word for the variable treatment line is ashi. The edge is harder than the back of the blade.

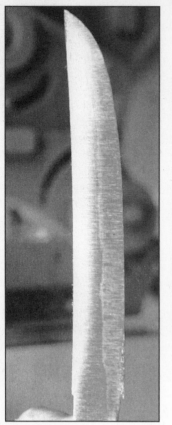

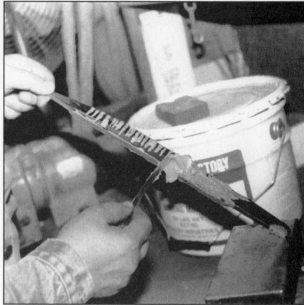

(Left) A rough Engnath blade before heat-treating and final polishing. The blade will curve more after heat-treating.

Bob Engnath is one of the most prolific sword makers in the U.S.—and one of the best.

Engnath's text outlines the thinking behind refractory cement placement near the tang/handle portion of a long blade.

no thin edges. This is a problem that can really discourage the knifemaker. "On one occasion, five swords left my shop with undetected cracks. It put me in such a state that I made no more for a year.

"I wouldn't tell this if there were not a way to fix it. You have to scrape the clay off the spine of the blade so that part of the back will harden just a bit, reducing the tendency to curve so much. Now the blades only curve about 3/4-inch. That, coincidentally, happens to be just about the correct curve for a Japanese sword."

The heat-treater has to do some adjustments. A proper sword is a little thinner at the tip than at the guard, according to Engnath. He will bend the tip down about 3/8-inch and the butt end upward about the same amount. "I pray a little when I do this," says the maker. "I even try Buddha. It pays to cover all the bases.

"The bending gadget in my shop is just a couple of 8-foot planks with bolts holding them together. There are spacers on the bolts, between the planks, so they are snug on the blade when I slide it in-between. If I put a 6-foot pipe on the other end of the blade, I can put a kink in 5/16-inch steel that is 1 1/2 inches wide.

"The last fly in the ointment is that the clay will not bend along with the steel when the sword starts to curve. That often makes the clay fall off, while there are still sections beneath it that are hot enough to harden. You do not necessarily want odd islands of hardened steel messing up the neat look of your cutting edge."

Custom knifemaker Kuzan Oda helped solve that problem by suggesting that wrapping mild iron wire right into the soft

clay would help it stay on tight enough to keep water from getting under it. It takes only about a dozen turns for a sword; thus, one is able to form the clay right back over the wire. If it appears to crack in drying, the sword maker can patch it the next day, before heat-treating the blade.

Engnath buys about fifty pounds at a time of the High Lumina Refractory Cement he calls glop. That should be enough for at least twenty swords. This material is already mixed and ready to use, and will keep soft for months if the lid is on tight.

"Getting clay onto the blade in a useful pattern is not too hard," declares Bob Engnath. "I need a couple of those plastic whipped topping containers my wife saves when they are empty. I next run down to the art store for an artist's palette knife. I usually get two; one is straight and small, the other longer. At the hardware store, I pick up some number 22 iron wire and a putty knife. I always add three or four shop rags.

"The work area need not be anything more involved than the workbench. I work while sitting, because putting clay onto a single sword might take as long as 45 minutes. One of those plastic containers should be full of the clay. Another container is filled with water, so the putty and palette knives can soak when not in use.

"Heap the clay in its container, so you can scrape a roll of it about the thickness of a wooden match onto the side of the small palette knife. If the clay is too stiff, dunk the little knife into the water bucket, pick up a few drops of water and stir it into the surface of a small patch of refractory cement. Too much water will cause the clay to shrink too much when it dries."

Custom knifemaker Bob Engnath designed his own brick-lined gas-powered furnace to accept the longest sword blades. This is hot work!

A water trough accepts the entire heated blade for uniform cooling. For some steels, an oil bath is preferred.

Dozens of sword blades have had the clay and wire applied. They wait for the clay to harden before heat-treatment.

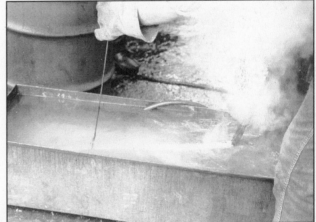

(Left) A typical Engnath sword is a thing of beauty. The variable heat-treatment lines are clearly visible on this sword blade. Japanese sword makers kept their process a secret for centuries.

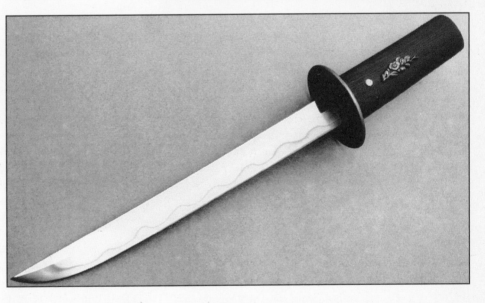

The typical curve in a Japanese sword blade is the result of selective hardening, rather than grinding. The treated blade is ready for final sanding and polishing.

Before starting the operation, Engnath says he likes to grind down the sharp edges of the tang before he must handle it too much. Such sharp edges can be painful.

The next step is to lay the clay-laden edge of the palette knife on the side of the sword with a brisk motion, transferring a line of clay to the blade so it runs from the cutting edge to the grind line. This move takes a bit of practice, according to Engnath. The grind lines and the clay should be approximately even and equal on both sides of the blade, but the material does not have to be symmetrical.

The lines, says Engnath, are called ashi lines. "Ashi means 'rat leg.' That puzzles me, too," admits the sword maker. "The Japanese used the lines to stop the edge from chipping. The softer sections of steel project down into the temper line.

"The ashi lines may be only 1/4-inch apart, to as much as 1/2-inch. They will have quite an effect on the upper shape of the

Custom knifemaker Jody Samson specializes in replicas of ancient edged weapons, many of which have been used in the movie industry.

Grinding long sword blades is a special skill that Samson has refined over the years.

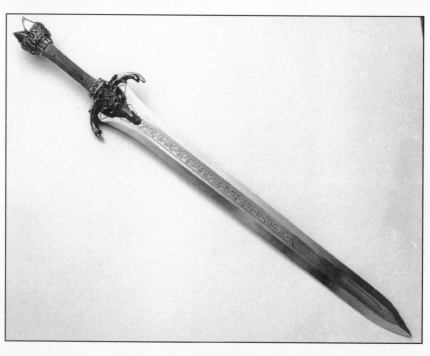

This is one of Jody Samson's Medieval replicas seen in *Conan the Barbarian*. (Photo by Dan Fitzgerald.)

temper line. They also have a bit to do with curvature, with fewer lines producing more pronounced curvature."

The maker now switches to the larger palette knife. It should be about the size of a small kitchen spatula. If the right size is not available at the art supply house, a larger one can be ground down to size.

The blade is reversed so the maker is holding the tip, and the tang is against the bench. Use care. The tip can cut.

Engnath says, "The clay you put on now will determine how high the temper line will go up the blade. The proper height is one-third of the total width, but I sometimes vary this. Begin plastering clay onto the side of the blade, stopping about halfway down. Once you have about 3/16-inch of clay on the

steel for some length, come back and work it down a bit lower. Take care not to cover the spine.

"As you get to within a few inches of the tang, make the temper line a little narrower by pushing the clay down farther. That's traditional. The temper line should extend into the tang about an inch past the end of the cutting edge. If you want to make the tang stiffer at the junction of the blade and handle, scrape about 1/2-inch of clay away along the top sides of the spine, tapering the cut in and out smoothly over about 6 or 8 inches."

The blade then is turned around and held by the tang as the clay application is repeated on the other side. When both sides are finished, a neat turnback is made of the clay at the tip.

Samson demonstrates the flexibility of one of his swords.

Samson likes to demonstrate the steel-piercing abilities of his swords by stabbing a steel drum.

"Stand the blade on its tip and wrap about a dozen turns of number 22 iron wire right into the clay, working from tang to tip," explains Engnath. "Do not let any clay get pushed around at the tip, because it will mess up that nice turnback you made there. Spatula the clay back over the cuts the wire made.

"You may heat treat immediately, unless you are using a coal-fire forge. If that is your method, it may be easier to wait until the clay has hardened, as there will be less chance of scraping the clay off the blade in the forge."

After the clay has hardened, Engnath is ready for heat-treating. He usually prefers to wait until he has at least a dozen, possibly two dozen long blades ready. The setup and the time consumed for several blades is considerably less than doing one blade at a time. Also, he has to have help in handling all the blades. His son is usually in the shop and some friends always stop by when he is treating sword blades. He is quick to enlist their help, too.

Engnath built his own gas-fired forge, which is long enough to accommodate the longest blades. He rigged up a set of multi-jet burners in the fire-brick-lined forge so the blades are heated uniformly and quickly. He can treat several at a time with his arrangement.

A cool, rainy winter day in Southern California is ideal for heat treating in the outdoor forge, because Engnath can judge the color of the heated blades more accurately before they are quenched. He places several blades along the brick shelf forge lining, turning them from time to time to assure even heat. As mentioned, he must use care to not knock any of the refractory clay from the blades during the process.

When the steel has reached the desired color denoting correct temperature in Engnath's judgment, he uses his heavy-duty tongs to pull out a blade, immediately plunging it into a water trough. The entire blade must be thrust into the water at once, so

Samson carves the fantastic figures on his sword handles out of jeweler's wax and then makes castings of them.

it all cools at the same speed. The action creates quite a bit of steam and sound. When the active steaming stops, the blade is pulled out of the water and placed on a rack to cool to air temperature. Later, the iron wire is unwrapped and the clay removed. That is when the final grinding, sanding and polishing begins.

Getting the long blade to the polish and contrast to produce a dramatic and beautiful Japanese sword is long and tedious work. But Engnath says he likes it. The results can be astonishing, and he has no trouble selling every sword he can turn out. Demand far exceeds production in any given year.

Back when Hollywood was making the movie *Conan the*

Jim Ferguson uses his Twisted Nickel process to produce long Damascus blades for collectors.

Custom knifemaker Chuck Stapel designed this long knife for the Los Angeles County Sheriff's Office Arson Explosives Detail—the bomb squad.

Barbarian, starring Arnold Schwarzenegger, a search was made of local knifemakers to find the artist who could—and would—produce the muscleman's big sword. The maker turned out to be Jody Samson, who at the time was working in a shop with Alex Collins and the late pioneer knifemaker John Nelson Cooper. Samson was already interested in medieval swords, armor, shields and other ancient weapons of war. He produced the sword Schwarzenegger used in the movie, as well as several more replicas for other movie scenes.

Samson is still turning out swords for the movies and for collectors nearly two decades after that motion picture was released. He has been involved in several other films, providing various unique tools of war. He also is associated with several renaissance groups, where there is a demand for his swords,

armor, chain mail, maces, daggers and the costume items he makes available.

Samson works out of a shop in the Hollywood area that is frequented by actors, producers, stunt men and women, directors, writers and others in the business. By now, Samson has gained a reputation for turning out some fine reality or fantasy swords for many uses.

Jody Samson specializes in ornate, fantastic hilts and handles. He uses the lost wax method to form the metal gargoyles, monsters, devils and dragons that decorate his swords.

He has some new equipment, but the task of grinding a straight, accurate sword blade is as tedious as it ever was, says Samson.

"One little slip, one lapse of concentration and you can ruin a blade that may have many hours of work in it," Samson says. "The really hard part is keeping the grind lines straight and even over the entire length of the blade. Even a slight relaxation at the wrong time will spoil the whole thing, especially on a complicated, triple-hollow-ground blade."

While Samson makes many swords for the movies, what he prefers are real swords. He likes to show off a bit by stabbing a newly finished sword into a steel drum out behind the shop. Samson has practiced the move, but a single thrust will push the blade completely through one side and into the far side of the drum. It takes considerable effort to remove. It is an impressive demonstration of the power of the sword.

Engnath, Hartsfield and Samson are not the only sword makers in America today, of course. There are dozens who produce excellent examples. There are hundreds of sword makers in other countries who make the blades for export to North America. Several factory production companies make knives with blades 9 inches long or more. Most are not considered short swords; they are simply long knives designed to make certain cutting chores easier.

The collector, the decorator, the martial artist, camper, hunter, explorer and the homeowner all may have use for a long knife or sword at certain times. Take some time to look over a number of mail-order knife catalogs, study the wares offered at the next knife show in your area and get acquainted with some of the makers. Learn about their philosophies and their skills in sword making. You might want to order one or two.

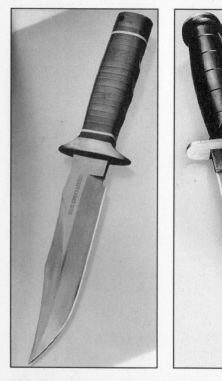

SOG Specialties has found a market for its big military-design knife for twenty years.

Damascus USA replicates a large military knife using forged-to-shape Damascus steel.

MACHINES FOR HANDMADE KNIVES

Modern knifemakers use power tools to save both time and effort

BELT SANDER. DISC grinder. Wheel grinder. Burr King. Baldor. Foredom. These names and others cover the equipment and brand names associated with knifemaking by both custom craftsmen and factory production workers. The terms can be confusing to beginners or to consumers. Are they necessary for a first-time knifemaker? How can we call it a handmade knife when power tools were used to make it?

A handmade or custom-made knife does not have to be made with hand tools only to qualify for the definition. Power tools are commonly found in 99 percent of custom knife-

makers' shops, some singly and some in multiples. As long as the knives are turned out one at a time and are produced by the craftsman, not by automated machines or on production lines, the product truly may be defined as a custom or hand-made knife.

There are certain power tools that are considered basic to most knifemakers. They are the genuine time- and work-savers that are used every day by the makers. Their value has been proven for decades. A custom knifemaker may visit the shop of another and recognize the machines and their function as the

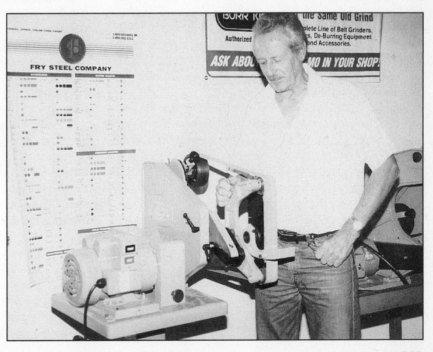

John Mallet, the man behind Tru-Grit, says the Burr King Model 960-200 is the most popular belt sander available to knifemakers. This version is complete with the Knifemaker attachment as standard equipment.

same as his own. There may be slight differences in the location and order in which they are set up, but the machines most likely will be the same. They are likely to be the same brand and model, too.

Your authors contacted one of our friendly purveyors of some of these power machines to learn what was popular. John Mallet has operated a small business he calls Tru-Grit in the Southern California area for several years. He is seen at most major knife shows displaying the newest machines, sanding belts, abrasives, wheels, buffing compounds, knife steels, handle materials, grinding discs, electric motors, sharpening stones and many other items knifemakers and knife owners might find handy.

The bulk of John Mallet's business is derived from the sale of three basic machines: Burr King Model 960-200 Knifemaker, Baldor electric grinders and, in more recent times, a Baldor motor-powered, Tru-Grit-designed disc grinder.

Of those items, the Burr King Knifemaker is the machine of choice by most custom knifemakers. It is powerful, adjustable, rugged and versatile. For some knifemakers, it is the only machine in the shop. Excellent knives may be produced using only one of these machines and various sanding belts. Mallet says other machinists or hobbyists do purchase a Burr King from time to time, but by far the largest number of them he sells goes to knifemakers, many of whom use several in their shops.

"The Model 960," says Mallet, "is the machine of choice for knifemakers who must be able to work fast and accurately while making their knives. There are several options and attachments for the machine that make it the most valuable tool in the shop."

The Burr King uses standard 2x72-inch sanding belts in grits ranging from the coarsest, used to rough-shape a blade or handle, to the finest micron grits for polishing and finishing blades. The Model 960 is available with a standard 1-horsepower, 1725-rpm electric motor or a $1\frac{1}{2}$-horsepower variable speed motor that has seen increasing popularity. The variable-speed motor will operate at speeds ranging from up to 2500 rpm. Some makers prefer the higher belt speed, while others swear by slower, controllable belt speeds. Other choices may include a single-speed $1\frac{1}{2}$-horsepower or 2-horsepower motor. With the latter, the manufacturer's model number is 1272—and the price moves up considerably.

Standard equipment for the Model 960, according to the Tru-Grit catalog, includes an adjustable belt-tension control for loose belt operation, positive belt-tracking, quick-change assembly for easy belt removal and replacement, an 8-inch contact wheel for profiling, hollow-grinding and other rapid stock removal, and a 2x8-inch platen directly behind the wheel. The platen will swing conveniently out of the way when not in use. Other standard equipment includes a precision-machined work table that is fully adjustable to the contact wheel and the rear backup platen.

As for optional equipment, the Burr King has several items of interest to knifemakers. One is a small wheel adapter to utilize $\frac{9}{16}$- to $1\frac{1}{2}$-inch wheels that are ideal for cutting handle finger grooves or any other tight radius work. A 10-inch contact wheel is also available, as is a knifemaker attachment with 2-

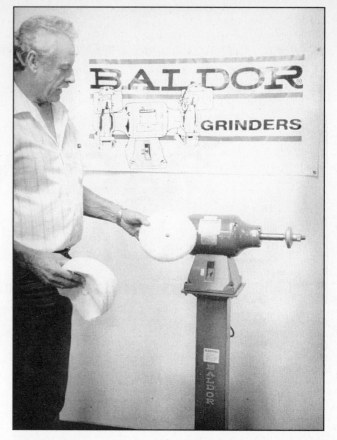

Wheel grinders and buffers from Baldor will accept a variety of wheels, stones and accessories for knifemakers.

inch and 5-inch contact wheels. An extra platen is placed between the two small wheels to be used for flat-grinding or tapering blade tangs.

John Mallet and his staff have developed a unique power tool based on the Baldor motor. The Tru-Grit disc sander is presented as ideal for those craftsmen who make folding knives, although it certainly has other uses. The standard motor is a $\frac{1}{3}$-horsepower reversible version, running at 1140 rpm, with the $\frac{1}{2}$-horse variable-speed optional. The disc grinder features a 45-degree calibrated adjustable tilt table, standard $\frac{7}{16}$-inch-thick 9-inch disc and base all machined from heavy 6061 anodized aluminum. Mallet says the Model TG-92 disc grinder has already proven popular with many knifemakers.

Another power machine common in knife shops and other facilities is a Baldor-powered buffer. The most popular is the $\frac{3}{4}$-horsepower model available at 1800 or 3600 rpm. Tru-Grit has several other options available in buffers. The company also carries a full line of grinding wheels, buffing wheels of various arbor sizes, thicknesses and diameters. Buffing compounds of several grit ratings are commonly available, too.

Mallet also offers a selection of knife steels in several widths and thicknesses. His favorite, and the favorite of most of his knifemaking customers seems to be ATS-34 stainless steel.

"ATS-34 is a pure sponge iron made from iron sand with low impurities," declares John Mallet. "ATS-34 is made using sophisticated steel-making technology, combined with ideal

Tru-Grit maintains a wide assortment of accessories, attachments, parts and options for the power tools sold.

(Right) Scott Sharpe smiles as he assists in inventory week at Tru-Grit. He was instrumental in setting up and maintaining supplies and equipment.

(Below) Mallet saw a need and filled it with the TG-92 disc grinder machine, already popular with some knifemakers.

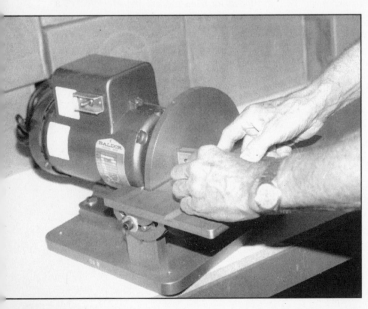

alloy element balancing. This steel is widely accepted as the highest-quality knife material."

In addition to the ATS-34, the company offers 440C, 416 pin stock, 416 annealed flat bar in various thicknesses and widths, plus a selection of Damascus steel for knifemakers.

John Mallet is not the only seller of Burr King knifemaking machines, of course, but he is one of the largest. There are several reputable dealers around the world with whom knifemakers deal for these products.

In 1996, Tru-Grit moved to a new location, several miles from the earlier location in Los Angeles. The move was made to avoid some of the crowds, traffic and smog of the big city. In addition, Scott Sharpe was named as the number two person in the company. John Mallet says Sharpe will be running the company in a "couple of years after I retire." Sharpe has full knowledge of the machines, their uses and the company's customers. There should be no change when Mallet decides to hang it up.

Catalogs and price lists are available from Tru-Grit.

DIXIE GUN WORKS' KNIVES

For the do-it-yourselfer,
these partially finished blades offer many possibilities

"THERE ARE FEW people who have the inclination to make a knife from scratch. One needs a bunch of specific tools, grinders and buffers, the list continuing until the costs incurred can be mind boggling. Knifemaking isn't cheap and the tools aren't, either." Those are the thoughts of C.R. Learn, an inveterate do-it-yourselfer.

Having made this profound statement, he was asked how the hobbyist can go about making a knife for his personal hunting and fishing needs.

"Well, you can take such materials as an ordinary metal-sharpening file and make a knife from it. Power hacksaw blades are good for a thin-bladed knife, but you still encounter the problem of power tools to work these into a good knife," Learn says.

One simply could take an appropriate piece of metal and shape it with a file, hacksaw and use some wood for a handle,

but then we run into the problem of heat-treating and finishing the knife.

This often leads one to give up the project entirely and buy a finished knife—but there are alternatives.

Dixie Gun Works has a series of ready-to-finish knives which are shown in an extensive catalog. They list several finished blades to which one needs to add a handle, and they are reasonably priced.

When a package containing two selected blades arrived at Bob Learn's California digs, it had an order form and information on other blades being offered under the name of E. Christopher Firearms Company. A call to Dixie revealed that to order one or two blades, one should use the Dixie catalog, but to order a quantity, it is done through Christopher Firearms.

These Dixie blades are finished, heat-treated to Rockwell 55-

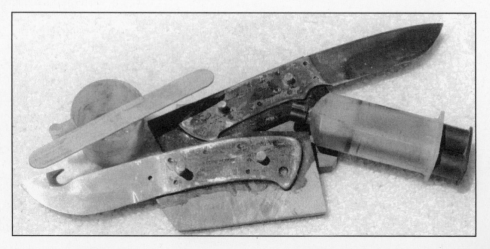

Some two-part epoxy, a stir stick, the unfinished handle and the rivets are all that's needed to complete the Dixie knife. Cover the wood handle and the metal with epoxy to get good adhesion. The rivets are longer than needed, but will be ground off later.

(Right) Dixie's full-tang knife has many holes drilled in it for rivet placement options. The two center ones were used for this project, but the maker could utilize any combination on the handle. Brazing rod will often fit any of these holes.

The Wapiti model gut hook knife is in position on the wood and a coat of epoxy is setting. The wood scale is larger than needed, but will be trimmed and cleaned up during finishing.

57C and each has its handle pre-drilled for several methods of installing the slabs or scales.

"Try to drill hardened Solingen steel and you will see why they give you many options," Learn opines. "You can't drill it with normal drill bits."

Dixie offers many blades and shapes, full-tang blades, as well as round tangs for those who prefer or want to try to install a slip-over style handle. There are over twenty blade and tang styles from which to pick in the Dixie catalog.

Learn feels a full-tang blade makes the strongest knife and two were ordered. One blade had the sweep of a skinner, with an added gut hook. The other was a straightforward blade for gen-

eral use and camp chores. Both knives had similar handle profiles and could be refined to become small easy-to-carry knives.

Next on Bob Learn's agenda was to find some good-looking wood for slabs or scales to serve as the handle.

"What was needed was a pair of wood scales that would cover the entire tang. Any excess material would be cut off, of course, during the finishing process, but there did need to be enough to extend forward on the blades, since no brass finger guards were ordered for these knives.

"Brass looks good and brightens up a knife handle, but when it goes green, it really looks bad. These would be made with no brass fixtures."

Here, the knives are set and curing under clamp pressure. Screw-down clamps give more pressure, but spring clamps are adequate.

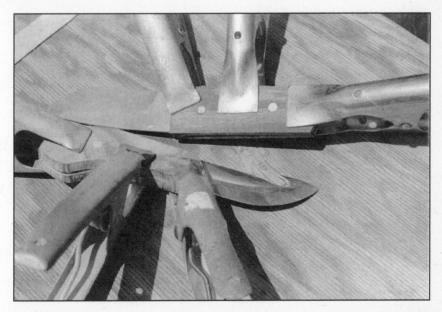

253

A quick check of the Learn exotic wood supply turned up a good scales possibility for the general blade Dixie calls Yellowstone. The handle material turned out to be ebony that was just thick enough to work. Another set of scales was sorted from the wood selection. These were of Oregon-grown myrtle, with some good, contrasting grain.

The blades were moved to an old belt sander, one of the wide shop sanders, introduced about twenty years ago. The forward edges of the scales were fitted together and clamped to keep them from slipping during sanding. This is the section that will be used for the finger guard and goes next to the blade where you just can't sand after they are epoxied into position. The ebony presented no problem, but the myrtle had the grain showing and the two sides for the handle had to be lined up and checked before sanding to a finish.

The forward section was completed before deciding which type of rivets to place in the handle for finishing. There were about a dozen holes of various sizes pre-drilled through the steel of the handle section, allowing the craftsman a variety of choices.

Perhaps a coffin handle around the outside might work, or two rivets set off-center. The two-hole style was selected and a brazing rod of proper size was selected from which to make the handle rivets.

"There was another hole near the butt one could use for attaching a lanyard, but the thought of a razor-sharp knife dangling near the body from a thong doesn't make good sense," Learn contends.

The items for the knives were collected and placed near the workbench. The scales were sanded as far as Learn could go before attaching them to the steel handle section. With the front edges finished and polished, he was ready to drill the brass center holes and epoxy the unit together.

"Use a drill bit just a touch smaller than the holes in the handles." Learn suggests.

Clamp the blade to the scale for drilling. Place the knife, blade up, on the drill press. Using the holes already in the steel as guides, drill two holes through steel and into the scale. Now place a pre-cut rivet from the brazing rod into the hole. Next, move to the other hole and drill it after proper alignment.

"You get only one chance at this, so take your time," Learn contends. When drilled, place the other rod rivet in the second hole. They should align.

To align the other side of the handle, place the rivets flush with those still held in the steel blade section. Clamp the handle with the two scales onto the blade section to make the two sides of the handle section.

Remove one rivet, and with the unit solidly clamped, drill the second handle section by passing the drill bit through the first section, the steel of the handle, and finally drilling the wood on the opposite scale. Keep the clamps in position and put the rivet into the drill hole. Remove the other rivet, align and drill so you now have the two handle sections fitted to the blade and the holes for the rivets are a precise fit.

"This is easier to do than explain," Bob Learn insists. The two rivet holes for the scales must fit the hole precisely, and you can only do it this way. "It is really simple, but the explanation gets more involved than the project. Now you have the first blade with handle scales ready to epoxy."

You now are ready to glue them together. Remove the rivets from the handles, but be certain to keep the right side of the handle on the right, the left side on the left or the drill holes may not

The handles have been shaped, but the hard edges are still there. They can be hard to use and will make your hand sore with much use, so they need to be rounded a bit.

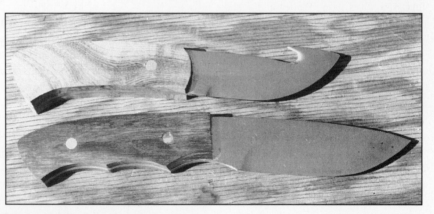

The finished knives are ready for use. The handles have been rounded for a comfortable grip, then buffed and finished. The blades have been buffed to a satin finish, and all they need is a final sharpening session on the stones.

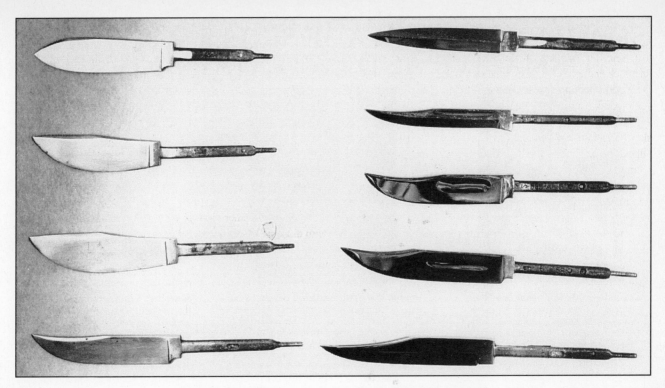

Round-tang models are also available, with threaded ends for handle assembly. The choice of handle material allows the builder to express his creativity.

fit. Mix a batch of the 24-hour-type epoxy, which seems to work best. Cover the steel handle area and the insides of the scales with the epoxy, insert the rivets and set the work aside to cure, making certain you have used enough clamps to hold them tightly together.

The rivets or pins are needed only to keep the scales from slipping. After the epoxy has cured, they will be tight to the steel handle section. Make certain you push the rivets a bit on one side so both sides have some rivet material protruding. You will grind this off and polish it later, but if it isn't extended beyond the scales now, it won't polish later.

After the epoxy has hardened, we are ready to finish sanding and forming the handles of the two knives. One can do this with a file and some sandpaper paddles or a power belt sander, if you have access to one. First, remove the handle material until flush with the steel of the handle. Do this all around the handle, bringing the wood down to the steel tang.

You can sculpt the wood with some fluting and finger grooves, but be careful. You are almost finished and can't afford mistakes.

The gut hook skinner was finished first by Learn, and the top and bottom edges of the handle were rounded slightly to fit the hand better. Straight, hard edges will make for sore hands while working the knife, so round them off gently. If you find later that you need more wood removed, you always can sand it then. Sand the brass rivets flush with the handles.

The Yellowstone general-purpose blade was treated in the same manner as was the other, but a bit more was taken off from the forward finger area so the fingers wrapped comfortably around the forward finger section. There was plenty of

handle with which to work, so some finger grooves were sanded in to make a good-fitting knife that won't slip in the hand while working with it.

The final step for the handle was to polish it with a soft, floppy buffing wheel. This polishes the handle wood and the blade. Some green grit was added to the wheel and the handles were buffed to a polished finish. The brass rivets in the mid-section of the handle also came out bright and shiny.

After inspecting the handle finish, one can move to the bright Solingen steel and buff it to an almost mirror finish. This buffing also puts a bit of an edge on the blade, but you will sharpen it later on a stone.

The finished knives look good and will be functional working tools for many years. The grip is solid, but the edges are rounded so the hand isn't uncomfortable in holding either model. The blade of the Yellowstone measures 4¼ inches with a cutting edge of 3½ inches. It's big enough to do the job on anything but maybe a moose, and overall length of the knife is 8½ inches.

The blade on the gut hook-equipped Wapiti measures 3⅜ inches, with a cutting edge of 3 inches; a curved skinning edge by the way. Overall length is 7½ inches.

These knives make a complimentary cutting pair and are of 57RC Solingen steel. Blade thickness is ⅛-inch, and they sharpen and hold an edge well.

With this project finished, if you like the end product well enough to try again—maybe this time a round tang—you can use one of the deer horns lying in a corner of the shop. They make great handles. Admit it, you're hooked and can't wait to get another project started!

SHARPEN YOUR BLADE SKILLS WITH THESE INFORMATIVE AND ENTERTAINING TITLES

NEW EDITION

NEW

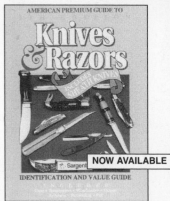

NOW AVAILABLE

Levine's Guide to Knives and Their Values, *The Complete Handbook of Knife Collecting, 4th Edition* by Bernard Levine
Stock the one book that's suitable for any knife collector. This handbook partners the latest knife values with pertinent historical overviews and expanded brand lists. Sets the standard for knife collectors worldwide. Numerous additions, significant pricing revisions and completely reworked sections head up the 4th edition that groups folding and fixed blades for simple identification. A traditional bible for collectors with a reputation for accuracy and excellence.
Softcover • 8-1/2x11 • 512 pages • 1,500 b&w illustrations • **LGKV4 $27.95**
Available February 1997

How to Make Multi-Blade Folding Knives, Eugene Shadley & Terry Davis This illustrated, step-by-step instructional book teaches knifemakers how to craft multiple blade folding knives. Every aspect of construction – from design to completion – is carefully explained and clearly shown in precise illustrations. Set up a workshop with all the right tools and equipment based on suggestions from the authors, preeminent knifemakers who have each earned several awards for their work. No other how-to on multi-blades exists! By the publisher of the world's #1 knife magazine, *Blade.* • SC • 8-1/2x11 • 192 pages • 200 b&w photos • **MBK01 $19.95**
Available April 1997

American Premium Guide to Pocket Knives and Razors, 4th edition, cuts to the Case – and Remington – knives in demand by collectors. Jim Sargent adds hundreds of rare photos and a huge section on Case sheath knives, plus ones on Pal and Browning. Updated values. 8-1/2x11 SC • 240p • fully illustrated • **APGP04 $22.95**

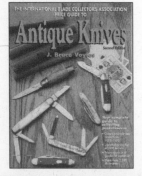

NOW AVAILABLE

The IBCA Price Guide To Antique Knives, edited by J. Bruce Voyles, is your complete guide to collecting pocketknives from 1800-1970. Get updated prices on 40,000 knives, in 6 grades of condition. Grading, trends and history of over 35 manufacturers included. 8-1/2x11 SC • 480p • 2,500+ photos • **KAK02 $17.95**

Battle Blades takes the work out of finding the fighting knife best suited to your needs and budget. Learn all the practical considerations that go with ownership. 8-1/2x11 HC • 168p • heavily illustrated • **BATB $30.00**

North American Indian Artifacts, 5th edition, pays tribute to the unique culture of Native Americans. Identify and value weapons, clothing, baskets, blankets, rugs, toys, ceremonial pieces, trade items and hundreds of other pieces of history. From renowned author Lar Hothem. 8-1/2x11 SC • 368p • fully illustrated • **INAFV $22.95**

These and other fine books available by calling Krause Publications
1-800-258-0929 Dept. 3CB1

Shipping: $3.25 for 1st book and $2.00 ea. add'l. Foreign addresses $10.00 for 1st book and $5.00 ea. add'l. WI res add 5.5%, IL res. add 7.75% sales tax.

Or mail Payment to: Krause Publications
700 East State St., Dept 3CB1, Iola, WI 54990-0001